Interpreting the Self

D1506355

PJ
7519
.A9
I58
2000

Interpreting the Self

Autobiography in the Arabic Literary Tradition

EDITED BY

Dwight F. Reynolds

COAUTHORED BY

Kristen E. Brustad • Michael Cooperson • Jamal J. Elias
Nuha N. N. Khoury • Joseph E. Lowry • Nasser Rabbat
Dwight F. Reynolds • Devin J. Stewart • Shawkat M. Toorawa

UNIVERSITY OF CALIFORNIA PRESS
Berkeley Los Angeles London

SAUK VALLEY CC
LRC

University of California Press
Berkeley and Los Angeles, California

University of California Press, Ltd.
London, England

© 2001 by the Regents of the University of California

Library of Congress Cataloging-in-Publication Data

Interpreting the self : autobiography in the Arabic literary tradition / edited by Dwight F. Reynolds ; coauthored by Kristen Brustad . . . [et al.].
p. cm.
Includes thirteen translated texts from Arabic.
Includes bibliographical references and index.
ISBN 0-520-22022-6 (cloth : alk. paper)—ISBN 0-520-22667-4(pbk. : alk. paper)
1. Arabic literature—History and criticism. 2. Autobiography. 3. Authors, Arab—Biography—History and criticism. 4. Arabic literature—Translations into English. I. Reynolds, Dwight Fletcher, 1956– II. Brustad, Kristen.
PJ7519.A9 I58 2000
892.7'09492—dc21 00-037411

Manufactured in the United States of America
9 8 7 6 5 4 3 2 1

10 9 8 7 6 5 4 3 2 1

The paper used in this publication meets the minimum requirements of ANSI/NISO Z39 0.48-1992(R 1997) (Permanence of Paper).

CONTENTS

ACKNOWLEDGMENTS

This work is unusual, perhaps even unique, in modern American letters, for it was collectively conceived, collaboratively researched, and cooperatively written by nine coauthors, not as an anthology of individual contributions, but as a single cohesive work. Although portions of the book were originally penned by one or another of our group (particularly the translations), the final product is the result of many readings, revisions, and discussions among all of the researchers. This approach is common in the physical and life sciences and, to a lesser extent, in the social sciences but remains rare in the humanities. The scope of this project, however, would have challenged the capacity of any single scholar, and the topic, once raised, was compelling. As a result, all of the coauthors took large amounts of time from their individual research plans to contribute to this joint effort.

The seeds of this project were first sown in 1990 during a summer getaway on the shores of Lake Sammamish outside Seattle, Washington, where Joseph Lowry's parents, Larry and Louise Lowry, graciously hosted a raucous bunch of young academics who at the time seemed equally interested in local viniculture and Derrida's writings on autobiography.

Having argued endlessly (or so we thought at the time) about whether the handful of medieval Arabic autobiographies we knew constituted a tradition, or indeed even constituted autobiographies at all, we spent two years seeking out and reading additional texts. In August 1992, with support from the University of California at Santa Barbara's Interdisciplinary Humanities Center, Center for Black Studies under the directorship of Charles Long, and Department of Religious Studies, we met for a week of presentations and discussions only to discover, somewhat to our dismay, that we had uncovered far more premodern Arabic autobiographies than we properly knew what to do with: not twenty or twenty-five, but well over fifty.

In summer 1993 and again in 1997, we were generously welcomed and hosted at the Middlebury Summer School of Arabic by then-director Mahmoud Al-Batal, whose boundless hospitality and encouragement greatly contributed to the completion of this work. Throughout those years our corpus of texts continued to grow—sixty, seventy, eighty—and our work in reading these newly uncovered texts, discussing recurring themes, and attempting to understand the motivations and worldviews of these medieval authors continued apace.

At the annual meetings of the Middle Eastern Studies Association in 1993 and again in 1994, the authors presented panels of papers exploring sample texts from the premodern Arabic autobiographical tradition. Under the insightful guidance of Julie Scott Meisami and Michael Beard, versions of these papers were published as a special edition of *Edebiyât: The Journal of Middle Eastern Literatures* (1997), guest edited by Dwight F. Reynolds under the watchful eye of his research assistant, Sandra Campbell.

Along the way, many others helped with their suggestions, encouragement, and guidance, among them ʿAbd al-Ḥamīd Ḥawwās, Roger Allen, Adel Allouche, Patricia Crone, Patricia Eisenlohr, Richard Hecht, Janet Gyatso, Michael Hopper, Stephen Humphreys, John Hunwick, Eve Troutt Powell, Werner Sollors, and Pei-Yi Wu. Their contributions are much appreciated.

We also wish to thank Ibrahim Muhawi for his meticulous comments and valuable suggestions on the manuscipt, as well as our anonymous reader. Lynne Withey, associate director of the University of California Press, provided inestimable encouragement and, more important, proved to be extraordinarily patient with our slow but steady process toward completion.

For their hours of research assistance and for cheerfully putting up with the editor's foibles, I personally wish to thank Sandra Campbell, Adrian DeGifis, and Linda Jones at the University of California at Santa Barbara, as well as our copyeditor, Sheila Berg, and our project editor, Rose Anne White.

It has fallen to me to do the final editing, and although my colleagues have rescued me again and again from errors I managed to introduce into various stages of the manuscript, both factual and interpretive, there are no doubt many that have not been expunged from the final text. These I claim as my own and hope that they may provide fodder for future publications by other scholars who will be able to revise, amend, and add to what we have assembled here as a first foray into a virtually untouched field.

The process of working as a collective on such a far-reaching project has at times been slow and awkward, for we did not always see eye to eye on all of the critical issues; but the overall richness of this extended collaboration, even if only measured by what I personally have learned from these scholars and friends, has far outweighed the additional work involved. At a time when our institutions often cut us off from our colleagues as much as they help to link us together, this project has provided a constant reminder of the joy and satisfaction that can and should grow out of the academic endeavor.

Dwight F. Reynolds
University of California at Santa Barbara

Introduction

When the Egyptian scholar Jalāl al-Dīn al-Suyūṭī sat down to pen his autobiography in about 1485, he began by situating his text within what was for him a recognized tradition of Arabic autobiographical writing. In the preface to his work he first considers the Qur'ānic injunction that one should speak of the blessings one has received from God ("And as for the bounty of your Lord, speak!" [Q 93:11]) and draws on traditions of the Prophet Muhammad (*ḥadīth*) and Qur'ānic commentaries to demonstrate that to speak of God's blessings, indeed to enumerate them in detail, is a means of expressing gratitude to God and thus a duty incumbent on every Muslim. He therefore titles his autobiography *al-Taḥadduth bi-niʿmat Allāh* (Speaking of God's Bounty) and closes his preface by noting both laudable and blameworthy motivations for writing an autobiography. He concludes by carefully identifying his own motivations as the former:

> Scholars from ancient to modern times have continually written biographical accounts of themselves [*yaktubūna li-anfusihim tarājim*]. They have done so with praiseworthy intentions, among which is "speaking of God's bounty" in thanks, and also to make known their circumstances in life so that others might emulate them in these, so that those who do not know of these circumstances should learn of them, and so that whosoever might later wish to mention them in works of history or in biographical dictionaries might draw upon their accounts.
>
> Among those who have done so before me are: [1] the Imām ʿAbd al-Ghāfir al-Fārisī [d. 1134], who was a gifted memorizer of the traditions of the Prophet; [2] al-ʿImād al-Kātib al-Iṣfahānī [d. 1201], who wrote an account of himself in an independent work which he titled *al-Barq al-shāmī* [The Syrian Thunderbolt]; [3] the jurist ʿUmāra al-Yamanī [d. 1175], who wrote an

> account of himself in an independent work; [4] Yāqūt al-Ḥamawī [d. 1229], who wrote an account of himself in his *Muʿjam kuttāb* [Biographical Dictionary of Writers]; [5] Lisān al-Dīn ibn al-Khaṭīb [d. 1374], who wrote an account of himself that occupies a half-volume of his book *Taʾrīkh Gharnāṭa* [The History of Granada], the whole work being eight volumes long; [6] the pious ascetic and accomplished legal scholar Abū Shāma [d. 1268], who wrote an account in his book [*The Sequel to the 'Two Gardens'*][1] in several fascicles; [7] the scholar of Prophetic traditions, Taqī al-Dīn al-Fāsī [d. 1429], who wrote an account of himself in his book, *Taʾrīkh Makka* [The History of Mecca], in several fascicles; [8] the scholar of Prophetic traditions, Ibn Ḥajar [d. 1449], who wrote an account of himself in his book *Taʾrīkh quḍāt Miṣr* [The History of the Judges of Egypt]; and [9] the Imām Abū Ḥayyān [d. 1344], who devoted to himself an account in an independent book which he titled *al-Nuḍār* [The Book of al-Nuḍār], a weighty volume.
>
> I have emulated them in this and have written this book in order to speak of God's bounty and to thank Him, not out of hypocrisy, nor for my own credit, nor out of pride. God is our source of help and to Him we entrust ourselves.[2]

In this simple preamble, al-Suyūṭī alludes to an entire world of literary conventions and traditions. He is, first of all, fully aware of a centuries-old tradition of autobiography in the Arabic language to which he was adding his own comparatively lengthy work (the Arabic printed text is two hundred fifty pages).[3] Al-Suyūṭī's various autobiographical works (he wrote at least three versions of his life) and similar introductions written by other autobiographers demonstrate that the genre of autobiography was clearly established in the Arabic literary tradition no later than the early twelfth century, although the earliest examples of Arabic autobiography can be traced back at least as far as the ninth century.

A second point of interest lies in al-Suyūṭī's list of previous autobiographies, for the texts cited are quite disparate. Some are short accounts of barely two pages that give scarcely more information than a curriculum vitae and are embedded in, or appended to, larger works on various topics; others are independent volumes of hundreds of pages devoted entirely to the author's life and works. Not only is al-Suyūṭī aware of this diversity, but he persistently calls our attention to it by singling out these very characteristics in his enumeration of predecessors. On the one hand, he is interested in, and carefully notes, the varying length and status of these texts; on the other, it is clear that he is primarily interested in earlier scholars, politicians, and religious figures who engaged in the act of writing about their own lives, regardless of the type of text produced. It is the act of writing an account of one's life and not the formal characteristics of the resulting text that defined autobiography for al-Suyūṭī and his contemporaries. In fact, al-Suyūṭī does not use a noun for the concept of autobiography but rather a verbal expression, *tarjama nafsahu* or *tarjama li-nafsihi,* which, among several interrelated meanings (see below), signifies "to compile a titled work/entry on oneself" or "to translate/interpret oneself," in the sense of creating a written representation of oneself, hence the title of this volume.

Al-Suyūṭī also allows us a glimpse of the rather ambiguous moral nature of the autobiographical enterprise, first in the four motivations he cites in the opening of this passage and then, more revealingly, in the personal disclaimers he presents to the reader at its close. The first motivation derives from the Qur'ānic injunction to speak of God's blessings in thanks; the importance al-Suyūṭī attaches to this motive is seen in the very title of his work, *Speaking of God's Bounty*. The second motivation is to provide an account of an exemplary life that can lead others to emulate one's virtues and meritorious acts, an idea found in many areas of Islamic intellectual and spiritual life. It springs, at least in part, from the idea of the Prophet Muhammad as an exemplar (*qudwa*), as the ideal human being whose life and acts (*sunna*) are to be imitated by believers.

These motivations for presenting one's life—as an act of thanking God and for others to emulate—stand in marked contrast to the confessional mode of some medieval and premodern European autobiographies that emphasize the public recognition ("confessions") of one's faults, sins, and shortcomings as a warning to others. One tradition seems to be framed to make the statement, "These are the ways in which I have enjoyed a moral and productive life—imitate me in them," while the other seems to imply, "These are the ways in which I have been deficient or in error—beware of similar pitfalls!" Each frame produced its own moral tensions and anxieties of representation, as well as literary strategies for resolving those issues. Although this comparison is a very broad one, and these general orientations certainly did not fully dictate the content of autobiographies in either context, it serves as a useful background against which to read contemporaneous autobiographies from European and Islamic societies in earlier periods.

Al-Suyūṭī's third motivation is the basic informational value of such accounts: they allow others to learn of one's life and conditions. And, finally, he presents a scholarly argument that these self-authored (and therefore presumably reliable) texts will be available to later writers who may use them in their biographical and historical works.

At the same time, al-Suyūṭī seeks to fend off potential criticism of his work by stating that he is not motivated by hypocrisy, self-interest, or pride. Herein lies a thread that wends its way through centuries of Arabic autobiographical writing: the tension between the portrayal of the self and self-aggrandizement, between recounting personal achievement and piously accepting the gifts bestowed on one by God that are to be publicized only for His greater glory. In al-Suyūṭī's case, this tension is in part alleviated by his strategy of linking his own book to a chain of works by pious and scholarly figures of the past: if such prominent men of the past have engaged in this act, then why should not he as well? To do so is thus framed as emulation of the actions of righteous men of the past, precisely one of the positive values al-Suyūṭī attributes to the act of autobiography itself: to write an autobiography is both an emulation of earlier respected figures and an act that will enable later generations to emulate the autobiographer. This strategy was successful enough to be copied by a number of later Arabic autobiographers, including Ibn Ṭūlūn of Damascus (d. 1546); al-Shaʿrānī, the Egyptian Sufi mystic (d. 1565); al-ʿAydarūs, the Arabo-Indian religious scholar (d. 1628); Ibn ʿAjība, the Moroccan Sufi shaykh (d. 1809); al-Muʿaskarī (d. 1823), the Algerian religious scholar; and even the Druze Pan-Arabist thinker and literary critic Amīr Shakīb Arslān (d. 1946), all of whom included similar lists of predecessors in the opening or closing passages of their autobiographies.

Al-Suyūṭī's emphasis on passing on knowledge of his "circumstances," "conditions," or "states" (*aḥwāl* or *aṭwār*), words commonly used by medieval Muslim scholars to describe the contents of autobiographies, reflects a widespread conceptualization of life as a sequence of changing conditions or states rather than as a static, unchanging whole or a simple linear progression through time. A life consists of stages dictated not merely by one's progression from childhood through youth to adulthood and old age but also by one's changing fortunes, which were often contrasted to those few areas of life in which genuine accrual over time was thought possible: the acquisition of knowledge and spiritual understanding, the creation of scholarly and literary works, and the fostering of offspring and students.

When al-Suyūṭī begins to recount his life, he presents it not in a chronological narrative but rather in categorized accounts describing different aspects of his identity and intellectual activity.[4] Consecutive sections discuss his genealogy, his geographic origin, his emulation of pious figures who had written about their own geographic origins, legal opinions of his father with which he disagreed (to demonstrate his independence of thought), his birth, the works he studied as a youth, the transmitters (more than six hundred, nearly a quarter of whom were women) from whom he collected *ḥadīth*,[5] the "rare" *ḥadīth* he collected as an adult scholar,[6] his pilgrimage to Mecca, his other travels, his teaching positions, the full text of one of his lectures, a list of his published works (283 of them), praise of his publications by contemporaries, the spread of his writings outside of Egypt, the description of a lengthy, bitter rivalry with an unnamed contemporary,[7] his claim to have reached the level of "independent legal theorist" (*mujtahid*) in Islamic law, and finally his claim to the title Renewer of the Faith (*mujaddid*) for the tenth Islamic century.[8]

This is clearly an account of an extremely rich and productive life; it is also presented as a comprehensive portrait of that life. However, it is an account that follows no pattern common to western autobiography.[9] Although it is filled with narratives of differing lengths, the work as a whole rejects the concept of ordering a life into a single narrative, a life "story" in the literal sense. Rather, it derives from an intellectual methodology in which classification, categorization, and description were the ultimate tools for the acquisition and retention of knowledge. Whereas western autobiography achieved its greatest popularity as a genre in tandem with its fictional counterpart, the novel,[10] the threads of the pre-twentieth-century Arabic autobiographical tradition were spun from the raw material of historical inquiry. It is fact and specificity, along with a fascination for individual accomplishments and intellectual production, that most interested and most commonly structured biographical and autobiographical texts of the Islamic Middle Ages. The organizing structure of al-Suyūṭī's text, however, in no way impedes the expression of his personality: no reader could leave this work with any doubt about al-Suyūṭī's vision of himself as a unique individual or the sheer force of his at times overweening personality.

Al-Suyūṭī's self-narrative represents but one of several distinct strands of Arabic autobiographical writing that emerged over the centuries. These strands derived from different models of intellectual endeavor and often stemmed from particularly influential works by specific writers. The diversity of literary form demonstrated by Arabic autobiographies from different time periods obviates the possibility of a single, simple description of the genre in formal terms, a situation similar to that which has emerged in the study of western autobiographical traditions.[11]

Al-Suyūṭī's work does serve, however, to alert us from the outset that in exploring self-narratives of different historical periods and different cultures, we shall encounter not only different ideas about the self and about the structure of a human life but also a wide range of differing literary conventions and discourses in which these selves and lives are represented. These encounters should provoke a series of complex questions concerning any specific culture or time period: What were considered the fundamental elements of a human individual? What were the purposes and motivations for the written representation of an individual life? Was the individual self deemed more truly represented by an account of an individual's personality (a set of psychological idiosyncrasies, habits, and internal emotions) or by an account of a person's acts and works? Indeed, did an individual indeed even possess a "personality"—a concept rooted in a model of malleability, development, and transformation? Or did an individual instead possess "character"—a concept that stresses continuity and a typical "manner of being" (cf. Greek *bios*)? Were those elements similar or different from the western concepts of individual, self, soul, mind, personality, and character?

The greatest challenge in reading and understanding Arabic autobiographical writings from different times and places is to distinguish the historical figures from their textual representations, and the textual representations from the consciousnesses that produced them, when all of these elements may or may not differ significantly from modern western models. Indeed, elucidating the relationships among authors, literary conventions, and historical transformations of consciousness remains the most challenging and yet perhaps the most fascinating task in all research on autobiography, whatever the culture or period.

This work consists of two parts: the first offers an analysis of a corpus of roughly one hundred forty Arabic autobiographical texts drawn from a period of just over one thousand years, from the ninth to the nineteenth century (including a small number of texts written or published in the early twentieth century, but which deal primarily with nineteenth-century lives); the second offers a selection of thirteen previously untranslated Arabic autobiographical texts that represent a variety of historical periods and literary styles. It is hoped that together these will serve not only to encourage further study of the Arabic autobiographical tradition but also to bring Arabic practices to the attention of a wider audience and thereby broaden critical discussion of autobiography in general.

The corpus on which this study is based contains all of the better-known Arabic autobiographies from the ninth to the nineteenth century, several of which are available in translation; it also includes a large number of additional texts that have remained unidentified or unstudied until now. Although this corpus is only a fraction of the tradition as a whole, it is difficult to estimate what portion it does in fact represent. Additional examples of Arabic autobiographies were being uncovered up until the completion of this volume, to say nothing of the many texts that remain in manuscript and the numerous works cited in indexes and bibliographies over the centuries that have not yet been located or may not have survived. A great deal of work remains to be done simply in the location and publication of these texts.

What links the texts in this study is their expression in the Arabic language. Thus this is a collection of Arabic autobiographies (autobiographies in the Arabic language) and not Arab autobiographies (autobiographies by Arabs), for many of the authors of these texts were of other ethnicities, including Berbers, Persians, Turks, West Africans, and even one Spanish Mallorcan. Arabic has served as a scriptural language, a language of intellectual and religious discourse, and a written lingua franca throughout the Islamic world for fourteen hundred years. It must be noted, however, that by restricting this study to texts written in Arabic, several premodern autobiographical traditions of the Islamic world will not be dealt with, traditions that may eventually prove significant to a broader understanding of autobiography in the regions of West, Central, and South Asia. These are the Turco-Persian traditions of Ottoman[12] and Iranian[13] political and religious memoirs, as well as the royal Moghul memoirs in Chagatay Turkish and Persian composed by Bābur, founder of the Moghul empire, and other members of his family in the Indian subcontinent.[14]

Although the boundaries of a literary tradition might at first seem easily definable by language, even a peremptory perusal of the Arabic tradition uncovers individual texts that challenge any notion of clear-cut borders. One such text is that of Princess Salmé of Oman who married a German and moved to Germany in the mid-nineteenth century. Her husband died only three years after her arrival there, leaving her with no means of support. Her memoirs are Arab by virtue of having been written by an Arab woman, and yet they were written in German and clearly composed for a European reading public despite the author's declaration that she wrote them for her children and only reluctantly acceded to pressure from friends to publish them.[15]

Another text that problematizes the boundaries of the Arabic tradition is the autobiography of Nubar Nubarian Pasha, one of Egypt's foremost statesmen of the late nineteenth century, who wrote his memoirs in French, the language of his secondary education. Nubarian, who was ethnically Armenian, was fluent in Turkish and educated in France but spent his life and career, which began at the age of seventeen, as an "Egyptian" politician in the Ministries of Commerce and Foreign Affairs. Nubarian is an intriguing example of a member of the cosmopolitan Ottoman elite who ruled much of the region now referred to as the Arab world while being both part of and yet removed from "Arab" culture.[16]

Although it falls outside the time frame of this study, an equally problematic text is that of the last khedive of Egypt, ʿAbbās II, who ruled from 1892 to 1914. His memoirs were first published in French, but the Arabic draft for the opening pages of the text in the khedive's own hand still exists and was published in facsimile with the Arabic translation of the entire text. It seems likely that the bulk of the text was dictated to a secretary; it is not known, however, whether that dictation was given in French or in Arabic.[17]

Other texts that defy simple classification are the Arabic slave memoirs of the nineteenth century. These texts were written in the Americas by Africans who had been enslaved in the antebellum United States and West Indies. They spoke various indigenous languages of their native West Africa (along with the English of their owners) and used Arabic as their religious and literary language. These life stories were produced at the instigation of white political activists who sought to use them in their campaigns to have these men set free (see chapter 3 below). Despite the unusual provenance of these works, several of them clearly deploy the classic conventions of the Arabic religious auto/biographical tradition. It is indeed a powerful moment of déjà vu to read in the terse autobiographical writings of a person considered mere chattel in early-nineteenth-century America formulas and phraseology reminiscent of those used by medieval philosophers, religious thinkers, and princes centuries earlier.[18]

The authors of the Arabic autobiographies included in this study were not only ethnically diverse, they were from a variety of religious backgrounds. Among them are Jewish authors, Christians of various denominations, and Muslims of Sunnī as well as Ismāʿīlī and Twelver Shiʿite orientations.[19] They were by vocation or avocation princes, philosophers, politicians, government functionaries, Shiʿite missionaries, physicians, professors, religious scholars, judges, mystics, historians, merchants, grammarians, slaves, a playwright, a princess from Zanzibar, an early Egyptian feminist, and an engineer. All of them wrote as members of the educated or social elites of their time, however humble their origins might have been. Some were multilingual and chose to write in Arabic as their language of intellectual exchange, and some were exclusively Arabophone; some wrote within the geographic confines of the modern Arab world, and some wrote in Arabic even though they were far away in India, Central Asia, or the Americas. One type of autobiographical text that did not surface in this survey was anything approaching an "Everyman" life story, the life narrative of a truly working-class or lower-class author who could offer a vision of society as seen "from below."[20]

Only three women autobiographers can be identified with certainty from this period: ʿĀʾisha al-Taymūriyya (d. 1902), the above-mentioned Princess Salmé of Zanzibar and Oman (d. 1924), and Hudā Shaʿrāwī (d. 1947), the famous Egyptian feminist, whose memoirs recount her life up to the year 1924. Although Salmé's text appears to be the earliest extant autobiography by an Arab woman, there is some fragmentary evidence for the existence of earlier texts. In particular, the first-person passages quoted in several Arabic biographical compendiums from the Sufi shaykha, legal scholar, and poetess ʿĀʾisha al-Bāʿūniyya (d. 1516) appear to be from an autobiographical notice; the original source, however, remains unidentified.[21]

The motivations of these authors for composing a written representation of their lives were complex and often multifarious: some included sections about themselves in larger works that were primarily biographical dictionaries (al-Fārisī, al-Jazarī, al-Bayhaqī, Ibn Ḥajar al-ʿAsqalānī, al-Sakhāwī) or in works on history (ʿImād al-Dīn al-Kātib al-Iṣfahānī, Abū Shāma, Mishāqa); some wrote of their own lives in the context of their family history (Ibn Buluggīn, ʿUmāra al-Yamanī, Ibn al-ʿAdīm, ʿAlī ibn al-ʿĀmilī); some wrote of themselves as characters in history interacting with the powerful and the mighty or as witnesses to great historical events (Jaʿfar al-Ḥājib, Ibn Ḥawshab, ʿImād al-Dīn al-Kātib al-Iṣfahānī, Ibn Khaldūn, Bābakr Badrī);

some wrote to preempt or redress criticism of their lives or works (Ḥunayn ibn Isḥāq, Ibn Buluggīn, al-Suyūṭī); some wrote their spiritual autobiographies as guides to later seekers of the true spiritual or philosophical path (al-Muḥāsibī, al-Rāzī, al-Ghazālī, Zarrūq, Ibn ʿAjība, al-Shaʿrānī); some wrote of their lives as a means of producing edifying entertainment (Usāma ibn Munqidh, al-Yūsī); some wrote of their lives as narratives of conversion to the true faith (Samawʾal al-Maghribī, ʿAbd Allāh al-Turjumān, al-Simnānī); some addressed their writings to their children, dead or alive (Abū Ḥayyān al-Andalusī, ʿAbd al-Laṭīf al-Baghdādī, Ibn al-Jawzī, Princess Salmé, Ṭāhā Ḥusayn); and some wrote as slaves trying to write themselves free (Abd al-Raḥmān, Abū Bakr, ʿUmar ibn Saʿīd).

In compiling this corpus, the question that arose at every turn was whether to conceive of these texts as autobiographies or to use a different, more neutral term, less burdened with literary expectations, such as "self-narratives" or "life representations." The first approach risked leading us (and our readers) to compare these medieval and premodern texts anachronistically to recent western autobiographies. The second approach, however, posed the greater risk of evading precisely those questions we wished to raise through the examination of this body of texts—questions concerning the history of consciousness, human personality, differing literary modes for representing the experience of a human life, and, ultimately, the modern western cultural construct of a radical and complete break in consciousness from earlier and "other" cultures.[22]

From the wide range of Arabic writings that might be termed first-person literature or self-narratives, the texts selected are those that appear to be closest kin to the western idea of autobiography, mostly from the Arabic genres of *sīra* and *tarjama*. The guiding criterion in this study for deeming a text an autobiography has been that the text present itself as a description or summation of the author's life, or a major portion thereof, as viewed retrospectively from a particular point in time.

For texts that met this basic description, no attempt has been made to pass judgment involving issues of which texts are "real" or "true" autobiographies based on subjective criteria such as the degree to which the author reveals his or her "inner self," or the degree to which the author stands back from and critically evaluates his or her earlier self, or which aspects of human life are portrayed in detail (all issues that are commonly raised in modern western literary criticism of autobiography). Nor has a sharp distinction been made between autobiography and memoir (the focus of the latter being the external events that took place during the author's life rather than the development of the author's life per se). Although the two categories appear to be separate and clear in the abstract, when addressing actual texts this clarity often proves ephemeral. The exclusion or inclusion of texts on the basis of length or other formal criteria has also been avoided.

This study deals with texts that are the results of acts of autobiography and attempts to focus on that species of text which al-Suyūṭī and his contemporaries would have classified under the rubric *tarjama li-nafsihi,* "he wrote an interpretation of himself," regardless of what judgments modern scholars may eventually render concerning the relationship between that genre and the genre of modern western autobiography. As Mary Sue Carlock has observed:

> Each scholar has applied the term [autobiography] according to his own standards or according to the definition which he himself has assigned to the term. . . . [C]onsequently this body of scholarly writings contains a variety of conflicting testimonies concerning what constitutes a bona fide autobiography.[23]

In short, in the spirit of a preliminary foray into a new field, the present work aims to err on the side of inclusiveness rather than exclusiveness.

This study stops at a point familiar to all scholars of Arab culture—the publication of the first volume of Ṭāhā Ḥusayn's autobiography in 1926–27—rather than at an arbitrary date such as the turn of the twentieth century.[24] *Al-Ayyām* (The Days), covers Ḥusayn's childhood in a village of southern Egypt and his migration from the countryside to Cairo to study at the al-Azhar Islamic University. Considered one of the foundational texts of modern Arabic literature, it is obligatory reading in schools in many countries of the Arab world and is certainly one of the most widely read and most influential Arabic literary works of that century.[25]

The publication of *al-Ayyām* marked a clear turning point in the development of the Arabic autobiographical tradition. After its publication, the Arabic literary landscape changed dramatically and the sheer number of autobiographies in Arabic increased exponentially. More significantly, the Arabic autobiography at this time came into direct contact with the novel, creating an ambiguous domain between fiction and nonfiction that had not previously existed in the Arabic autobiographical tradition. Several nineteenth-century literary experiments can be said to have engaged the fictional mode to some degree (e.g., Aḥmad Fāris al-Shidyāq's *al-Sāq ʿalā al-sāq* or ʿAlī Mubārak's *ʿAlam al-Dīn*), but they produced no imitators.[26] Huṣayn's text, in contrast, wedded the Arabic autobiography to certain conventions of European fictional narrative in a manner that has been imitated by the vast majority of twentieth-century Arab autobiographers. The dramatic rise of the autobiographical novel and the emergence of autobiographies with novel-like qualities immediately following the publication of *al-Ayyām* raises a number of critical questions not generally applicable to earlier Arabic autobiographical texts.[27]

In addition, questions of direct and indirect western literary influence, the conscious revival and transformation of classical Arabic literary forms, the new sociopolitical context of resistance to the European colonial powers, the struggle for political independence, the rise of Arab nationalism, and the sudden emergence of a strong Arab women's autobiographical tradition, as well as new regional and national identities, all combined to create a context in which the Arabic autobiography changed not only as a literary form but also as a means of sociopolitical expression. For these reasons, we have chosen to exclude the remainder of the twentieth century from the present work as a topic that merits and requires independent study.[28]

Notes

1. Blank in the original; the intended work is *Dhayl al-rawḍatayn* (The Sequel to 'The Two Gardens'), Abū Shāma's thirteenth-century historical chronicle.

2. Dates and numerals added. Selections from *The Syrian Thunderbolt,* by ʿImād al-Dīn al-Kātib al-Iṣfahānī, as well as the complete texts of the autobiographical sections of *The Sequel* by Abū Shāma and *The History of Judges of Egypt* by Ibn Ḥajar appear in English translation in this volume.

3. Western translations of classical Arabic texts are typically longer than the original, often by half again as many pages; the difference arises from the compactness of Arabic-script texts as well as the frequency of cultural referents that require paraphrasis in English.

4. For a discussion of the ordering of these sections, see E. M. Sartain, *Jalāl al-Dīn al-Suyūṭī* (Cambridge: Cambridge University Press, 1975), 1:142 ff.; and Kristen Brustad, "Imposing Order: Reading the Conventions of Representation in al-Suyūṭī's Autobiography," *Edebiyât: Special Issue—Arabic Autobiography,* N.S. 7, no. 2 (1997): 327–44.

5. *Ḥadīth* are accounts of the words and actions of the Prophet Muhammad. The study of *ḥadīth,* and in premodern times, collecting them orally from reliable transmitters, formed an integral part of a Muslim scholar's education. Ideally, a *ḥadīth* was transmitted and later passed on to others complete with a list of all of the names in the chain of transmission from the Prophet himself to the speaker.

6. Arabic *ʿawālin,* i.e., *ḥadīth* with the fewest number of transmitters stretching back to the Prophet Muhammad or the Companions. These *ḥadīth* were prized for their rarity and relatively short chains of transmission. In al-Suyūṭī's times, a millennium after the lifetime of the Prophet, a *ḥadīth* that had passed through fewer transmitters had come to represent both a form of authenticity and an intellectual find.

7. Excerpts from this chapter of al-Suyūṭī's text are translated in this volume.

8. A well-known Islamic tradition holds that a "renewer" of the faith will appear in each century.

9. The closest parallel among European autobiographies was written, curiously enough, by a contemporary of al-Suyūṭī, Girolamo Cardano (d. 1576), who divided his work into chapters with titles such as "Friends," "Marriage and Children," "Health," and "Sports." Girolamo Cardano, *The Book of My Life,* trans. J. Stoner (New York: Dutton, 1930).

10. Rousseau (d. 1778), whose work is considered by many scholars to be the single most significant breakthrough in the development of modern western autobiography, composed his *Confessions* only after fictional life stories had been popular in French literature for nearly half a century. Fictional explorations preceded and irrevocably shaped western concepts of the literary self.

11. See, for example, Philippe Lejeune, "The Autobiographical Pact," trans. Katherine Leary, in *On Autobiography* (Minneapolis: University of Minnesota Press, 1989), 3–30. The fulcrum point of Lejeune's "solution," the title page of a published autobiography, is not applicable to premodern Arabic texts. The Chinese autobiographical tradition also encompasses a number of subgenres from different historical periods and styles and thus similarly resists a single formal description; see Pei-Yi Wu, *The Confucian's Progress: Autobiographical Writings in Traditional China* (Princeton: Princeton University Press, 1990).

12. For an overview, see Cemal Kafadar, "Self and Others: The Diary of a Dervish in Seventeenth-Century Istanbul and First-Person Narratives in Ottoman Literature," *Studia Islamica* (1989): 121–50. Kafadar identifies and cites texts from a variety of genres including autohagiography, memoirs, diaries, dreambooks, captivity memoirs, and autobiographies. For one of the more famous authors, Muṣṭafā ʿAlī, see Cornell H. Fleischer, *Bureaucrat and Intellectual in the Ottoman Empire: The Historian Muṣṭafā ʿAlī (1541–1600)* (Princeton: Princeton University Press, 1986). Although this work is in part based on a short autobiography by Muṣṭafā ʿAlī appended to his *Counsel for Sultans,* Fleischer makes little reference to the text itself; see, however, the edition and translation of Andreas Tietze, "Muṣṭafā ʿAlī's Counsel for Sultans of 1581," *Österreichische Akademie der Wissenschaften, Philosophisch-Historische Klasse Denkschriften,* Bd. 137, Bd. 158 (Vienna, 1979, 1982). Robert Dankoff, *Seyahatname: The Intimate Life of an Ottoman Statesman, Melek Ahmad Pasha (1588–1662) as Portrayed in Evliya Celebi's "Book of Travels"* (Albany: SUNY Press, 1991), gives an overview of the autobiographical elements in Evliya Celebi's work.

13. Shāh Ṭahmāsp, *Tazkira-i Shāh Ṭahmāsp* (*The Autobiography of Shah Ṭahmāsp I of Iran [1514–1576]*) (Teheran: Intishārāt-i Sharq, 1984); German trans. by Paul Horn, *Die Denkwurdigkeiten schah Tahmasp's des Ersten von Persien* (Strassburg: K. J. Trubner, 1891). See also Ṭahmās Khān (d. 1803), *Ṭahmāsnāmah,* ed. Muhammad Aslam (Lahore: Panjab University, 1986), available in translation as *Tahmas Nama: The Autobiography of a Slave,* abridged and trans. by P. Setu Madhana Rao (Bombay: Popular Prakashan, 1967); Bert G. Fragner, *Persische Memoirliteratur als Quelle zur neueren Geschichte Irans* (Wiesbaden: Franz Steiner, 1979), for nineteenth-century examples; and C. M. Naim, trans., *Zikr-i Mir: The Autobiography of the Eighteenth-Century Mughal Poet, Mir Muhammad Taqi "Mir" (1723–1810)* (New Delhi: Oxford University Press, 1999).

14. Ẓāhiruddīn Muḥammad Bābur (d. 1530) ruled portions of Central Asia, Afghanistan, and Iran and was the founder of the Mughal empire of India. *The Book of Bābur* (Bābur-nāmah) is part official chronicle and part personal memoir. Although much of the narrative concerns affairs of state, the number of intimate glimpses into Bābur's personality have caused some western scholars to rank it among the great autobiographies of the world (it has been available in translation

since 1826), and its most recent American translator has been moved, somewhat effusively, to declare it "the first—and until relatively recent times, the only—true autobiography in Islamic literature" (Wheeler M. Thackston, trans., *The Bāburnāma* [Oxford: Oxford University Press, 1996], 9). See, however, the recent edition, concordance, and translation of Eiji Mano, *Bābur-nāma (Vaqāyiʿ)* (Kyoto: Syokado, 1995, 1996), for a trenchant critique of the Thackston text. Additional memoirs or journals were written by Bābur's daughter, Gulbadan Bēgum, and his great-grandson, the emperor Jahāngīr (r. 1605–27).

15. *An Arabian Princess between Two Worlds: Memoirs, Letters Home, Sequels to My Memoirs, Syrian Customs and Usages,* ed. E. van Donzel (Leiden: E. J. Brill, 1992); *Raised in a Harem: Memoirs of an Arabian Princess from Zanzibar, Emily Ruete, Born Salmé, Princess of Zanzibar and Oman* (New York: Marcus Weiner, 1989).

16. *Mémoires de Nubar Pacha,* introd. and notes by Mirrit Butros Ghali (Beirut: Librairie du Liban, 1983).

17. See *ʿAhdī: mudhakkirāt ʿAbbās Ḥilmī al-thānī, khidīw Miṣr al-akhīr* (Cairo: Dār al-Shurūq, 1993).

18. The best coverage of these texts and their authors is found in Allan Austin, *African Muslims in Antebellum America: A Sourcebook* (New York: Garland, 1984); and Marc Shell and Werner Sollors, eds., *The Multilingual Anthology of American Literature* (New York: New York University Press, 2000).

19. An early rift over the issue of political and religious succession to the Prophet Muhammad led to a general division in Islam between Sunnī Muslims and Shiʿite Muslims. In later periods the primary distinction came to be the issue of spiritual authority and guidance for the Muslim community, with the Shiʿite community believing in a series of Imāms, spiritual leaders who were thought to have direct inspiration from God, while the Sunnīs recognized no such role. The Shiʿite community further split into groups that followed different lineages of spiritual leaders. A number of the autobiographers dealt with in this study wrote their autobiographies primarily as an expression of their roles in proselytizing for or fomenting rebellion against one or another of these sectarian groups.

20. The texts closest to this genre in Arabic literature are the historical chronicles written by lower-class figures such as the "soldier's daybook" of Aḥmad al-Damurdashī. See al-Damurdashī's *al-Damurdashī's Chronicle of Egypt, 1688–1755,* trans. and annot. Daniel Crecelius and ʿAbd al-Wahhāb Bakr (Leiden: E. J. Brill, 1991), and the chronicle of Syria penned by a Damascene barber, Aḥmad al-Ḥallāq al-Budayrī (18th c.), *Ḥawādith Dimashq al-yawmiyya,* A.H. *1154–1175* (Daily Events in Damascus, 1741–1762), ed. Aḥmad ʿIzzat ʿAbd al-Karīm (Cairo: Maṭbaʿat Lajnat al-Bayān al-ʿArabī, 1959).

21. Muḥammad al-Ghazzī, *al-Kawākib al-sāʾira bi-aʿyān al-miʾa al-ʿāshira,* 3 vols. (Beirut: al-Maṭbaʿa al-Amrīkāniyya, 1945–59), 1:287–92; see also ʿAbd al-Ḥayy Ibn al-ʿImād, *Shadharāt al-dhahab fī akhbār man dhahab,* 8 vols. (Cairo: Maktabat al-Qudsī, 1931–33), 8:111–13; and passages cited in ʿUmar Bāshā Mūsā, *Taʾrīkh al-adab al-ʿarabī: al-ʿaṣr al-mamlūkī* (Beirut: Dār al-Fikr al-Muʿāṣir, 1989), 437–42.

22. This element of modern western thought is explored and critiqued in Bruno LaTour's *We Have Never Been Modern* (Cambridge, Mass.: Harvard University Press, 1993).

23. Mary Sue Carlock, "Humpty Dumpty and Autobiography," *Genre* 3 (1970): 345–46.

24. First published in the Egyptian journal *al-Hilāl* in 1926–27, then in 1929 and 1933 in book form at the Imad Press in Cairo, and translated into English by E. H. Paxton, *An Egyptian Childhood, the Autobiography of Taha Hussein* (London: Routledge, 1932).

25. Fedwa Malti-Douglas begins her study of *al-Ayyām* with the question: "The most read work in Arabic literature?" to which she answers, "[T]he best-known work may well be the autobiography of the Egyptian intellectual Ṭāhā Ḥusayn." *Blindness and Autobiography: al-Ayyām of Ṭāhā Ḥusayn* (Princeton: Princeton University Press, 1988), 3. Similarly, John Haywood declares it "the most celebrated book in modern Arabic literature," in *Modern Arabic Literature 1800–1970* (New York: St. Martin's Press, 1971), 196.

26. Aḥmad Fāris al-Shidyāq, *al-Sāq ʿalā al-sāq fī mā huwa l-Fariyāq,* 2 vols. (Paris: Benjamin Duprat, 1855); ʿAlī Mubārak, *ʿAlam al-Dīn,* 4 vols. (Alexandria: Maṭbaʿat Jarīdat al-Maḥrūsa, 1882).

27. Arabic autobiographical novels published immediately following the appearance of *al-Ayyām* include Ibrāhīm ʿAbd al-Qādir al-Māzinī's *Ibrāhīm al-kātib* (1931), Tawfīq al-Ḥakīm's *ʿAwdat al-rūḥ* (1933), and Ṭāhā Ḥusayn's own *Adīb* (1935). In another cross-fertilization between fiction and autobiography, the author Bayram al-Tūnisī published a series of autobiographies of fictional characters drawn from the lower classes of Egyptian life in the 1920s and 1930s that he used as vehicles for social commentary and criticism. See Martina Häusler, *Fiktive ägyptische Autobiographien der zwanziger und dreissiger Jahre* (Frankfurt: Peter Lang, 1990).

28. Until recently, there was only one lengthy treatment of modern Arabic autobiography: Yaḥyā Ibrāhīm ʿAbd al-Dāyim, *al-Tarjama al-dhātiyya fī al-adab al-ʿarabī al-ḥadīth* (Autobiography in Modern Arabic Literature) (Beirut: Dār Iḥyāʾ al-Turāth al-ʿArabī, 1975). Three recent works, however, mark growing scholarly interest in this area: Muʾayyad ʿAbd al-Sattār, *al-Sīra al-dhātiyya: dirāsa naqdiyya* (The Autobiography: A Critical Study) (Uddevalla, Sweden: Dār al-Manfā, 1996); Robin Ostle, Ed de Moor, and Stefan Wild, eds., *Writing the Self: Autobiographical Writing in Modern Arabic Literature* (London: Saqi Books, 1998); and Tetz Rooke, *"In My Childhood": A Study of Arabic Autobiography* (Stockholm: Stockholm University, 1997).

For the emergence of women's autobiography, see Hudā Shaʿrāwī, *Harem Years: The Memoirs of an Egyptian Feminist (1879–1924),* trans., ed., and introd. Margot Badran (London: Virago Press, 1986); Margot Badran, "Expressing Feminism and Nationalism in Autobiography: The Memoirs of an Egyptian Educator," in *De/Colonizing the Subject: The Politics of Gender in Women's Autobiography,* ed. Sidonie Smith and Julia Watson (Minneapolis: University of Minnesota Press, 1992), 270–93; and Margot Bardran, *Feminists, Islam and Nation: Gender and the Making of Modern Egypt* (Princeton: Princeton University Press, 1995).

PART I

A Thousand Years of Arabic Autobiography

CHAPTER ONE

The Fallacy of Western Origins

European scholars from the late eighteenth through the first half of the twentieth century, including Goethe, Herder, and Dilthey, called for the collection and study of autobiographical writings. They conceived of this as a broad category of literary production that encompassed writings from both earlier historical periods and other cultures; however, in the mid-twentieth century, autobiography was dramatically reconstructed in western literary criticism as a cultural product unique to modern western civilization. This new formulation appeared abruptly, fueled perhaps by the impending collapse of the colonial encounter and perhaps also by the "threat" of cultural relativism. In the simplest of terms, immediately after World War II, western literary critics suddenly ceased to write of autobiography as a literary category parallel to "novel" or "biography," both of which easily admit of cross-cultural and historical comparisons, and began instead to treat it as the exclusive creation of the modern West. One of the clearest assertions of this new stance was penned by Georges Gusdorf in a 1956 article that has been characterized as the very foundation of modern autobiography studies.[1]

> It would seem that autobiography is not to be found outside our cultural area; one would say that it expresses a concern peculiar to Western man, a concern that has been of good use in his systematic conquest of the universe and that he has communicated to men of other cultures; but those men will thereby have been annexed by a sort of intellectual colonizing to a mentality that was not their own. . . .
>
> The concern, which seems so natural to us, to turn back on one's own past, to recollect one's life in order to narrate it, is not at all universal. It asserts itself only in recent centuries and only on a small part of the map of the world.[2]

Gusdorf's assertions have been reiterated many times in subsequent works by other scholars such as Roy Pascal.

> It is beyond my scope to suggest why autobiography does not come into being outside Europe, and the existence of such a work as Babur's memoirs of the sixteenth century, which would occupy a significant place in the history of autobiography had it belonged to Europe, makes one hesitate to generalise. But there remains no doubt that autobiography is essentially European. Where in modern times members of Eastern civilisations have written autobiographies, like Gandhi for instance, they have taken over a European tradition.[3]

The French critic Georges May adds a further claim—that autobiography emerged uniquely within the cultural influence of Christianity. He asserts, albeit with some minor reservations, that as a literary form the autobiography is a western phenomenon invented by modern Europeans and linked inextricably with Christianity.[4] The assumptions evident in the work of Gusdorf, Pascal, and May recur in most western writings on the topic of autobiography, even those focused on discrete aspects of the subject, such as childhood memoirs.

> The Childhood [autobiography] is a genre which presupposes a sophisticated culture. *It is inconceivable among primitives; even in the contemporary Third World, it emerges only in imitation of culturally more advanced models.* It demands a sense of form, and the intellectual ability to adapt the ill-balanced and misshapen material of experience to the harmony of literary expression without overmuch distortion of the original truth. It requires a grasp of the epic dimension, and the severe discipline of a controlled rhythm. . . . It demands self-knowledge. (Emphasis added)[5]

The canon of pre-twentieth-century autobiographies that has emerged in the West over the past century, the body of texts deemed by scholars to represent the genre's most noteworthy and significant examples—including those of Augustine, Abelard, Suso, Margery Kempe, Petrarch, Cellini, Cardano, Montaigne, Rousseau, Goethe, Benjamin Franklin, and others—has remained for historical, political, and academic reasons predominantly modern western European, overwhelmingly male, and in that already relatively narrow category, predominantly French, German, and English. Although notable additions in recent years have included surveys of women's autobiographies, African American slave autobiographies, working-class autobiographies, and modern autobiographical traditions from other regions, the myth of origins constructed by Gusdorf, May, Pascal, and others remains fundamentally unchallenged.[6]

Autobiography's shift from a general category of literature as conceived by Goethe, Herder, and Dilthey to the culturally specific genre advocated by Gusdorf, May, and Pascal represents a highly significant, and politically suspect, turning point in western intellectual history. It marks a reorientation that seeks to distinguish fully formed, authentic, modern western selves from the incomplete individual consciousnesses of earlier periods and inauthentic, facsimile selves produced by modern nonwestern cultures in imitation of their superiors. Seen in this light, autobiography is positioned at the very crux of literary scholarship's relationship to earlier historical periods and to other cultures and is currently privileged as a defining discursive marker for what it is to be "modern" and what it is to be "western."

How many exceptions are needed to cast doubt on the assumption of western origin and exclusivity and allow it to be critically reexamined? While the established canon includes many texts significant for the study of French or English autobiography, the validity of such a restricted corpus as the basis for statements extended to autobiography in cross-cultural and even global contexts is both problematic and underdetermined. Although there is an obvious need for western scholars to gain access to nonwestern traditions, the theory-generating bodies of the western literary academy are resolutely entrenched, even now, within the confines of European languages and literatures.

Western scholarship *on* autobiography thus recapitulates the act *of* autobiography. It views literary history as leading inevitably to a predetermined end point—the modern western autobiography—much the way the autobiographer views the passage of larger historical events only as they have affected himself or herself, and the random events contributing to the development of his or her personality as leading, as if by design, inexorably and directly to the moment of writing. Both view the past teleologically.

Western literary scholars and social historians have also consistently imputed changing forms of literary expression, somewhat ingenuously, to historical changes in "self-consciousness." Thus the structural and rhetorical characteristics of the western chronological, narrative-based autobiography have become the gauge by which scholars seek to measure the level of "self-consciousness" and "individual identity" present in other historical periods and other cultures, bypassing the changing literary conventions that mediate these expressions of the Self. The almost inevitable result is that other, particularly nonwestern, forms of autobiography are discounted as immature and underdeveloped, as pale shadows of the "real" or "true" autobiography known only in the modern West, and therefore as literary productions clearly not born of the same sense of individual identity.

Western Reception of Arabic Autobiography

Until recently, there existed only two serious treatments of premodern Arabic autobiography in western scholarship: one by Georg Misch and the other by Franz Rosenthal.[7] Their pioneering work merits close attention, as their writings established both the parameters and the tone for subsequent studies in this area by western and Arab scholars. Both Misch and Rosenthal approached their research armed with philosophical assumptions that, though now dated and even condemned, are critical for understanding and evaluating their work. Both sought, not to analyze a history of changing literary conventions for the representation of the human life experience (i.e., autobiographies as literary texts), but rather an essentialized self that they deemed easily and directly discernible through the literary representation. In addition, they believed firmly in the historical development of a culturally defined "Western self," the superiority of which was assumed unquestioningly, as were the existence of a modern western "individualism" and "self-awareness" not found in other societies or other historical periods. Their work thus focused as much on disproving the existence of "true" autobiography in other cultures as it did on tracing the history of autobiography. In the sixty years since the publication of their works, little new scholarship on the topic of premodern Arabic autobiography has appeared. As a result, even later scholars who clearly do not share the philosophical and social assumptions of Misch or Rosenthal have continued to cite their readings of specific texts while ignoring the larger arguments within which those readings were originally situated.

Georg Misch was the student, research assistant, and son-in-law of the famous nineteenth-century German philosopher Wilhelm Dilthey. Dilthey believed in the central importance of autobiography as a historical document and indeed that the autobiography furnished the basic, indivisible building block of all historical writing. He saw in it the "most direct expression of reflection on life."[8] Misch not only shared his teacher's utilitarian view of autobiography as the foundation of the study of history but also saw himself as one in a long line of German scholars concerned with the history of the autobiography as an important aspect of the history of humanity:

> Herder stimulated a whole group of scholars to collect superb self-portraits *from the most diverse lands and ages.* He explained, in the foreword to such a collection, which first appeared in Germany in 1790, that a "library of authors writing about themselves" would make an excellent "contribution to the history of mankind." Goethe then conceived of the idea of a "comparison of the so-called confessions *of all the ages*": the great progression of the liberation of the human personality would be thereby illuminated. (Emphasis added)[9]

Misch's massive *Geschichte der Autobiographie* (The History of Autobiography) traces autobiographical writing and self-depiction from its ancient roots to what is, for Misch, its emergence as a mature, historically useful, engaging expression of an individual's ability to reflect on his or her age in the writings of Rousseau. He sets out to tell the story of how the autobiography metamorphosed into perfection with Rousseau and portrays that development in decidedly teleological fashion as parallel to, and resulting from, the development of self-consciousness and individual personality in the West. This progression, as Misch sees it, moves from a general absence of a sense of individual self to a self-conscious concern with the subject. According to Misch, the autobiography "belongs, in its essence, to the recent formations of higher stages of culture."[10] He investigates the autobiography as an important aspect of the stage-by-stage development of the "western" psyche. Autobiographical writings marginal to this progression are swept aside, albeit not without some difficulties.

Nevertheless, and contrary as it would seem to his stated intention, Misch devotes considerable space to ancient "Oriental" autobiographical writing, launching his multivolume study with a treatment of autobiographical writings from such traditions as those of ancient Egypt, the Fertile Crescent, and the Old Testament Books (specifically Ezra and Nehemiah). Although he concedes that the autobiographical writings of the ancient Orient are "unexpectedly numerous," there is in this richness an "infinite poverty of a sense of the individual."[11] It is not until he reaches Greece in the "post-Homeric" and "Attic" periods that Misch speaks of "development."[12]

Misch notes that the autobiography appears as a genre unto itself in Greece in the fourth and fifth centuries C.E.[13] Although many of the authors of autobiographies in this period and slightly before were inhabitants of the eastern Mediterranean (e.g., Galen, Nicholas of Damascus), Misch is careful to portray the autobiography as a product of the West. He dismisses the idea that eastern cultures may have added to the development of western autobiography with a discernible degree of awkwardness: No one, he claims, "would consider the new autobiography as an Oriental outgrowth merely because its representatives and some isolated traits of its physiognomy stemmed from provinces with especially strong Oriental strains."[14] Such conclusions notwithstanding, Misch devotes hundreds of pages to various periods of Arabic autobiographical writing. He could not read Arabic, however, so his analysis of individual works (for which he relied on translations or on Rosenthal's work; see below) is less important for our purposes than his general cultural orientation. Particularly instructive in this regard is the procedure by which he dismisses pre-Islamic Arabic poetry.

Misch begins his treatment of Arabic autobiographical writing with an exhaustive survey of pre-Islamic poetry as an expression of the voice of the individual.[15] He is initially enthusiastic about the individualistic quality of the pre-Islamic corpus and goes to great lengths to explain it; in the final analysis, however, the Bedouins' individuality as expressed in pre-Islamic poetry reflects, for Misch, a profound conformism, despite all appearances to the contrary. The perspective of the pre-Islamic poet is not that of one who looks outward from within but rather that of one who views himself as an elemental, integrated part of the environment and his social group.[16] The pre-Islamic poet suffers from the fact that he lives in a "one-dimensional intellectual realm."[17] Thus Misch dispenses with the poetry itself, apparently disregarding his initial instincts, and proceeds to base his conclusions on a suspect anthropologism applied to an area in which he has no expertise.

If Misch feels compelled to solve the "problem" of individuality in pre-Islamic poetry, the far larger corpus of autobiographical material in the Islamic Middle Ages presents him with even greater difficulties. He confesses the existence of "an astonishingly great number" of such autobiographies "when compared to the state of formal autobiographies from the corresponding time of the Christian Middle Ages."[18] He concludes, however, that "the Arabic scholarly biographies are characterized, just as are the Byzantine, by a stage of self-consciousness in which development, as far as we can see, has come to a standstill." He finds a "paucity of human sentiment" to be their most basic characteristic.[19]

There was a degree of cross-fertilization between Misch and Rosenthal, who were researching and writing about Arabic autobiographies at the same time. Rosenthal hails Misch's achievement as "a classic work of Classical scholarship,"[20] and Misch in turn welcomes the materials provided by Rosenthal, for they added to and reinforced his own conclusions. Although Misch's treatment of Arabic autobiographical writings is more wide-ranging and ambitious than Rosenthal's, Rosenthal was the first Arabist to turn his attention to the question of the Arabic autobiography as such.

In contrast to Misch, Rosenthal concentrates on a modest collection of Arabic texts that appear to have unambiguous pretensions to autobiography. Rosenthal does not explicitly develop a genre definition, nor does he concern himself with other manifestations of autobiographical writing, although he acknowledges that they take many forms in Arabic. He speaks simply of a collection of "actual, coherent autobiographies," whose number appears significant standing alone, yet pales in comparison to the totality of Arabic literary production in the Middle Ages.[21]

Rosenthal examines these texts one by one, after a brief and useful discussion of possible Greek and Persian influences on the Arabic autobiographical tradition. He ascribes primary influence to later classical authors such as Galen. But Rosenthal, like Misch, finds the source material wanting.

His views are perhaps best summarized in the opening and closing remarks to his study:

> The autobiographical tradition in Islam is bound less to personality than to the subject matter. The experiences of the individual, as such, do not offer the incentive for their being communicated, but rather do so only through their generally applicable pedagogic content.[22]

> None of the autobiographies came into being out of a consciousness of the individual value of the uniquely personal.[23]

These views of Misch and Rosenthal are even more curious when seen against the background of nineteenth-century European scholarship in which the Arabs were noted for their concept of the individual in contrast to the Europe's lack thereof before the Renaissance.

> In the Middle Ages . . . Man was conscious of himself only as member of a race, people, party, family, or corporation—only through some general category. . . . In Italy this veil first melted into air. . . . [M]an became a spiritual individual, and recognized himself as such. In the same way the Greek had once distinguished himself from the barbarian, and the Arabian had felt himself an individual at a time when other Asiatics knew themselves only as members of a race.[24]

Similar to the historical shift in the definition of autobiography noted at the beginning of this chapter, this image of the individuality of the Arabs dropped out of western scholarly discourse and was replaced by its diametric opposite.

Rosenthal thus operates within categories very similar to those used by Misch, positing an idealized autobiography (perhaps typified by Rousseau, possibly deriving from Augustine) never to be realized in Arabic. This idealization is part unarticulated genre theory (successful autobiographies have a certain relationship to personality not found in Arabic examples) and part unarticulated theory of personality or of individuality (those incidents of individuality worth observing, depicting, and so on, are not to be found in the Arabic examples, perhaps because their authors did not experience them). Neither of these mutually reinforcing preconceptions is made explicit in Rosenthal's monograph. They appear clearly, however, in the judgments he renders about individual texts and about the genre as a whole. The following examples are characteristic of the uniformly negative evaluations he offers about many of the texts he discusses.

In the opening passage of his most autobiographical work, *al-Munqidh min al-ḍalāl* (The Deliverer from Error), al-Ghazālī (d. 1111) describes having explored a series of competing schools of religious thought before finding spiritual satisfaction in mysticism. Rosenthal declares that the description is "markedly . . . improbable" and that therefore "psychological veracity is not touched upon."[25] Ultimately, Rosenthal feels compelled to point out how unfavorably al-Ghazālī's autobiography compares to that of Augustine. Rosenthal's judgments about Samawʾal al-Maghribī's autobiography are particularly harsh. Samawʾal (d. 1174), a Jewish convert to Islam, is said by Rosenthal to lack "the religious drives necessary for the inner veracity of a religious conversion."[26] Further, Rosenthal all but accuses Samawʾal of lying about the dreams he had portending his conversion to Islam.[27] Usāma ibn Munqidh (d. 1188), author of a highly entertaining book-length autobiography, is faulted for failing to possess insight into the "world-historical meaning" of the events that he witnesses and also for being unable to distinguish between meaningful and meaningless events.[28] The autobiography of Abū Shāma (d. 1268), perhaps because it is written in the third person, is called "the first proof of how . . . the expression of consciousness of the self [in the Arabic tradition] has loosed itself totally from any relationship at all to inner worth." The work has, for Rosenthal, the effect of the "most meaningless, emptiest exaggeration."[29]

Obviously, a student of literature might today perceive these same characteristics—accepting for the sake of argument that Rosenthal's caustic barbs correctly describe some aspects of the texts addressed—as features to be analyzed: the autobiographer's manipulation of the narrative in a way that might not correspond to the actual order of the events experienced (al-Ghazālī); the question of the autobiographer's veracity and the role of autobiography as "conversion narrative" (Samawʾal); the selection of both large historical events and minute personal details with which to construct a portrait of a life (Usāma); and the relationship between the author's conception of self and the literary structure of the autobiographical text (Abū Shāma). Indeed, Rosenthal's own categories of thought, such as "psychological veracity," "religious drives," "the inner veracity of conversion," "meaningful" versus "meaningless" events, and the "world-historical meaning" of witnessed events, might today require more intellectual archaeology than those of the medieval texts he finds so unilluminating.

Despite Rosenthal's categorical judgments, his achievement must not be overlooked: he was the first modern scholar to identify the genre of Arabic autobiography and to collect many of its important texts. He also, along with Misch, underscored the connection between the Greek and Arabic traditions of autobiographical writings. Without his monograph on the subject, which for all its archaisms was nevertheless pioneering and magisterial, the present study might never have been undertaken. A remarkable indication of the significance of Misch's and Rosenthal's work is that neither has been superseded in more than half a century of subsequent scholarship. Indeed, the small body of texts they examined became an accepted canon in scholarly circles, and their conclusions have been echoed for decades in many contexts.

Arabic Scholarship

The first scholarly treatments of the Arabic autobiographical tradition in twentieth-century Arabic scholarship owe much to Rosenthal's original presentation of the corpus and refer to only a handful of texts not treated by him; understandably, however, they do not agree with some of Rosenthal's unremittingly negative evaluations of the texts themselves. Iḥsān ʿAbbās's monograph, *Fann al-sīra* (The Art of the *Sīra*), explores the Arabic literary genre *sīra,* which combines both biographical and autobiographical dimensions (see below). The last chapter of the work focuses on premodern Arabic autobiographies and describes seventeen texts in some detail.[30] ʿAbbās groups the texts into five large categories: (1) purely anecdotal texts (*akhbārī maḥḍ*); (2) texts of explanation, elucidation, warning, or justification (*tafsīr, taʿlīl, iʿtibār, tabrīr*); (3) texts of spiritual struggle; (4) texts recounting the author's adventures; and (5) other. In the same year, Shawqī Ḍayf published a study of Arabic autobiography the title of which, *al-Tarjama al-shakhṣiyya* (The Self-Authored *Tarjama*), refers to a different, though related, genre of Arabic literature, the *tarjama,* or biographical notice (see below).[31] He, too, groups these self-narratives into five categories: (1) philosophical, (2) scholarly and literary, (3) spiritual/mystical, (4) political, and (5) modern. Both works are primarily descriptive, and, although they provide readings of the texts that are more grounded in the conventions of the Arabic literary tradition, neither successfully opened up the field of autobiographical studies among Arab scholars in the disciplines of Arabic literature or Middle Eastern history.

A more recent study of modern Arabic autobiography by Yaḥyā Ibrāhīm ʿAbd al-Dāyim, *al-Tarjama al-dhātiyya fī al-adab al-ʿarabī al-ḥadīth* (The Autobiography in Modern Arabic Literature), addresses the premodern autobiographical tradition in a rather different manner.[32] First, ʿAbd al-Dāyim categorizes the texts primarily by the authors' motivations for writing them, and second, he addresses the literary dimensions of the texts more directly. Although dealing with nearly all of the same texts as his predecessors, ʿAbd al-Dāyim sees a significant connection between the premodern and modern traditions of Arabic autobiography, albeit with a noticeable dislocation caused by the rapid adoption of certain western cultural forms in the late nineteenth and early twentieth century. Treating autobiography primarily as a literary (rather than historical) form, he deems many medieval texts to have reached a high level of literary development. Among those he cites as communicating a sense of "literary pleasure" similar to modern texts are

SAUK VALLEY CC
LRC

the autobiographies of al-Mu'ayyad al-Shīrāzī, Ibn Buluggīn, Ibn al-Haytham, al-Rāzī, Usāma ibn Munqidh, Ibn Khaldūn, and al-Shaʿrānī.[33]

General Misconceptions

In the field of Middle Eastern studies, Arabic autobiographies became "orphan texts," dismissed by literary scholars, historians, and political scientists for conflicting reasons. Three primary assumptions seem to have hindered recognition of this tradition and greater scholarly attention to this corpus. The first has been the assumption that autobiography is extremely rare in Arabic literature. Edward Said, for example, writes, "Autobiography as a genre scarcely exists in Arabic literature. When it is to be found, the result is wholly special."[34] Stephen Humphreys refers to autobiography as "a very rare genre in Islamic literature."[35] Albert Hourani wrote of Rashīd Riḍā, the early-twentieth-century Egyptian reformer: "He has left us something which is rare in Arabic, a fragment of autobiography which in fact is a history of his intellectual and spiritual formation during the first thirty years or so of his life."[36] However, the idea that autobiography is almost nonexistent in Arabic literature may already be changing, for in the revised edition of Hourani's work (1983), this line was altered to read: "He has left us something *which is not so rare in Arabic as was once thought,* a fragment of autobiography [emphasis added]."[37]

The assumption that premodern Arabic autobiography is a rarity has been repeated in even more categorical terms in one of the few recent works to address the topic directly, the edited volume *Middle Eastern Lives: The Practice of Biography and Self-Narrative.*[38] For example, Marvin Zonis writes:

> Those works from the region that achieve the "true potential of the genre" are few in number, limiting the utility of autobiography for illuminating Middle Eastern conceptions of the self. But not only is autobiography generally lacking; biographies, indigenous to the region, are also in relatively short supply. . . . It is no wonder, then, that autobiography and biography are not yet part of the genres of literature in the Middle East.[39]

Zonis goes on to lament the problems that the lack of Middle Eastern autobiographies causes the historian:

> The relative absence of autobiographies deprives investigators of the Middle East, both Western and Middle Eastern scholars, of the opportunity to examine first-person data on the life course as it is lived in the Middle East.[40]

Zonis's conclusions are vastly overstated. Leaving aside the question of biography, if we search only for modern, politically oriented autobiographical texts (the field that most interests Zonis), we find from Egypt alone autobiographies by ʿAbbās II (the last khedive, r. 1892–1914), Muḥammad Najīb (first president of Egypt), Anwar al-Sādāt (third president of Egypt), Jihān al-Sādāt (first lady), ʿAlī Mubārak (statesman and cabinet minister under several successive governments), Ibrāhīm Fawzī Pasha (military general), Nubar Nubarian (statesman and minister), Rashīd Riḍā (political and social reformer), Hudā Shaʿrāwī (early feminist), Bābakr Badrī (Sudanese leader of the Mahdist movement that opposed Anglo-Egyptian rule), Aḥmad ʿUrābī (leader of the 1881–82 rebellion), Salāma Mūsā (social and political thinker), Ṭāhā Ḥusayn (cultural figure and minister of education), ʿUthmān Aḥmad ʿUthmān (political figure and commercial developer), Aḥmad Amīn (literary historian), Khālid Muḥammad Khālid (religious reformer), Muḥammad ʿAbduh (the single most influential religious reformer of the nineteenth century), Muḥammad Farīd (nationalist political figure), and Sayyid Quṭb (religious reformer of the Muslim Brotherhood), as well as ʿAbd al-ʿAẓīm Ramaḍān's full-length study of twentieth-century Egyptian political memoirs covering many less famous examples.[41]

The overall impression that Arabic autobiography is an extremely rare phenomenon is due primarily to the small number of examples that have been available to scholars. Rosenthal treats twenty-three texts in his article.[42] The *Cambridge History of Arabic Literature* cites seventeen of these texts[43] and Bernard Lewis lists twenty-one of them in his survey, "First-Person Narrative in the Middle East."[44] Iḥsān ʿAbbās treated seventeen texts, and Shawqī Ḍayf broadened the field slightly by treating twenty-six.[45] A 1989 dissertation by Saleh al-Ghamdi presents twenty-seven autobiographical works dating from the ninth to the sixteenth century.[46] Thus the same corpus of approximately two dozen texts has provided the foundation for all twentieth-century studies of the genre of Arabic autobiography up to the present. Although a large number of premodern Arabic autobiographical texts have been edited from manuscript and published in Arabic in the sixty years since the publication of Rosenthal's study, there simply has not been a conceptual category for premodern Arabic autobiography in either western or Arab scholarship that would cause them to be grouped together and thereby draw the attention of scholars.

A second major assumption follows from the supposed rarity of Arabic autobiographies: those few texts that have attracted scholarly attention have been presumed to be, and have therefore been studied as, anomalies rather than as part of a literary genre or historical tradition. Ironically, al-Suyūṭī, writing in 1485, was far more aware of the Arabic autobiographical tradition than most Arab or western scholars are today. This tendency to examine autobiographical texts as isolated, unrelated texts has even affected the scholarly understanding of the course of twentieth-century Arabic literature. Although several modern autobiographies, particularly that of Ṭāhā Ḥusayn, are considered to be among the greatest works of modern

Arabic literature, surveys of that literature have completely ignored the genre. Instead, the attention of the literary establishment, influenced by the prestige of the novel in the West, has been focused almost entirely on the development of the Arabic novel. Modern Arabic autobiographies are thus most often dealt with as *romans manqués*.[47] The *Cambridge History of Arabic Literature* contains no separate treatment of modern autobiography and notes only that several early Arabic novels were autobiographical[48] and that Ṭāhā Ḥusayn's work, *al-Ayyām*, is an autobiography.[49] Pierre Cachia, author of a study on Ṭāhā Ḥusayn, does not mention any other autobiographies in his collection of essays surveying modern Arabic literature.[50] And M. M. Badawi, who briefly treats the ubiquitous *al-Ayyām*, finds it disappointing for not being more of a novel:

> But despite the fact that it is one of the most attractive literary works in modern Arabic, *al-Ayyām* is not a novel. For all its irony and detachment, its vivid characterization, its humorous and pathetic situations, it is still no more than an inspired autobiography.[51]

This treatment of autobiographies, both medieval and modern, as a collection of unrelated texts, on the one hand, and as awkward (mis)representations of other genres such as biography, historical writings, or novels, on the other, has led scholars to ignore both the historical links between these texts and the literary discussions and evaluations of the genre of autobiography penned by premodern Arab authors. The late medieval critical discourse in which writers addressed issues such as whether an autobiography is more historically reliable than a biography, whether it is more virtuous to leave the writing of one's life to others (thus avoiding charges of vanity and self-aggrandizement), whether one should write an autobiography as a separate work or embed it in larger work, and so forth, has been completely ignored.

The third major hindrance to the study of Arabic autobiography has been the early judgments of Misch and Rosenthal that these Arabic texts do not constitute "true" autobiographies. Their opinions have been accepted as authoritative and repeated uncritically in survey works for more than half a century, a state of affairs that has successfully discouraged any serious reevaluation of the genre. This alleged shortcoming is variously formulated as the absence of any depiction of the author's personality or personal life or as a sweeping generalization that Arabic biographies and autobiographies deal only with types and classes rather than with individuals. Gustave von Grunebaum, for example, writes:

> Much of Arabic autobiography is limited to the listing of significant dates: birth, study, public appointments. The personality behind the events remains shrouded. . . . Only rarely does a scholar—and all the Muslim autobiogra-

> phers are scholars or theologians of one sort or another—describe his personal character.[52]

Thus western scholarship has created out of the Arabic autobiographical and biographical traditions a literary construct in which we find individual texts describing "types" rather than a type of text describing individuals. This construction is based on a model so steeped in a particular modern western conception of biography and autobiography that scholars are unable to address effectively an auto/biographical tradition possessed of different literary conventions. This line of thought derives in part from modern expectations that an autobiography should reveal an interior self different from, and even at odds with, the exterior public self. In short, the reader confronted with statements such as those cited above could easily conclude that autobiography and even biography are either nonexistent or exceedingly rare in Arabic and that the few examples that do exist are completely devoid of merit or interest. Such a conclusion would be, quite simply, false.

Against this prevailing current, a few dissenting voices have occasionally been raised, most often by scholars of other traditions who have on the whole been more impressed with the Arabic texts in question than have western Arabists. The *University Library of Autobiography* (1918) included not only translations of the autobiographies of Ibn Sīnā (Avicenna), al-Ghazālī, and Tamerlane but also a sympathetic introduction by Charles Bushnell.[53]

> The wonderful "confession" of Saint Augustine created no school, was imitated by no successors until, some six hundred years having passed, we begin to trace the rising culture of the Middle Ages. We then find the first autobiographical successors of Saint Augustine not among Christians, nor even among Europeans, but among the Arabic scholars of the Mohammedan Empire.[54]

Nearly sixty years later, Aldo Scaglione noted with surprise that, although they had been readily available in translation for decades, none of these texts had yet been treated in any existing western study of autobiography. In his own study devoted to the question, Is there really no true autobiography outside of Christian Europe? in which he examines the texts cited above as well as a fourth medieval Arabic autobiography, that of the famous fourteenth-century historiographer Ibn Khaldūn, Scaglione felt it necessary to substantiate his case by comparing each of these texts with contemporary European texts generally accepted as classic autobiographies.[55] He argues that because the Islamic texts can be shown to share basic characteristics with the canonical European texts, they must therefore also be deemed autobiographies. Though the arguments he presents are compelling, his conclusions have had little impact.

S. D. Goitein's opinion similarly offers a remarkable contrast to those of his contemporaries regarding the nature of the Arabic auto/biographical tradition. He states in reference to al-Balādhurī's *Ansāb al-ashrāf* (Genealogies of the Descendants of the Prophet Muhammad):

> First and foremost, I was impressed by the endless number of individuals whose personality is clearly brought out, in one way or another, by those ancient Arabic narratives. In the case of prominent actors on the scene, this is being done in monographs, composed of consecutive accounts, complemented by longer or shorter disconnected anecdotes, and concluded, usually subsequent to the story of his death, by a formal description of his character, illustrated again by the narration of relevant deeds, dicta, or incidents.[56]

This work by al-Balādhurī (d. 892) is not strikingly different from the rest of the Arabic tradition; Goitein's reading, however, *is* notably different from those of many of his peers. He sees in the compound nature of these texts (narratives, disconnected anecdotes, quotations, formal descriptions of character, deeds, dicta, etc.), not a chaotic jumble devoid of personalities, but a discourse of multiple texts that is, in part, deeply concerned with the portrayal of character.

Only as more Arabic autobiographical writings find their way into print and translation will scholars be able to evaluate this tradition from a firmer foundation. In comparison to the extraordinary corpus of premodern Arabic biographical materials, the strand of autobiographical writings will always appear a weaker step-sibling. In comparison to the corpus of European autobiographical texts for many of the same periods, however, the Arabic corpus is a tradition of substance clearly worthy of further exploration. Its study seems particularly vital as its very existence calls into question many western assumptions about the representation of self, consciousness, personality, and identity.

A reading of the corpus used as the basis for this study, a far larger body of texts than previously assembled, leads to a number of initial conclusions: (1) Arabic autobiographies—defined as texts that present themselves as a description or summation of the author's life, or a major portion thereof, as viewed retrospectively from a particular point in time—are far more numerous than has been assumed, even though they constitute a minor genre when contrasted with the vast body of Arabic biographical and prosopographical writings; (2) premodern Arabic autobiographers reveal considerably more about their personal and "inner" lives in their texts than has been previously documented, but much of this information is made manifest only through careful, close reading of the texts and a thorough awareness of their social milieus and literary strategies; and (3) a general literary "autobiographical consciousness" became firmly established in the medieval Arabic literary tradition, an awareness that is articulated in passages of Arabic autobiographies that address various motivations for writing autobiographies, the works of earlier autobiographers, and the ethical and religious implications of writing autobiographies.

Redefining the Issues

In attempting to provoke a reevaluation of autobiography in world literature, two courses of action are possible. One is to unearth the noncanonical elements subversively present in the current western canon and so recover or reemphasize these aspects of cultural diversity. It is rarely stressed, for example, that Galen and Nicholas lived and wrote in Asia Minor (in modern-day Turkey and Syria) or that Augustine, whose work is held to rest so squarely within the western European tradition of autobiography, wrote from North Africa and that it is a North African childhood and youth that he describes so intensely in his *Confessions.* Nor is it often stressed, although modern scholars often construct Augustine's work as the foundation of the western autobiographical tradition, that more than seven centuries passed before a "true" European was to write an autobiography that approached the works of these figures. Thus, both geographically and historically, these writers of seminal autobiographies must be insinuated into the western tradition by adjusting the (sometimes suspiciously) flexible boundaries of "western culture." Why, for example, should Europeans construe themselves as any more the heirs to Greek thought than Islamic culture when Islamic culture, in Arabic linguistic form, adopted, nurtured, and added to that body of knowledge for centuries before its transmission to Europe proper?

Even in the body of texts written by Europeans as conventionally defined, there are some intriguing moments of possible contact with other traditions. Several scholars have pointed out, for example, that one of the few autobiographies by a medieval European monarch, the *Libre dels Feyts* of James I of Aragon (1208–76), appears to be heavily influenced by, if not overtly modeled on, medieval Arabic literary forms. There were as yet few European examples of autobiography to be imitated and none at all for the autobiography of a king.[57]

The other more ambitious and potentially more fruitful course of action is to open up nonwestern traditions of autobiography for closer examination. Chinese literature offers an example of an autobiographical tradition that endured for centuries and underwent a number of rises and falls in popularity and several major transformations in terms of form and genre, yet has scarcely been touched on in western scholarship.[58] The Chinese tradition appears to present a fascinating parallel to the Arabic tradition in that it, too, has provoked little attention among modern native scholars and both traditions may be said to have been far better known among late medieval literati than among twentieth-century academics. The Tibetan tradition presents itself as another interesting candidate for in-depth study. Tibetan spiritual autobiographies are not only numerous and extremely sophisticated but also constitute a major portion of the earliest known Tibetan texts.[59] Thus the Tibetan autobiographical tradition seems to offer us a remarkable counterexample in which spiritual autobiography is not a late-developing genre but rather one of the foundational genres of an entire literary tradition. A reexamination of medieval and early modern Japanese *nikki* works (inadequately referred to in English as "diaries") and other autobiographical texts seems to be equally promising. Such works as the eleventh-century Heian literary diaries of Murasaki Shikibu, Sarashina, and Izumi Shikibu and, from later periods, texts such as the autobiography of Arai Hakuseki (1657–1725) and the spiritual autobiography of his contemporary, Hakuin Ekaku (1686–1769), all seem ripe for reevaluation with fewer Eurocentric and presentist assumptions about the literary conventions of "true" autobiography and a less parochial conceptualization of ideas such as the self, the human personality, and "individualism."[60]

Given the importance accorded autobiography for the understanding of culture, personality, and society, it is imperative to study nonwestern traditions both for their own sake and comparatively. This path of study will highlight previously overlooked aspects of European autobiographies and should provoke new and insightful readings. The present work is designed as a step in this direction.

The Arabic autobiographical tradition presents itself as a particularly important example by virtue of both its historical and its textual dimensions. It is a tradition that originated early (ninth–eleventh centuries), has endured for more than a millennium, evolved in a number of different directions in terms of formal characteristics, and, perhaps most important, articulated itself in discussions and critical writings about the autobiographical act.

With this background in mind, the simple phrase of our fifteenth-century Arab autobiographer, Jalāl al-Dīn al-Suyūṭī, "Scholars from ancient to modern times have continually written biographical accounts of themselves," stands as a significant challenge to the views of late-twentieth-century literary scholarship on the history of autobiography in world literature and the act of portraying the self in human culture.

Notes

1. "In the beginning, then, was Georges Gusdorf." See "Autobiography and the Cultural Moment: A Thematic, Historical and Bibliographic Introduction" in James

Olney, ed., *Autobiography: Essays Theoretical and Critical* (Princeton: Princeton University Press, 1980), 8.

2. Georges Gusdorf, "Conditions and Limits of Autobiography," trans. James Olney, in Olney, *Autobiography,* 29.

3. Roy Pascal, *Design and Truth in Autobiography* (Cambridge, Mass.: Harvard University Press, 1960), 22.

4. Georges May, *L'autobiographie* (Paris: Presses Universitaires de France, 1979), 17–25.

5. Richard N. Coe, *When the Grass Was Taller: Autobiography and the Experience of Childhood* (New Haven, Conn.: Yale University Press, 1984), 40.

6. One recent work which does aim at reevaluating the limitations of this corpus is Roy Porter, ed., *Rewriting the Self: Histories from the Renaissance to the Present* (New York: Routledge, 1997). It succeeds, however, in delineating the historical development of this canon far more than in challenging it.

7. Georg Misch, *Geschichte der Autobiographie,* 4 vols. (Bern and Frankfurt: A. Francke and Gerhard Schultke-Bulmke, 1949–69); Franz Rosenthal, "Die arabische Autobiographie," *Studia Arabica* 1 (1937): 1–40.

8. Wilhelm Dilthey, *Der Aufbau der geschichtlichen Welt in den Geisteswissenschaften* (Frankfurt: Suhrkamp, 1970), 242.

9. Misch, *Geschichte,* v. I.1, 4–5.

10. Ibid., v. I.1, 6.

11. Ibid., v. I.1, 22.

12. Ibid., v. I.1, 63 ff.

13. Ibid., v. I.2, 551.

14. Ibid., v. I.2, 552.

15. Ibid., v. II.1, 179–303.

16. Ibid., v. II.1, 213.

17. Ibid., v. II.1, 224. At this point, Misch quotes with approval from an article by Gustave von Grunebaum, "Die Wirklichkeitsweite der früharabischen Dichtung. Eine literaturwissenschaftliche Untersuchung," *Wiener Zeitschrift für die Kunde des Morgenlandes,* Beifheft 3 (1937).

18. Misch, *Geschichte,* v. III.2, 980.

19. *Ibid.,* v. III.2, 908. The citation is to Rosenthal's "Die arabische Autobiographie," 3.

20. Rosenthal, "Die arabische Autobiographie," 5.

21. Ibid., 3.

22. Ibid., 11.

23. Ibid., 40.

24. Jacob Burckhardt, *The Civilization of the Renaissance in Italy,* trans. S. G. C. Middlemore (London: Harrap, 1929), originally published in German in 1869.

25. Ibid., 13.

26. Ibid., 27.

27. Ibid., 28.

28. Ibid., 30.

29. Ibid., 32. Abū Shāma's text appears in translation in this volume; readers are free to evaluate the text on their own.

30. Iḥsān ʿAbbās, *Fann al-sīra* (Beirut: Dār al-Thaqāfa, 1956), 111–39.

31. Shawqī Ḍayf, *al-Tarjama al-shakhṣiyya* (Cairo: Dār al-Maʿārif, 1956).

32. Beirut: Dār Iḥyāʾ al-Turāth al-ʿArabī, 1975.

33. Yaḥyā Ibrāhīm ʿAbd al-Dāyim, *al-Tarjama al-dhātiyya fī al-adab al-ʿarabī al-ḥadīth* (Beirut: Dār Iḥyāʾ al-Turāth al-ʿArabī, 1975), 39.

34. Edward Said, *Beginnings* (Baltimore: Johns Hopkins University Press, 1987), 81.

35. R. Stephen Humphreys, *Islamic History: A Framework for Inquiry,* rev. ed. (Princeton: Princeton University Press, 1991), 194.

36. Albert Hourani, *Arabic Thought in the Liberal Age: 1798–1939* (Oxford: Oxford University Press, 1962), 224.

37. Albert Hourani, *Arabic Thought in the Liberal Age: 1789–1939,* 2d ed. (Cambridge: Cambridge University Press, 1983), 224.

38. Martin Kramer, ed., *Middle Eastern Lives: The Practice of Biography and Self-Narrative* (Syracuse: Syracuse University Press, 1991).

39. Marvin Zonis, "Autobiography and Biography in the Middle East: A Plea for Psychopolitical Studies," in Kramer, *Middle Eastern Lives,* 61.

40. Ibid., 63.

41. ʿAbd al-ʿAẓīm Muḥammad Ramaḍān, *Mudhakkirāt al-siyāsiyyīn wa-l-zuʿamāʾ fī Miṣr 1891–1981* (Beirut: al-Waṭan al-ʿArabī; Cairo: Maktabat Matbūlī, 1984); a shorter but useful survey of Iraqi memoirs is found in Werner Ende, "Neue arabische Memoirenliteratur zur Geschichte des modernen Iraq," *Der Islam* 49 (1972): 100–109. See also Elie Kedouri, *Arabic Political Memoirs and Other Studies* (London: Cass, 1974).

42. Rosenthal, "Die arabische Autobiographie."

43. M. J. L. Young, "Medieval Arabic Autobiography," in *Cambridge History of Arabic Literature: Religion, Learning, and Science in the ʿAbbasid Period,* ed. M. J. L. Young, J. D. Latham, and R. B. Serjeant (Cambridge: Cambridge University Press, 1990), 183–87.

44. In Kramer, *Middle Eastern Lives,* 20–34.

45. ʿAbbās, *Fann al-sīra,* and Ḍayf, *al-Tarjama.*

46. Saleh al-Ghamdi, "Autobiography in Classical Arabic Literature: An Ignored Genre" (Ph.D. diss., Indiana University, 1989).

47. This situation is even stranger given that, in contrast to the number of premodern Arabic autobiographies, the number of twentieth-century Arabic autobiographies available in translation in western languages has been growing rapidly: see recently published translations of works by Fadwā Ṭūqān, Salāma Mūsā, Aḥmad Amīn, Hudā Shaʿrāwī, Anwar al-Sādāt, Jihān al-Sādāt, Fadhima Amrouche, Leila Abu Zeyd and others; dozens of other twentieth-century autobiographies are readily available in the original Arabic.

48. Roger Allen, "The Beginnings of the Arabic Novel," in *Cambridge History of Arabic Literature: Modern Arabic Literature,* ed. M. M. Badawi (Cambridge: Cambridge University Press, 1992), 191.

49. Hilary Kilpatrick, "The Egyptian Novel from Zaynab to 1980," in Badawi, *Cambridge History of Arabic Literature,* 226.

50. Pierre Cachia, *An Overview of Modern Arabic Literature* (Edinburgh: Edinburgh University Press, 1990).

51. M. M. Badawi, *Short History of Modern Arabic Literature* (Oxford: Clarendon, 1993): 111.

52. Gustave von Grunebaum, "Self-Expression: Literature and History," in *Medieval Islam: A Study in Cultural Orientation* (Chicago: University of Chicago Press, 1956), 270.

53. *University Library of Autobiography* (15 vols.); vol. 2: *The Middle Ages and Their Autobiographers,* with an introduction by Charles Bushnell (New York: F. Tyler Daniels Co., 1918; rpt. National Alumni, 1927). The autobiography of Tamerlane has been discredited by recent scholars as a forgery probably created a century or more after Tamerlane's death.

54. Ibid., ix.

55. Aldo Scaglione, "The Mediterranean's Three Spiritual Shores: Images of Self between Christianity and Islam in the Later Middle Ages," in *The Craft of Fiction: Essays in Medieval Poetics,* ed. Leigh A. Arrathoon (Rochester, Mich.: Solaris Press, 1984), 453–73.

56. S. D. Goitein, "Individualism and Conformity in Classical Islam," in *Individualism and Conformity in Classical Islam,* ed. Amin Banani and Spyros Vryonis (Wiesbaden: Otto Harrassowitz, 1977), 5.

57. Robert I. Burns, "The King's Autobiography: The Islamic Connection," in *Muslims, Christians, and Jews in the Crusader Kingdom of Valencia* (Cambridge: Cambridge University Press, 1984), 285–88; Samuel Armistead, "An Anecdote of King Jaume I and Its Arabic Cogener," in *Cultures in Contact in Medieval Spain: Historical and Literary Essays Presented to L. P. Harvey,* ed. David Hook and Barry Taylor (London: King's College, 1990), 1–8; Juan Vernet, *La cultura hispanoárabe en Oriente y Occidente* (Barcelona: Ariel, 1978), 333.

58. Pei-Yi Wu, *The Confucian's Progress: Autobiographical Writings in Traditional China* (Princeton: Princeton University Press, 1990).

59. The authors would like to thank Janet B. Gyatso for sharing with them her paper, "Autobiography in Tibetan Religious Literature: Reflections on Its Modes of Self-Presentation," which provided a window onto another nonwestern tradition of autobiography, one that appears both substantial and fascinating.

60. See, for example, John C. Maraldo, "Rousseau, Hakuseki, and Hakuin: Paradigms of Self in Three Autobiographers," in *Self as Person in Asian Theory and Practice,* ed. Roger T. Ames (New York: SUNY Press, 1994), 57–86; Marilyn J. Miller, *The Poetics of Nikki Bungaku: A Comparison of the Traditions, Conventions, and Structure of Heian Japan's Literary Diaries with Western Autobiographical Writings* (New York: Garland, 1985); Annie Shepley Omori, trans., *Diaries of Court Ladies of Old Japan* (Tokyo: Kenkyusha, [1935] 1961); Joyce Akroyd, trans., *Told Round a Brushwood Fire: The Autobiography of Arai Hakuseki* (Princeton: Princeton University Press, 1979); Norman Waddell, trans., "Wild Ivy: The Spiritual Autobiography of Hakuin Ekaku," *Eastern Buddhist* 15, no. 2 (1982): 71–109; and 16, no. 1 (1983): 107–39; Richard Bowring, trans., *Murasaki Shikibu: Her Diary and Poetic Memoirs* (Princeton: Princeton University Press, 1982); Edwin A. Cranston, trans., *The Izumi Shikibu Diary: A Romance of the Heian Court* (Cambridge, Mass.: Harvard University Press, 1969).

CHAPTER TWO

The Origins of Arabic Autobiography

Biographical Traditions: Early Prototypes

The Arabs of pre-Islamic times practiced a type of oral biography in the form of short narratives called *akhbār* (sing. *khabar*). When reciting his genealogy, a tribesman would add identifying remarks and accounts of memorable incidents associated with certain figures in the lineage.[1] Similarly, a poem would be transmitted along with reports about the poet and the occasion for the composition of the verses. These paired elements, the informational *khabar* and the transmitted text (whether a list of names or a poem), affirmed each other's authority and authenticity, and the joined elements of anecdote and poem, or anecdote and genealogy, commonly remained together in oral tradition as a single discursive unit. For this reason, perhaps, the *khabar* remained unitary and limited in focus and never expanded to the point of becoming the summation of a life.[2] With the advent of Arabic writing and the proliferation of literacy, it was primarily by the accumulation and combination of *akhbār* that biographies (along with various sorts of extended history accounts) were first constructed. The pattern of linking poetry and prose into a single discourse imprinted itself very strongly on early Arabic written literature and greatly influenced the formation of written historical and literary genres during the early Islamic period (seventh–ninth centuries).[3]

From the rich but fragmentary materials of oral tradition, a written scholarly tradition of compilation and anthologization emerged. Under the early caliphs of the Umayyad dynasty (661–750), the historical lore of the pre-Islamic Arabs, along with reports of events in early Islamic history, was committed to writing. Massive collections of poems, place-names, genealogies, rare and obscure vocabulary, and many other types of knowledge were compiled directly from oral sources. The tenth-century bibliographer Ibn al-Nadīm has left a catalog of these early works, which also included lists of caliphs, compilations of anecdotes about poets, and incidents from the lives of early political figures. From such early collections of *akhbār*, later historians compiled the first dynastic and annalistic histories, sometimes juxtaposing conflicting accounts in a single work and leaving the reader to choose among them. Finally, reports of the words and actions of the Prophet Muhammad were collected in authoritative compendiums that listed the transmitters of each report by name. Eventually, the written tradition began to generate its own distinctive genres, less dependent on the form of the raw data being collected, among which were a number of genres that can be more properly termed biographical in varying degrees.

Influenced perhaps by the genealogical model, the earliest independent biographical listings take as their subject groups of specialized professionals such as *ḥadīth* transmitters, poets, singers, and so forth, rather than single individuals.[4] The treatment of subjects as members of a group, however defined, remained the most common technique of Arabic biographical writing. The major exception was the life of the Prophet Muhammad, recensions of which date back to the eighth century. Early versions of his life story, called *maghāzī* (military expeditions), deal primarily with his campaigns, while later compilations, called *siyar* (see below), offer accounts of his career from birth to death.[5] Although biographies of later figures were never as detailed as those of the Prophet, the *siyar* provided a model of life narration whose influence is evident in the biographical as well as the autobiographical writings of later centuries.

By the seventh century, the reports of the Prophet's career had been collected and arranged into a sequential narrative. But many scholars were interested in such reports only to the extent that they could support, or produce, a particular interpretation of the law. Reports of legal, ritual, and theological importance were thus separated out and given the name *ḥadīth*, "reports of the Prophet's exemplary words and deeds." To confirm the reliability of *ḥadīth* reports, it was necessary to examine the men and women who had transmitted them. Did the scholar cited as the transmitter of a particular report have a reputation for veracity and good character? Could he have met the teacher from whom he claimed to have heard the *ḥadīth*? Were the two men actually in Mecca (or Medina, or Kufa) at the same time? Did he receive authorization (*ijāza*) to transmit this particular report? And so forth. To keep track of such information, *ḥadīth* scholars compiled lists of the Prophet's companions and of those Muslims of subsequent generations who transmitted on their authority. Many such lists contain little more than names, in chronological or alphabetical order; others, however, notably the compilation of Ibn Saʿd (d. 845), contain extensive *akhbār* about many of their subjects. As crucial elements in the authentication of transmitted knowledge, biographical data were rapidly assimilated to, and developed within, the domain of historical writing.[6]

Biographical Writing: Literary Genres

The most significant types of Arabic biographical writing that present themselves as complete summations of a life in one fashion or another are *sīra, tarjama, barnāmaj, fahrasa,* and *manāqib.* The *sīra* and *tarjama* were both geographically and historically quite widespread and are dealt with in detail below; the terms *barnāmaj* and *fahrasa,* however, have been limited to specific regions and periods. The term *barnāmaj,* in the sense of biography, was used almost exclusively in Islamic Spain (eighth–fifteenth centuries) and later, to a much lesser extent, in North Africa,[7] while the use of *fahrasa* or *fihrist* to denote a biography or autobiography is restricted to North Africa and particularly to Sufi contexts.[8] For brevity's sake, as the *barnāmaj* and *fahrasa* refer to texts that are structurally almost identical to the *tarjama,* they are addressed here as regional variants of that basic form.

As we shall see, the genres *sīra* and *tarjama* (in its several variant forms) eventually developed recognized subgenres in which the author recorded his own life rather than that of someone else. These constitute the two genres of early medieval Arabic literature that most closely resemble the western concept of autobiography. The last of the biographical forms mentioned above, however, the *manāqib* (lit. "virtues"), never seems to have been used for autobiographical purposes; the form was apparently too explicitly linked to praise and encomia to be adapted for use in autobiographical writings. *Manāqib* works were written about religious and political figures, groups of people, occasionally of cities, and even of the Islamic religion itself.[9] The vast majority, especially in later centuries, were focused on religious figures, particularly Sufi mystics. Other terms associated with the biographies of religious figures are *akhbār* (accounts), *akhlāq* (morals), *faḍā'il* (superior qualities), *khaṣā'iṣ* (attributes), and *ma'āthir wa-mafākhir* (glorious deeds and gracious qualities). These forms, however, along with the *manāqib,* remained entirely biographical in nature and never seem to have developed parallel *auto*biographical traditions, as did the *sīra* and *tarjama* forms.

Sīra (Exemplary Life Story)

The *sīra* is the earliest of the full biographical forms, dating at least to the second Islamic century (eighth century) with the works of Ibn Isḥāq (d. 767) and Ibn Hishām (d. 828 or 833) on the Prophet Muhammad. Derived from the verb *sāra,* meaning "to go" or "to travel," the noun *sīra* denoted a path or journey, one's manner of proceeding, and by extension, the behavior or conduct of an individual.[10] It eventually came to mean a biography, in particular that of the Prophet Muhammad. The form soon came to serve as a vehicle for the retelling of other famous lives, such as Ibn Shaddād's *sīra* of Saladin (Ṣalāḥ al-Dīn al-Ayyūbī), Badr al-Dīn al-ʿAynī's biography of the Mamluk sultan al-Mu'ayyad, *al-Sayf al-muhannad fī sīrat al-malik al-Mu'ayyad* (The Fine Indian Blade on the Life of King al-Mu'ayyad), and many others.

The *sīra* thus became an independent work devoted to the biography of an individual; although there are far fewer of these texts than the hundreds of thousands of shorter biographical notices that have come down to us, they still constitute a sizable body of literature. In addition, the term *sīra* appears to have carried the connotation of an exemplary life, such as that of the Prophet Muhammad or his son-in-law, ʿAlī, and in certain later periods is found predominantly among Shiʿite writers. In the late medieval and premodern periods, the title *manāqib* (virtues) became the most common term for single-subject biographies of religious exemplars. Despite the change in nomenclature, *manāqib* works often proceeded in the manner of a *sīra*, documenting the subject's career from birth to death using eyewitness testimony and lists of teachers, students, family members, and works composed.

The term *sīra* grew to encompass autobiographies as well, as seen in the case of the work of another al-Mu'ayyad, al-Mu'ayyad al-Shīrāzī (d. 1077), who recounts the events of his own life, although it is difficult to determine whether the title *Sīrat al-Mu'ayyad* was originally used by the author or applied to the text by later copyists. In any case, the two types of *sīra*, biographical and autobiographical, were not initially distinguished from one another. The genre, as such, consisted of the literary representation of a life as a subgenre of history and did not differentiate between first-person and third-person texts; and as some autobiographical texts were also written in the third person, the texts themselves were at times not formally different. Although a *sīra* might be given a formal, often flowery, title when composed, it later often came to be known simply as "The *Sīra* of so-and-so" in medieval bibliographies, indexes, and cross-references in other works.[11]

The term *sīra* in reference to an independent auto/biographical text became less and less common over the centuries (with the exception of its continual use in reference to the biography of the Prophet), and fifteenth- and sixteenth-century writers such as al-Suyūṭī, Ibn Ṭūlūn, and al-Shaʿrānī do not even mention it in their discussions of autobiography. One reason for this disappearance may be that by this later period the term *sīra* had also come to designate a genre of folk epic, such as the epics of the poet-warrior ʿAntar ibn Shaddād, the heroine Dhāt al-Himma, and the Bedouin tribe of the Banī Hilāl.[12] This extension of the term may well have grown out of the idea of the exemplary life, for the genre consists primarily of highly romanticized accounts of larger-than-life heroes and their adventures. The term was revived in the twentieth century, however, in modern Arabic both as a term for biography and as part of a compound neologism, *al-sīra al-dhātiyya* (self-*sīra*), now the most common term for autobiography.

Most Arabic biographical writings from the early medieval to the modern period, however, do not take the form of independent works, that is, as individual *sīra*s (Ar. pl. *siyar*), but rather in various forms of biographical collections and anthologies. The production of biographical dictionaries (*ṭabaqāt*), annalistic histories (*tawārīkh*), which included biographical notices, and biographical materials preserved in anecdotal form (*akhbār*) reached stupendous proportions during the Islamic Middle Ages. Some of the larger biographical compendiums contain well over ten thousand biographical notices, and the number of compendiums themselves is in the thousands. Biographical writing was for centuries one of the most widespread genres of Arabic literature.[13]

Ṭabaqāt (Biographical Dictionaries)

Most Arabic biographies are found in special collections, referred to in English as "biographical dictionaries" or "biographical compendiums." The earliest of these were devoted to the generations (Ar. sing. *ṭabaqa*) in a category or class of people, hence the Arabic name for the genre, *ṭabaqāt* (lit. "generations"). A great number of different "classes" (sing. *ṣinf* or *ṭā'ifa*) provided the framework for such compendiums in the Islamic Middle Ages: Qur'ān reciters, physicians, caliphs, scholars of *ḥadīth*, jurists of the Shāfiʿī legal tradition, theologians of the Muʿtazilī school, Shiʿite scholars from Bahrain, grammarians from Yemen, famous women scholars of Egypt, poets of the sixteenth century, poets the author met personally, teachers of the author, and so on. Occupations, geographic origins, sectarian and dogmatic affiliations, historical periods (particularly centennial compilations), tribal and family groupings, and even first names and nicknames were all used as parameters for defining a particular group to be covered in a given biographical dictionary. Women scholars were commonly included in medieval biographical compendiums, and some collections devoted special sections to various classes of women including poets, religious scholars, and mystics.[14] The variety as well as the number of *ṭabaqāt* works is at times overwhelming. Medieval Islamic society preserved massive amounts of biographical data, and these data were accessed, referenced, and cross-referenced in a multitude of ways.

The organization of these biographical works and other reference works from the same period reflects an intellectual milieu in which classification and categorization, often involving the marshaling of astonishing amounts of specific detail such as dates, names, book titles, and lists of teachers represented the predominant methodology for the acquisition, organization, authentication, and transmission of knowledge. The ubiquity of this intellectual methodology has led some modern scholars to decry the entire Arabic autobiographical and biographical tradition as one concerned only with human beings as representatives of classes or (stereo)types and not with individuals and individual characteristics.

This judgment misses the point of classical Arabic biographical writing as its practitioners understood it. Beginning in the ninth century and possibly earlier, Muslim scholars elaborated competing visions of (religious) authority according to which various groups of qualified practitioners (e.g., *ḥadīth* scholars, jurists, Sufis) claimed responsibility for the maintenance of aspects of the Prophetic legacy. Given this framework, the biographer's primary task consisted of establishing the specific group's claim to the Prophetic legacy and then documenting the transmission of that legacy from one generation of practitioners to another. This paradigm carried over even to groups whose relation to the Prophet and the Revelation were tenuous or nonexistent (physicians, singers, poets, etc.), all of whose biographers wrote of them as members of professional collectivities. Especially in the more obviously religious contexts, the biographer had little incentive to document his subjects' idiosyncrasies. Thus *ṭabaqāt* do not *fail* to take account of individuality; rather, they *succeed* in excluding it.[15]

This does not mean that *ṭabaqāt* entries entirely lack individuation; indeed, many of them contain vivid incident and evocative detail. The amount of individuation and detail varies according to both the "class" of the person represented and his or her social and historical prominence: famous figures almost invariably receive more detailed treatment; biographical notices of poets generally feature more clearly delineated personalities than those of *ḥadīth* scholars. Yet even these elaborations must be understood in the context of collective and contrastive self-definition through biography. A figure who attained exemplary status in his professional collectivity, or who became a subject of dispute in the controversies that erupted between scholarly and professional groups, attracted to himself or herself evidentiary narratives pro and con, all of which found their way into his or her biographical entry. Disputation, competition, and contention prompted a similar expansion of autobiographical narrative, as the works of Ḥunayn ibn Isḥāq, Ibn Buluggīn, and al-Suyūṭī—among others—show.

Seen in this light, the relationship of autobiography to biography appears to be rather ambiguous. On the one hand, biography provided a literary framework for the emergence of autobiographical literary forms. On the other hand, if the overall project of biography tended to downplay and even exclude "individuality," it is difficult to see how the emergence of autobiography as a literary act can be traced directly to the biographical endeavors that preceded it. Even so, the raw material and research methodologies used by compilers of these biographical dictionaries eventually gave rise to autobiographical writings in the form of the *tarjama,* an individual (biographical or autobiographical) entry in a larger compilation.

Tarjama (Biographical Notice)

Most of the entries found in biographical compendiums belong to the genre *tarjama,* a term with Aramaic origins that can be referred to simply as a "biographical notice."[16] In modern Arabic the term literally means a "translation" (cf. Aramaic *targum*) or an "interpretation," a sense that was also present in medieval Arabic. But in medieval Arabic the verb *tarjama* also meant to give a work, or an individual section of a work, a title or heading, as seen in the introduction to a work by the famous Andalusian judge, al-Qāḍī ʿIyāḍ: "I have given it the title [*wa-tarjamtuhu bi-*] *Madhāhib al-ḥukkām fi nawāzil al-aḥkām* [The Methods of Judges in the Judgment of Cases]."[17] By extension, the term may have come to mean a work that was divided into sections with headings.

The term *tarjama* thus contains three central and interrelated ideas, that of explanation or interpretation, that of transformation into a different medium, and that of clarification by means of division into sections and labeling. The *tarjama* as biographical notice may be taken to be a representation of a person, to be distinguished from the physical being; it is an inexact, imperfect copy of a life, just as a commentary cannot represent the original text, or a translation represent the Qur'ān.[18] But it is a key to the person, a clarification, an attempt to label and explain his or her actions and accomplishments and make them comprehensible to posterity and accessible to the student. To reach the original person in a more direct fashion can only be accomplished by reading the original text, that is, his or her works, or by receiving his or her teachings through oral transmission, passed down through generations of teachers. The biography may therefore be seen as a commentary on an original, a key to a great thinker, past or present.

The basic constituent parts of a *tarjama* usually consisted of an account of the subject's name and ancestry, date of birth (and death, if applicable), a catalog of teachers (*mashyakha, muʿjam,* or *thabat*),[19] a bibliography of works written by the subject (*fihrist* or *fahrasa*),[20] travel and pilgrimage accounts (*riḥla*),[21] and collections of entertaining or illuminating anecdotes (*nawādir* and *akhbār*).[22] In addition, depending on the subject's professional affliation, a *tarjama* might include collections of personal letters and formal epistles (*rasāʾil* and *ikhwāniyyāt*),[23] selections of poetry (*shiʿr*),[24] accounts of visions and dreams (*manāmāt* or *manāẓir*),[25] and accounts of minor miracles (*karāmāt*) and virtues (*manāqib*).[26]

These sections of the *tarjama* were also composed and published in certain contexts as independent works completely separate from any entry in a biographical compendium. These forms (both as traditional sections of a *tarjama* and as independent works) merit careful study both for the information they contain about Islamic society in different time periods and as the means for representing dimensions of an individual's life. Unfortunately, however, most of them have attracted little scholarly attention because they fall outside the primary lines of modern historical and religious research. It is astonishing how little information is available about the historical development of these forms despite their status as the primary vehicles through which an enormous amount of knowledge about premodern Arabo-Islamic society has come down to us. Literary scholars have rejected them as more properly the realm of historians, and historians have, on the whole, treated them as transparent and unproblematic, deeming the literary conventions either obvious or uninteresting.[27]

The Arabic *tarjama* represents a carefully categorized frame for depicting the most crucial information about a person in an intellectual context that focused on a person's value as a transmitter and contributor to knowledge and to a shared academic and spiritual heritage. The categories in which this information was presented existed both as constituent parts of the *tarjama* itself and, when expanded, as independent literary genres that could circulate on their own.

Curiously, the portion of the *tarjama* for which the least articulated terminology developed was the opening narrative segment, which provided the historical "life story" of the subject, although some sources do refer to this section of a *tarjama* as the *sīra.* Here a sharp contrast with the western tradition becomes quite clear, for it is only the "life story" that is generically labeled and developed in the western tradition as auto/biography. In the West, it is relatively rare for this narrative to be coupled directly with a person's literary, artistic, or intellectual output; even personal letters are often edited and published separately. In a lengthy medieval Arabic *tarjama,* however, the basic historical information was often combined directly with the biographer's (or autobiographer's) selection of the subject's best poetry, letters, and bons mots; the subject's life story and literary production were thus often represented side by side and traveled through time together as the *tarjama* was quoted, expanded, or summarized by later biographers and compilers.

Autobiographical Subgenres

When the author of a biographical compendium came to a point where it was logical or desirable to write his own entry, he did so in either the first- or third-person voice, and the result was termed a *tarjamat al-nafs,* "self-*tarjama,*" or the author was said to have written a *tarjama* of himself (*tarjama nafsah* or *tarjama li-nafsih*). Even more widespread as a practice was the writing of a self-*tarjama* so that it could be included in a biographical compendium edited by someone else. At times these autobiographies were produced at the direct request of the compiler of the biographical dictionary. Many such texts are included in collections that consist primarily of biographies and are sometimes only identified as *auto*biographies by a single line or phrase such as "the following text that he wrote about himself." The autobiographical text mught appear in its complete form, or the compiler might present only selections from the autobiography, which are then interspersed with material from other sources confirming, contradicting, or supplementing the autobiographical passages. At times the result is a seamless account in which it is quite difficult to distinguish between the hand of the biographer and the hand of the autobiographer; at other times the final product may clearly reproduce the voice of the autobiographer separate from that of the biographer and those of additional sources.

One rich example of this process is the "autobiography" of Ibn al-ʿAdīm (d. 1262) as told to Yāqūt al-Ḥamawī (d. 1229), which includes passages, carefully distinguished as such, from Ibn al-ʿAdīm's written autobiography (produced at the request of Yāqūt), oral material collected from Ibn al-ʿAdīm in an interview with Yāqūt about the written autobiography, as well as a variety of other sources, both written and oral.[28] Yāqūt (one of the major biographical compilers of his day and himself the author of an autobiography) meticulously reproduces all of these separate voices in this text and in a number of similar examples. The resulting texts reveal a great deal about Yāqūt's methodology in conducting interviews, gathering information, and assembling texts from oral and written primary sources. Through these texts we can catch glimpses of the autobiographical substrata of the mass of biographical writings that have come down to us in anthologized form. A thorough examination of the biographical compendiums should provide more concrete indications as to the nature and extent of such autobiographical practices, even though many of the autobiographical texts referred to are no doubt lost.

Thus the biographical *tarjama,* like the *sīra,* developed an autobiographical subgenre. At first, these self-composed autobiographical notices were scarcely distinguishable from their biographical siblings; this subgenre continued to exist for centuries. Eventually, however, the self-*tarjamas* provided a major impetus for the development of independent autobiographies and began to take on distinguishing characteristics of their own.

Other Influences

Discussions of the contribution of ancient Greek and Persian literatures to the development of Arabic autobiography focus primarily on the impact of works by the Greek physician Galen of Pergamon (d. ca. 200) and the Persian physician Burzōē (sixth century).[29] Arabic translations of these texts circulated widely in the Middle Ages, and references to them appear in several Arabic autobiographies written between the tenth and twelfth centuries. The philosophers al-Rāzī (Latin Rhazes) and Ibn Sīnā (Latin Avicenna), the physicians Ibn Riḍwān and Ibn al-Haytham, and Samawʾal al-Maghribī, a Jewish convert to Islam, all note their familiarity with one or another of these texts in their own autobiographical writings.[30]

Burzōē is best known as the translator of the famous collection of animal fables, the *Panchatantra,* from Sanskrit into Middle Persian. His Persian text was then translated into Arabic by Ibn al-Muqaffaʿ (d. 755 or 756) in the early eighth century and retitled *Kalīla wa-Dimna.* All that is known about Burzōē's life comes from the short texts prefaced to various redactions and translations of *Kalīla wa-Dimna,* which include at least five different versions of his travels to India and two versions of his autobiography. One of the most common of the accounts of his journey to India relates that the Persian king Khusraw Anūshirawān (r. 531–79) had heard of a fabulous collection of tales in India and charged Burzōē with the task of obtaining it. Once in India, Burzōē resides in the court of the Indian king for a time before daring to attempt to see this marvelous book. He befriends an Indian by the name of Azawayh and discourses lengthily with him on the nature of true friendship. Finally, he makes his request, and Azawayh brings him the book from the king's chambers. Burzōē copies it, translates it, and then returns to Persia. King Khusraw is so pleased that he offers Burzōē whatever reward he should desire, but Burzōē accepts only a cloak as recompense and requests that his own life story be appended to the work. The king orders this done.

Another version has Burzōē traveling to India in search of powerful herbs that grow in the mountains there, which, when properly prepared, are capable of reviving the dead. Despite many attempts, Burzōē fails in this task. He then meets a group of Indian sages, however, who explain that this legend is but an allegory: the mountains are wise men, the herbs their books, and the dead the ignorant of the earth. Satisfied with this explanation, Burzōē returns to Persia and presents a large number of books he has translated to King Khusraw.[31]

Burzōē's autobiography offers yet another version of the events narrated in the account of his journey to India. An accomplished physician, Burzōē despairs of his craft because, in the end, he can only cure disease temporarily and all of his wards eventually succumb to death. He seeks spiritual solace, but none of the religions he turns to offers an answer to his malaise. In the text he twice mentions that he traveled to India, presumably as part of his spiritual quest, and once notes that he translated books there. Eventually, however, he renounces the world and becomes an ascetic.

Burzōē's life story is recounted in an ahistorical mode devoid of such details as names, dates, or places and is structured in a manner that evinces little sense of chronology. It can scarcely be said to have influenced the vast majority of Arabic autobiographies, which are specifically devoted to documenting the historical details of their authors' lives. Yet one text in particular, by al-Ghazālī (d. 1111), does bear some resemblance to Burzōē's text. Al-Ghazālī was a religious scholar and professor at the pinnacle of his highly successful career when he suffered a crisis that literally left him unable to speak. According to his autobiography, *al-Munqidh min al-ḍalāl* (The Deliverer from Error), as a result of this episode he retired from public life in pursuit of Truth.[32] None of the known schools of religious thought satisfied him, however, until he encountered Sufi mysticism, which provided the spiritual peace he craved. He withdrew from the world to live the life of an ascetic but eventually, years later, returned to his post and wrote his autobiography as a guide to other seekers. Thus, unlike Burzōē's nihilistic despair, al-Ghazālī's text draws on Islamic traditions of didacticism and emulation and offers itself as a guide to the true path.

Galen of Pergamon included personal references and autobiographical details in a number of his writings, but two works in particular are thought to have had some influence on the early Arabic tradition: *On My Books* and *On the Ordering of My Books*. In the former, Galen sought to provide a definitive list of his own works after having noted in the book markets of Rome that some of his works were circulating under the names of other authors and still other works were being falsely attributed to him. In the latter, however, Galen did more than simply list his works. In the opening section he attempted to order them as they should be read by students, from the most basic texts to the most difficult and complex, while in a subsequent section he provides brief accounts of his reasons for writing certain works and the time and place in which he did so. In this rough chronology Galen includes brief references to his travels and education and his lengthy conflicts with rivals jealous of his success.[33]

Autobibliographies similar to Galen's *On My Books* did indeed become one of the common features of Arabic autobiography. At times these book lists circulated independently, but more often, unlike Galen's work, they were included in a larger autobiographical work that also documented other aspects of the author's life such as his birthdate, genealogy, teachers, and travels. Although *On the Ordering of My Books* includes more in the way of personal detail, no Arabic autobiography is structured in a manner similar to Galen's text. The one element for which there are numerous parallels, however, is Galen's account of his jealous rivals. Ḥunayn ibn Isḥāq's autobiography (translated in this volume) is very similar in tone to passages in Galen, and Ḥunayn, the preeminent translator of Galen of his day, was certainly familiar with this text; however, Ḥunayn's account is more closely patterned on the biblical/Qur'ānic account of Joseph, which he, as a Christian, would have known equally well (see the introduction to the translation). Another account of intellectual rivalry is found centuries later in the autobiography of al-Suyūṭī, also translated in this volume.

It is clear that the autobiographical writings of both Burzōē and Galen circulated widely and may thus have helped to set the stage for the emergence of the Arabic autobiographical tradition; however, other than the autobibliography subgenre noted above, neither text seems to have influenced in any direct manner the form, structure, style, or content of Arabic biographical or autobiographical writing.

A final thread that played a critical role in the rise of Arabic autobiography was that of spiritual, particularly Sufi, autobiographical writings the origins of which are traced by Rosenthal as far back as al-Muḥāsibī (d. 857) and al-Tirmidhī (d. 898), and continue through al-Ghazālī's *al-Munqidh min al-ḍalāl* and the works of many later Sufi autobiographers such as al-Simnānī, Zarrūq, al-Shaʿrānī, al-Yūsī, and Ibn ʿAjība.[34] In these works the author's path of spiritual development constitutes the central focus of the text. They are thus by definition texts that portray primarily an "inner self" and are constructed on a model of transformation and development. They are also, even more clearly than their scholarly counterparts, constructed as models for emulation in the sense that embedded in the text is a call or an invitation to the reader to travel the same spiritual path. Several of these texts culminate with the author's "conversion" to the spiritual or mystical life and may thus also be linked to conversion autobiographies such as those by Samaw'al al-Maghribī, who converted to Islam in the twelfth century, and the Christian writer Fray Anselmo Turmeda, who converted to Islam in the fourteenth century.

Autobiography as a specific type of Arabic literature thus evolved mainly in the context of the Arabic biographical tradition, which in turn had emerged primarily as a branch of historical writing. Autobiographical writing developed first within two primary forms: *sīra* and *tarjama*. Limited exposure to pre-Islamic Greek and Persian models in Arabic translation exerted some influence on physicians and philosophers of the tenth to twelfth centuries—the two classes of scholars most directly involved with ancient Greek and Persian thought. The Sufi spiritual autobiography also emerged as a recognizable subtradition of its own, which in turn influenced even some nonspiritual autobiographical texts. The two recognized indigenous Arabic genres, self-*sīra* and self-*tarjama,* took on numerous modified forms in different social and literary contexts, but they continued to be understood by late medieval and premodern writers as constituting a single recognizable act of writing an account of one's life for posterity regardless of the formal differences in the resulting texts.

Notes

1. See Ignaz Goldziher, *Muslim Studies,* trans. C. R. Barber and S. M. Stern, 2 vols. (London: George Allen and Unwin, 1967), 1:168, 170; Werner Caskel, *Ǧamharat an-nasab: Das genealogische Werk des Hišam ibn Muḥammad al-Kalbī* (Leiden: E. J. Brill, 1966), 1:35; and, for a discussion of this form in its modern living context, Andrew Shryock, *Nationalism and the Genealogical Imagination: Oral History and Textual Authority in Tribal Jordan* (Berkeley: University of California Press, 1997).

2. However, for arguments to accept *akhbār* accounts as autobiography, see Hilary Kilpatrick, "Autobiography and Classical Arabic Literature," *Journal of Arabic Literature* 22 (1991): 1–20, and Jamal J. Elias, "The *Ḥadīth* Traditions of ʿĀʾisha as Prototypes of Self-Narrative," *Edebiyât: Special Issue—Arabic Autobiography,* N.S. 7, no. 2 (1997): 215–33.

3. See Wolfhart Heinrichs, "Prosimetrical Genres in Classical Arabic Literature," and Dwight F. Reynolds, "Prosimetrum in 19th- and 20th-Century Arabic Literature," in *Prosimetrum: Crosscultural Perspectives on Narrative in Prose and Verse,* ed. Joseph Harris and Karl Reichl (Suffolk: Boydell and Brewer, 1998), 249–75, 277–94.

4. On lists and narratives, see Stefan Leder, *Das Korpus al-Haiṯam b. ʿAdī (st. 207/822). Herkunft, Überlieferung, Gestalt früher Texte der ahbār Literatur* (Frankfurt: Vittorio Klostermann, 1991), 197 ff.

5. See Martin Hinds, *Studies in Early Islamic History,* ed. Jere Bacharach, Lawrence I. Conrad, and Patricia Crone, Studies in Late Antiquity and Early Islam, 4 (Princeton: Darwin Press, 1996), 188–98.

6. On *ḥadīth* and biography, see Otto Loth, "Ursprung und Bedeutung der Ṭabaqāt," *Zeitschrift der Deutschen Morgenländischen Gesellschaft* 23 (1869): 593–614; on the development of the historiographical genres, see Tarif Khalidi, *Arabic Historical Thought in the Classical Period* (Cambridge: Cambridge University Press, 1994).

7. ʿAbd al-ʿAzīz al-Ahwānī, "Kutub barāmij al-ʿulamāʾ fī al-Andalus," *Majallat maʿhad al-makhṭūṭāt al-ʿarabiyya* 1 (May 1955): 91–120.

8. *Fihrist* and *fahrasa* are originally Persian. In Arabic, *fihrist* means "index" or "listing." Within a *tarjama,* however, it took on the special sense of a bibliography of works written by the author. The development specific to Islamic Spain and North Africa was that the term was applied to an entire biography or autobiography rather than to one of the constituent parts. See Charles Pellat, "Fahrasa," *EI*² 2:743–44; ʿAbd al-Ḥayy al-Kattānī, *Fihris al-fahāris wa-muʿjam al-maʿājim wa-al-mashyakhāt wa-al-musalsalāt,* 3 vols. (Beirut: Dār al-Gharb al-Islāmī; 2d ed., 1982–86).

9. Charles Pellat, "Manāḳib," *EI*² 6:349–57.

10. Bravmann argues persuasively from a variety of early texts that the term *sīra*, in the early Islamic period, was essentially a synonym of the term *sunna* and referred to the specific personal "practice" of a figure, particularly the Prophet Muhammad; see M. M. Bravmann, *The Spiritual Background of Early Islam: Studies on Ancient Arab Concepts* (Leiden: E. J. Brill, 1972), 123–39.

11. The term *sīra* also refers to at least two other concepts in early Arabic literature. The first is the legal sense of "the conduct of state" or "international law" as in the works titled *Kitāb al-Siyar* by al-Shaybānī (d. ca. 805) and by al-Awzāʿī (d. 770) preserved in the recension of al-Shāfiʿī (d. 820). The second is the sense of a "doctrinal position" or "stance," a usage found from the early eighth century onward that is retained in the Omani Ibāḍī use of the term in reference to a "doctrinal treatise" (see Patricia Crone and Friedrich W. Zimmermann, *The Epistle of Sālim B. Dhakwān* [Oxford: Oxford University Press, 1999]).

12. For a historical overview of this genre, see Dwight F. Reynolds, *Heroic Poets, Poetic Heroes: The Ethnography of Performance in an Arabic Oral Epic Tradition* (Ithaca: Cornell University Press, 1995), 5–9; see also, Peter Heath, *The Thirsty Sword: Sīrat ʿAntar and the Arabic Popular Epic* (Salt Lake City: University of Utah Press, 1996).

13. On the biographical compendiums, see Wadād al-Qāḍī, "Biographical Dictionaries: Inner Structures and Cultural Significance," in *The Book in the Islamic World: The Written Word and Communication in the Middle East,* ed. George N. Atiyeh (Albany: SUNY Press, 1995), 93–122; Khalidi, *Arabic Historical Thought,* 204–10; Paul Auchterlonie, *Arabic Biographical Dictionaries: A Summary Guide and Bibliography* (Durham: Middle East Libraries Committee, 1987); Ibrāhīm Hafsi, "Recherches sur le genre Ṭabaqāt dans la littérature arabe," *Arabica* 23 (1976): 227–65; 24 (1977): 1–41, 150–86; Malik Abiad, "Origine et développement des dictionnaires biographiques arabes," *Bulletin d'Études Orientales* 31 (1979): 7–15; H. A. R. Gibb, "Islamic Biographical Literature," in *Historians of the Middle East,* ed. Bernard Lewis and P. M. Holt (London: Oxford University Press, 1962), 54–58; and for a sociopolitical interpretation of the use of biographical compendiums, Michael Chamberlain, *Knowledge and Social Practice in Medieval Damascus, 1190–1350* (Cambridge: Cambridge University Press, 1994); and Michael Cooperson, *The Heirs of the Prophet in the Age of al-Maʾmūn* (Cambridge: Cambridge University Press, 2000).

14. Ruth Roded, *Women in the Islamic Biographical Dictionaries: From Ibn Saʿd to Who's Who* (Boulder: Lynne Rienner, 1994).

15. See Michael Cooperson, "Ibn Ḥanbal and Bishr al-Ḥāfī: A Case Study in Biographical Traditions," *Studia Islamica* 86, no. 2 (1997): 71–101.

16. Although no definitive "first" for the genre has been identified, ʿAbd al-Dāyim, *al-Tarjama al-dhātiyya,* attributes the earliest use of the term *tarjama* in reference to a biographical notice to Yāqūt (d. 1229) in his *Muʿjam al-udabāʾ.*

17. Al-Qāḍī ʿIyāḍ, *Madhāhib al-ḥukkām fī nawāzil al-aḥkām,* ed. Muḥammad ibn Sharīfa (Beirut: Dār al-Gharb al-Islāmī, 1990), 30.

18. In Islamic thought the Qurʾān is held to be untranslatable both in that it contains a multitude of meanings only a fraction of which can be conveyed in a translation and in that its beauty and stylistic features are inimitable. A rendering

into another language can thus only remain a specific human interpretation of the divine utterance and not a translation, which is only possible when transforming one human text into another human text.

19. A published example is that of Ibn al-Jawzī (d. 1200): *Mashyakhat Ibn al-Jawzī,* ed. M. Maḥfūẓ (Beirut: Dār al-Gharb al-Islāmī, 1980). An excellent survey of the rich but widely scattered medieval "teacher lists" is found in Jonathan Berkey, *The Transmission of Knowledge in Medieval Cairo: A Social History of Islamic Education* (Princeton: Princeton University Press, 1992), 33 n. 50.

20. See Pellat, "Fahrasa," *EI*².

21. The best recent overview of the subject is J. F. P. Hopkins, "Geographical and Navigational Literature," in *The Cambridge History of Arabic Literature: Religion, Learning, and Science in the ʿAbbāsid Period,* ed. M. J. L. Young, J. D. Latham, and R. B. Serjeant (Cambridge: Cambridge University Press, 1990), 301–27. The standard Arabic secondary sources on the subject are Aḥmad Abū Saʿd, *Adab al-riḥlāt* (Cairo: n.p., 1961) and Shawqī Ḍayf, *al-Riḥlāt* [= *Funūn al-adab al-ʿarabī: al-fann al-qaṣaṣī IV*] (Cairo: Dār al-Maʿārif, 1969).

22. See, for example, *Ṣayd al-khāṭir* (The Mind Trap) (Amman: Maktabat Dār al-Fikr, 1987) by ʿAbd al-Raḥmān Ibn al-Jawzī, which closely resembles Pascal's *Pensées.*

23. Anīs al-Maqdisī, *Taṭawwur al-asālīb al-nathriyya fī al-adab al-ʿarabī* (Beirut: Sarkis Press, 1935); Zaki Mubarak, *La prose arabe au IVe siècle de l'Hégire (Xe siècle)* (Paris: Maisonneuve, 1931); Zakī Mubārak, *al-Nathr al-ʿarabī fī l-qarn al-rābiʿ* (Cairo: Dār al-Maʿārif, 1966).

24. Nearly all of the surveyed autobiographers up to the nineteenth century were also poets; indeed, knowledge of, and the ability to compose, poetry were considered an essential element of basic education. Many of these authors included selections from their poetry as portions (even the major portion) of their autobiography. It was also common to include samples of, or refer to, a person's poetic output in the Arabic biographical tradition.

25. See, for example, the recent study on the dreambook of Abū ʿAbd Allāh al-Zawāwī al-Bijāʾī, which includes accounts of 109 separate dreams and visions of the Prophet Muhammad: Jonathan G. Katz, *Dreams, Sufism, and Sainthood: The Visionary Career of Muhammad al-Zawāwī* (Leiden: E. J. Brill, 1996); also J. Katz, "Visionary Experience, Autobiography, and Sainthood in North African Islam," *Princeton Papers in Near Eastern Studies* 1 (December 1992): 85–118.

26. See, for example, the *Rasāʾil* of the Moroccan Sufi shaykh al-ʿArabī al-Darqāwī (d. 1823) portions of which are available in French, translated by Titus Burckhardt, "Le Sheikh al-ʿArabī Ad-Darqāwī. Extraits de ses lettres," *Études Traditionnelles* 394 (March–April 1966): 60–80; "Le Sheikh Ad-Darqāwī: Nouveaux extraits de ses lettres," *Études Traditionnelles* 402–3 (July–October 1967): 192–210; and in English, *Studies in Comparative Religion* 16, nos. 1–2 (Winter–Spring 1984): 108–10. See also Pellat, "Manāḳib," *EI*².

27. For a demonstration of how classical Arabic biography may be usefully read by modern historians, see R. Stephen Humphreys, *Islamic History: A Framework for Inquiry,* rev. ed. (Princeton: Princeton University Press, 1991), 187–208.

28. See Nuha N. N. Khoury, "The Autobiography of Ibn al-ʿAdīm as Told to

Yāqūt al-Rūmī," *Edebiyât: Special Issue—Arabic Autobiography,* N.S. 7, no. 2 (1997): 289–311.

29. Franz Rosenthal, "Die arabische Autobiographie," *Studia Arabica* 1 (1937): 5–7, 10; Saleh al-Ghamdi, "Autobiography in Classical Arabic Literature: An Ignored Genre" (Ph.D. diss., Indiana University, 1989), 42–51. Von Grunebaum, however, argued that foreign influences were minimal and that the major impulse for the rise of Arabic autobiography lay within the indigenous Arabic literary tradition. See Gustave von Grunebaum, *Medieval Islam: A Study in Cultural Orientation* (Chicago: University of Chicago Press, 1946), 261 ff.

30. For Arabic versions of the life of Galen, see Max Meyerhof, "Autobiographische Bruchstücke Galens auz arabischen Quellen," *Sudhoffs Archiv für Geschichte der Medizin* 22 (1929): 72–86. For the life of Burzōē, see François de Blois, *Burzōy's Voyage to India and the Origin of the Book of Kalīlah wa Dimnah* (London: Royal Asiatic Society, 1990).

31. For synopses of the remaining versions, see Blois, *Burzōy's Voyage,* 40–43.

32. Abū Ḥāmid Muḥammad al-Ghazālī, *al-Munqidh min al-ḍalāl* (Cairo: al-Maktab al-fannī, 1961).

33. For extracts in English translation, see Arthur J. Brock, *Greek Medecine, being extracts illustrative of medical writers from Hippocrates to Galen* (London: Dent and Sons, 1929), 174–81; full translations into French are found in Paul Moraux, *Galien de Pergame: souvenirs d'un médecin* (Paris: Belles Lettres, 1985).

34. The autobiographies of al-Tirmidhī and al-Simnānī appear in translation in this volume.

CHAPTER THREE

Toward a History of Arabic Autobiography

If the origins of Arabic autobiographical writing in the *sīra* and *tarjama* traditions seem to be clear, the historical time frame for the emergence of a general recognition of the autobiographical act within the Arabic literary tradition is more difficult to determine. One of the major obstacles to the study of Arabic autobiography so far has been the tendency to view autobiographical texts as isolated anomalies rather than as examples of a literary-historical tradition. The sheer number of premodern Arabic autobiographical texts now available effectively negates this approach. Even more telling than the raw numbers, however, are the direct historical connections linking many of these texts and their authors and the recurring pattern of historical "clusters" of autobiographical production. These relationships not only establish the familiarity of authors with earlier autobiographies and autobiographers but also provide the groundwork for an understanding of the development of literary conventions in Arabic autobiographical writing. This chapter provides a basic historical overview of several discrete dimensions of the development of Arabic autobiography by surveying, first, historical connections among texts and authors; second, diverse authorial motives for writing autobiographies as expressed in the texts themselves; and third, the emergence of a general "autobiographical anxiety" as reflected in texts written in justification and defense of the autobiographical act by Arabic autobiographers.

Historical Clusters

The first "proto-autobiographies" appear to have been composed in isolation from each other. Ḥunayn's ninth-century "Trials and Tribulations" account (translated in this volume) focuses on a defense of himself and his reputation against charges of iconoclasm; al-Muḥāsibī's spiritual manual, *Kitāb al-Naṣā'iḥ* (The Book of Advice), from the same century is significant primarily as a model for later writers assessing and evaluating their spiritual progress; and al-Tirmidhī's text (translated in this volume), *Buduww sha'n abī ʿAbd Allāh* (The Beginning of the Affair of Abū ʿAbd Allāh), consisting of a very brief life narrative accompanied by a series of dream accounts, seeks primarily to establish the spiritual authority and status of its author.[1]

If these earliest Arabic autobiographical writings seem to have been composed in isolation from one another, already by the tenth and early eleventh century, short autobiographies by the philosophers and physicians al-Rāzī, Ibn al-Haytham, Ibn Sīnā, and Ibn Riḍwān were circulating in well-known anthologies and would have been familiar to many scholars over a large geographic expanse. In the same period, the politically and polemically oriented autobiographies of Ibn Ḥawshab (d. 914) and Jaʿfar al-Ḥājib (d. ca. 954) were circulating in Shiʿite circles; these two texts survive only as fragments, but internal textual evidence indicates that the complete texts were of substantial length.

In the late eleventh and twelfth century, there appears to have been a flowering of autobiographical writing and personal record keeping, which, if these did not constitute full autobiographies as such, were widespread enough for biographers such as Yāqūt to draw on extensively in compiling their biographical dictionaries. Autobiographical writings by al-Dānī, al-Fārisī, al-Bayhaqī, Ibn Ma'mūn, Yāqūt himself, and others circulated in this manner. Two lengthy, independent autobiographies from the beginning of this period, those of Ibn Buluggīn and al-Ghazālī, were composed within a few years of each other (ca. 1095 and 1107), the former being a political family history in which the author's life occupies well over half the work and the second a systematically organized account of the author's spiritual crisis, exploration of differing schools of religious philosophy, and eventual acceptance of Sufi teachings. The life story of Samaw'al al-Maghribī (d. 1174), which recounts his conversion from Judaism to Islam and is attached to an anti-Jewish polemical treatise, also dates to this period.

In the late twelfth and early thirteenth century, there appears a cluster of distinctive and noteworthy autobiographical texts written by a group who lived in Damascus and Aleppo during and immediately after the time of Saladin, among whom we can establish a number of direct personal links:

1. ʿUmāra al-Ḥakamī al-Yamanī (d. 1175), poet, diplomat, and historian executed by crucifixion for treason and/or heresy on the orders of Saladin;
2. Usāma ibn Munqidh (d. 1188), nobleman who fought in the counter-Crusades as one of Saladin's commanders;
3. ʿImād al-Dīn al-Kātib al-Iṣfahānī (d. 1201), Saladin's personal secre-

tary and later chronicler of his reign (selections translated in this volume);

4. Yāqūt al-Ḥamawī (d. 1229), literary historian and prominent biographer who compiled an enormous biographical encyclopedia of literary figures, including several of his fellow autobiographers;[2]
5. ʿAbd al-Laṭīf al-Baghdādī (d. 1231), prominent physician and teacher who met Saladin and was rewarded with a position and government stipend (autobiography translated in this volume);
6. Ibn al-ʿAdīm (d. 1262): prominent historian of Aleppo and personal friend of Yāqūt (autobiography translated in this volume);
7. Abū Shāma (d. 1268), historian of Saladin's reign and dynasty (autobiography translated in this volume); and
8. Saʿd al-Dīn ibn Ḥamawiyya al-Juwaynī (d. 1276), military governor, historian, and finally Sufi mystic.[3]

Given their prominence and fame, this group of literati were well aware of one another's careers and writings; and, indeed, several of them met face-to-face. ʿImād al-Dīn quotes from ʿUmāra's autobiography in his own work, *Kharīdat al-Qaṣr* (The Pearl of the Palace), referring to it as the book that ʿUmāra wrote (*muṣannafuhu*).[4] Although he cites primarily ʿUmāra's poetry, he presents the poems for the most part in the order in which they occur in ʿUmāra's autobiography, rather than in that of his *dīwān* (collected poems).[5] On one of his frequent trips to Cairo, ʿImād al-Dīn actually had ʿUmāra's poetry recited to him by the son of Usāma ibn Munqidh, who had heard it from the poet himself—the poetry of one autobiographer recited to another autobiographer by the son of a third autobiographer![6] In addition, passages from Abū Shāma's historical work, *Kitāb al-Rawḍatayn* (The Book of the Two Gardens), the supplement to which includes his autobiography, seem to indicate a familiarity with both ʿUmāra's work[7] and Saʿd al-Dīn Juwaynī. ʿAbd al-Laṭīf al-Baghdādī describes meeting ʿImād al-Dīn al-Kātib al-Iṣfahānī in his autobiography, and Yāqūt personally commissioned the autobiography of his close friend, Ibn al-ʿAdīm, for inclusion in his compendium.

The production of multiple autobiographical texts from this rather close-knit literary and scholarly group may have been prompted by these many personal connections, or the large number of autobiographies known from this period may only reflect the fact that it has been more intensely researched than most other periods of Islamic history. Another possibility, noted by Rosenthal, is that the tremendous political instability of the period may have helped to foster a fertile context for autobiographical production.[8]

As a result of the considerable attention devoted to the period of Saladin and the Crusades by both Arab and western historians, most of these texts are well known, commonly used as historical sources, and usually recognized and treated as autobiographies. Among them, however, the work of ʿImād al-Dīn al-Kātib al-Iṣfahānī stands out, for it is ostensibly a biography of Saladin. Yet later Arab sources such as al-Suyūṭī and al-Shaʿrānī consistently refer to it as an autobiographical work.[9] They clearly assessed the work from its contents and not from the formal framing device of its title and dedication. Since ʿImād al-Dīn wrote of himself extensively in this work, it was deemed an act of self-*tarjama.*

Two other historical clusters appear in Spain. The autobiographer Ibn Saʿīd al-Maghribī (d. 1286) knew of the earlier autobiographical notices of Ibn al-Imām (d. 1155), al-Ḥijārī (d. 1155), and Ibn al-Qaṭṭāʿ (d. 1121).[10] Later, Lisān al-Dīn Ibn al-Khaṭīb (d. 1374) states that he saw and read the autograph copy of the eleventh-century autobiography of Ibn Buluggīn when he visited southern Morocco, where Ibn Buluggīn had died in exile, and then returned home to write his own autobiography. He might also have been familiar with the autobiography of Abū Ḥayyān al-Andalusī (d. 1344) who lived a generation earlier, the text of which—although now lost—achieved some fame in the late Middle Ages and was still being cited two centuries later by al-Suyūṭī and al-Shaʿrānī in Egypt as a lengthy autobiographical work; it was probably written during Abū Ḥayyān's sojourn in Egypt. Only a few years after Lisān al-Dīn ibn al-Khaṭīb wrote his text, the famous historiographer Ibn Khaldūn (d. 1406), whose family was originally from Spain, and who had met and worked with Ibn al-Khaṭīb in Spain in 1363, also wrote an autobiography.[11] It is clear that by the end of the fourteenth century there were numerous examples of independent, lengthy autobiographies circulating throughout the Arabic-speaking world.

A more tenuous, but still intriguing, connection lies in an encounter that took place between Ibn Khaldūn and Tamerlane (Timur-lenk) outside of Damascus in 1401. Ibn Khaldūn was trapped inside the city during Tamerlane's siege, but Tamerlane had heard of Ibn Khaldūn's presence and wished to meet him. Ibn Khaldūn describes in a dramatic scene in his autobiography being lowered over the city walls by rope in the middle of the night. Over a period of six weeks, the two met several times and discussed a variety of topics, including Ibn Khaldūn's life story, Tamerlane's genealogy and place in history, the kings of the ancient world, and the geography of the Maghreb. At Tamerlane's request, Ibn Khaldūn wrote out a great deal of information, including a book-length description of the Maghreb. Ibn Khaldūn was eventually released and allowed to return to Cairo.

It seems plausible that when Tamerlane questioned Ibn Khaldūn about his life, as they had discussed Ibn Khaldūn's other writings, Ibn Khaldūn may have mentioned that he had penned an account of it. And Ibn Khaldūn, as a historian, might well have asked whether an official biography (or autobiography) of Tamerlane was available, or in the process of being written, that he could consult. In any case, soon thereafter Ibn Khaldūn decided to expand his earlier autobiography so as to include his encounter with Tamerlane and republish it as an independent volume, for it had previously existed only as a chapter in a larger historical work.[12] An autobiography of Tamerlane also appeared and was for centuries accepted as authentic, although in recent decades most modern scholars have come to agree that it was probably created a century or more after Tamerlane's death and was perhaps written by one of his descendants.[13]

One of the largest clusters of texts is that associated with Ibn Ḥajar al-ʿAsqalānī and his pupils. Ibn Ḥajar (d. 1449) wrote several brief autobiographies (one of which is translated in this volume). His student al-Sakhāwī (d. 1497) wrote a thirty-page autobiography that he included in his celebrated biographical compendium of the ninth Islamic century as well as an independent autobiography that remains in manuscript,[14] and two of al-Sakhāwī's students, Ibn Daybaʿ (d. 1537) and Zarrūq (d. 1493), each wrote autobiographies. Another of Ibn Ḥajar's students, al-Suyūṭī, wrote a substantial autobiography that was then emulated by Ibn Ṭūlūn al-Dimashqī (d. 1546) and al-Shaʿrānī (d. 1565). At more than seven hundred printed pages, al-Shaʿrānī's text is the longest premodern Arabic autobiography known to us. These texts circulated widely and were cited by later autobiographers as far afield as India (al-ʿAydarūs; d. 1628) and Morocco (Ibn ʿAjība; d. 1809).

A later thread links members of Sufi circles in North Africa. Ibn al-ʿAjība (d. 1809) was familiar with the autobiographical works of al-ʿArabī al-Darqāwī (d. 1823),[15] Zarrūq (d. 1493), al-Shaʿrānī (d. 1565), and al-Yūsī (d. 1691). Still another cluster is found in the Shiʿite community in Jabal ʿĀmil (now southern Lebanon) during the sixteenth and seventeenth centuries, including Zayn al-Dīn ibn ʿAlī al-ʿĀmilī (d. 1558), his great-grandson, ʿAlī ibn Muḥammad al-ʿĀmilī (d. 1692), and Muḥammad ibn al-Ḥasan al-Ḥurr al-ʿĀmilī (d. 1688).

One fascinating cluster of Arabic autobiographies written by enslaved West Africans appeared in the early nineteenth century in the United States and the Caribbean. These were made famous by the American popular press and played prominent roles in several political causes célèbres. Although the authors were not personal acquaintances, they may very well have known of one other. It seems that those who solicited these autobiographical texts did in fact know of the other cases; thus, if the texts themselves were not directly linked, the political forces that motivated their composition certainly were. The best documented are those written by Abū Bakr al-Ṣiddīq, ʿAbd al-Raḥmān, and ʿUmar ibn Saʿīd.[16]

Abū Bakr al-Ṣiddīq (d. 1850), later renamed Edward Donellan, was originally from Timbuktu and educated in Jennah. As a child he traveled extensively with his teacher but was captured at the age of fourteen or fifteen by the Ashanti and sold to Christian slave traders. He arrived in the West Indies in 1807 or 1808 and ended up keeping the accounts for the plantation where he was a slave. He kept these records in Arabic script, which he then read aloud each evening to the plantation owner in pidgin English. A visitor to the plantation, Dr. Madden, was so moved by Abū Bakr's literacy, his faith in the One True God, his highborn rank (he was later often referred to as a prince), and his desire to return to his homeland that he fought for his manumission, which was eventually granted in a British court. On his route homeward, in August 1835, Abū Bakr stopped in England. There, at the request of his hosts, he wrote out his life story in Arabic. Though only a few pages long, it offers a vivid description of his childhood education, his travels, his capture and sale as a slave, and his experiences among the Christians.

ʿAbd al-Raḥmān (d. 1829), known as "Prince," originally from the region of Futa Jalloun, was educated in Timbo, Jennah, and Timbuktu. He was captured at the age of twenty-one while leading a military expedition, sold into slavery, and then purchased by a landowner in Tennessee. He ran away but could not manage to live in the wild and so finally returned. Eventually he married and had several children. In 1807, in an astonishing development, he encountered in the Natchez market John Coates Cox, a man who had lived in Timbo twenty-five years earlier as a guest of his father. Cox recognized ʿAbd al-Raḥmān and tried to buy him but was rebuffed. He then petitioned the governor for the slave's manumission but failed. Finally he launched a publicity campaign with the help of a local newpaper that promised to publish and deliver to ʿAbd al-Raḥmān's father a letter written by his son in Arabic. The U.S. State Department became involved, and ʿAbd al-Raḥmān was freed, but he did not wish to return to Africa without his wife and children. With help from friends, he launched a lecture tour across the northern United States to raise money to buy his family's freedom. For a year he was probably the most famous African American in the nation. During his tour he was constantly asked to write things in Arabic (when asked to write the Lord's Prayer, he would dutifully copy out the opening chapter of the Qur'ān). At the request of those fighting for his cause, ʿAbd al-Raḥmān wrote a short autobiography in Arabic that was translated into English and reprinted as part of the newspaper war that had erupted after his liberation. Eventually his wife was freed, and the two of them sailed for Liberia in February 1829. On arrival they were delayed by the rainy season, and, tragically, ʿAbd al-Raḥmān died of fever before being able to complete the final leg of his journey home. His brief autobiography, written in Arabic and broken English, recounts his life up to the death of his friend, Mr. Cox.

ʿUmar ibn Saʿīd (d. 1864), also known as "Prince Moro," was originally from the region of Futa Toro. Accounts of how he ended up being sold as a slave vary, but he eventually arrived in South Carolina, probably in 1807. Reporters portray him as a man of royal lineage and as a converted and faithful Christian. In 1831 he composed an autobiography in Arabic, later translated in two different versions, both of which were published. He even entered into correspondence with Francis Scott Key, author of the "Star-Spangled Banner." He remained in the United States until his death; the Arabic text of the autobiography, lost since 1925, resurfaced in 1998 and has been published with an introductory analysis.[17]

In all three cases, the popular press constructed these slaves as "Moors," as opposed to "Africans"; as royalty (all three were again and again referred to as princes); and as Muslims who worshiped God, in contrast to pagans. The popular press also sought to portray them as potential (or actual) converts to Christianity. But it was their ability to write in Arabic that set each of them on the road to celebrity. In the 1820s even many staunch supporters of slavery were shocked that literate men of noble rank and education were being maintained as slaves; much of the encouragement for setting these men free came from Southern slave owners. In all three cases, the autobiographies were produced at the request of white friends, but the texts clearly draw on features of the Arabic religious biographical tradition (although it is unclear, from the evidence available, whether any of these men had read an Arabic *auto*biography).

In the nineteenth century, the advent of Arabic printing assured the more rapid dissemination of new texts in the Arab Middle East. The semi-autobiographical accounts of travels to Europe such as al-Ṭahṭāwī's *Takhlīṣ al-ibrīz ilā talkhīṣ Bārīz* (Purified Gold from an Account of Paris Told), published in 1834, as well as experiments in autobiographical fiction such as Aḥmad Fāris al-Shidyāq's *al-Sāq ʿalā al-sāq fī mā huwa al-Faryāq* (Thigh upon Thigh on the Question of Who Am I), published in 1858, found substantial readerships. In scholarly circles ʿAlī Mubārak published an account of his life in his massive geographic-biographical compendium of Egypt, *al-Khiṭaṭ al-tawfīqiyya* (1888–89), which was later imitated by Muḥammad Kurd ʿAlī in his six-volume geographic-biographical compendium of Syria, *Khiṭaṭ al-Shām* (1925–28), which concludes with Kurd ʿAlī's autobiography. In 1898 the famous poet Aḥmad Shawqī prefaced his autobiography to his four-volume anthology of poetry, *al-Shawqiyyāt,* which unleashed a storm of newspaper commentary. And a wave of political memoirs by figures such as Ibrāhīm Fawzī Pasha (who wrote a personal, and at the time highly controversial, account of the Anglo-Egyptian Sudan campaigns) and, later, Nubar Nubarian Pasha (Armenian-Egyptian civil servant), Saʿd Zaghlūl (Egyptian nationalist leader), and Bābakr Badrī (Sudanese nationalist leader) and a putative autobiography by Aḥmad ʿUrābī (leader of the Egyptian rebellion of 1881–82), also originated in this period.

In short, these historical clusters of autobiographical production and the myriad individual links among various authors and texts make it clear that Arabic autobiographical writing constituted an often tightly knit literary tradition over many centuries. It is important to note, however, that in only a few of the cases do the autobiographies in these historical clusters actually resemble one another as texts. While the biographical branches of the *sīra* and *tarjama* genres remained in formal terms often rigidly conventional, their autobiographical counterparts expanded and evolved beyond the original conventions and purposes of their type. Whereas biographers usually accepted the conventions of earlier examples in their own fields, autobiographers found precedents but did not view them as binding formal models. As a result, the corpus of Arabic autobiographies displays a high degree of formal variety and includes a number of highly idiosyncratic texts. Perhaps this was possible precisely because the production of autobiographical texts remained limited in comparison to that of biographies and prosopographical notices. This degree of variation may also explain why the establishment of different categories or types for Arabic autobiographies in the medieval and premodern periods has proved of such limited usefulness.[18] Such divisions group together texts that have few formal similarities and at the same time obscure precedents and influences that cut across the boundaries of these heuristic categories.

Whether contact took place between authors or through reading another autobiographer's text, what seems to have been communicated is the autobiographical act as precedent, rather than specific formal characteristics or a sense of what the style or content of an autobiography should be. To whatever degree these authors influenced, motivated, or inspired one another to interpret their lives in literary representations, they did so in a manner that left themselves free to tailor their interpretations to their own individual needs and desires. This history of formal innovation seems to be indicative of an individualistic impulse that is connected in a very significant way to self-portrayal in the Arabic literary tradition.

Authorial Motivations

The earliest autobiographical texts covered in this survey, those from the ninth through the eleventh century, present themselves directly, with little in the way of framing or justification and no overt concern about how the reader will interpret the fact that the author is writing of himself: Ḥunayn ibn Isḥāq and al-Rāzī write to defend themselves against their critics; al-Muḥāsibī's brief autobiographical passage is of a spiritual nature and located in a larger guide to his followers; al-Tirmidhī wrote to establish his own spiritual status and did not provide any introduction or dedication for his text; the works of Ibn Ḥawshab, Jaʿfar al-Ḥājib, and al-Mu'ayyad al-Shīrāzī are all memoirs of Shiʿite religiopolitical activities of the tenth and eleventh centuries; Ibn al-Haytham, al-Dānī, and Ibn Riḍwān wrote scholarly reports of their lives without framing devices to articulate the authors' aims beyond the overtly historical. Two texts from the eleventh century, by Ibn Sīnā and Ibn Buluggīn, are notable from the point of view of the emergence of autobiography as a literary act.

The autobiography of Ibn Sīnā has been well known among western scholars for quite some time and has been edited and published from several different sources.[19] Although written as a scholarly autobiography, it is more detailed than other contemporary examples of this type.[20] The autobiography focuses on Ibn Sīnā's childhood and youth and ends while he is still a young man. Ibn Sīnā's student, al-Jūzjānī, later continued the text as a biography, providing an account of the remainder of Ibn Sīnā's life.

The appearance of the text in the biographical dictionary *ʿUyūn al-anbāʾ fī ṭabaqāt al-aṭibbāʾ* (The Sources of Knowledge about the Generations of Physicians), by Ibn Abī Uṣaybiʿa (d. 1270), provides an example of how such texts were transmitted during the Middle Ages. The entry on Ibn Sīnā includes a short introduction by the compiler, the text of the autobiography itself, the biography by al-Jūzjānī, a short bibliography of Ibn Sīnā's works, a selection of his poetry, and a bibliographical addendum.

The autobiography proper has come down to us without any formal preface or dedication. In the various medieval biographical compendiums in which it appears, however, compilers prefaced the text in a way that reveals how it was received. Ibn Abī Uṣaybiʿa, for example, wrote:

> He related his experiences and described his life so that everyone else could dispense with his own account. And therefore we have confined ourselves for that reason to what he related about himself and also to those of his experiences described by Abū ʿUbayd al-Jūzjānī, the companion of the Shaykh.[21]

Al-Qifṭī (d. 1248) included Ibn Sīnā's text in his biographical compendium of scientists and physicians, *Taʾrīkh al-ḥukamāʾ* (History of Scientists), which may have been Ibn Abī Uṣaybiʿa's source, and prefaced the text with the statement: "One of his pupils asked him about his past, and so he dictated what has been recorded from him to [the pupil], which was that he said . . ." A number of the compilers use the Persian term *sar-guzasht* (recollections) in presenting the text of the autobiography proper, which may well indicate a lingering sense of ambiguity in that period about what Arabic term should be used to describe such a text.[22]

The remark by Ibn Abī Uṣaybiʿa that Ibn Sīnā composed his own account of his life so that others would not do so reflects a concern echoed by a number of later writers. For them, the issue was not to write an (auto)biographical text so that such a text would exist but rather to write an account of their lives before others should do so, thus asserting control over the content and presentation of the material and preventing the spread of factual errors. Ibn ʿAjība (d. 1809), for example, writes that he discovered that his colleagues and pupils were gathering biographical notes about him: "And therefore, fearing that they might allow some addition or omission to slip into their work, I decided to report, with God's assistance, what I have seen with my own eyes and heard with my own ears, for that which is transmitted is not that which was actually seen."[23] Al-Sakhāwī (d. 1497) notes of ʿAbd al-Ghānī al-Maqdisī that a certain Makkī ibn ʿUmar ibn Niʿma al-Miṣrī "collected a *tarjama* of him before he could collect one himself."[24]

The frame created by al-Qifṭī for Ibn Sīnā's autobiographical text, that of writing in response to a request from someone else, is a common prefatory device found in many genres of writing in the Islamic Middle Ages. Whether the request was real or simply a rhetorical device, this opening was deployed by autobiographers and then reused and transmitted by later compilers of biographical compendiums. Al-Sakhāwī, for example, writes that he wrote "a *tarjama* of himself in response to those who asked him concerning it [*ijābatan li-man sa'alahu fīhā*]."[25]

In contrast, the autobiography of ʿAbd Allāh Ibn Buluggīn (d. after 1094) provides explicit, self-conscious justifications for the autobiographical act. In his introduction, Ibn Buluggīn explains that he wishes to portray the truth and that the "intention in this enterprise of mine is not to narrate some entertaining tale [*nādira mustaṭrafa*] or some strange anecdote [*ḥikāya mustaghraba*] or an edifying or profitable notion [*maʿnā yu'addī ilā ta'addub wa-intifāʿ*]."[26] Rather, he declares that he shall eschew fancy language and embellishment and relate the events of his life directly: "I believe that a continuous narrative is better in both form and composition than one which is cut into pieces. I would like, therefore, to write this work in a manner that flows [smoothly] from topic to topic."[27] Among his motives for writing are "to enumerate the blessings of God and to thank Him as is His due, as God has urged in addressing His Prophet: 'And as for the bounty of your Lord, speak!' [Q 93:11]"[28] and to defend the reign and reputation of his dynasty. These concerns are reiterated in the closing chapter of the work. Perhaps the most striking detail in this passage is that Ibn Buluggīn felt it necessary to justify not the act of recording his life or the history of his family but rather the technique of presenting his work as a coherent narrative instead of as a sequence of carefully substantiated historical anecdotes along with their sources.

The reference here to Qur'ān 93:11 as part of the motivation for writing an autobiography is intriguing. The same verse is quoted in an earlier, well-known work by another Andalusian writer, Ibn Ḥazm (d. 1064), *Ṭawq al-ḥamāma fī al-ulfa wa-l-ullāf* (The Neckring of the Dove on Lovers and Love). In the context of discussing fidelity, Ibn Ḥazm writes: "I do not say what I am about to say in order to boast, but simply relying upon the precept of God Almighty Who says, 'And as for the bounty of your Lord, speak!' "[29] The verse appears to have been deployed as a disclaimer of pride or arrogance when speaking about oneself. Ibn Buluggīn's text provides the earliest-known use of this verse in connection with the writing of an autobiography, but it was later used by a number of Arabic autobiographers in other regions. They could not have picked up this usage from Ibn Buluggīn's autobiography, however, because it did not circulate widely; in fact, it appears to have remained in the original autograph copy of the author or possibly in a single copy made directly from the original. Only one manuscript of the work is extant, that discovered in the library of the Qarawiyyīn Mosque in Fez, Morocco, which was published by E. Lévi-Provençal in the 1930s.[30] Lisān al-Dīn Ibn al-Khaṭīb saw the autograph copy of Ibn Buluggīn's work on a visit to Aghmāt, Morocco, where he had been held in captivity. Apart from two other brief references to the work, also by fourteenth-century writers, the book seems to have remained completely unknown, uncited, and unreferred to, until this century.[31]

The next occurrence of Qur'ān 93:11 in an autobiographical text appears to be in Abū Shāma's thirteenth-century work written in Syria, followed by its use nearly two centuries later in the title and preface of al-Suyūṭī's text from Egypt. The use of this verse in three geographically and historically separate instances raises several questions. Are these parallel citations coincidental or related? If the latter, are they related to each other via other autobiographical texts, through Qur'ānic commentaries, or perhaps through other channels such as popular usage of this verse in oral discourse, public sermons, and the like?

The connection between Qur'ān 93:11 and the act of writing an autobiography is not as direct as might appear at first glance. In the context of this particular chapter of the Qur'ān, "The Morning Light " (Sūrat al-ḍuḥā), the command "And as for the bounty of your Lord, speak!" is addressed to a singular, male interlocutor identifiable as the Prophet Muhammad:

In the Name of God the Merciful, the Compassionate!

1. By the morning light!
2. By the darkening night!
3. Your Lord has not forsaken you, nor does He feel spite.
4. The Hereafter is better for you than this [first] life!
5. Your Lord will lavish [bounties] on you and you will know delight.
6. Did He not find you an orphan, then give you respite?
7. Find you unaware, then guide you aright?
8. Find you wanting, and then provide?
9. So as for the orphan, wrong him not!
10. And as for the beseecher, shun him not!
11. And as for the bounty of Your Lord, speak![32]

Discussion in many Qur'ānic commentaries is restricted to whether the term "bounty" (*niʿma:* the Arabic is singular, although commonly translated as "blessings") refers to the Qur'ān itself, so that "speak" would mean "recite," or, alternatively, to the status of prophethood, in which case "speak" would mean "inform people that you are God's messenger." The generalization of this verse to apply to anyone other than the Prophet himself is therefore a secondary development, not a close or literal interpretation of the text.[33]

A preliminary study of the major Qur'ānic commentaries only partly answers these questions. Al-Ṭabarī's tenth-century commentary offers only a synonym for the word "speak," *dhakara,* meaning "to mention" or "to state." It is nonmainstream scholars such as the Muʿtazilites (a theological school that advocated free will, divine justice, and allegorical interpretation of the Qur'ān) and Shiʿites (who recognized a series of spiritual leaders after the Prophet Muhammad possessing direct inspiration from God) who first concerned themselves with broader issues and questions. In the case of Qur'ān 93:11, one early treatise, that of the Muʿtazilite al-Qāḍī ʿAbd al-Jabbār (d. 1025), extends the message of the verse beyond the immediate addressee, the Prophet, to all Muslims, thereby generalizing the obligation of showing one's gratitude for God's blessings to the entire Islamic community. One century later, the commentator al-Zamakhsharī (d. 1144), also a Muʿtazilite, not only included this broader interpretation but also supported it with a number of Prophetic traditions. More significantly, his text includes the term *iqtidā',* "to take as an example or model," along with an anecdote involving ʿAlī (fourth caliph of the Islamic community and son-in-law of the Prophet Muhammad) being asked to speak of himself. When he at first refuses, he is reminded of this Qur'ānic verse and only then agrees.

In most of the major commentaries subsequent to al-Zamakhsharī (with the exception of al-Bayḍāwī's paraphrastic commentary), passages concerning this verse include an ever-larger number of Prophetic traditions in support of the broader interpretation, including examples of members of the Prophet's family speaking of themselves in response to questions and referring directly to the concept of exemplarism. Chronologically, this development roughly parallels the proliferation of autobiographies beginning with the twelfth and thirteenth centuries. The large cluster of autobiographies written in the fifteenth and sixteenth centuries by Ibn Ḥajar and his students follows immediately on Ibn Ḥajar's own study of the Prophetic traditions cited in al-Zamakhsharī's commentary. Ibn Ḥajar's student al-Suyūṭī includes in his commentary on the Qur'ān a greater number of *ḥadīth* concerning this verse than any previous or later commentator; and he himself, as already mentioned, inspired several of his own students to write autobiographies. The increasing number of *ḥadīth* cited in support of this interpretation of the verse may have been inspired by the proliferation of autobiographical writings, and it is clear that the interpretation of this verse as applicable to all Muslims and all blessings, the concomitant growth of autobiographical writings, and the increased anxiety demonstrated in those texts in the fourteenth to the sixteenth century all reflect broader developments in medieval Islamic society and thought.

From the twelfth to the fourteenth century we encounter autobiographical texts written in a number of different forms: scholarly vitas, spiritual guides, conversion narratives, belletristic works, and historical works in which the author plays the central role. Almost none, however, betrays any misgivings on the part of its author about engaging in the act of writing about himself. One exception is Ibn Saʿīd al-Maghribī (d. 1286), who wrote: "I excuse myself for this desire to write my own biography [*tarjamatī*] here with the same excuse used by Ibn al-Imām in [his book] *Simṭ al-jumān* [The String of Pearls], and the excuse of al-Ḥijārī in his book *al-Mushib* [The Lengthy Account], and Ibn al-Qaṭṭāʿ [d. 1121] in *al-Durra* [The Pearl]."[34]

By the end of the fifteenth century, Arabic writers displayed increasing awareness of earlier autobiographical writings. Al-Sakhāwī, writing in 1466, gives a long list of noteworthy Arabic biographies beginning with those of the Prophet in the introduction to his biography of his teacher, Ibn Ḥajar. This list also contains the following references to autobiographies:

1. The historian al-Ṣārim Ibrāhīm ibn Duqmāq al-Ḥanafī collected a *tarjama* of himself [*jamaʿahā li-nafsih*].
2. Ibrāhīm ibn ʿAbd al-Raḥīm ibn Jamāʿa collected a *tarjama* of himself.
3. Iftikhār al-Dīn Ḥāmid ibn Muḥammad ibn Muḥammad al-Khwārizmī al-Ḥanafī wrote a *tarjama* of himself in one fascicle [*tarjama li-nafsih fī juz'*].
4. Al-Ṣalāḥ Abū al-Ṣafī Khalīl ibn Aybak al-Ṣafadī collected a *tarjama* of himself.
5. I saw a booklet [*kurrāsa*] in the script of al-Samaw'al ibn Yaḥyā ibn ʿAbbās al-Maghribī, later al-Baghdādī, in which he states the cause for his conversion to Islam, and it is like a *tarjama* of himself [*wa-huwa shibh al-tarjama li-nafsih*].
6. Abū Muḥammad ʿAbd Allāh ibn Muḥammad ibn Hārūn al-Ṭā'ī. I think he himself wrote it [*aẓunnuhā li-nafsih*].
7. Al-Ḥāfiẓ ʿAbd al-Ghanī ibn ʿAbd al-Wāḥid al-Maqdisī . . . Makkī ibn ʿUmar ibn Niʿma al-Miṣrī collected a *tarjama* of him before he could collect one on himself [*sabaqahu ilā jamʿihā li-nafsih*].
8. Muḥammad ibn Abī Bakr ibn ʿAbd al-ʿAzīz ibn Muḥammad al-ʿIzz ibn Jamāʿa wrote a fascicle [*juz'*] which he called *Ḍaw' al-shams fī aḥwāl al-nafs* [The Light of the Sun on the States of the Self] in which he gave a *tarjama* of himself [*dhakara fīhā tarjamat nafsih*].
9. The compiler [of the present work], Abū al-Khayr Muḥammad ibn ʿAbd al-Raḥmān al-Sakhāwī, collected a *tarjama* of himself in response to those who asked him to do so [*ijābatan li-man sa'alahu fīhā*].

10. Al-Shams Muḥammad ibn Muḥammad ibn al-Khiḍr al-ʿAyzarī al-Dimashqī collected a *tarjama* of himself.[35]

Of these nine autobiographies, cited haphazardly in the introduction to a biography, only two have come down to us.

As we have seen, authors had begun to write autobiographical texts for a wide variety of purposes by the eleventh and twelfth centuries, and these diverse purposes were reflected in the development of a number of innovative forms: political autobiographies (Ibn Buluggīn, Ibn Ḥawshab, al-Ḥājib Jaʿfar), belletristic autobiographies (ʿUmāra al-Yamanī, Usāma ibn Munqidh), conversion autobiographies (the Jewish convert Samawʾal al-Maghribī and his later counterpart, the Christian convert ʿAbd Allāh al-Turjumān [= Fray Anselmo Turmeda]). By the late fifteenth century, when Jalāl al-Dīn al-Suyūṭī was writing his autobiography, the various threads of development had cross-fertilized and influenced one another such that different types of texts and different authorial motivations are difficult to distinguish. Al-Suyūṭī's autobiography touts scholarly and intellectual achievements; in it the traditional elements of the *tarjama* have been drastically expanded, reframed as a spiritual duty, and then validated by his citation as precedents of three scholarly autobiographies (al-Fārisī, Ibn Ḥajar, Abū Shāma), two political autobiographies (al-Iṣfahānī, Ibn al-Khaṭīb), one belletristic autobiography (ʿUmāra), and two texts that have not come down to us (Yāqūt, Abū Ḥayyān). Notably missing from his list is any overtly spiritual autobiography, although he himself had been ceremonially invested as a Sufi.

A half century later when the Sufi shaykh al-Shaʿrānī wrote his autobiography demonstrating spiritual rather than intellectual achievements, he borrowed al-Suyūṭī's list of earlier autobiographers and added four new names (Abū ʿAbd Allāh al-Qurashī, Abū al-Rabīʿ al-Mālaqī, Ṣafī al-Dīn ibn Abī al-Manṣūr, Jalāl al-Dīn al-Suyūṭī) and discreetly dropped ʿUmāra al-Yamanī, whom Saladin had crucified for heresy and possibly treason.[36] Al-Shaʿrānī, however, recasts the entire list of writers as religious scholars by including the appropriate religious title—shaykh, imām, or mujtahid—for each. He then discusses his reasons for writing an autobiography both in scholarly terms, also borrowed from al-Suyūṭī, and in mystical terms, taken from the works of his Sufi masters. Finally, he composes the body of his text in a completely idiosyncratic manner by listing separately each blessing he has received from God. Not only were the formal features of the textual tradition flexible, but the entire tradition was liable to differing portrayals; it could equally well be characterized as one of scholarly, textual precedents (al-Suyūṭī) or as one of spiritual predecessors (al-Shaʿrānī).

Autobiographers of the late fifteenth through the nineteenth century, such as al-Sakhāwī, al-Suyūṭī, Ibn Ṭūlūn al-Dimashqī, Ṭāshköprüzāde, al-

Shaʿrānī, al-ʿAydarūs, ʿAlī ibn Muḥammad al-ʿĀmilī, and Ibn ʿAjība, all demonstrate their familiarity with the Arabic autobiographical tradition in a variety of ways: by including lists of previous autobiographers in the introductions to their works, by incorporating earlier autobiographies into their own historical or *ṭabaqāt* works, or by borrowing justifications for writing an autobiography from the prefaces of earlier texts.[37] On the whole, beginning in the late fifteenth century, Arabic autobiographers become more and more concerned with the careful framing of their texts, the articulation of their motivations, and defending themselves from potential charges of vanity, falsification, and innovation.

Autobiographical Anxieties

Todorov remarks that "the historical existence of genres is signaled by discourse on genres."[38] Autobiography, in the form of *tarjamat al-nafs,* engendered a scholarly and religious discourse in Arabic literature at least as early as the fifteenth and sixteenth centuries. This was the era of al-Suyūṭī, al-Sakhāwī, Ibn Ṭūlūn al-Dimashqī, and al-Shaʿrānī, all of whom included discussions of autobiography in their writings.

The passage cited in the introduction to this volume from one of al-Suyūṭī's autobiographical works presents his justifications for writing an autobiography. These were the obligation to enumerate the blessings one has received from God as an act of thanks, emulation of the many respected figures who had previously composed autobiographical works, and the laudable nature of writing whereby one passes on information of one's life to subsequent generations, to which he appended his claim that he did not write his book out of pride or conceit. Implicit in al-Suyūṭī's argument about autobiography as historical writing is his belief that a firsthand account by the author is more reliable than an account written by others.

Four decades later, Ibn Ṭūlūn al-Dimashqī (d. 1546) was to write the following in the introduction to his autobiography:

> The author of a *tarjama* sometimes sets it apart in a separate work, as did our teacher Abū al-Fatḥ al-Mizzī (and I have followed him in this here); and sometimes someone else writes a separate work about him (and this is better), as the expert on prophetic tradition Shams al-Dīn al-Sakhāwī did in his work *al-Jawāhir wa-l-durar* [Jewels and Pearls], a *tarjama* about his teacher, the great scholar of Islam, Ibn Ḥajar. Our teacher, the historian Muḥyī al-Dīn al-Nuʿaymī followed him in this by writing an independent *tarjama* of his teacher and ours, the *ḥadīth* scholar Burhān al-Dīn al-Nājī. But sometimes a *tarjama* is not set apart in a separate work, but is found within another of the author's works, as our teacher, the consummate scholar Jalāl al-Dīn al-Suyūṭī, did by mentioning himself in his medium-sized book *Ṭabaqāt al-nuḥāt* [The Generations of Grammarians]. In it he said:

> I hoped that there would be some mention of my name in this book to be blessed by, and in imitation of, the deeds of those of my predecessors who mentioned their own names within their writings on history, such as the Imām ʿAbd al-Ghāfir in his *al-Siyāq* [Continuation],[39] Yāqūt al-Ḥamawī in his *Muʿjam al-udabāʾ* [Biographical Dictionary of Writers], Ibn al-Khaṭīb in his *Taʾrīkh Gharnāṭa* [History of Granada], and al-Taqī al-Fāsī in his *Taʾrīkh Makka* [History of Mecca]—these latter two wrote their *tarjamas* at great length—Ibn Ḥajar in his *Quḍāt Miṣr* [The Judges of Egypt], and innumerable others.[40] Then there are those who wrote of themselves [in a biographical compendium] under the first letter of their name, such as al-Fāsī and Ibn Ḥajar, and I have followed them in this. There are also those who wrote of themselves at the end of a book, and in the case of Yāqūt this involved a fortunate coincidence since his name begins with *Y* [the last letter of the Arabic alphabet].

> And I [Ibn Ṭūlūn] say: This coincidence also happened to our teacher, the *ḥadīth*-scholar Jamāl al-Dīn Yūsuf ibn ʿAbd al-Hādī when he wrote an entry on himself and inserted it into his compendium of Ḥanbalī scholars in his book *Manāqib Imām Aḥmad ibn Ḥanbal* [Praiseworthy Qualities of the Imām Aḥmad ibn Ḥanbal]; he wrote a lengthy autobiography [*aṭāla fī tarjamatih*].[41] I have even heard him recite this aloud and at that time he mentioned to me what the *ḥadīth*-scholar Abū ʿAbd Allāh al-Bukhārī said in his *Ṣaḥīḥ*, quoting Rabīʿa[42]: "It is not fitting that anyone who possesses even a small amount of knowledge should allow himself to be forgotten."[43]

When Ibn Ṭūlūn declares that it is "better" that someone else write one's biography than to write a text about oneself, it seems clear that it is better, not from a historical, factual point of view, but from a moral or ethical point of view; it spares the author the temptations of pride or arrogance and being accused thereof. It was in fact standard practice for a student to compile a biography of his teacher, sometimes on the basis of autobiographical materials supplied by the teacher. Ibn Ṭūlūn, however, curiously states that he wrote his autobiography at the request of his teacher, Shaykh Muḥyi al-Dīn al-Nuʿaymī, rather than at the far more usual request of a student.

Another major Arabic autobiographer of the sixteenth century, the Sufi shaykh ʿAbd al-Wahhāb al-Shaʿrānī, pulls all of these threads together in his lengthy defense of autobiography. He asserts that autobiography enables others to emulate one's good characteristics, functions as an enduring act of thanks to God that outlives the author, and provides useful information for future generations. Al-Shaʿrānī firmly supports the idea that a firsthand account is more reliable than someone else's rendering and substantiates this argument with quotations from the Prophet Muhammad, the Qurʾān, and the mystical philosopher Ibn al-ʿArabī. His final argument reiterates that, in writing an autobiography, one is following the example of great figures of the past. He closes with a spirited denial that an autobiography is written out of pride.[44]

Ibn ʿAjība, a Moroccan Sufi writing in 1807, also cites the desire for historical accuracy as the primary justification for writing an autobiography. Rather than allow his students to compile a biography—a task that they had apparently already begun—he forestalled their work by writing his own text, preferring to provide a more reliable account himself: "Fearing that they might allow some addition or omission to slip into their work, I decided to report, with God's assistance, what I have seen with my own eyes and heard with my own ears, for that which is transmitted is not that which was actually seen."[45] Ibn ʿAjība also cites the Qur'ānic injunction to speak of God's bounty and gives a list of famous Sufis who had previously written autobiographies to further justify his undertaking.

The judgment that an autobiography is a more reliable account than a biography fits quite closely with the structure of Islamic historiography and religious sciences in general, where eyewitness accounts were carefully transmitted for centuries in both oral and written form. This advantage from the point of view of historical methodology, however, did not entirely outweigh the fear of stumbling into the moral pitfalls involved in writing about oneself.

This brief historical survey provides a rough sense of how the writing of autobiography became an ever more conscious act within the Arabic literary and historical traditions, an act at times fraught with significant "autobiographical anxieties." Paradoxically, the need to justify the writing of such a text appears to have grown most intense in the fourteenth through sixteenth centuries, a period in which the autobiographical act itself had become fully established and quite widespread. Nevertheless, it also seems reasonable that critical debate over a literary genre should intensify after it achieves a certain currency. In any case, just as autobiography itself grew out of a genre, the *tarjama,* concerned with maintaining the lines of inheritance back to exemplary figures including the Prophet, eventually it too came to carry a legacy, to which its inheritors staked their own claims.

Notes

1. These were first identified as the starting points of different strands of Arabic autobiographical writing in Franz Rosenthal, "Die arabische Autobiographie," *Studia Arabica* 1 (1937): 11–12, 15–19.

2. Although referred to by several later writers, the autobiography of Yāqūt has not come down to us. In the appendix to his recent edition of Yāqūt's compendium, Iḥsān ʿAbbās states that he was unable to locate the author's autobiography in any manuscript of the work. See Iḥsān ʿAbbās, ed., *Muʿjam al-udabāʾ* (Beirut: Dār al-Gharb al-Islāmī, 1993), 7:2881.

3. This work is available only in a reconstruction by Claude Cahen: "Une source pour l'histoire ayyubide: Les mémoires de Saʿd al-dīn ibn Ḥamawiya al-Juwaynī," *Bulletin de la Faculté des Lettres de Strasbourg* 7 (1950): 320–37; rpt. in Cahen, *Les peuples musulmans dans l'histoire médievale* (Damascus: Institut Français, 1977), 457–82.

4. ʿImād al-Dīn al-Kātib al-Iṣfahānī, *Kharīdat al-qaṣr* (Damascus: al-Maṭbaʿa al-Hishāmiyya, 1964), 112.

5. Hartwig Derenbourg, *ʿOumâra du Yémen, sa vie et son oeuvre* (Paris: Leroux, 1897), xii–xiv; al-Iṣfahānī, *Kharīdat al-qaṣr,* 101–44.

6. Derenbourg, *ʿOumâra du Yémen,* xiv; al-Iṣfahānī, *Kharīdat al-qaṣr,* 107.

7. Derenbourg, *ʿOumâra du Yémen,* xiv–xv.

8. Franz Rosenthal, *A History of Muslim Historiography* (Leiden: E. J. Brill, 1968), 175.

9. [*tarjama nafsahu fī ta'līfin mustaqillin sammāhu al-barq al-shāmī*] in al-Suyūṭī; cited in English in the introduction of this work.

10. See ʿAli Ibn al-Qaṭṭāʿ, *al-Durra al-khaṭīra fī shuʿarāʾ al-jazīra,* ed. Bashīr al-Bakkūsh (Beirut: Dār al-Gharb al-Islāmī, 1995), 232 n. 3. Ibn al-Imām (d. 1155) was a compiler of biographies of Andalusian poets (see Hussain Monés, "Ibn al-Imām," *EI*[2] 3:807). ʿAbd Allāh ibn Ibrāhīm Ibn al-Ḥijārī is the author of *Kitāb al-Mushib fī gharīb al-maghrib.*

11. In his autobiography, Ibn al-Khaṭīb includes the text of one of his letters to Ibn Khaldūn.

12. For a translation of Ibn Khaldūn's version of this famous encounter as well as useful information concerning the different versions of his autobiography and conflicting accounts found in the works of other medieval Arab historians, particularly Ibn ʿArabshāh, see Walter J. Fischel, *Ibn Khaldūn and Tamerlane* (Berkeley: University of California Press, 1952).

13. An English translation of this text is found in *University Library of Autobiography,* vol. 2: *The Middle Ages and Their Autobiographers* (New York: F. Tyler Daniels, 1918), 171–206.

14. Carl Brockelmann, *Geschichte der arabischen Litteratur* (Leiden: E. J. Brill, 1943–49), Supp. vol. 2, p. 31: *Irshād al-ghāwī bal* [sic] *isʿād al-ṭālib wa-l-rāwī li-l-iʿlām bi-tarjamat al-Sakhāwī;* in addition, he wrote a lengthy biography of his teacher, Ibn Ḥajar.

15. See Titus Burckhardt, "Le Sheikh al-ʿArabī Ad-Darqāwī: Extraits de ses lettres," *Études Traditionnelles* (March–April 1966): 60–80; "Le Sheikh Ad-Darqāwī: Nouveaux extraits de ses lettres," *Études Traditionnelles* 402–3 (July–October 1976): 192–210.

16. See Allan Austin, *African Muslims in Antebellum America: A Sourcebook* (New York: Garland, 1984); and Marc Shell and Werner Sollors, eds., *The Multilingual Anthology of American Literature* (New York: New York University Press, 2000).

17. Shell and Sollors, *Multilingual Anthology of American Literature,* 58–93.

18. Al-Ghamdi, for example, classifies medieval Arabic autobiographies into spiritual, political, and academic; Ḍayf, into philosophical, scholarly/literary, Sufi, political and modern.

19. For a detailed discussion of the history of the manuscripts, published

editions, and translations, see William E. Gohlman, *The Life of Ibn Sina: A Critical Edition and Annotated Translation* (Albany: SUNY Press, 1974).

20. There is an ongoing debate about whether this text should be read as an autobiography or as a demonstration of the author's "epistemological theory" concerning intuition and study. For the latter argument, see Dimitri Gutas, *Avicenna and the Aristotelian Tradition: Introduction to Reading Avicenna's Philosophical Works* (Leiden: E. J. Brill, 1988): 194–98; and for a response, see Michael E. Marmura, "Plotting the Course of Avicenna's Thought," *Journal of the American Oriental Society* 111, no. 2 (1991): 333–42.

21. Gohlman, *The Life of Ibn Sina*, 7–8.

22. Ibid., 7.

23. Aḥmad Ibn ʿAjība, *L'autobiographie (Fahrasa) du Soufi Marocain Ahmad ibn ʿAgîba (1747–1809)*, trans. into French by J.-L. Michon (Leiden: E. J. Brill, 1969), 33. Reprinted from *Arabica* 15–16: 1968–69; Engl. trans. of cited passage by D. F. Reynolds.

24. Al-Sakhāwī, *al-Jawāhir wa-l-durar;* cited in Rosenthal, *Muslim Historiography,* 603.

25. Al-Sakhāwī in Rosenthal, *Muslim Historiography*, 606; it is worth noting that Galen's *On My Books* is framed as the response to a similar request.

26. Ibn Buluggīn, *The Tibyān: Memoirs of ʿAbd Allāh b. Bulluggīn, Last Zirid Amīr of Granada,* trans. Amin Tibi (Leiden: E. J. Brill 1986), 33.

27. Ibid., 34.

28. Ibid., 41.

29. Adapted from A. J. Arberry, *The Ring of the Dove* (London: Luzac, 1953), 158.

30. Ibn Buluggīn, *Tibyān,* 9.

31. Ibid., 8.

32. Our translation.

33. A number of theological discussions took place among early scholars concerning the obligation of thanking God, but these do not seem to have involved the verse in question. For an extensive description of this debate, see Kevin Reinhart, *Before Revelation: The Boundaries of Muslim Moral Thought* (Albany: SUNY Press, 1995).

34. This passage is quoted in Aḥmad al-Maqqarī (d. 1632), *Nafḥ al-ṭīb min ghuṣn al-Andalus al-raṭīb,* ed. Iḥsān ʿAbbās (Beirut: Dār Ṣādir, 1968), 2:262, from the autobiography of Ibn Saʿīd (d. 1286) in *al-Mughrib fī hulā al-Maghrib;* however, the versions of *al-Mughrib* that have come down to us independently do not appear to include the passage. See Ibn al-Qaṭṭāʿ (d. 1121), *al-Durra al-khaṭīra fī shuʿarāʾ al-jazīra,* ed. Bashīr al-Bakkūsh (Beirut: Dār al-Gharb al-Islāmī, 1995), 232 n. 3.

35. Al-Sakhāwī, in Rosenthal, *Muslim Historiography,* 586–610.

36. Al-Qurashī and al-Mālaqī remain unidentified.

37. Qur'ān 93:11, for example, is mentioned by al-Suyūṭī, al-Shaʿrānī, Ṭashköprüzāde, al-ʿAydarūs, and Ibn ʿAjība.

38. Tzvetan Todorov, *Genres in Discourse,* trans. Catherine Porter (Cambridge: Cambridge University Press, 1990), 17.

39. *Al-Siyāq li-ta'rīkh Nīsābūr,* ʿAbd al-Ghāfir al-Fārisī's "Continuation" of Muḥammad ibn ʿAbd Allāh al-Ḥakīm al-Nīsābūrī's (d. 1014) *Ta'rīkh Nīsābūr* (History of Nishapur).

40. *Al-Fulk al-mashḥūn fī aḥwāl Muḥammad ibn Ṭulūn* (Damascus: Maṭbaʿat al-Taraqqī, 1929), 6. Ibn Ṭulūn's citation from al-Suyūṭī is from a different text than that quoted at the beginning of this volume.

41. Many collections were organized alphabetically by first name; thus the author's autobiography would fall under *Y* for Yūsuf, the last letter of the Arabic alphabet.

42. Possibly Rabīʿa ibn ʿAlī ʿAbd al-Raḥmān (d. 753).

43. [*lā yanbaghī li-aḥadin ʿindahu shayʾun min al-ʿilmi an yuḍayyiʿa nafsah*], al-Bukhārī, *Bāb al-ʿIlm* (The Chapter on Knowledge).

44. ʿAbd al-Wahhāb al-Shaʿrānī, *Laṭāʾif al-minan wa-l-akhlāq* (Cairo: ʿĀlam al-Fikr, 1976), 6–8; al-Shaʿrānī's preface is translated in Dwight F. Reynolds, "Shaykh ʿAbd al-Wahhāb al-Shaʿrānī's Sixteenth-Century Defense of Autobiography," *Harvard Middle Eastern and Islamic Review* 4, nos. 1–2 (1997–98): 122–37.

45. Ibn ʿAjība, *L'autobiographie,* trans. J.-L. Michon, 33.

CHAPTER FOUR

Arabic Autobiography and the Literary Portrayal of the Self

The two previous chapters traced the history of Arabic autobiographical writing from its emergence in the ninth century through its development into a self-conscious critical discourse in the late fifteenth century. This chapter takes a closer look at the texts themselves, addressing issues of the literary portrayal of the self.

Western scholarship is far from unanimous on a definition of "true" autobiography (Arabic or otherwise). In recent years, scholars have deployed a variety of (often conflicting) criteria involving the literary portrayal of the author's "personal," "inner," or "private" life as the measure of real autobiography. These criteria are more often than not latent and unarticulated; however, a revealing pattern emerges from discussions of which text constitutes the first "true" autobiography in a given tradition.

The pioneer of critical study of the Arabic tradition, Franz Rosenthal, sees the beginnings of Arabic spiritual autobiography in the writings of al-Muḥāsibī (d. 857) and considers the earliest secular autobiography to be that of Ḥunayn ibn Isḥāq (d. 873 or 877).[1] Anwar al-Jundī declares that al-Ghazālī (d. 1111) was the first Arab to write his memoirs,[2] whereas Marshall G. S. Hodgson states that al-Ghazālī was the only true premodern Arab autobiographer.[3] Philip Hitti and Nikita Elisséeff say that Usāma ibn Munqidh (d. 1188) was the first;[4] ʿAlī ʿAbd al-Wāḥid and Ṭāhā Ḥusayn consider Ibn Khaldūn (d. 1406) the first;[5] and ʿIzz al-Dīn Ismāʿīl claims that it was Ṭāhā Ḥusayn himself (d. 1973).[6] For Thomas Philipp, a pre-twentieth-century Arabic autobiography is an impossibility: "It would be misleading to attempt the reconstruction of the history of the [Arabic] autobiography."[7] This, in his opinion, is because "true" autobiography in Arabic springs without predecessor or precedent, fully formed and completely modern, from the pen of Jurjī Zaydān in 1908. He rejects as autobiographies texts by Zaydān's contemporaries ʿAlī Mubārak (d. 1893), Mikhāʾil Mishāqa (d. 1888), and Ibrāhīm Fawzī Pasha (d. 1902). For Philipp, the boundary between proto-autobiography and real autobiography in Arabic literature can be drawn at one specific moment in time.

There is a distinct tendency for scholars to identify more and more recent texts as the first "true" autobiography; in essence, the definition of autobiography among scholars of Arabic literature is becoming more tightly constrained by modern western concepts of the genre, many of which have been generated by critics only in the past thirty years. This general tendency is, in methodological terms, self-defeating: by imposing ever more modern definitions of "true" autobiography, scholars have set ever more recent historical limits for the genre and its presumed concomitant cultural manifestations, including individual identity and self-awareness. This categorization renders the "true" autobiography an extremely recent phenomenon in both western and Islamic societies. From this perspective, autobiography can possess—exactly as Philipp claims—no history. By accepting only the most recent concept of western autobiography, literary historians have created an ever-receding horizon whereby only the nearest historical examples of either culture are acceptable as mature examples of the genre.

Another significant methodological problem plagues approaches that seek to define the genre of autobiography by establishing a specific starting point: nearly all such studies presume that an era of "true" autobiography is subsequently and universally ushered in with the publication of the first real exemplar of the genre. In the western tradition, for example, scholars have identified Rousseau over and over again as the first "true," "real," or "modern" autobiography. Paradoxically, if scholars were to apply the same criteria they use so stringently in distinguishing Rousseau from his close predecessors (e.g., Cellini and Cardano) with equal assiduousness to autobiographies produced after Rousseau, there would remain remarkably few "true" autobiographies to study.

Nor do any of these scholars seem willing to address the vacuum that their opinions leave behind: once the line has been drawn at the first "true" autobiography (Arabic or otherwise), what status is to be accorded the many earlier self-conscious, self-authored texts that purport to give a complete representation of the author's life? The critical issue becomes whether to address these earlier texts as autobiographies, in the sense of a portrayal of the self, or as some other category of life representation. The answer to this question hinges both on our modern expectations of autobiography as a genre—that it should reveal a private, psychological inner self beyond an exterior, public self—and on our expectations of autobiography as a portrayal of an individualized identity or personality. To what extent are these modern expectations generalizable across cultures and literatures? Any eventual judgment will necessarily involve the interaction between two opposing approaches to the study of autobiography.

The first approach is to seek in these texts elements that we, as twenty-first-century readers, readily identify as the portrayal of an inner self: the emotional life of the author, his or her private behavior, the disclosure of motivations and reactions, and the evaluation of the author's personality, sexuality, and so forth. The first section of this chapter operates entirely at this level of analysis. The second section pursues a rather different course, one based on different assumptions about the relationship between literary representation and the "self."

Essentializing the Self: Private Life and Personality in the Memoirs of Ibn Buluggīn

Assuming for the sake of argument that concepts such as "private," "personal," and "inner self" are unchanging and ahistorical, and that what appears to us to be personal (versus public) is in fact so, then a number of the Arabic texts in this survey may certainly be judged true autobiographies, even by such presentist standards. These texts possess many of the criteria sought by modern western scholars such as direct portrayal of the author's thoughts, emotional reactions, and an awareness of psychological development and maturation from childhood through adulthood to old age. One such text is the autobiography of Ibn Buluggīn (d. after 1094).

The eleventh-century prince Ibn Buluggīn was the last member of the Berber Zīrid dynasty to rule the kingdom of Granada in southern Spain. After he was deposed in 1090 by the invading Almoravids, he was sent into exile in Aghmāt, Morocco, where he lived out the rest of his life as a captive and wrote his memoirs in about 1094. The first third of the text consists of an apologia for Ibn Buluggīn's dynasty. The initial four chapters of the work deal with his forebears and their reigns. In chapters five through twelve Ibn Buluggīn describes his own life and reign. One fascicle, which included a discussion of Ibn Buluggīn's ascension to the throne, is missing in the single known manuscript. As mentioned above, Ibn Buluggīn felt it necessary to justify not the writing of his autobiography per se but the continuous narrative style that he used in writing it.

The final chapter is of most interest to us here, for, having recounted the events of his life in chronological order, he now stops to evaluate his experiences.

> I have now described some of the events that took place in al-Andalus [Islamic Spain], the role of our dynasty and the end to which our fates brought it, as best my memory and ability have allowed, right up to the present. Let me now mention some of the poetry I composed concerning all this, in periods when

> my mind was unoccupied by troubles and my soul at ease, which left me free to ponder all manner of beautiful things and to experience joy at the sweetness of all news. I have never presumed to possess any particular talent as a poet, however, nor was I much concerned with it, for I composed only when I discovered something that caught my attention or sought to produce an eloquent description of something I wished to portray.[8]

Unfortunately, no samples of Ibn Buluggīn's poetry are included in either the Arabic published edition or the English translation.

Ibn Buluggīn then turns to the horoscope cast by the court astrologers in his youth and compares it to his life as it actually unfolded.

> Everything is set at one's conception and birth. In the predictions calculated from the hour of my birth, I have read of characteristics that I have indeed noted in my nature and disposition, despite the fact that those who made those predictions wrote them down when I was but a child and could not have known anything of my circumstances in life [*aḥwālī*]. This document was hidden from me by [the minister] Simāja for a time, until it came into my hands against his will. This disturbed him, for he feared I would grow vain from the good fortune foretold therein. In it I read of wondrous and strange things.[9]

He notes that the horoscope correctly predicted that his children would be born late in his life, that he would have a lifelong attraction to boys with mercurial characteristics but at the same time harbor an aversion to any unlawful relations with them, and that he was, as predicted, afflicted with melancholy and other frightful psychological ailments. He does not concur, however, with the enduring good fortune the astrologers foresaw for him, for in reality his life had been filled with quite the reverse.

Ibn Buluggīn discusses at some length the topics of medicine, health, eating habits, sexual mores and appetites, whether astrology is a true science or quackery, whether it is good to be informed of the hour of one's death ahead of time, the existence of jinn and angels, and the role of pleasure and love in life. After citing earlier authorities on each topic, he gives his own opinion. On wine drinking, for example, he writes:

> My opinion about wine is that if someone's mood grows more composed by drinking a lot of it, then no one should say to him, "Drink less!" And to someone for whom it is pleasing to drink but a little, no one should say, "Drink more!" A reasonable person detects this on his own and, knowing what is not in harmony with his nature, does not exceed that. . . .
>
> People say that drinking relieves anxieties, but I say that it only excites them, depending upon one's mood when one begins to drink: if one is happy, drinking will arouse feelings that one had previously pacified, and if one is beset with cares, it will remind one of the situation one is in and of even worse situations, and lead one down evil paths.[. . .] Sadness comes from what has happened in the past, and sometimes wine will distract one from that, but

> nothing brings on sleep like sadness coupled with remembering what has gone before or looking through a book seeking only to read of what has happened in the past.[10]

In discussing life's trials, wealth, power, and happiness, Ibn Buluggīn portrays himself poignantly as a man who at one point had possessed everything, then had it all taken from him by his enemies, and who now writes as a prisoner in exile from his native land.

> I myself have been afflicted with such troubles, for human nature is indeed one and varies only slightly, which is why humans have been ordered [by God] to love each other as they love themselves, in hopes of justice and fairness [from Him].
>
> I find my feelings toward great wealth now, having possessed it and then lost it, more abstemious than before I gained it, though I was at that time better off than I am now. I feel similarly about all that I possessed in the way of power to command and forbid, the amassing of treasures, elegant foods, clothing, riding animals, and buildings, and the other luxurious circumstances among which I was raised; indeed, they were so luxurious that one could not wish for or even imagine something of which I was not given the very best and even more. These riches were not suddenly cut off, nor did they disappear after only a brief moment, that I should linger in sorrow over them and think of them as having existed only in my dreams. I possessed them for a period of twenty years [during my reign], and nearly that long [before my reign] while I was growing up in the very lap of luxury.
>
> I find myself now, after having lost all this, more desirous of having children than of anything I have described, since I did not have any before. I have said to myself: I already obtained the goals that people strive for in this world, and in doing so acquired fame from horizon to horizon. But there is no escape from losing these things, sooner or later, during one's lifetime or at one's death. So I reckon those twenty years as one hundred—they are gone "as if they had not flourished yesterday!" [Q 10:24]. Now it is more fitting for me to contemplate what it is I seek. And it is God's prerogative to order what He wills![11]

On the birth of his children, he writes:

> One of the blessings God bestowed upon me was that He made my firstborn child a girl. Our entire tribe still considers themselves blessed by her and strongly dislike having sons as their firstborn. I saw that the joy of my father, Sayf al-Dawla—May God have mercy on him!—was not fulfilled by similar good fortune.[. . .] After this God granted me two sons, but we did not celebrate their births, so that our fears for them would not be joined with [the misfortune] of my own path. This was a kindness granted me by the Beneficent in His graciousness and generosity. To enumerate God's blessings is an act of giving thanks for them [*fa-taʿdād niʿam Allāh shukr lahā*], and to proclaim this with gratitude and devotion, not out of pride or vanity, is among the most important duties a person undertakes.

> [. . .] I then turned my attention to composing this book which—by my life—shall take the place of a son who causes the memory of his father to live on in the world. In it, I have explained aspects of myself, for those who are uninformed, that have been obscured by evil things that have been said and by what the envious have claimed led to my downfall. [. . .] I have written this book for people of kindness and truth who have been confused by the matter, for those who love me and wish me well.[12]

The final passages of the text contain an impassioned plea to the reader to judge the author well and to disdain the malicious slanderers who have attacked his reputation. A last angry tirade is addressed directly to his detractors. Unfortunately, the very last lines of the text are illegible in the manuscript.

Ibn Buluggīn situates his life within the history of his dynasty, evaluates his own reign, and discusses the political and military intrigues of his day. But as an author, he also steps back from that "public" life and evaluates its course, comparing it to earlier astrological predictions and examining his own personality and emotions, his private habits and behavior, his likes and dislikes, his hopes and desires, and how these changed as he aged.

Ibn Buluggīn's text is not an isolated example of such self-revelatory writing. Many autobiographers tell us of the trials and tribulations they faced in their careers and evaluate their causes at a very personal level. Ḥunayn ibn Isḥāq (ninth century) devotes his entire autobiographical work to a description of the difficulties he experienced as a result of the slander of his rivals and how he eventually survived to overcome them. Ibn Riḍwān (eleventh century) recounts his poverty as a youth pursuing his studies, bemoans the fact that he did not have enough money to marry until comparatively late, and expresses general pessimism about the state of scholarship, particularly in the field of medicine, in his day. Al-Jazā'irī (seventeenth century) on the one hand takes pride in the amount of suffering he has endured and on the other recounts these tribulations with a great deal of wit and humor often directed at himself.[13] Al-Baḥrānī (eighteenth century) traces his life through periods of hardship and misfortune until he finally succeeds in accumulating the material wealth with which he, as a narrator, is obsessed throughout his account (translated in this volume).

Many authors also give overt portrayals of dramatic moments in their emotional lives. Abū Ḥayyān al-Andalusī (fourteenth century) wrote his autobiography (text not extant) as an act of mourning the untimely death of his daughter Nuḍār; in it he recorded what he would have wished to have told her of his life. Ibn al-Jawzī (twelfth century) wrote an account of his life for his son as a legacy, exhorting him to lead a good and productive life. Much later, Princess Salmé of Zanzibar (nineteenth century) and Ṭāhā Ḥusayn (twentieth century) also addressed their autobiographies to their children. The Sufi shaykh Zarrūq (fifteenth century) writes that the early death of his mother completely reoriented his life, causing him to devote himself to his studies and to the pursuit of a pious way of life, to the astonishment of his family and relatives. ʿAlī al-ʿĀmilī (seventeenth century) writes poignantly and at some length of the tremendous grief he experienced at the death of his twenty-two-year-old son and of how it changed his attitude toward life and includes the poem he wrote as an elegy (translated in this volume). Aḥmad Fāris al-Shidyāq (nineteenth century) interrupts his prose narration to include the elegaic poem he wrote in grief at the death of his young son.

Several authors express their awareness of the passing stages of life and find in the onset of old age a motivation for looking back over the life they have lived. Usāma ibn Munqidh (twelfth century) penned his autobiography at the age of ninety and waxed eloquent in describing the onset of old age and senility, how he could at the time of writing scarcely recognize in himself the younger Usāma, and how he continually bemoaned his past life. He includes one of his own poems on this theme and then begs the reader's pardon for the digression. Abū Shāma (thirteenth century) places the moment in which his hair suddenly turns gray—at the age of twenty-five—at the very center of his autobiography, likening it to old age and evaluating its significance. At this point in the text he also includes a poem about the event (translated in this volume).

Private personal habits also find their place in a number of these texts. Ibn Sīnā (eleventh century), in a frequently cited example, recounts that he used to drink a glass of wine when he felt overcome by sleep while studying late at night, which would revive him and allow him to continue his work. Al-Yūsī (seventeenth century) relates that when he first got married as a young man, the pleasures of his nuptial bed kept him from concentrating on his studies for months and describes the great effort with which he finally mastered his physical desires and was able to return to his education. Ibn ʿAjība (eighteenth century) writes that he was a handsome youth and that many women attempted to seduce him with their charms but that with God's help he did not fall into temptation. Jurjī Zaydān (nineteenth century) recounts his early experimentation with masturbation and how, on overhearing adult men say that it weakened the body, he thereafter decided to refrain from it.

Portrayals of close relationships with parents, siblings, and spouses also appear; at the same time, there is a notable lack of depictions of close friendships in these texts. Al-Tirmidhī (ninth century) provides an intriguing portrait of his wife's close involvement in his spiritual life and progress; indeed, by the end of his autobiography, his wife assumes the primary role in the narrative (translated in this volume). Ibn Buluggīn (eleventh century) tells early in his memoirs of the tenderness and affection his grandfather felt for his father, who was an only son, and how after the death of his father at just twenty-five that affection was transferred to himself. His grandfather took him out of school when he was still a child so that he could sit in court and learn the ways of kings. The father of Usāma ibn Munqidh (twelfth century) is a very powerful figure in his memoirs, and many anecdotes depict a close and enduring friendship between father and son. Zarrūq (fifteenth century) is saddened that his father died before he was old enough to know him but refers to his mother harshly, as "a wasteful woman." In contrast, he speaks very fondly of his grandmother, who raised him after he was orphaned. Ibn ʿAjība (eighteenth century) devotes a brief chapter of his autobiography to listing his wives and children; although his account is on the whole very sparse, it does touch, rather diplomatically, on how his favorite wife, unlike the other women he married, was not of high rank. ʿAlī Mubārak's father (nineteenth century) constantly rescued him from his escapades by helping him out of prison, allowed him to leave harsh teachers who beat him, and at one point endangered his entire family by trying to sneak his son out of the government school in Cairo where ʿAlī Mubārak lay deathly ill in the infirmary (translated in this volume). Princess Salmé (nineteenth century) recounts numerous anecdotes describing her intense love for her father, the ruler of Zanzibar, and family relations at the royal court.

It appears, then, that authors of autobiographies chose to include information about their private lives based to a great extent on individual impulse rather than on established literary convention. It is clear that although the tradition of Arabic autobiography did not require that authors reveal their private selves in detail, neither did it preclude this, even when we define these terms as the depiction of behavior, relationships, and reactions that modern western readers deem "personal" or "private."

Historicizing the Self: Deciphering the Autobiography of Ibn Ḥajar

Another approach to the issue of literary representations of the self is to ask whether our modern conceptualizations of such terms as "personal," "private," and "inner self" are completely applicable to premodern texts, whether they are as obvious and as unchanging as they may at first appear. We live in a time characterized by an intense dichotomy in the conceptualization of the self into public and private. Was this true in earlier periods? Is this true in other cultures? In the post-Freudian western world, for example, sexual acts and sexuality have come to constitute a major portion of the private self and of personal identity and are seen as a window into the subconscious. Did they do so in premodern worldviews, or were they instead similar to table manners, bathing, and toiletry, that is, personal and bodily behaviors that, although private, play no great role in defining the self? Should we instead be looking more closely at recurring elements in premodern texts that may have played significant roles in representing the self similar to the role now played by sex and sexuality? The problematization of terms such as "personal," "private," and "inner self" requires of us far more intense study of the changing constraints of literary representation through which such conceptualizations make themselves known.

In the work of Ibn Buluggīn we found many of the qualities modern readers would expect from an autobiography: an author's critical evaluation of his own personality, a retrospective examination of the course of his life, and even a sense of imparting some of the hard-learned lessons of that life to posterity. Far more problematic, however, are those texts that are but brief accounts of the external events of a life and which apparently offer us little of the author's personality. Among later medieval Arab authors, one of the most famous—and driest—of these texts was that of Ibn Ḥajar al-ʿAsqalānī (d. 1449). The text constitutes little more than an encyclopedia entry, written in the third person, located in the author's biographical compendium of the judges of Egypt. It is short enough to be cited in its entirety.

Ibn Ḥajar al-ʿAsqalānī: Aḥmad b. ʿAlī b. Muḥammad b. Muḥammad b. ʿAlī b. Aḥmad. From the town of ʿAsqalān by origin, Egyptian by birth and upbringing, resident of Cairo. He was born in the month of Shaʿbān in the year A.H. 773 [1372 C.E.] and his father died in the month of Rajab 777 [1375 C.E.]. His mother had already died while he was still a young child, so he was raised an orphan. He did not enter Qurʾān school until he was five years old and only completed memorizing the Qurʾān when he was nine. He was not prepared to pray the *tarāwīḥ* prayers of the holy month of Ramadan publicly until the year 785 [1383 C.E.], when he had already turned twelve.[14]

His guardian was the famous Raʾīs Zakī al-Dīn Abū Bakr b. Nūr al-Dīn ʿAlī al-Kharrūbī, the head of the merchants' guild in Egypt who had become a neighbor that year and who took him in when he had no one to support him. In that year he studied the *Ṣaḥīḥ* of al-Bukhārī with the greatest authority in the Ḥijāz, ʿAfīf al-dīn ʿAbd Allāh al-Nishāwarī, the last of the companions of Raḍī al-Dīn al-Ṭabarī, Imām at the Maqām [of Abraham in Mecca]. But he did not complete his studies, for it happened that he did not hear the entire work, though he received a certificate for his teacher's teachings anyway.

He also studied it with Shaykh Shams al-Dīn Muḥammad b. ʿUmar al-Sallāwī al-Dimashqī, who taught beneath the living quarters of al-Kharrūbī in a house which was at the Ṣafā Gate, on the right when heading out towards Ṣafā, known as the House of ʿAynāʾ the Sharīfa [descendant of the Prophet Muhammad], daughter of the Sharīf ʿAjlān. In this house there is a window which looks out over the Holy Mosque in Mecca and whoever sits there can see the Kaʿba and the Black Stone in its corner. The reader and the listener used to sit there without a bench beneath the aforementioned window. The teacher of the author [of this autobiography] would sit there along with the others who studied with him. When the reciter read, the teacher would order them to listen until he had finished reading to the very end of the book. But the author [of this autobiography] occasionally went out to take care of some need or other and there was no one taking roll. So my source for [the *Ṣaḥīḥ* of al-Bukhārī] is Shaykh Najm al-Dīn al-Murjānī, who taught it to me properly much later; I have relied upon him by virtue of my trust in him.

After that [the author] memorized books of abridgments [*mukhtaṣarāt*] of the fields of study. It was necessary that someone take him in hand, and this fell to Shaykh Shams al-Dīn Muḥammad b. ʿAlī b. Muḥammad b. ʿIsā b. Abī Bakr b. al-Qaṭṭān al-Miṣrī, so [the author] attended his lessons. Al-Qaṭṭān revealed to him works of history while he was still studying in the children's Qur'ān school and filled his mind with many things about the lives [Ar. *aḥwāl*, lit. "conditions"] of the *ḥadīth* transmitters.

Meanwhile he also heard lessons from Najm al-Dīn b. Razīn and Ṣalāḥ al-dīn al-Ziftāwī and Zayn al-Dīn b. al-Shiḥna and he looked into the literary arts starting from the year 792 [1390 C.E.]. He composed poetry and wrote odes in praise of the Prophet as well as short occasional pieces.

Then he met with the greatest transmitter [of *ḥadīth*] of the era, Zayn al-Dīn al-ʿArāqī, in the month of Ramadan in the year 796 [1394 C.E.]. He stayed on with him for ten years while the art of *ḥadīth* was revealed to him. Before that year had ended, he produced for his Shaykh, the authority [*musnid*] of Cairo, Abū Isḥāq al-Tanūkhī, the work *al-Mi'a al-ʿUshāriyya* [a collection of one hundred Prophetic *ḥadīth*].

The first person to read it in full was the transmitter Abū Zarʿa b. al-Ḥāfiẓ al-ʿArāqī [son of his teacher, the famous *ḥadīth* scholar just mentioned].

Then [the author] traveled to Alexandria and attended lessons from its authorities at that time. Later he went on the pilgrimage and traveled through Yemen. He attended lessons from scholars in Mecca, Medina, Yanbuʿ, Zabīd, Taʿizz, Aden, and other cities and villages.

In Yemen he met the great scholar of Arabic lexicography, a man without rival, Majd al-Dīn b. al-Shīrāzī, and received from him one of his most famous works called *al-Qāmūs fī al-lugha* [Dictionary of the Arabic Language]. He met many of the learned men of those cities and then returned to Cairo. Next he traveled to the Levant and heard lessons from scholars in Qaṭiyya, Gaza, Ramla, Jerusalem, Damascus, al-Ṣāliḥiyya, and other villages and cities.

His stay in Damascus was one hundred days, and what he heard in that period amounted to nearly one thousand fasicles of *ḥadīth,* among which were some from the great books: *al-Muʿjam al-awsaṭ* [The Middle Collection] by al-Ṭabarānī, and *Maʿrifat al-ṣaḥāba* [Knowledge of the Companions] by Abū ʿAbd Allāh b. Manda, most of the *Musnad* of Abū Yaʿlā and others.

Then he returned and completed his own book, *Taʿlīq al-taʿlīq,* about the lives of the greatest of his teachers, and so others began to take *ḥadīth* dictation from him. He remained the protégé of Shaykh Sirāj al-Dīn al-Bulqīnī until he granted him a certificate [to teach law and grant legal opinions]. After al-Bulqīnī granted him a certificate [*adhina lahu*] he obtained the certificate of Shaykh al-Ḥāfiz Zayn al-Dīn al-ʿArāqī.

Then he began to compose his own works. He dictated *al-Arbaʿīn al-mutabāyina* [Forty Variant *Ḥadīth*] in the Shaykhūniyya college starting in the year 808 [1406 C.E.], then he dictated from *ʿUshāriyāt al-ṣaḥāba* approximately one hundred sessions over a number of years. Then he was given charge of the teaching of *ḥadīth* at the al-Jamāliyya al-Jadīda college, and he dictated there, but he cut short his dictation when he left in the year 814 [1411 C.E.]. He worked at writing books and was then appointed to the position of shaykh of the Baybarsiyya college, then with the teaching of Shāfiʿite law at the al-Mu'ayyadiyya al-Jadīda college. Then he was appointed judge on the seventeenth of the month of Muḥarram in the year 827 [1423 C.E.]. Thereafter, he convened a new dictation session from the beginning of the month of Ṣafar of that year until the present.[15]

This is precisely the type of text that helped to generate the image among western scholars of an utterly impersonal auto/biographical tradition. Yet we have only to examine the autobiographies of Ibn Ḥajar's own students to realize that Ibn Ḥajar's text is at the far end of the spectrum in the Arabic tradition in terms of its brevity and laconic style. Even in the case of this text, however, a careful reading reveals several noteworthy features.

First, the author carefully positions himself from the opening passages in a very modest stance concerning his intellectual achievements: he did not enter school until age five, did not finish memorizing the Qur'ān until age nine, did not pray the *tarāwīḥ* prayers until age twelve, and so forth. His language leads us to believe that he was somehow constantly behind schedule either because of his status as an orphan or because he was a slow student; yet from the information that can be gleaned from contemporary biographies and autobiographies, none of these ages are older than average. We know from other sources that his leading the *tarāwīḥ* prayers during Ramadan was delayed for a year by a trip to Mecca that he made in the company of his guardian, but it is probable that he is more concerned with projecting a self-effacing attitude.[16]

It is also striking that the only passage with any material detail at all is the one in which he describes his early attempts to master the *Ṣaḥīḥ* of al-Bukhārī. Suddenly, in this passage we have a house, its location, a window, a view of the Kaʿba, and students and teacher sitting on the floor beneath that window. Equally sudden is the shift to the first-person voice: "So my source for [the *Ṣaḥīḥ* of al-Bukhārī] is Shaykh Najm al-Dīn al-Murjānī, who taught me properly much later; I have relied upon him because of my trust in him."

The terminology of the Arabic passage directly reflects medieval Islamic teaching methods—"I heard this work from," "I completed my audition of such and such a work," "I mastered my audition," "I was granted a certificate to transmit such and such a work"—in which a teacher or reciter read aloud a work that was then taken down in dictation by pupils (hence the use of terms such as "hearing" and "audition") and discussed; and if a student wished to receive an *ijāza,* or certification, as a transmitter of that work, he then read the work back to the teacher and answered his questions about the text.[17] The work in question, the *Ṣaḥīḥ* of al-Bukhārī, is a collection of the traditions [*ḥadīth*] of the Prophet Muhammad, the field of study in which Ibn Ḥajar himself became the greatest authority of his time. It is not just any collection, however, but one of the canonical "Six Books."[18] That Ibn Ḥajar should recount to us his failure to master this basic work first from Shaykh al-Nishāwarī and then from Shaykh al-Sallāwī, and both times for completely unsubstantial reasons, is somewhat akin to Einstein recounting that he failed mathematics over and over again in school. And his meticulous description of this particular scene as being literally within sight of the Kaʿba in Mecca—the single most sacred spot on earth in Islam—adds more than a hint of irony.

Ibn Ḥajar may have had a number of different motivations for narrating these specific events in greater detail than the rest of his text. He may have wished to document meticulously his own authority to transmit this work; given his stature at the time of writing, however, it hardly seems likely that this would have been questioned. Alternatively, he may have been motivated by a desire to establish his own modesty concerning his intellectual achievements in a continuation of the rhetoric of the opening passage. He may even have wished to be an encouraging example to later striving students, particularly those who experienced hardships in childhood and began their schooling at a disadvantage.

When we read this passage against the background of Arabic autobiography as a whole, however, a far more important observation emerges. Among those premodern autobiographical texts that treat the author's childhood, a very large portion recount anecdotes of childhood embarrassments, failings, misbehavior for which they were punished, incidents in which they played the role of fool or were the butt of a joke, and so forth. Even those texts that uncritically laud the adult autobiographer as a major intellectual or spiritual authority often include rather detailed anecdotes of the authors as ordinary and quite fallible children. Over and over again Arabic autobiographers include humorous, often endearing, stories of themselves as children, even when they continue their accounts in the most serious tones when dealing with their adult lives and achievements. It is one of the most enduring and often-repeated motifs of premodern Arabic autobiography.[19]

Al-Tirmidhī (ninth century) begins his autobiography (translated in this volume) by admitting that he had to be pressed to study by his father until he finally acquired the habit and left off childish games and play. He also notes that he was twenty-seven years old when he finally succeeded in memorizing the Qur'ān after a "conversion experience" while returning from the pilgrimage. This late beginning in religious life is all the more remarkable in that the focus of al-Tirmidhī's autobiographical work is to demonstrate his status as a spiritual authority.

Ibn Sīnā (late tenth/early eleventh century) confesses that although he had mastered all of the other sciences, he was unable to comprehend Aristotle's *Metaphysics* even after having read it "forty times," until he finally came across a copy of al-Fārābī's commentary that enlightened him. It has been argued that the stages of Ibn Sīnā's education should be read as an allegorical treatise on the intellect;[20] whatever the case, this story, which portrays the hitherto insatiable student as utterly confounded, is one of the most memorable scenes in the narrative.

ʿAbd al-Laṭīf al-Baghdādī (late twelfth/early thirteenth century) recounts that, despite the best preparation at home, he could understand nothing of the teacher's "incoherent babbling" when his father first took him to school and that only when he was turned over to the teacher's assistant was he able to make sense of the lessons. He later describes in detail the warm friendship and camaraderie that developed between himself and this blind teaching assistant and how they later studied as colleagues under this same teacher (translated in this volume).

Zarrūq (fifteenth century) tells of being caught listening to storytellers in the marketplace and being rebuked by a male relative for his idleness; he never returned to hear their performances. He also recounts that when he experimented with being decorated with henna, he was scolded by a female relative for wearing the mark of a woman and never again adorned himself. He was also reprimanded for reaching out toward the food at a meal before their family's guest had begun to eat. Orphaned at an early age, his grandmother raised him using a number of clever ruses to inculcate good behavior. To encourage him to pray, she placed a dirham coin under his pillow as reward, a trick that also kept him from looking at the possessions or wealth of others with greed or envy. To teach him to appreciate their daily sustenance, she would cook food and hide it, then tell the young Zarrūq that they had no food that day. Together they would pray for God's beneficence and the food would miraculously appear. Zarrūq's childhood memories evoke both the naïveté of youth and the experience of gradually learning right from wrong.

Al-Yūsī (seventeenth century) tells us that he was so bashful about having to excuse himself to answer nature's call while in school and having to relieve himself in the proximity of others that he frequently stayed out of school rather than face that embarrassment. To conceal his ploy, he would wait along the road for his schoolmates and join them as they walked home, pretending that he had spent the entire day with them. The scoldings he received did not change his behavior; rather, the early death of his mother and the resulting emotional crisis he experienced motivated him to conquer this shyness, attend school, and devote himself so assiduously to his studies that his acquaintances found him unrecognizable as his former self.

Yūsuf al-Baḥrānī (eighteenth century) tells of being educated by his father but confesses that he was unfortunately not a very good pupil, as he was at that time still dominated by "the ignorance of youth" (translated in this volume).

Ibn ʿAjība (eighteenth century) used to get himself and his clothing so wet doing his ablutions before prayer that his mother tricked him into believing that it was permissible to do ablutions with a stone (by Islamic law this is only acceptable when traveling where water is not available and in certain other cases); he did not discover the truth until much later in life. On the whole, Ibn ʿAjība recounts primarily anecdotes that demonstrate his precocious piety and serious demeanor; some of the gullibility of a child attempting to impress the adults around him, however, still manages to shine through.

ʿAlī Mubārak (nineteenth century) describes his childhood misbehavior at length. He constantly ran away from teachers and various employments, eventually even ending up in jail, until he finally found his way into a goverment school in Cairo as a teenager. Mubārak offers numerous explanations for his misadventures and in doing so carefully shepherds our sympathies even when portraying himself as a most troublesome child (translated in this volume).

Mubārak, who went on to play a prominent role in Egypt as an educational reformer, also tells us that his first encounter with geometry left him totally bewildered. The mystical drawings seemed to resemble the strange talismans of folk healers and wandering dervishes. His confusion was only alleviated later by a superlative teacher who opened his mind and heart. He praises at some length the excellent techniques of this teacher. Later, he is again frustrated in his studies as a member of a delegation to France, where Egyptian officials insisted that the delegation be taught engineering in French before they had studied the French language! He also describes the personal study habits he developed in order to succeed.

Jurjī Zaydān (nineteenth century) writes of learning to read, write, and recite the Psalms, at which time his father declared his education to be complete, although he could not understand a word of the text (which may in fact have been in Syriac rather than Arabic). He also describes the ongoing tension between himself and his father concerning the amount of schooling he should have and what occupation he should take up.

Finally, in the most famous avatar of this motif, Ṭāhā Ḥusayn (late nineteenth/early twentieth century) relates in detail his experience of memorizing the Qurʾān as a blind child. Despite his great pride in this achievement, through lack of practice he forgot it and to his shame was found out in a very painful moment in front of his father and a guest. He then memorized it again and again forgot it, and finally, only on the third try, did he succeed in memorizing and retaining it.

Ibn Ḥajar thus includes in his fourteenth-century text a motif found in Arabic autobiographies in the centuries both before and after his own. Whether this is due to an awareness of earlier autobiographical writings or to literary convention, or whether it was simply a habit of medieval scholars and teachers to share such anecdotes, we do not know. But again and again, Arabic autobiographers who confess no real failings as adults begin their autobiographies with accounts of childhood failings or embarrassments, portraying themselves as slow or inept students, as having started their schooling late or having lagged behind their classmates in their studies, and as having possessed a child's naive or ridiculous beliefs. While the inclusion of such anecdotes hardly constitutes deep analysis of psychological development, it is equally clear that the weltanschauung of these authors is far from what has been previously claimed: "a person is viewed as a type rather than an individual and . . . this view is static: there is no awareness of the development of a person's character."[21] Even the terse scholarly prose of Ibn Ḥajar reveals the inaccuracy of such a statement.

One critical issue emerges from these passages that confide intimate information to the reader about the author's childhood: they establish the autobiographical authority of the text and mark it as distinct from a biography. Such information was known to the author alone. Even if a scholar shared such stories with his closest disciples, out of respect students refrained from including them in their biographical accounts of their teacher. It was apparently unacceptable for anyone but the author himself to present this type of self-effacing anecdote. What might at first glance seem to detract from an autobiographer's authority as an intellectual or religious figure may well have aided in establishing the authority of the autobiographical text. Moreover, as autobiographies were written in either the first-person or third-person voice, such passages may have played a critical role in projecting the autobiographical nature of a text.

Ibn Ḥajar is, moreover, one of many writers who included far more information about his life in his other works than he did in his formal autobiography; in fact, very little of what we know about him comes from this short text.[22] He was, for example, also a poet, and his collected poetic works were disseminated and transmitted along with his scholarly works on *ḥadīth* and his famous biographical dictionary covering the eighth Islamic century, the first of the great all-inclusive centenary biographical collections.[23]

Despite its brevity and impersonal nature, this text set a powerful precedent. Ibn Ḥajar's credentials as a scholar were unassailable. That he had written a biography of himself, however brief, was immediately noted by his students, who later imitated him. His rival protégés, al-Sakhāwī and al-Suyūṭī, each wrote autobiographies, and al-Sakhāwī's two students, Ibn Daybaʿ and Zarrūq, then each wrote an autobiography. Al-Suyūṭī's student Ibn Ṭūlūn al-Dimashqī wrote an autobiography, and ʿAbd al-Wahhāb al-Shaʿrānī wrote his seven-hundred-page autobiography on the basis of al-Suyūṭī's, carefully excluding all mention of the autobiographies of al-Sakhāwī and his students (the rival lineage) when listing autobiographies by respected predecessors in his introduction. Finally, later writers such as al-ʿAydarūs and Ibn ʿAjība were able to cite all of these texts as precedents for their own.

Ibn Ḥajar's sketch of his life is clearly meant to be read against the backdrop of his other works; no amount of careful reading will turn this into a detailed portrait of the author's personality. Yet we have seen that a close reading grounded in comparison with other Arabic autobiographies does demonstrate that there is more to this text than first meets the eye. It is noteworthy that such an expanded reading is possible even with an autobiographical text couched in this sparse format. Applying this approach to lengthier, more detailed texts is not only more easily accomplished, but the resulting insights are proportionally greater as well.

Reading for Stylistic Convention in the Autobiography of al-Suyūṭī

Another example of the close reading of literary conventions can be found in a recent analysis of the representation of the author's emotions in the autobiography of al-Suyūṭī.[24] In this case, insight is derived not from a broad-based comparison with other texts but rather close attention to the details of a single author's style. At several critical points in the author's life, where a modern reader might expect a description of the author's innermost emotions, al-Suyūṭī tells us what he did, rather than how he felt, deploying a rhetoric of action rather than of emotion. In one incident that demonstrates this narrative mode, the author prepares to deliver his first public lecture. We are given information about which teachers are to be present, his mentor's approval, setting the date of the lecture, the open invitation sent out to the public, and even the author's preparatory notes for the lecture itself. Rather than describe his nervousness, however, al-Suyūṭī reports: "I went to the tomb of the Imām al-Shāfiʿī—May God be pleased with him!—and requested him to intercede for me for God's help."[25] This account of his actions, though devoid of explicit references to emotions, would have conveyed much to his contemporary readers about his state of mind before this dramatic moment in his life.

Another device used several times in the same text is the author's description of the emotions of those around him rather than his own. In a poignant scene describing his father's final illness, he notes that a female relative sent for a holy man to come and pray for the father's recovery—testament to the state of fear prevailing in the household—and that the other members of his family were in despair. When he notes his father's death, when he himself was but five years and seven months old, he concludes the passage laconically, "And thus I grew up an orphan."[26] This last image occurs immediately after a reference to the Qur'ān and would have resonated strongly with contemporary readers. The Prophet himself was raised an orphan, and the Qur'ān contains several frequently cited passages relating to the treatment of orphans. Indeed, the chapter of the Qur'ān from which al-Suyūṭī drew the title of his work (*Speaking of God's Bounty*) contains two such passages, including "So as for the orphan, wrong him not!" (Q 93:6).[27] When it comes to the portrayal of his own emotions, al-Suyūṭī as autobiographer consistently prefers to report his actions rather than describe his mental state.

Two different sets of insights emerge from the examples above: (1) by studying premodern Arabic autobiographies as a series of linked texts, we have noted a commonly recurring motif, that of childhood failure or embarrassment, which seems to occur only in autobiographical writings and with a regularity that invites further analysis; and (2) a close examination of those moments that appear to be emotionally charged in a single text reveals how one autobiographer succeeds in communicating his emotional state without departing from the event-based mode of his account. Applying a similar strategy to the corpus of texts assembled here, and seeking out motifs and devices that seem within the context of this tradition to indicate some form or representation of inner emotion or private experience—though they may not coincide precisely with modern western ideas of that realm of human experience—points to two recurring features as particularly deserving of further analysis: the narration of dreams and the use of poetry.

Dreams, Visions, and Unseen Voices

Medieval Arabo-Islamic culture possessed a rich literature on dreams and their interpretation.[28] The early dream manuals of Ibn Sīrīn (d. 728), Ibn Abī al-Dunyā (d. 894), and Ibn Qutayba (d. 889) circulated widely for centuries; these were adapted and added to by many later writers. A twelfth-century biographical dictionary by al-Ḥasan ibn al-Ḥusayn al-Khallāl (d. 1127), *The Generations of Dream Interpreters* (Ṭabaqāt al-muʿabbirīn), listed more than six hundred famous practitioners of the craft of dream interpretation.[29] The Old Testament, the Qur'ān,[30] the *ḥadīth* of the Prophet Muhammad,[31] as well as the neighboring cultures of Greece, Persia, and India, all provided extensive material for the development of Arabo-Islamic beliefs and practices concerning dreams and their interpretation. One Arabic autobiographer, Ḥunayn ibn Isḥāq (d. 873 or 877), translated the dream manual of Artemidorus (second century C.E.) from Greek into Arabic in about 873. Ibn Sīnā, another autobiographer, wrote a dream interpretation treatise of his own.[32] The surviving thirteen-month fragment of the diary of Ibn al-Bannā᾽ (d. 1078) includes some twenty-five narratives of dreams seen by the author, his family and friends, for which he provides interpretations. Ibn Khaldūn, also an autobiographer, ranked dream interpretation among the sciences of Islamic religious law.[33] The erudition of Arabic writers in the matter of dream interpretation acquired such renown that by the tenth century a Byzantine author seeking to lend his Greek dream manual additional authority pretended to be an Arab writer, though his ignorance of Islamic religious practice and his detailed knowledge of orthodox Christian practice combine to reveal his true identity.[34]

Most early Arabic authorities state that a dream (*manām*) or vision (*ru᾽yā*) can originate either with God or with the Devil; some held that the Devil was capable of producing dreams only at night and that therefore dreams seen during the day were from God. (It should be noted that the language of these texts does not always allow us to determine whether the "dreams" or "visions" in question are experienced in the state of sleep or wakefulness.) In addition, a famous *ḥadīth* of the Prophet Muhammad states: "Whoever sees me in a dream has indeed seen me, for the Devil is incapable of assuming my form [*man ra᾽ānī fī l-manām fa-qad ra᾽ānī laysa li-l-shayṭān ʿan yatamaththala ṣūratī*]."[35] Thus visions of the person of the Prophet himself assumed a character separate from that of other dreams and came to play a major role in spiritual biography and autobiography.[36]

Almost all early sources recognize at least two categories of dreams: literal dreams, which require no extensive interpretation, and symbolic or allegorical dreams, which require specialized interpretation. Since the first category is taken to be self-evident, the majority of oneirocritical works deal exclusively with the latter category (Ibn Abī al-Dunyā being a notable exception). The most common type of treatise on dreams was the dream manual or dictionary, which listed instances of dreams and their interpretations or specific symbols and their meanings.[37] In accounts of literal dreams, the entry concerns how and when the event actually took place, and these dreams are often tied to specific persons; in accounts of allegorical dreams or symbols, the entry includes the interpretation or meaning, and most often no information is given concerning an actual occurrence of this dream. One additional category of dreams, sometimes subsumed under the category of literal dreams, is that of messages, often in the form of poems, that are delivered to the dreamer by figures such as angels, prophets, dead relatives, or former teachers. In these dreams the act of interpretation concerns only the text rather than any form of visual imagery. This category is in turn closely related to the concept of the "unseen caller" or "unseen voice" [*hātif*], which was common already in pre-Islamic poems and narratives.[38] In all of these categories, the most common functions for dreams (as portrayed in dream manuals) are either as portents of future events, in which case the act of interpretation is an attempt to decipher the event before it actually occurs, or as the affirmation or legitimization of an act or a person's status.[39]

The growing body of recent scholarship on Arabo-Islamic dream literature deals almost exclusively with the areas of dream theory and interpretation. The questions posed by the analysis of Arabic autobiographies, however, are somewhat different and center on dreams as they appear in a specific narrative context: How do Arabic autobiographers deploy dreams in their texts? When and why are they included? What do they represent, and what function do they serve?

A large number of the texts in the present corpus include dream narratives; indeed, in two cases (al-Tirmidhī and Abū Shāma) dream narrations occupy well over half the body of the text. Modern readers might be tempted to see the inclusion of dreams as a portrayal of the author's "inner experience" and even as a potential reflection of the author's innermost personality ripe for psychological interpretation. The textual evidence suggests otherwise. Arabic autobiographers most often do not include dreams as reflections of their personalities but rather as messages from outside themselves that act as portents of the future or as authoritative testimony affirming or legitimizing a particular action or an individual's status. The deployment of the dream thus betrays a moment of "anxiety" reflected not so much in the content and symbolism of the dream itself but rather at the point of its inclusion in the text. What assertion or action in the account does the author feel requires this supporting testimony? Interpretive theory of the period most often understood symbolic dreams to be related not to the personal life of the dreamer but to that area of life that was indeed filled with uncertainties—one's political, social, and financial status. In the medieval Arabic tradition dreams about sex, for example, were interpreted as being about political and social life. In modern western cultures one may have dreams about one's public life, but these are often interpreted as betraying anxieties about sex or other private matters, while in the Islamic Middle Ages if one had dreams about sex, they were thought to reveal insights about one's public life. The vast majority of the dreams found in this corpus of autobiographies, however, are of the literal type that require little or no symbolic interpretation.

The dream narrative that provides the dramatic high point of the account (translated in this volume) attributed to Ḥunayn ibn Isḥāq (d. 873 or 877) of his trials and tribulations is one such literal dream.[40] Ḥunayn, a physician and translator, recounts his experiences in the pattern of the biblical/Qur'ānic Joseph story. He, like Joseph, is wrongly accused and imprisoned. The ruler, in this case the caliph, is ailing and has a dream that eventually leads to Ḥunayn's release, the restoration of his possessions, and his elevation to a position of power. The dramatic moment comes not in the interpretation of the dream, as in the scriptural versions, but in the caliph's public narration of the dream before the court. In his dream he sees two figures who are identified as Jesus and Ḥunayn. Jesus tells the caliph that he must pardon Ḥunayn, who has been falsely accused, and should call him to his side and take whatever medication Ḥunayn prescribes. Although the dream requires no interpretation, it is critical to the narrative as a whole, as it provides the only motivation for Ḥunayn's release and restoration to favor.

Al-Simnānī (d. 1336) (text translated in this volume) lived a sumptuous life in his youth as an intimate companion in the court of Sultan Arghūn in northeastern Iran. At the age of twenty-four, just at the moment of charging into battle, he heard a "rebuking voice" and saw a vision of the Hereafter. The experience left him gravely ill and eventually led him to abandon the life of the court and to pursue a life of asceticism and mysticism.

The Jewish scholar Samaw'al al-Maghrībī (d. 1174) saw the prophets Samuel (his namesake) and Muhammad in dreams immediately before his conversion from Judaism to Islam. However, in his autobiography, which he appended to a polemic tract against Judaism, stung by criticism that he might have converted because he had been "deceived by jumbled dreams" [*aḍghāth aḥlām;* see Q 12:44], he asserts that the dreams were not the cause for his conversion but rather a warning:

> The reader of these pages should now understand that it was not the dream that had induced me to abandon my first faith. A sensible man will not be deceived about his affairs by dreams and visions, without proof or demonstration. . . . It was those proofs and demonstrations that were the cause of my conversion and for taking the right path. As to the dream, it served merely to alert and to prod me out of my procrastination and inertia.[41]

Despite Samaw'al's need to clarify that he converted on the basis of rational arguments and proofs of Islam's status as the true faith rather than solely because of his visions, he obviously considered the dreams significant and persuasive for at least some of his readers, for he would not otherwise have included them in his text.

Samaw'al al-Maghribī's dream of the Prophet Muhammad and al-Simnānī's vision in the midst of battle provide the background to the authors' religious conversions. Samaw'al converted from Judaism to Islam and al-Simnānī gave up worldly life to devote himself to mysticism. Rosenthal, as we have seen, deemed Samaw'al's account of his vision unconvincing. But the important point is that these authors, and others we shall discuss below, reported these experiences with the clear expectation that their readers (or at least some of them) would find these accounts convincing. They are reported as acts of suasion and, in these two cases, provide the sole motivation offered in the text for one of the most important decisions of the authors' lives. These reported experiences, in this sense, function much as an act of personal confession or divulgence functions in a modern western autobiography: the author reveals a previously hidden and completely personal motivation for a dramatic act in his past.

A similar dream that motivates the author's action is that of ʿImād al-Dīn al-Kātib al-Iṣfahānī (d.1201) (text translated in this volume). He was accompanying Saladin's uncle, Nūr al-Dīn, when they arrived at a mosque that had recently been damaged in an earthquake. Nūr al-Dīn pledged to have the mosque restored and to have the prayer niche decorated in gold and mosaic, but he died before carrying out his plans. Nūr al-Dīn later appears to ʿImād al-Dīn in an admonitory dream saying that the prayer niche needs his attention. ʿImād al-Dīn replies that he has appointed someone to take care of it, but Nūr al-Dīn repeats his message. ʿImād al-Dīn immediately writes to his retainer, who indeed had not yet begun the work, and tells him to begin the restoration forthwith.

Another function of dreams is not the legitimation of an act or decision by the author but an affirmation of his spiritual or scholarly status. Al-Tirmidhī (d. between 905 and 910) (text translated in this volume) recounts his conversion experience to the mystical life while in Mecca on pilgrimage. In this case, the conversion itself is not occasioned by a vision; however, when he is later describing how he immersed himself in fasting and prayer, secluded himself from society, and took long walks in the wilderness, amid the ruins and in cemeteries, he begins recounting a series of dream narratives. First, he tells us of his own visions of the Prophet Muhammad. Next he recounts his wife's dreams (which occur sometimes in Arabic and sometimes in Persian) in which she encounters angels who give her messages to pass on to her husband. These dreams were, according to al-Tirmidhī, "always so clear and so obvious that they needed no interpretation." Finally, he recounts dreams of acquaintances and friends about him ("I saw the Prophet—may God bless him and grant him peace!—surrounded by light and praying with [the author] right behind him, praying along with him").

Similarly, the scholar Abū Shāma (d. 1268) (text translated in this volume) recounts his own dreams and then those of his mother, his brother, and a number of acquaintances, all of which point to Abū Shāma's high standing as a scholar. In his case, several of the dreams are explained in the text by various devices, including by figures in the dream itself. For example, the author's brother dreamed that he saw Abū Shāma dangling from a rope hanging down from heaven; he asks a figure in the dream the meaning of this and is whisked off to the Dome of the Rock where the figure explains to him that his brother has been given knowledge similar to that which had been given to Solomon.

The single most common dream motif in this corpus of autobiographies, however, is a dream seen by one of the author's parents that is a harbinger of his birth and that, in addition, sometimes leads to the choice of name or profession for the child.[42] Ibn al-ʿAdīm (d. 1262) (text translated in this volume) reports that his father was deeply saddened by the death of his first son at an early age, but then he had two dreams. In the first the dead child appears and says, "Father, tell my mother that I want to come to you," and in the second he sees a shaft of light emerge from his male organ and hang over their house. The dream is interpreted to mean the arrival of a son, and shortly thereafter the mother gives birth to the author. Similarly, the father of al-ʿAydarūs (d. 1628) had a dream two weeks before the author's birth in which he saw gathered a number of Muslim mystics. Because of this dream, his father was convinced that his son would become an important man and gave him three names from those of the two saints he saw in his vision: ʿAbd al-Qādir and Muḥyī al-Dīn after Shaykh al-Jīlānī and Abū Bakr after Shaykh Abū Bakr al-ʿAydarūs.

Only a small number of the dreams cited in these texts are complex enough to be susceptible in any interesting way to psychoanalytic interpretation. Dream accounts are found, however, in a wide variety of sources in premodern Arabo-Islamic culture, and such interpretation might prove more useful elsewhere. In this particular body of texts, dreams at times communicate the author's justification for earlier actions or affirmation of his status and occasionally serve as portents of the future. Almost all are tied, one way or another, to the issue of textual authority. They function as the displaced authority of the authorial "I": what the author cannot say merely on his own authority, he can support with testimony from an outside source through the narration of a dream or vision. This interpretation does not address the "reality" of the dreams themselves or even the author's sincerity but rather the selection of dream accounts and the occasion for their inclusion in texts that purport to be a truthful representation of the author's life.

Poetry: An Alternative Discourse

The vast majority of Arabic autobiographies contain at least some examples of the author's poetry. The inclusion of representative or remarkable samples of someone's poetry is standard practice in Arabic biography, the purpose of which is usually to demonstrate the subject's literary achievement and cultivation. Autobiographers followed suit by including selections from their poetry in their texts, but in many cases this poetry marks a significant and highly emotional event in the author's life. Thus, while modern editors and scholars of medieval and premodern autobiographies for a variety of reasons have often deleted or ignored these verse passages, in fact poetry should be understood as a central—not merely "decorative"—element in the Arabic autobiographical tradition.

The practice of poetry in Arab culture differs significantly from its practice in western societies. First, poetry emerged as the earliest and most highly prized literary form in the pre-Islamic era, particularly the formal "ode" (*qaṣīda*), and, in general terms, has retained that position until the present time.[43] Second, up until the nineteenth and twentieth centuries, poetry and prose interacted in a close and interesting manner in Arabic literature. Although poetry was often collected and published in works containing virtually no prose, there were few genres of prose that did not contain occasional and sometimes quite substantial amounts of verse.

In the oral culture of the pre-Islamic Arabian peninsula, poetry was the mode of authoritative discourse whereas prose was often denigrated as unfixed in form and therefore unreliable. Poetry, because of its formal structure in meter and rhyme, is more impervious to change in oral transmission; prose, because of its lack of structure, is more susceptible to alteration. The earliest Arabic prose narratives from oral tradition to find their way into writing were accompanied by poems. *The Battle Days of the Arabs* (Ayyām al-ʿarab) took a bipartite discursive form: each historical narrative was validated and confirmed by its accompanying poem(s), while the context for the composition and original performance of the poem(s) was spelled out in the prose narrative.[44] Many of the early genres of Arabic literature (seventh–tenth centuries) directly reflected oral origins in their formal features, and the vast majority of medieval Arabic literary genres assimilated prose and poetry into a single style that moved back and forth between the two with great ease (see, e.g., the selections from ʿImād al-Dīn al-Kātib al-Iṣfahānī's *al-Barq al-shāmī* [The Syrian Thunderbolt] translated in this volume).

Poetry communicated ideas in a "marked" discourse separate from prose. As mentioned above, it could be used to delineate a formal or authoritative speech act, but it could also be used to express deeply felt emotions: love, grief, loneliness, anger, yearning. All these were themes more often expressed in poetry than in prose. Because of its durability, its perceived beauty, and the amount of control it demonstrated on the part of the author, poetry functioned as an acceptable code for expressing things that, if expressed in plain language or in actions, might be culturally unacceptable.[45] Though it might be unseemly to lose control of one's emotions, to express those same raging feelings in verse offered a socially satisfactory alternative. In contrast, poetry could also degenerate into a language of clichés and mannerisms, with the same motifs and images recurring over and over. What functioned very well as emotional release for a yearning lover or a bereaved parent might later simply not be deemed a "good poem" from the viewpoint of the literary historian.

An excellent example of the significant role of poetry in public life is found in the career of ʿUmāra al-Yamanī, the only one of our medieval autobiographers to have earned fame primarily as a poet. Born in Yemen, ʿUmāra had a tumultuous career as a scholar and a merchant, then as a diplomat (he was sent to Cairo as ambassador to the Fatimid dynasty), and finally as a court poet.[46] He fell in and out of favor with the Fatimid authorities, even to the point of being kept under house arrest in the southern Egyptian city of Qūṣ for several months. His autobiography recounts that during his stay among the Fatimids he was often pressured, unsuccessfully, to profess the Shiʿite creed of that dynasty. Despite the vicissitudes of his career under the Fatimids and his refusal to accept their religious doctrine, he is portrayed by later sources as having maintained a noteworthy fidelity to that house even after its fall. After Saladin's ascension to the throne, which officially reestablished Sunnī Islam in Egypt, ʿUmāra was viewed as a Fatimid sympathizer and suspected of being a Shiʿite himself. He composed a number of formal odes of praise to Saladin and other Ayyūbid princes, but none of these seem to have earned him favor in Saladin's eyes. Finally, he addressed an ode of "complaint" (*shakwā*) to Saladin that quickly achieved renown. It opened with the lines:

> O Ear of the Days, if I speak, pray listen to
> the choking of this consumptive, the moaning of this miserable man!
> And retain every sound whose call you hear,
> for there is no use in asking you to lend an ear if what it hears is not retained.

But even this formal sixty-four-verse ode did not bring him Saladin's favor or attention. At approximately the same time, ʿUmāra composed an elegaic ode for the fallen Fatimid dynasty that achieved even more fame. One critic wrote of it: "Never has a better poem been written in honor of a dynasty which has perished."[47]

> O Fate, you have stricken the hand of glory with paralysis,
> and its neck, once so beautifully adorned, you have stripped bare.

As if in a premonition of his own end, the poet concluded:

> Wretched ʿUmāra spoke this ode,
> fearful of murder, not fearful of error!

Biographical sources recount two differing, though possibly related, reasons for his dramatic death. In one version, ʿUmāra is accused of being part of a political conspiracy aimed at reinstating the Fatimid regime and is sentenced to death along with the other plotters. In the more widely circulated version, and that subscribed to by his contemporary and fellow autobiographer ʿImād al-Dīn, he provoked the anger of Saladin by composing an ode said to contain a heretical verse:

> The origins of this religion spring from a man
> who strove so much that they addressed him as 'Lord of Nations'!

ʿImād al-Dīn notes that the verse is probably spurious and was most likely falsely attributed to ʿUmāra.[48] Even so, Saladin had ʿUmāra executed in 1175, either by hanging or crucifixion. Poetry was, at times, a very serious business. Whether or not the story is true, the fact that ʿUmāra's crucifixion over a verse of poetry gained enough credence to be accepted conveys some of the importance assigned to poetry in Arabic literary practices.

Though ʿUmāra was the most renowned poet-autobiographer in the Arabic tradition until Aḥmad Shawqī in the late nineteenth century, poetry played a role in the lives of nearly all of these writers, and even in the texts of many of their autobiographies. In premodern Arab societies nearly all educated literary, political, and religious figures composed poetry at least occasionally. Some composed enough poetry that their verses survived independently in collected or anthologized works, but for most, the poems live on embedded in their other writings, including their biographies or autobiographies. Almost all of the autobiographers represented in this corpus are known to have composed poetry. Some, such as Lisān al-Dīn Ibn al-Khaṭīb and ʿUmāra al-Yamanī, included many pages of their poetry in their autobiographies; others made only passing reference to theirs. Even autobiographers who did not include a selection of their poetry as a separate section of their texts occasionally resorted to poetry to mark an emotional event or moment in their narratives.

When the ninety-year-old Usāma ibn Munqidh (twelfth century) muses lyrically on old age, he closes his thought with a poem followed by an apology to the reader for his digression.

> Little did I realize at that time that the disease of senility is universal, infecting everyone whom death has neglected. But now I have climbed to the summit of my ninetieth year, worn out by the succession of days and years, I have become myself like Jawād the fodder dealer, and not like the generous man [Ar. *jawād*] who can dissipate his money. Feebleness has bent me over to the ground, and old age has made one part of my body enter through another, so much so now that I can now hardly recognize myself. Here is what I have said in describing my own condition:
>
> When I attained in life a high stage,
> for which I had always yearned, I wished for death.

Longevity has left me no energy
by which I could meet the vicissitudes of time when hostile to me.
My strength has been rendered weakness, and my two confidants,
my sight and my hearing, have betrayed me since I attained this height.
When I rise, I feel as if laden with a mountain;
and when I walk, as though I were bound with chains.
I creep with a cane in my hand which was wont
to carry in warfare a lance and a sword.
My nights I spend in my soft bed, unable to sleep,
wide awake as though I lay on solid rock.
Man is reversed in life: the moment he attains perfection and
completion, he reverts to the condition from which he started.[49]

When ʿAbd al-Laṭīf al-Baghdādī (thirteenth century) waits at the deathbed of his lifelong companion and intellectual alter ego, Shaykh Abū al-Qāsim al-Shāriʿī, their final exchange (as reported in the autobiography) occurs in verse.

I stayed with Abū al-Qāsim—we were inseparable morning and night—until he passed away. When his illness grew worse, and his head cold turned to pneumonia, I advised him to take medication, but he recited the following verse:

I do not chase away the birds from trees
whose fruit I know from experience is bitter.

Then I asked him about his pain and he said:

More pain cannot be caused
than that of a dying man's wound.

When al-ʿAlī al-ʿĀmilī (seventeenth century) is distraught over the loss of his son, Ḥusayn, who died at the age of twenty-two, he begins to express his grief in prose but then shifts to poetry.

By God, the sun has neither risen nor set,
but that you have been my heart and my concern,
Never have I sat addressing a group,
but that you were my speech to my companions,
Nor have I sighed, happy or sad,
but that your remembrance was linked with my breaths,
Nor have I been about to drink water out of thirst,
but that I saw your image in the glass.
O star whose life was so short!
thus it is with shooting stars;
Eclipse came to him in haste, before his time,
overwhelming him before it reached the haunt of moons.
The crescent of days past did not fill out,
and did not tarry till the new moon.

I mourn for him, then say, hoping to console,
"You are fortunate; you have left behind the world and its pain."
I remain among enemies and he is with his Lord:
how different are our neighbors!
As if no living creature had died but he,
and no mourner wailed for anyone but him.

Aḥmad Fāris al-Shidyāq (nineteenth century) likewise finds it appropriate to express his grief at the death of his young son in verse; after describing the boy's illness and death, he concludes with a seventy-two-verse elegy composed in his memory that opens with the lines:

My tears after your passing, at every remembrance of you flow;
my memories of you are a hidden pyre.
O departed one, you have abandoned a soul
which burns with grief in the fiercest fire.[50]

ʿAlī Mubārak (nineteenth century) recounts that when he was a teenager, as he lay on what he thought was his deathbed, locked in a school infirmary in Cairo, he heard that his father was conspiring to sneak him out by bribing the guards. Despite his joy at the possibility of freedom, he felt he must refuse because the government punished severely not only those students who ran away from the schools but also their entire families. At this moment he cites a single verse of poetry to signal his emotion:

Could perhaps the sorrows which now beset me
conceal behind them approaching release?

Similarly, when Mubārak is forced out of his powerful political posts by an envious rival during the reign of the khedive Saʿīd, he bitterly cites an aphoristic line of verse to sum up the situation:

Like the secondary wives of a beautiful first wife, they say of her face,
out of envy and spite, that it is unlovely.

But perhaps the role of poetry as a discourse of emotion is most poignantly captured in a simple phrase by ʿImād al-Dīn al-Kātib al-Iṣfahānī (twelfth century) in his autobiography: "I missed my family dreadfully and expressed my feelings in verse at every stop on the road."[51]

In the Arabic literary tradition poetry has also been used for other purposes—as artistic embellishment, as formal speech, as authoritative speech, as a means of persuasion—but its role as a rhetoric of emotion is most significant here. It acts both as an alternative discourse that expresses personal feelings and as a means of lending emotional weight to the recounting of an event in a biographical or autobiographical narrative.

In addition, the capacity to be moved to compose poetry by beauty, grief, joy, pride, or spiritual experience was taken as a measure of a person's inner feelings and sensitivity. Rather than see the raw expression of one's emotional reactions as a significant act that revealed the heart or soul, it was the reflection of these feelings in "art," in the composition of poetry, that was deemed meaningful. In this sense the Arabic aesthetic of poetry might far more fruitfully be compared to that found in tenth-century Heian Japan than to that of modern western societies.[52]

Poetry is found both alongside autobiographical texts (that is, appended in a separate chapter or section) and embedded in autobiographical accounts. These passages or sections would often have been understood by premodern readers to reflect the author's emotional, inner life. Poetic passages might include courtly praise poems or occasional poems that reveal little of the author's personality; others, however, reflect poignant moments of love, loss, or great joy. Medieval and modern readers had, and continue to have, the choice of evaluating such passages for their artistic merit or for their impact in the context of the author's life; that is, in terms of their formal features or as a moment in which to identify directly with the author's feelings. If such moments at are times clichéd, the power to impress with poetic excellence may be impaired, but not necessarily the potential to move the reader emotionally.

The study of premodern Arabic autobiographical texts is hampered by a historical shift in Arabic literary discourse. Beginning in the late nineteenth century, Arab cultures began to adapt a view parallel to that prevalent in the West—that poetry and prose are separate discourses that should not intermingle.[53] Before that, a very large percentage of Arabic literature of all kinds, including autobiographies and biographies, were part poetry and part prose. The interaction between the two was a significant feature of the text. In the late nineteenth century, some of the first Arab attempts at writing novels maintained this dual dimension and the prose narrative was often interrupted by lengthy sections of verse.[54] By the turn of the twentieth century, however, poetry and prose had separated irrevocably and prosimetric forms all but disappeared from high literature, although they continue to exist in folk genres.[55] As a result, modern editions of premodern Arabic autobiographies at times do not include the poetry that was part of the original text. We have already noted that the autobiographies of Ibn Sīnā and Ibn Buluggīn, for example, now circulate in editions without the poetry that accompanied them in medieval times. This is a development that deprives the modern scholar of an important insight into the personal, emotional side of premodern authors.

Notes

1. Franz Rosenthal, "Die arabische Autobiographie," *Studia Arabica* 1 (1937): 11–12, 15–19; Saleh al-Ghamdi, "Autobiography in Classical Arabic Literature: An Ignored Genre" (Ph.D. diss., Indiana University, 1989), 31–33, concurs.

2. Anwar al-Jundī, *al-Aʿlām al-alf* (Cairo: Maṭbaʿat al-Risāla, 1957), 1:100.

3. M. G. S. Hodgson, *The Venture of Islam* (Chicago: University of Chicago Press, 1984), 2:180.

4. Philip Hitti, introduction to *Kitāb al-iʿtibār* (1930; rpt. Baghdad: Maktabat al-Muthannā, 1964), 25; Nikita Elisséeff, *Nūr al-Dīn: Un grand prince musulman de Syrie au temps des croisades* (Damascus: Institut Français de Damas, 1967), 1:22.

5. ʿAlī ʿAbd al-Wāḥid, ed., *Muqaddimat Ibn Khaldūn,* 2d ed. (Cairo: Lajnat al-Bayān al-ʿArabī, 1965), 1:152; Taha Hussein [Ṭāhā Ḥusayn], *ʿIlm al-ijtimāʿ,* vol. 8 of *al-Majmūʿa al-kāmila li-muʾallafāt Ṭāhā Ḥusayn* (Beirut: Dār al-Kitāb al-Lubnānī, 1973), 27.

6. ʿIzz al-Dīn Ismāʿīl, *al-Adab wa-funūnuh,* 3d ed. (Cairo: Dār al-Fikr al-ʿArabī, 1965), 235.

7. Thomas Philipp, "The Autobiography in Modern Arab Literature and Culture," *Poetics Today* 14, no. 3 (Fall 1993): 583.

8. Ibn Buluggīn, *Mudhakkirāt al-Amīr ʿAbd Allāh ākhir mulūk, banī zīri bi-Gharnāṭa al-musammā bi-kitāb al-tibyān,* ed. E. Lévi-Provençal (Cairo: Dār al-Maʿārif, 1955), 178; cf. *The Tibyān: Memoirs of ʿAbd Allāh b. Buluggīn, Last Zīrid Amīr of Granada,* trans. Amin T. Tibi (Leiden: E. J. Brill, 1986), 174.

9. Ibn Buluggīn, *Mudhakkirāt,* 179; cf. Tibi, *Tibyān,* 174.

10. Ibn Buluggīn, *Mudhakkirāt,* 184, 187; cf. Tibi, *Tibyān,* 178, 180.

11. Ibn Buluggīn, *Mudhakkirāt,* 196–97; cf. Tibi, *Tibyān,* 187–88.

12. Ibn Buluggīn, *Mudhakkirāt,* 199–200; cf. Tibi, *Tibyān,* 189–90.

13. Devin J. Stewart, "The Humor of the Scholars: The Autobiography of Niʿmat Allāh al-Jazāʾirī (d. 1112/1701)," *Iranian Studies* 22 (1989): 47–50.

14. The reference is to the tradition of having boys who have finished memorizing the Qurʾān recite the Holy Book publicly during Ramadan by leading the congregation in the special evening prayers (*tarāwīḥ*) of that month.

15. "Ibn Ḥajar went on to finish his work *Rafʿ al-iṣr* but did not complete his own biographical notice. The remainder of his biography is found in al-Suyūṭī's *Ḥusn al-muḥāḍara.*" Editor's note in *Rafʿ al-iṣr ʿan quḍāt miṣr* [History of the Judges of Egypt] (Cairo: al-Maṭbaʿa al-Amīriyya, 1957), 85–88.

16. Sabri K. Kawash, "Ibn Ḥajar al-Asqalānī (1372–1449 A.D.): A Study of the Background, Education, and Career of an ʿĀlim in Egypt" (Ph.D. diss., Princeton University, 1969), 75–76.

17. See George Makdisi, *The Rise of Colleges: Institutions of Learning in Islam and the West* (Edinburgh: Edinburgh University Press, 1981); Johannes Pedersen, *The Arabic Book* (Princeton: Princeton University Press, 1984); Jonathan Berkey, *The Transmission of Knowledge in Medieval Cairo: A Social History of Islamic Education* (Princeton: Princeton University Press, 1992); Michael Chamberlain, *Knowledge and Social Practice in Medieval Damascus, 1190–1350* (Cambridge: Cambridge University Press, 1994).

18. In addition to al-Bukhārī, the "Six Books" included another *Ṣaḥīḥ* by Muslim and four books of *Sunan* by al-Sijistānī, al-Tirmidhī, al-Nasāʾī, and Abū Mājah.

19. Dwight F. Reynolds, "Childhood in One Thousand Years of Arabic Autobiography," *Edebiyât: Special Issue—Arabic Autobiography,* N.S. 7, no. 2 (1997): 379–92.

20. See Dimitri Gutas, *Avicenna and the Aristotelian Tradition: Introduction to Reading Avicenna's Philosophical Works* (Leiden: E. J. Brill, 1988).

21. E. M. Sartain, *Jalāl al-Dīn al-Suyūṭī* (Cambridge: Cambridge University Press, 1975), 1:137.

22. Franz Rosenthal, "Ibn Ḥadjar al-ʿAsḳalānī," *EI*² 3:776–78.

23. Ibid., 776; see Ibn Ḥajar al-ʿAsqalānī, *Uns al-hujar fī abyāt Ibn Ḥajar* (Beirut: Dār al-Rayyān li-l-Turāth, 1988); and Kawash, "Ibn Ḥajar."

24. Kristen Brustad, "Imposing Order: Reading the Conventions of Representation in al-Suyūṭī's Autobiography," *Edebiyât: Special Issue—Arabic Autobiography,* N.S. 7, no. 2 (1997): 327–44.

25. Ibid., 332.

26. Ibid.

27. Autobiographers who were orphaned of one or both parents in early childhood include Ibn Ḥajar, al-Suyūṭī, Zarrūq, Ibn Daybaʿ, al-Yūsī, Ibn ʿAjība, Babakr Badrī, and ʿAlī al-ʿAmilī, whose father left when he was six years old and died when he was sixteen.

28. See, for example, the 181 titles cited by Toufic Fahd, "Inventaire de la littérature onirocritique arabe," in *La divination arabe* (Leiden: E. J. Brill, 1966; rpt. Paris: Sindbad, 1987), 330–63; also, Gustav von Grunebaum and R. Callois, eds., *The Dream and Human Societies* (Berkeley: University of California Press, 1966); and John C. Lamoreaux, "Dream Interpretation in the Early Medieval Near East (Ph.D. diss., Duke University, 1999).

29. Cited in M. J. L. Young, "Arabic Biographical Literature," in *Cambridge History of Arabic Literature: Religion, Learning and Science in the ʿAbbasid Period,* ed. M. J. L. Young, J. D. Latham, and R. B. Serjeant (Cambridge: Cambridge University Press, 1990), 174. Al-Khallāl's original work apparently listed 7,500 practitioners of the craft; a summary of it including 600 dream interpreters was consulted by the scholar al-Dīnawarī around the year 1000. See Lamoreaux, "Dream Interpretation," 29–31.

30. See, for example, Qur'ān 37:101–5 (Abraham's dream); 12:4–7 (Joseph's dream); 12:36–37 (prisoners' dreams interpreted by Joseph); 12:43–49 (Pharaoh's dream); 48:27 (the vision of Muhammad).

31. Fahd, *La divination arabe,* 256–68.

32. M. A. M. Khan, "A Unique Treatise on the Interpretation of Dreams by Ibn Sina," in *Avicenna Commemoration Volume* (Calcutta: Iran Society, 1956), 255–307.

33. Ibn Khaldūn, *The Muqaddimah,* trans. F. Rosenthal (New York: Pantheon, 1958), 3:103.

34. Steven M. Oberhelman, *The Oneirocriticon of Achmet: A Medieval Greek and Arabic Treatise on the Interpretation of Dreams* (Lubbock: Texas Tech University Press, 1991).

35. Ibn Abī Dunyā, *Morality in the Guise of Dreams: Ibn Abī al-Dunya, a Critical Edition of Kitāb al-manām,* ed. Leah Kinberg (Leiden: E. J. Brill, 1994), 81. Shiʿite sources claim the same status for the Imāms *(man ra'ānā fa-qad ra'ānā fa-inna al-shayṭāna lā yatamaththalu binā)*, ʿAlī al-ʿĀmilī, *al-Durr al-manthūr,* 2 vols., ed. Aḥmad al-Ḥusaynī (Qom: Maktabat al-Marʿashī al-Najafī, 1978), 2:197.

36. See Jonathan G. Katz, *Dreams, Sufism, and Sainthood: The Visionary Career of*

Muhammad al-Zawāwī (Leiden: E. J. Brill, 1996); Ignaz Goldziher, "The Appearance of the Prophet in Dreams," *Journal of the Royal Asiatic Society* (1912): 503–6.

37. An English collation of several medieval Arabic works into a single dream dictionary is available in Yehia Gouda, trans., *Dreams and Their Meanings in the Old Arab Tradition* (New York: Vantage Press, 1991).

38. See the autobiography of al-Simnānī (translated in this volume) for an example of the *hātif.*

39. See Leah Kinberg's series of articles on this topic: "The Legitimization of *Madhāhib* through Dreams," *Arabica* 32 (1985): 47–79; "The Standardization of Qur'ān Readings: The Testimonial Value of Dreams," *The Arabist: Budapest Studies in Arabic* 3–4 (1991): 223–38; and "Literal Dreams and Prophetic *Ḥadīth* in Classical Islam—A Comparison of Two Ways of Legitimization," *Der Islam* 70 (1993): 279–300.

40. The text poses a number of problems and may not even have been written by Ḥunayn himself. See Michael Cooperson, "The Purported Autobiography of Ḥunayn ibn Isḥāq," *Edebiyât: Special Issue—Arabic Autobiography,* N.S. 7, no. 2 (1997): 235–49.

41. Samaw'al al-Maghribī, *Ifḥām al-yahūd, Silencing the Jews,* ed. and trans. Moshe Perlmann (New York: American Academy for Jewish Research, 1964), 87–88.

42. Galen of Pergamon reports that he was trained in medicine and philosophy as a result of powerful dreams dreamed by his father. Arthur J. Brock, *Greek Medecine, being extracts illustrative of medical writers from Hippocrates to Galen* (London: Dent and Sons, 1929), 180.

43. In reading western treatments of modern Arabic literature, one might assume that the novel has long been the most prestigious form of literary expression in Arabic. This is a view promulgated primarily in western scholarly discussion and certainly did not hold true in the Arab world itself, with the possible exception of Egypt, until very recently. Indeed, many of the objections voiced about the awarding of the 1989 Nobel Prize for literature to the Egyptian novelist Naguib Mahfouz were raised precisely because the prize was being given for a form (which many view as adopted from the West) that has played a far less significant role in Arab culture and society than poetry.

44. A fascinating modern echo of this is found in the words of a Jordanian Bedouin versed in tribal histories: *al-guṣṣa illī mā ʿindhā gaṣīda kidhib* (A story without a poem is a lie!), quoted in Andrew Shryock, "History and Historiography among the Belqa Tribes of Jordan" (Ph.D. diss., University of Michigan, 1993), 295.

45. This aspect of poetry is analyzed in a modern context in Lila Abu-Lughod, *Veiled Sentiments: Honor and Poetry in a Bedouin Society* (Berkeley: University of California Press, 1986); however, it has been a general characteristic of Arabic poetic discourse since the pre-Islamic period.

46. ʿUmāra was also the author of a fascinating history of Yemen about which his translator has written: "ʿOmārah has preserved for us an exceedingly curious picture of Arab life and manners, such, I may perhaps venture to say, as is only excelled in Arabic literature by the tales of the Thousand and One Nights." Henry Cassels Kay, *Yaman: Its Early Medieval History* (London: E. Arnold, 1892), x–xi.

47. Quoted in Jawad Ahmad ʿAlwash, *Umara al-Yamani the Poet* (Baghdad: al-

Maʿārif Press, 1971), 120, drawn from Aḥmad al-Maqrīzī, *al-Khiṭaṭ* (Cairo: B. al-Suluk, 1914), 2:392.

48. ʿImād al-Dīn al-Kātib al-Iṣfahānī, *Kharīdat al-qaṣr* (Damascus: al-Maṭbaʿa al-Hishāmiyya, 1964), 104.

49. *An Arab-Syrian Gentleman and Warrior in the Period of the Crusades: Memoirs of Usāmah ibn-Munqidh,* trans. Philip K. Hitti (Princeton: Princeton University Press, 1987), 190–91.

50. Aḥmad Fāris al-Shidyāq, *al-Sāq ʿalā al-sāq fī mā huwa al-Faryāq* (Paris: Benjamin Duprat, 1855), 614.

51. ʿImād al-Dīn al-Kātib al-Iṣfahānī, quoted in al-Fatḥ al-Bundarī, *Sanā al-barq al-shāmī,* ed. Ramazan Şeşen (Beirut: Dār al-Kitāb al-Jadīd, 1971), 114.

52. Marilyn J. Miller, *The Poetics of Nikki Bungaku: A Comparison of the Traditions, Conventions, and Structure of Heian Japan's Literary Diaries with Western Autobiographical Writings* (New York: Garland, 1985).

53. Dwight F. Reynolds, "Prosimetrum in 19th- and 20th-Century Arabic Literature," in *Prosimetrum: Cross-Cultural Perspectives on Narrative in Prose and Verse,* ed. Joseph Harris and Karl Reichl (Suffolk: Boydell and Brewer, 1998), 277–94.

54. See, for example, the novels of Salīm al-Bustānī (d. 1884). For a treatment of the life and work of al-Bustānī, see Constantin Georgescu, "A Forgotten Pioneer of the Lebanese 'Nahḍah': Salīm al-Bustānī" (Ph.D. diss., New York University, 1978).

55. One modern echo of the use of poetry in Arabic autobiography can be found in Bint al-Shāṭiʾ [ʿĀʾisha ʿAbd al-Raḥmān], *ʿAlā jisr bayna al-ḥayāh wa-l-mawt* (Cairo: al-Hayʾa al-ʿĀmma al-Miṣriyya li-l-Kitāb, 1967), which both opens and closes with selections from the author's poetry.

PART TWO

Translations

The Autobiography of Ḥunayn ibn Isḥāq

(809–873 or 877)

Introduction

Ḥunayn ibn Isḥāq was a Nestorian Christian from the Iraqi town of al-Ḥīra. He traveled to Baghdad to seek a career in medicine but quarreled with his teacher and left the city. Several years later he returned, having learned classical Greek so well that even his former teacher came to rely on him for translations of Greek medical texts. Ḥunayn may have learned his Greek in Alexandria or Constantinople; he was also proficient in Arabic, Syriac, and possibly Persian. Muslim as well as Christian scholars sought his services as a translator, and he reportedly enjoyed the patronage of the ʿAbbāsid caliphs. Working from older Syriac translations of the classical texts or (as he preferred) the original Greek, Ḥunayn rendered into Arabic works by Plato, Aristotle, Hippocrates, and Galen, in addition to composing more than seventy scientific treatises of his own. As a translator, he broke with the older practice of word-by-word rendition, and his translations are remarkable even today for their clarity and precision. He and his successors created a new scientific vocabulary for Arabic and made possible the successful appropriation and naturalization of Greek thought into the intellectual life of the Islamic world.

As the autobiography ascribed to him explains, however, his fame provoked his rivals to plot against him. The text of the autobiography appears in a biographical entry on Ḥunayn compiled by Ibn Abī Uṣaybiʿa (d. 1270), a historian of medicine. After bemoaning the treachery of his fellow Christians and describing their envy of his superior abilities, Ḥunayn tells the tale of how his coreligionist and fellow physician Jibrīl ibn Bakhtīshūʿ tricked him into spitting on an icon in the presence of the caliph al-Mutawakkil. Such an offense made Ḥunayn an iconoclast, and the head of the Nestorian church recommended that the caliph punish him. Ḥunayn was accordingly flogged and imprisoned. His rivals then pressed the caliph to execute him. The sovereign was reportedly on the verge of doing so when a miraculous intervention persuaded him to relent.

Ḥunayn's epistle on his trials and tribulations resembles, to some degree, the Greek genre of apologetic autobiography, but it is also highly reminiscent of the biblical/Qur'ānic story of Joseph. Both Ḥunayn and Joseph are betrayed by their "brothers" (coreligionists in the case of Ḥunayn), falsely accused and imprisoned, and finally released, absolved, and rewarded as a result of a ruler's dream. The epistle thus presents a fascinating amalgam of Greek and biblical elements in an Arabic literary form. The conspicuously literary character of the text—as manifested, for example, in the narration of conversations Ḥunayn cannot possibly have overheard—has led some scholars to doubt its authenticity. Gotthard Strohmaier, for example, concludes that one of Ḥunayn's disciples composed it to defend his teacher against charges of iconoclasm. Indeed, Ḥunayn's iconoclastic opinions are attested in several other sources, although none of these is entirely trustworthy either. In any event, the epistle remains one of the earliest prose works in Arabic in the autobiographical mode. If it was in fact composed by another hand, it is remarkable that this later author should have chosen such an innovative and, at the time, virtually unknown form of Arabic writing when seeking to clear Ḥunayn of the accusations brought against him by the Church.

Bibliography

Cooperson, Michael. "The Purported Autobiography of Ḥunayn ibn Isḥāq." *Edebiyât: Special Issue—Arabic Autobiography,* N.S. 7, no. 2 (1997): 235–49.

Gutas, Dimitri. *Greek Thought and Arabic Culture: The Graeco-Arabic Translation Movement in Baghdad and Early ʿAbbāsid Society (2nd–4th/8th–10th Centuries).* London: Routledge, 1998.

Ibn Abī Uṣaybiʿa. *ʿUyūn al-anbāʾ fī ṭabaqāt al-aṭibbāʾ.* Ed. Nizār Riḍā. 2 vols. Beirut: Dār Maktabat al-Ḥayāt, 1965. 257–74.

Rosenthal, Franz. "Die arabische Autobiographie." *Studia Arabica* 1 (1937): 15–19.

Salama-Carr, Myriam. *La traduction à l'époque abbaside: L'école de Hunayn ibn Ishaq et son importance pour la traduction.* Paris: Didier, 1990.

Strohmaier, Gotthard. "Ḥunayn ibn Isḥāq und die Bilder." *Klio* 43–45 (1965): 525–33.

Epistle on the Trials and Tribulations Which Befell Ḥunayn ibn Isḥāq
[*ʿUyūn*, pp. 257–74]

Ḥunayn ibn Isḥāq writes:

My enemies so tormented me that I was no longer able to sleep. I would lie awake at night, and during the day I was too distracted to work. My persecutors felt neither remorse for their cruelty nor gratitude for all the favors I had bestowed upon them in the past. They attacked me and wronged me because they envied my learning and resented the preeminence that God Almighty had granted me over my contemporaries. Most of my tormentors were members of my own family; in fact, it is with them that my trials and sufferings began. Those I favored over other members of the profession came next. I trained them, directed their studies, advanced their careers, treated them well, and introduced them to [the works of] Galen, but they repaid my kindness with a malice compelled by their natures.

They slandered me in the ugliest possible ways, spreading the most sordid kind of rumors about me and keeping important confidences from me, until suspicions were aroused and opinion turned against me. Everywhere I found prying eyes. I was observed so closely that my very words were cataloged and used against me. On the basis of malicious insinuations, meanings I had not intended were painstakingly extracted from my words and accusations against me multiplied. My enemies stirred up hatred for me among peoples of all sects, not just the members of my own denomination. Councils were convened on my account where people offered invidious interpretations of my behavior. Every time I learned of such things, I praised God anew, and bore with fortitude what I could not change.

The situation eventually reached the point where I found myself utterly ruined and heartbroken, in prison, and reduced to the narrowest of circumstances. During that time I was unable to obtain even the smallest amount of gold or silver, a book, or even a single sheet of paper to peruse.

Then God Almighty cast His glance of mercy upon me and restored His favor to me, restoring His bounty, which I had once known so well. The restoration of my wealth was due to a certain person who had been especially zealous in his hatred. This aptly illustrates Galen's remark that "the best people are those who can turn the animosity of evil men to advantage."[1] This person turned out to be the best enemy I ever had!

Now I shall recount what happened to me in the incidents I have just described:

How could it have been otherwise? How could I not have provoked such animosity, stirred up so much envy, and set the councils of the great abuzz with slander and abuse? Money was paid to have me killed, those who insulted me were honored, and those who treated me generously were humiliated. And yet all this happened, not because I had offended or ill-treated a single one of them, but because I had risen above them and surpassed them in learning and in labor, and transmitted to them precious knowledge from languages that they knew poorly, that they would not have been led to on their own, or of which they knew nothing. All this I did with the greatest possible eloquence and felicity of expression, without fault or flaw, without sectarian tendentiousness, and without obscurantism or vulgarity. This is attested by the Arab rhetoricians, specialists in syntax and rare expressions. My readers never stumbled over a solecism, a wrongly voweled word, or a poorly expressed thought. I used the most elegant and yet the easiest phrases. A lay reader who knew nothing of philosophical methods and belonged to no Christian sect would still appreciate my work and realize its importance. In fact, such people spend a great deal of money on works I have translated, preferring them to works translated by all others before me. Furthermore, let me say without fear of contradiction that all men of culture—regardless of religious affiliation—befriend me and take my part, treat me with honor, receive what I teach them with gratitude, and reward me with many favors. But as for those Christian physicians, most of whom themselves learned from me, and whom I watched grow up, it is they who cry for my blood, even though they could never manage without me.

Sometimes they would say: "Who is Ḥunayn, after all? Just a man who translates books for a fee—no more than a tradesman; at least, we can't see any difference. A knight can pay a smith a dinar to forge a replica of his sword, and the smith might make one hundred dinars a month. Ḥunayn only services our tools, but he does not work with them himself, just as a swordsmith is no good at handling swords, no matter how skilled he may be in making them. Imagine a swordsmith trying to take the field with knights! That's Ḥunayn for you. What does he know about medicine, having never diagnosed a disease in his life? All he wants is to be like us, so people will call him 'Ḥunayn the physician' instead of 'Ḥunayn the translator.' The best thing would have been for him to stick to his own profession and keep his nose out of ours. He would get more money out of us, and we would treat him better, if only he would stop holding consultations, peering at bottles, and prescribing drugs." Or they would say: "Ḥunayn cannot enter anyone's house, high or low, without them mocking him and tittering to one another as he leaves the room."

Every time I heard things like this I would feel a tightness in my chest, and I would contemplate killing myself out of anger and frustration. There was nothing I, a lone man standing against a horde of enemies, could do to stop them. Yet I knew in my own mind that it was their envy that drove them to do what they were doing, although even they realized how ugly it appeared. Malicious envy is a perennial human failing. As anyone with any idea of religion knows, the first act of envy was Cain's murder of his brother Abel after God refused Cain's sacrifice and accepted Abel's. Since envy has always existed, it is hardly surprising that I too should have been one of its victims. As they say: "Envy is punishment enough for him who feels it," and, "The envious one punishes himself more than he punishes his rival." Arabic poetry has much to say about malicious envy, for example:

> They may envy me, but I do not reproach them.
> Many virtuous men before me have been envied.
>
> I shall remain as I am—they shall continue to feel as they feel;
> Indignant and resentful are most of us buried.
>
> I am the one they resent, but I shall not change.
> I lie heavy on their hearts while my own is unworried.

What this and other poets have said on this subject would take a long time to relate without adding much to the point.

Ironically, many of the same people, when baffled by a difficult case, would make their way to me and ask me to confirm their own diagnoses or have me prescribe medicines and treatments. The soundness of my recommendations was confirmed again and again. But the ones who came to seek my opinion were at the same time my most vituperative enemies; I shall do nothing more for them until the time comes when I have God to judge between them and me. I said nothing at the time, however, for I was not dealing with one or two rivals, but with fifty-six, all Nestorians like myself, and all in much greater need of me than I of them. Furthermore, as so many of them were in the service of the caliph, their influence was great. They were virtually in charge of the kingdom. My position was weaker than theirs in two respects: first, I was alone, and second, those people who had my interests at heart depended on my rivals' patron, the caliph.

The whole time, I complained to no one of my sufferings, great as they were. Instead, I would express my gratitude toward my persecutors on every public occasion and in the presence of high-ranking persons. When it was pointed out to me that they were deriding me and slandering me in their assemblies, I dismissed the notion. Affecting disbelief, I would say that we—my rivals and I—were as one, bound by the ties of faith, birthplace, and profession, and that I could not imagine that such people could speak ill of anyone, much less of me. When my remarks reached them, they would say: "He's trying to allay his fears by pretending not to hear." The more they slandered me, the more I praised them.

I shall now tell of the final trap they set for me (not counting what happened before with the Banū Mūsā, the Galenites, and the Hippocratics regarding the matter of the first accusation).[2] Here then, is the story of my last tribulation:

Bakhtīshūʿ the physician[3] succeeded in setting in motion a plot against me by which he was able to place me in his power. This he did by means of an icon depicting the Madonna holding Our Lord in her lap and surrounded by angels. It was beautifully worked and most accurately painted, and had cost Bakhtīshūʿ a great deal of money. He had it carried to the court of the caliph al-Mutawakkil,[4] where he positioned himself to receive the icon as it was brought in, and to present it personally to the caliph, who was extremely impressed with it. Bakhtīshūʿ, still in the caliph's presence, began kissing the icon repeatedly.

"Why are you kissing it?" asked Mutawakkil.

"If I do not kiss the image of the Mistress of Heaven and Earth, your Majesty, then whose image should I kiss?"

"Do all the Christians do this?" asked Mutawakkil.

"Yes, your Majesty," replied Bakhtīshūʿ, "and more properly than I do now, because I am restraining myself in your presence. But in spite of the preferential treatment granted the Christians, I know of one Christian in your service who enjoys your bounty and your favors, but who has no regard for this image and spits on it. He is a heretic and an atheist who believes neither in the oneness of God nor in the Afterlife. He hides behind a mask of Christianity, but in fact denies God's attributes and repudiates the prophets."

"Who is this person you are describing?"

"Ḥunayn the translator," said Bakhtīshūʿ.

"I'll have him sent for," said Mutawakkil, "and if what you say turns out to be true, I'll make an example of him. I'll drop him in a dungeon and throw away the key; but not before I've made his life miserable and ordered him tortured over and over until he repents."

Bakhtīshūʿ said, "With your Majesty's permission, might his summons be delayed until such time as I return?" Mutawakkil assented to his request.

Bakhtīshūʿ left the palace and came to see me.

"My dear Ḥunayn," he said, "you should know that someone has presented the caliph with an icon. He's quite taken with it and thinks it's of Syrian origin. He keeps saying how marvelous it is. If we let him keep it, and praise it in his presence, he'll never stop dangling it in front of us and saying, 'Look! It's a picture of your god and his mother!' He has already said to me, 'Look at this wonderful image! What do you think of it?' I told him, 'It's a picture like the ones they paint on the walls of bathhouses and churches or use in decorations; it is not the kind of thing we are concerned about or pay any attention to at all.' He said, 'So it means nothing to you?' 'That's right,' I said. 'Spit on it, then, and we shall see if you are telling the truth,' he said. So I spat on it and left him there laughing up a storm. Of course I did this just so he would get rid of it and stop provoking us with it and making us feel different from everyone else. If someone gives him the idea of using it against us, the situation can only get worse. So, if he calls for you and asks you questions like the ones he asked me, the best thing to do is to do what I did. I have spread the word among the rest of our friends who might see him, and told them to do the same."

I fell for this stupid trick and agreed to follow his advice. Barely an hour after he left, the caliph's messenger arrived to summon me. When I entered the caliph's presence, I saw the icon before him.

"Isn't this a wonderful picture, Ḥunayn?"

"Just as you say, your Majesty."

"What do you think of it? Isn't it the image of your god and his mother?"

"God forbid, your Majesty! Is God Almighty an image, can He be depicted? This is a picture like any other."

"So this image has no power at all, either to help or to harm?"

"That's right, your Majesty."

"If it's as you say, spit on it."

I spat on it, and he immediately ordered me thrown in prison.

Then he sent for Theodosius, the head of the Nestorian church.[5] The moment he saw the icon, he fell upon it without even saluting the caliph and held it close, kissing it and weeping at length. A retainer moved to stop him, but the caliph ordered him away. Finally, Theodosius—after much weeping—took the icon in his hand, stood up, and pronounced a long benediction on the caliph. The caliph answered the greeting and ordered him to take his seat. Theodosius sat down holding the icon in his lap.

Mutawakkil said, "What do you think you are doing taking something from in front of me and putting it in your lap without permission?"

"Your Majesty," said Theodosius, "I have more right to it. Of course the caliph—may God grant him long life!—has precedence over us all, but my faith does not allow me to leave an image of the Holy Family lying on the ground, in a place where its sanctity is unrecognized, or even in a place where its sanctity might not be recognized. It deserves to be placed where it will be treated as it deserves, with the finest of oils and most fragrant incense burning before it continually."

The caliph said, "Then you may leave it in your lap for now."

"I ask your Majesty to bestow it as a gift to me, and to deem it equivalent to an annual income of a hundred thousand dinars, until I can discharge the debt I owe your Majesty. Your Majesty will find me ready to grant any request he may make of me in the future."

"I give you the image," said the caliph. "But I want you to tell me how you deal with someone who spits on it."

Theodosius replied, "If he is a Muslim, then there is no punishment, since he does not recognize its sanctity. Nevertheless, he should be made aware of it, reprimanded, and reproached—in accordance with the severity of the offense—so that he never does it again. If he is a Christian and ignorant, people are to reproach and rebuke him, and threaten him with awful punishments, and condemn him, until he repents. At any rate, only someone totally ignorant of religion would commit such an act. But should someone in full command of his own mind spit on this image, he spits on Mary the Mother of God and on Our Lord Jesus Christ."

"And how must you deal with such a person?"

"I, your Majesty, can do nothing, having no authority to punish with whip or rod, nor do I have a deep dungeon to imprison him in. But I can excommunicate him and forbid him to enter the church and to partake in Communion, and I can prohibit Christians from intercourse or conversation with him, and I can make life a severe trial for him. He would remain an outcast among us until he repents and recants. Then he must move through the community and disburse a part of his wealth in alms to the poor and the downtrodden, and observe all the prayers and fasts. At that point we invoke our Scripture—'If ye forgive not the sinners, your own sins will not be forgiven you'—and lift the ban of excommunication on the offender, and all would be as it was before."

Then the caliph ordered Theodosius to take the icon, and told him to do as he liked with it, and gave him a hundred dirhams, telling him to spend it on his icon. After he had left, the caliph sat a while marveling at him and his love and adoration for his god.

"This is a truly amazing thing," said the caliph, and then ordered me brought in. He called for the ropes and the whip, and ordered me stripped and spread before him. I was struck a hundred lashes. Then the caliph ordered that I be confined and tortured, and that all my furnishings, riding animals, books, and the like be carried off. My houses were destroyed and the wreckage was dumped in the river. I remained confined in the palace for six months under conditions so appalling that I was transformed into an object of pity for those who saw me. The beatings and the tortures were repeated every few days.

I remained thus until the fifth day of the fourth month of my imprisonment, when the caliph fell ill. He became so ill that he was unable to move or stand: everyone, including him, gave up any hope of his recovery. Nevertheless, my enemies the physicians were at his bedside day and night to attend to him and administer his medicines. All the while, they would continue to bring up my case to him: "If your Majesty would only rid us of that heretical atheist, he would be ridding the world of a great menace to religion."

They continued pressing him to do something about me, accusing me of all sorts of vile things in his presence, until finally he said, "So what would you have me do with him?" "Get rid of him once and for all," they replied. In the meantime, whenever one of my friends came to ask about me or tried to intercede for me, Bakhtīshūʿ would say, "That, your Majesty, is one of Ḥunayn's disciples; he holds the same opinions as his master." Thus, the number of people who could help me diminished whereas the number of people plotting against me increased, and I despaired of my life. At last, in the face of their persistent demands, the caliph said, "I'll kill him first thing tomorrow morning and spare you any more trouble on his account." The whole lot of them were greatly relieved and returned cheerfully to their own affairs.

A palace functionary informed me that I had been condemned. With distraught mind and aching heart, in terror of what was to befall me on the morrow, innocent, having done nothing to deserve such a punishment, nor committed any offense other than falling victim to a plot and playing into the hands of my enemies, I beseeched God Almighty to vouchsafe me such providence as He had shown me in the past. I prayed: "Dear God, You know I am innocent, and You are the one to save me." At last my anxiety gave way to sleep.

Then I felt someone shaking me, and heard a voice say, "Rise and praise God, for He has delivered you from the power of your enemies. He will cure the caliph at your hands so put your heart at rest."

I awoke terrified. "Since I invoked Him while awake," I thought, "why deny having seen Him in my sleep?" And so I prayed continuously until the break of day.

When the eunuch arrived and opened my door earlier than usual, I thought, "The time is all wrong—they are going ahead with it after all. My enemies' triumph is at hand." I begged God for His help.

The eunuch had been sitting only a moment when his page arrived accompanied by a barber. "Come, fortunate one," said the eunuch, "and have your hair cut." After the haircut, he took me to the bath and had me washed and cleaned and perfumed on the caliph's orders. When I emerged from the bath the eunuch put splendid clothes on me and left me in his booth, where I waited until the rest of the physicians arrived. Each took his appointed place. The caliph called out, "Bring in Ḥunayn!"

Those assembled had no doubt that he was calling me in to have me executed. Seeing me, he had me approach closer and closer until I at last sat directly before him. He said, "I have gratified a well-wisher of yours and forgiven you your crimes. Give thanks to God for your life, then treat me as you see fit, for I have been ill too long."

I took his pulse and prescribed cassia pods, handpicked off the stalk, and manna, which were the obvious things to prescribe for his constipation.[6]

"God help you, your Majesty, if you take his medicine," clamored my rivals, "it can only make your condition much worse."

"Do not try and argue with me—I have been commanded to take whatever he prescribes," said the caliph. He ordered the drug prepared and took it at once.

Then he said, "Ḥunayn, acquit me of all I have done to you. The one who interceded for you is powerful indeed."

"His Majesty is blameless in his power over me. But how is it that he spared my life?"

The caliph spoke up: "Everyone must hear what I am about to say." They gave him their full attention and he said:

"As all of you know, you left last night under the impression that I was going to execute Ḥunayn this morning, as I had promised. Last night, I was in too much pain to fall asleep. About midnight, I dropped off, and dreamed that I was trapped in a narrow place, and you my physicians, along with my entire retinue, were far off in the distance. I kept saying, 'Damn you, why are you staring at me? Where am I? Is this a place fit for me?!' But you sat silent, ignoring my cries. Suddenly a great light shone upon me as I lay there, a light that terrified me. And there stood before me a man with a radiant face, and behind him another man dressed in sumptuous clothes. The man before me said, 'Peace be with you,' and I answered his greeting. 'Do you recognize me?' he asked.

'No,' I said.

'I am Jesus Christ,' he said.

I trembled and shuddered in terror and asked, 'Who is that with you?'

'Ḥunayn ibn Isḥāq.'

I said, 'Forgive me—I cannot rise to greet you.'

He said, 'Pardon Ḥunayn, and absolve him of his crime, for God has forgiven him. Take what he prescribes for you and you will recover.'

"I awoke unable to stop thinking about what Ḥunayn had suffered at my hands, and marveling at the power of his intercessor. Now it is my duty to restore to him what was rightfully his. You are all dismissed; it is he who shall attend me. Every one of you who asked me to take his life shall bring me ten thousand dirhams as blood-price. Those who were not present need pay nothing. Whoever fails to bring this amount will lose his head."

Then he spoke to me: "You may take your appointed seat."

The group dispersed and each member returned with the ten thousand dirhams. When all they had brought had been collected, the caliph ordered that a like amount be added from his own treasury, for a total of more than two hundred thousand dirhams, and ordered it handed over to me.

By the end of the day, the medicine had moved his bowels three times, and he felt the onset of recovery. "All you wish, Ḥunayn, is yours," he said, "for your standing is much enhanced in my eyes, and you are far more important to me than ever before. I shall restore your losses many times over, reduce your rivals to abject dependence upon you, and elevate you above all of your colleagues."

Then he commanded that three houses belonging to him personally be renovated. They were houses the likes of which I had never occupied in all my days, nor known any of my fellow physicians to own. Everything I needed—furniture, bedding, utensils, books, and the like—was delivered as soon as the houses were made over to me. This was confirmed in the presence of notaries in view of the substantial value of the houses—a figure in the thousands of dinars. In this way, the caliph, out of concern and affection for me, wanted to ensure that the houses would belong to me and my children without anyone being able to contest our right to them.

When all his instructions regarding the transport of the property to the houses had been carried out, including the installation of curtains and hangings, and there remained only the matter of actually moving in, the caliph ordered the money due me, multiplied many times over, brought before me. He then had me conveyed in a train of five of his best mules, with all their trappings. He also gave me three Greek retainers, and granted me a monthly stipend of fifteen thousand dirhams, which, in addition to my accumulated back pay from my time in prison, added up to a substantial sum. Furthermore, his servants, the women of the harem, and the rest of his family and retainers, contributed countless moneys, robes of honor, and parcels of land. In addition, the services I used to perform outside the caliphal residence were transferred, in my case, to the interior of the residence. I became the leading representative of the physicians—my allies as well as the others. This crowned my good fortune; this is what the enmity of evildoers wrought. As Galen said, "The best of people are those who can turn the animosity of evil men to advantage."

It is certainly true that Galen suffered great tribulations, but they were never as bad as mine.[7]

I can indeed tell you that, time and again, the first people to scurry to my door and to ask me to intercede for them with the caliph, or to consult me on an illness that had baffled them, were the same rivals who had inflicted upon me the miseries I have already described to you. And I swear by the God I worship, the First Cause, that I would show them goodwill, and hasten to do favors for them. I bore no grudges against them, nor did I ever avenge myself on them for what they did to me. Everyone marveled at the goodwill with which I performed services for my rivals, especially when people heard what my rivals were saying about me behind my back, and in the presence of my master, the caliph. I would also translate books for them on request, without profit or reward, whereas in the old days I used to earn the weight of the translated work in gold dirhams.[8]

I have recounted all this for no other reason than to remind the wise man that trials may befall the wise and the foolish, the strong and the weak, the great and the small. Those trials, although they respect no differences of degree, must never give him cause to despair of that Divine Providence which shall deliver him from his affliction. Rather, he must trust, and trust well, in his Creator, praising and glorifying Him all the more. Praise the Lord, then, Who granted me a new life, and victory over my oppressors, and Who raised me above them in rank and prosperity. Praise Him ever anew and always.

This is Ḥunayn's entire statement as given in his own words.

Notes

1. The title of a treatise by Galen.

2. The Banū Mūsā—Aḥmad, al-Ḥasan, and Muḥammad—were the sons of Mūsā ibn Shākir, astronomer at the court of the caliph al-Ma'mūn (r. 813–33). They wrote on the sciences, particularly geometry, and patronized translators, including Ḥunayn. The incidents in question remain unidentified.

3. Bakhtīshūʿ ibn Jibrāʾīl, like Ḥunayn, was a Nestorian Christian court physician. He was known for his enormous wealth and his "erudition, loyalty, integrity, charity and perfect adherence to manly conduct" (Ibn Abī Uṣaybiʿa, *ʿUyūn al-anbāʾ*, 201–9). Ironically, he is said to have had his own difficulties with the caliphs: both al-Wāthiq and al-Mutawakkil dismissed him and confiscated his property, in both cases because of plots hatched by jealous or suspicious rivals.

4. The tenth ʿAbbāsid caliph, reigned 847–61.

5. The head of the Nestorian ecclesiastical heirarchy was called the *catholicos*. Theodosius held this office from 853 to 858 C.E.

6. Cassia pods (Ar. *khiyār shanbar*) are produced by the "Pudding Pipe tree" (*Cassia fistula*) and pulped for medicinal use; "manna" (Ar. *taranjubīn*) is the sugary exudate of the flowering ash (*Fraxinus ornis*), collected from cuts in the bark. Cassia and manna were used as purgatives or laxatives.

7. Galen is said to have lost his library in a fire.

8. Ibn Abī Uṣaybiʿa (d. 1270) notes: "I have come across many of these books, and acquired a good number of them for myself. They are written in Muwallad Kūfī script, in the hand of al-Azraq, Ḥunayn's scribe. They are written in a broad hand, with a thick stroke, and in widely separated lines, on sheets twice and three times as thick as today's paper, and cut to a size one-third of standard Baghdādī paper. Ḥunayn produced his books in this way to increase the size and weight of the volumes because he was paid their weight in gold dirhams. Since the paper he used was so thick, it is little wonder that his works have survived all these many years." Ibn Abī Uṣaybiʿa, *ʿUyūn*, 270–71.

The Autobiography of al-Ḥakīm al-Tirmidhī

(b. before 830, d. between 905 and 910)

Introduction

The account of ʿAbd Allāh Muḥammad ibn ʿAlī, known as al-Ḥakīm al-Tirmidhī ("the Sage of Tirmidh") is one of the earliest surviving spiritual autobiographies in the Arabic tradition. The author was born between 820 and 830 in Tirmidh, in what is today southern Uzbekistan. He studied the religious sciences of his day but became aware of his mystical calling only while performing the pilgrimage rites in Mecca. Thereafter, he embarked on a rigorous program of prayer, austerity, and meditation, culminating in a vividly described experience of closeness to God. Unfortunately, his expressions of devotion provoked accusations of heresy similar to those leveled against his mystical contemporaries. Eventually, however, al-Tirmidhī's charisma won him a devoted following. He died sometime between 905 and 910, leaving behind a number of works that offer mystical interpretations of *ḥadīth* and religious law.

One of al-Tirmidhī's works, *Khatm al-awliyā'* (The Seal of the Saints), helps to clarify some of the unusual features of his autobiography. In the *Khatm,* he explains that the soul or the self must begin by suppressing its desires and concentrating on the fulfillment of religious duties. Neither good deeds nor a reputation for piety will succeed in bringing one closer to God. Rather, the sincere seeker must attain an exemplary degree of self-control and resist all engagement with the transient world. Eventually, the seeker will find himself in a "wasteland of perplexity" and cry out to God in despair. Should He respond by carrying off the seeker's heart to a place near Him in heaven, the seeker will become a *walī Allāh,* an "ally" or a "friend" of God.

In keeping with al-Tirmidhī's emphasis on spiritual development rather than scholarly work or worldly rank, his autobiography passes quickly over his youth and religious training, as well as his travails at the hands of his rivals and detractors, and focuses instead on a series of dreams and visions that he construes as indicators of his spiritual status. Although he evidently believed himself to be a *walī Allāh,* he was reluctant to say so explicitly, preferring to let the dream-visions speak for him.[1] Indeed, he attributes the most powerful of these visions to others, including several male companions as well as his wife. The visions are narrated in the text exactly as they were related to al-Tirmidhī, necessitating abrupt shifts from the autobiographical "I" to the first-person "I's" of the other dreamers. The increasing importance of dreams in the text leads ultimately to al-Tirmidhī's surrender of the narrative to other voices.

The most important of these voices is that of his wife, who is given no other name. Many of her dream-visions affirm her husband's high standing; others, however, deal exclusively with her own spiritual journey. In one vision, a visiting angel hands her a branch of myrtle and tells her that her husband is not yet ready to receive such a gift. In another, she is granted knowledge of the names of God. These dreams are narrated in a mixture of Arabic and Persian, the latter being the couple's native language and probably the only one al-Timidhī's wife could speak. Although al-Tirmidhī does not say so, his wife's ascent to the highest spiritual state affirms the contention that formal education is not a prerequisite for attaining mystical knowledge. It is she who reports to him that a mysterious figure called "the prince" has identified him as the leading *walī* of his time. And it is she who has the last word: in a series of waking visions, she learns the meaning of the sacred names of God. At this point, having given her the floor, al-Tirmidhī the narrator—if not al-Tirmidhī the man—is overshadowed by his wife and her mystical experiences.[2]

Bibliography

Radtke, Bernd, and John O'Kane. *The Concept of Sainthood in Early Islamic Mysticism: Two Works by al-Ḥakīm al-Tirmidhī.* Richmond, Surrey: Curzon Press, 1996.

Abū ʿAbd Allāh Muḥammad al-Tirmidhī. "Buduww sha'n Abī ʿAbd Allāh." In *Khatm al-awliyā',* ed. ʿUthmān Yaḥyā. Buḥūth wa-dirāsāt bi-idārat maʿhad al-ādāb al-sharqiyya fī Bayrūt, 19. Beirut: al-Maṭbaʿa al-Kāthūlīkiyya, 1965. 14–32.

The Beginning of the Career of Abī ʿAbd Allāh [the Sage of Tirmidh]
[*Khatm al-awliyāʾ*, pp. 14–32]

My career began because God favored me with a father[3]—God rest his soul—who pressed me to take up the pursuit of knowledge. When I was eight years old, he began to instruct me and to encourage me to study. This he did with unvarying vigor both when I was disposed to heed him and when I was not, until study became a habit for me and took the place of the games and play of childhood. He thus acquainted me, still a youth, with the sciences of *ḥadīth* and legal reasoning.

When I reached the age of twenty-seven, or thereabouts, I suddenly felt the need to make the pilgrimage. Fortunately, the means to do so became available to me, and I set off, stopping for a time in Iraq to collect *ḥadīth*. I then traveled to Basra and from there I left for Mecca in the month of Rajab, arriving toward the end of Shaʿbān. God provided me with the means to remain in Mecca until pilgrimage time. I came, by God's grace, to pray at the *multazam* [the area near the door of the Kaʿba where all prayers are said to be answered], every morning at the first light of dawn. There I was truly converted in my heart, and made to see past the clash of questions great and small. I performed the pilgrimage and returned, having effected in myself a change of heart.

At those times when I prayed at the *multazam*, I would ask God to make me righteous, inspire me with an aversion for the things of the world, and grant me the ability to know His Book by heart. At that time, this was all I felt the need to ask for.

I set off for home, God having instilled in me the desire to memorize the Qurʾān while on the road. I learned a good portion of it while traveling, and, after I had returned home, God by His grace eased my task, and I succeeded in memorizing all of it. I would stay up late reading, but I never wearied of the Qurʾān, even when I had been up all night, and I discovered the sweetness of it.

I began reading books of the praises of God—blessed be His name—and collecting phrases with which to admonish myself and to inspire thoughts of the Hereafter. Meanwhile, I was searching the nearby towns, but could find no one to guide me along the path, or preach to me and strengthen my resolve. I was confused; I did not know what God wished for me. Nevertheless, I pursued my fasting and my prayer, until at last the words of a man of [mystical] knowledge reached my ears. I came across the book of al-Anṭākī and examined it, and was thus guided to some knowledge of the discipline of the soul. I took up this practice and God helped me. Inspired to deny myself my desires, I found that I could train myself to do one thing after another, even to the point of denying myself cool water. I would refrain from drinking from the river, thinking, "Perhaps this water had flowed here wrongfully." So I would drink from a well or from a big watercourse.

I became enamored of solitude at home and of walking in the wilderness. I took to wandering amid the ruins and the cemeteries on the outskirts of town. I sought for trustworthy friends to support me, but could find none, and so I withdrew to those ruins and lonely places.

While in this state, I dreamt that the Prophet—God bless him and grant him peace—entered the Friday mosque in our town. I followed him inside. He continued walking until he reached the enclosed area with me close behind him, almost touching his back, and placing my feet exactly where he had placed his, until I too reached the enclosed area. The Prophet ascended the pulpit, and I followed behind him, step for step. He reached the top step and sat down, and I sat on the next step down. To my right was the Prophet, in front of me were the doors that open onto the market, and to my left was the congregation. I then woke up while I was still in that state.

One night, a little time later, I was praying and felt sleepy, so I put my head down on the prayer rug next to my bed. I saw an enormous stretch of desert, in some place I did not know, and I saw an enormous court, with a place prepared at the head, and a tent or booth set up there, made of cloths and curtains I cannot describe. Then I seemed to hear someone saying, "You are being taken to your Lord." I entered the tent. I could see no one at all, no shape or figure, but I was terrified as I passed behind the curtains. I was certain, even as I slept, that I was standing in His presence. Soon after, I saw myself emerging from the tent, standing near the outermost curtain, and saying, "He has forgiven me" [or: "May He forgive me!"]. I found that I had stopped breathing, I was so terrified.

I continued in my practice of self-denial, pushing aside my desires, staying at home to be away from people, and constantly addressing myself to God in supplication. In this way, one thing after another was opened up to me. I discovered strength and awareness in myself, and I sought out those who could help me. We would meet at night, practicing the remembrance of God, praying, and abasing ourselves in supplication at the first light of dawn.

At this time I fell into trouble on account of slander and baseless rumors about me. Certain persons, of the sort who pretend to knowledge, made themselves heard at my expense. They slandered and persecuted me, accusing me of freethinking and heresy. Rumors spread, but I was indifferent. I remained on my own course, day and night, never changing, always the same. But matters took a turn for the worse: I was denounced to the governor at Balkh, who sent someone to investigate. "Here," it was reported to the governor, "is someone who talks of Love [*al-ḥubb*], corrupts the people, preaches heresy, and claims to be a prophet," and other things that I had never even thought, much less said. Finally, I went to Balkh, where I was forbidden by the governor to speak of Love.

Sorrow purifies the heart, and thus did God—blessed be His name—provide me with the means to purify myself. I recalled the saying of David—God bless him and grant him peace: "O Lord, Thou hast commanded me to purify my body by fasting and prayer, but how do I purify my heart?" God said: "With trouble and sorrow, David!" [cf. II Samuel 16]. Troubles came upon me from all sides, but I finally found in them the path to the mortification of my soul. In the past, I had tried to mortify my soul in various ways: I had ridden a donkey through the marketplace, walked barefoot through the streets, worn shabby clothes, and carried burdens like a poor man or a slave; but my soul would recoil and refuse to submit. This was upsetting to me, but when these slanders came to afflict me, the perversity of my soul disappeared. My soul bore all these things and was humbled, and obeyed me; and at last, I experienced in my heart the sweetness of humility.

One night during this time, a group of us gathered for the remembrance of God, on the occasion of a visit by one of our brethren. After some part of the night had passed, I left to return home. On the road, my heart opened up in a manner I cannot describe: as if something had touched my heart, something which cheered and delighted my soul. I was so happy that, as I walked, I feared nothing in my path: the dogs barked at me and I treasured their barking, because of some delight I felt in my heart. It even seemed to me that the sky with its moon and all its stars had drawn near the earth. All the while, I was invoking God, and I felt as if something had been set firmly within my heart. As I experienced this sweetness, my stomach wriggled and twisted and turned over on itself, and contracted, so powerful was this delight. The sweetness spread down my spine and through my veins. It seemed to me as if I were as close to God as His throne.

Every night I would stay awake until morning, unable to sleep, and I grew to bear this easily. I was still perplexed, however; I did not know what this experience was, but I grew stronger and more assiduous in my activities.

At that time an insurrection occurred in the area and civil strife ensued. All those who were persecuting and defaming me in the nearby towns fled. They suffered in the conflict and were forced into exile, and the country was rid of them.

It was during this period that my wife said to me:

> I dreamt I saw someone walking in the air, coming out of our house and walking above the path. He looked like a young man with curly hair, dressed in white, wearing sandals. He was calling to me from the air, and I was opposite him on the bench. He said, "Where is your husband?" "He has gone out," I

> replied. He said, "Tell him the Prince commands him to act justly." Then he was gone.

A short while later, a large number of people, including the elders of the town, gathered at my doorstep. I did not realize they were there until they started banging on the door. I went out and found them asking me to teach and hold assemblies for them on a regular basis. These people were the very same ones who had been spreading nasty rumors about me among the population, rumors so malicious that I had come to think of these people—or most of them in any case—as a sort of infectious disease. They had cast aspersions on my way of life and accused me of heretical beliefs that I had never held or even imagined holding.

Now here they were asking me to do this for them. Eventually, I gave in. When I spoke to them, it was as if the words came to me like ladlefuls of water from the sea and captivated their hearts. More and more people gathered round me. They filled the house and formed crowds in the street and the mosque. Finally, they carried me off to the mosque and it was as if all those lies and falsehoods about me had never been. Then the conversions began and disciples appeared and leadership, with all of its trials, fell to me as a Divine tribulation.

When the aforementioned slanderers returned from exile, they found that I had become a powerful man with many students and followers. In the past, they had turned the government and the people against me so effectively that I did not dare show my face in public, but God saw to it that their plots came to nothing. Now it was clear that they had acted out of malice and envy, and that no one was listening to them any more, so they gave up hope of harming me further.

In the meantime, my wife continued to have visions. They always came before dawn, and they came one after the other, like a Divine message. They were always so clear and so obvious in their meaning that they need no interpretation. One of these visions went like this:

> I saw a big pool, in a place I had never been before. The water in the pool was as clear as spring water. Where the water was flowing into the pool, we saw bunches of grapes, all white. My two sisters and I were sitting at the head of the pool eating the grapes, with our legs in the water, but floating without sinking or disappearing from sight. I said to my little sister, "Here we are eating grapes, but who do you think is sending them to us?"
>
> Suddenly a man appeared, curly haired, dressed in white, with a white turban on his head and his hair hanging loose behind him. He asked me, "Who would have a pool like this or grapes like these?"
>
> Then he took my hand and helped me to my feet, and, leading me away from my sisters, said: "Tell [your husband] Muḥammad ibn ʿAlī [al-Tirmidhī] to stop reading the verse, 'We have placed the balanced scales for the Day of

Resurrection . . .'" [Q 21:47] and so on to the end of the verse. "Those scales are not for flour nor for bread; they weigh the speech that comes from here"—pointing to his tongue—"and the deeds that come from here and here"—pointing to his hands and feet. "You do not know that an excess of words, like the drinking of wine, produces a kind of intoxication."

I asked him: "Who are you?"

He replied: "I am an angel. We roam the earth, and we reside in the Holy Temple at Jerusalem." In his right hand, I saw a sprig of fresh green myrtle, and in his other hand, sweet basil. He was holding these as he spoke to me.

"We walk the earth," he said, "and seek out the servants of God. We place this basil on the hearts of the servants of God, that they arise to serve and worship Him. And we place the myrtle on the hearts of the True and Certain Ones, that they may know sincerity. Sweet basil is green even in summer, and the myrtle never changes, no matter what the season. So ask [your husband] Muḥammad ibn ʿAlī, 'Would you not be happy to have these?'—pointing to the myrtle and the basil. "God can increase the piety of the God-fearing to the point that they need fear no longer, but He places these on their hearts to teach them piety first."

Then he continued, "Tell him to purify his home."

I replied, "I have small children and it is hard to keep the house clean."

He answered, "I don't mean free of urine. I mean this"—pointing to his tongue.

"Why don't you tell him all this yourself?" I asked him.

"I will not tell him myself," he said, "because the matter is not important enough for that, at least, not for other people. When he transgresses, though, it is important. Why does he trangress, then? Because this"—he gestured with the myrtle—"is still a long way off for him."

Then he pulled off some of the myrtle from the bunch in his hand and gave it to me.

"Should I keep this for myself, or give it to him?" I asked.

He laughed and his teeth sparkled like pearls. "Take it," he said, "and I'll bring the rest to him myself. What you have is for both of you—the two of you are of equal rank. And tell him, 'Let this be my last exhortation to you.' Peace be with you." But then he added, "God will give you, you and your sisters, a garden, but not because of your fasting and prayer; rather, because of the goodness of your hearts, and because you love good and shun evil"—or, in Persian, "You do not accept evil and you love the good."

"Why didn't you say this in front of my sisters?" I asked him.

"Because neither of them measures up to you." Then he said, "Peace be with you," and was gone, and I woke up.

Another time she dreamt that she was in the big room of our house:

In the room were couches upholstered with silk. One of these big couches was next to the prayer room. I looked and behind the couch I saw a tree growing out of the *qibla* end of the prayer room [the wall facing Mecca]. The tree grew as high as the height of a man, and then stopped. It was dry and shriveled up, with branches like a palm tree, looking like tent-pegs or shavings. Then fresh green branches, about five in number, sprouted from the trunk. When the new branches started growing about halfway up the trunk, the tree suddenly shot up into the air, about three times as high as a man, carrying the new sprouts up with it. Then bunches of fresh dates appeared on the branches.

I said to myself in my sleep, "This tree is mine. No one in the world, even in Mecca, has a tree like this." I stepped closer to it, and I heard a voice coming out of the trunk of the tree. I could see no one, so I looked at the trunk of the tree, and I noticed that it was growing out of a rock. It was a big rock and it filled half the room, with the tree growing out of the center of it. Next to this rock was another one, hollowed out like a basin. Water was flowing from the trunk of the tree into the hollow rock. This water was utterly clear and pure, like sap.

Then I heard a voice calling to me from somewhere near the tree: "Do you promise to watch over this tree and to make sure that no one touches it? For this tree is yours. Once it grew in sandy soil, and so many hands touched it that its fruit drooped and withered, but we placed a rock around it and sent a bird to watch over its fruit. Look!"

I looked and I saw a green bird the size of a dove on one of the branches of the tree, not on one of the fresh shoots that had sprouted from the trunk, but on one of the withered limbs just above. The bird flew from branch to branch, working its way upward. Whenever it landed on one of the dry branches that looked like pegs, the branch would turn green and fresh, and sprout bunches of dates.

The voice said, "Guard this tree until the bird reaches the top and makes the whole tree green or else it will have to stop there in the middle."

"I will guard it," I said, not seeing who I was speaking to. The bird went up the tree branch by branch, and each one turned green. When the bird reached the top of the tree, I said in wonder, "There is no god but God! Where is everybody? Don't they see this tree? Don't they know where it is?"

From the top of the tree the bird cried, "There is no god but God!"

I wanted to pull a date from the tree, but the voice said, "Not yet! Wait until they ripen." Then I woke up.

Then another time she dreamt she was sleeping next to me on the roof:

I heard voices from the garden. I cried aloud in dismay, "We've neglected our guests! I'd better go and give them something to eat." I walked over to the edge of the roof to find my way down, and then the whole side of the house simply lowered itself and left me standing upright on the ground.

Two men were sitting there, awe-inspiring in their dignity. I approached them and apologized, but they smiled back. One of them said, "Ask your husband why he is so preoccupied with this *furuzd,* meaning 'grass.'[4] Your duty is to succor the weak, and be a support to them. And tell him, 'You are one of the pegs [that hold up] the earth, and a large segment of mankind is in your care.' "

"Who are you?" I asked.

"I am the Prophet Muḥammad Aḥmad,[5] and this is Jesus." Then he said, "Tell him: 'When you say—O King! O Holiness! Have mercy on us!—you bring holiness upon yourself. Every land you bless will grow strong and mighty, and every land you do not bless will grow weak and feeble.' And tell him: 'We have given you a dwelling place and the *frequented house* [Q 52:4—a reference to the Kaʿba in Mecca], so treat them well.' " Then I woke up.

Then, on the twenty-fourth night of the month of Ramadan, she dreamt that she heard my voice from afar . . .

. . . but sounding like no voice I had ever heard. I followed the sound and came to the door of a palace full of light. I went in. The prayer room was raised up, higher than the congregation and higher than the building around it. There you were, in something that resembled a prayer niche, standing and facing Mecca. You were praying, with the light shining all around you. I thought, "His voice is enough to save the people, but he keeps himself from them."

Abū Dawūd the tailor dreamt he saw people gathering around a stairway, or ladder, set in a wall that rose to the skies:

I approached and found a crowd of people at the base of the ladder. I wanted to climb up, but a voice said, "You shall not ascend until you obtain permission." I looked up and there was a man standing in my way.

I thought to myself, "How am I supposed to obtain permission?" Then I noticed a piece of paper in my hand. I showed it to the man, and he stepped aside. I climbed the high wall. At the top, I saw only a few other people. Beyond the wall was a sea, and beyond the sea was an enormous, dizzying expanse of emptiness. I said to the others at the top of the wall, "Who are you? What are you doing here?"

"On the other side of the sea," they said, "in that great space, is Muḥammad ibn ʿAlī [al-Tirmidhī]." I stared as if staring at the crescent moon, until at last I saw you a great distance away. Again and again I rubbed my eyes and stared. I noticed the people with me were keeping away from the sea. I threw myself into it and almost immediately found myself on the other side. I walked until I found you, and there you were, sitting in that emptiness with your hood wrapped around your head. I wondered how I had come to find you in this place. Then I woke up.

Then Aḥmad ibn Jibrīl the whole-cloth dealer told me that he had dreamt of me as well:

I saw you walking around the Holy Kaʿba. Something like a shelf, or a wing, had come out of the walls, about two cubits below the roof. You were making

> your circumambulations on this shelf, with the top of the wall just higher than your waist. Then you rose up into the air until you were higher than the roof, and you kept on walking around the Kaʿba, up in the air like that. Then, astonished, I woke up.

And Muḥammad ibn Najm the lumber dealer had a dream:

> I saw the Prophet—may God bless and grant him peace—surrounded by light and praying with Muḥammad ibn ʿAlī [al-Tirmidhī] right behind him, praying along with him.

At one point during those years, I became much occupied with computing the declinations and learning to calculate using the zodiac and the astrolabe, and had become immersed in these matters. Then Muḥammad ibn Najm told me of a dream he had had:

> I heard a voice say, "Tell Muḥammad ibn ʿAlī [al-Tirmidhī], 'These things you are doing are not part of your calling or your way, so avoid them!' " I was terror-stricken by the awful splendor of the man who spoke these words. He appeared to me as an old man with white hair and beard, sweet smelling, handsome, and I imagined somehow that he was an angel.
>
> Then he said, "Tell Muḥammad ibn ʿAlī to cast those things aside, for I suspect they will become a veil between him and the Lord of Majesty. Remember to fear God in this world—you are not a base wretch, you are merely distracted [?]. Tell him this and do not neglect to pass on God's counsel to His creatures."

Then my wife dreamt that the two of us were sleeping in one bed and the Prophet of God—may God bless him and grant him peace—entered and lay down in our bed with us. Another time she dreamt that he came to our house. She said:

> I was overjoyed and bent to kiss his feet, but he stopped me. He gave me his hand and I kissed it. I was trying to think of what to ask him for. I used to suffer from an inflammation in one of my eyes, so I said, "O Prophet of God, sometimes my eye becomes inflamed." He replied, "Whenever that happens, put your hand over your eye and say, 'There is no god but God, alone, without partner; His is the power and His is the praise. He brings life and death. Goodness is in His hands, for He is All-Powerful.' " Then I woke up. After that, whenever my eye became inflamed, I would say these words and the inflammation would subside.

Then my wife dreamt that she was on Sakiba Street, looking at the cemetery, a long way off:

> Then suddenly I could see even farther—as far as Dawdabad, it seemed—and I saw an uncountable number of people, as if the world had suddenly become

> crowded with people, even clinging to walls and treetops, like birds. I thought, "What is all this?"
>
> A voice said, "The prince has invaded without warning. No one knew he was coming. For twelve days his armies were advancing upon us, and we sensed nothing, and now they have covered the earth."
>
> I looked at all the people. They were pale-faced and speechless with terror. Then I saw you coming into the room. You undressed, asked for water, and then washed yourself with water from the brass ewer. You put on a waist-wrapper and a cloak. You were wearing sandals. I asked you, "What are you doing?" You replied, "What a marvel! Do you know what this prince wants?"
>
> The people had fallen into a stunned and terror-stricken silence. It was as if they no longer knew one another—as if, in their fear, they had all become strangers. But you were calm and fearless. You were saying to me, "What a marvel! The prince will choose, from all the people on the earth, forty souls to speak to."
>
> I said, "Why aren't you going?"
>
> "God's will be done," you replied.
>
> The whole world was watching you (this she said in Persian). The people were saying, "Unless Muḥammad ibn ʿAlī comes to our rescue we shall all perish. He must find these forty people, wherever they are, and if he does not take his place among them, then all these people will be destroyed."

She said that forty people were to be found, from all over the world, and if I was not among them, then all these people would go to ruin. But how would the prince know me and when would he find me? At any rate, it seemed I was needed to complete the forty myself, for there was still one missing. The story was that the prince had come with Turkish troops to search out these people. She said that I put on a white shirt and cowl, and sandals, and went out:

> It seemed to me in my dream—she said—that when you reached the prince, you found the people jostling to get away from the Turks, but the Turks were not beating anyone, and the people's fear seemed to have disappeared. I called out, as I stood at the end of the street, "Are you one of the forty?"
>
> Someone said, "By those forty we shall be saved."
>
> "Muḥammad ibn ʿAlī will save us," said someone else. I started to weep. "What are you weeping about? He's the one who is going to save us," they said. "Not because something bad is going to happen to him," I said, "but because of his kind heart. How can he bear to look at the sword?" I was thinking that the forty would be executed, so I wept.
>
> Then I went back to the house. I felt that somehow a whole day had passed. When I reached the front door, I turned and I saw you there. "Thank God!" I said. "How were you spared?"
>
> You gestured as if to say, "If only I had been!" Then, "Just wait until you hear the whole story."
>
> You seemed to be covered in white, and you seemed twice your normal

> height. Your cheeks were flushed and shining, and your forehead and eyebrows were covered with something that looked like dust. I looked more closely and saw that there was no dust, only the traces of your terror. "How were you spared?" I asked again.
>
> "Don't you realize? I am the first of the forty. It was me he recognized and me he chose. He touched me here"—you pointed to your chest—"and he shook me so hard I thought my whole body was going to be torn apart. Then he said to me in Persian, 'You are a great lord. . . . You are at the head of the world.' "
>
> "You saw the prince? You actually saw him?!"
>
> "No. I got as far as the pavilion, where there was an enclosure set up before his door, and the prince put his hand out—or so it seemed—and he touched me, and shook me, and spoke to me. Then we went out into the courtyard, which looked like the festival enclosure they set up in the cemetery. The prince said, 'Take these forty souls out to the courtyard, and hold them there. Keep them standing, do not let them sit.'
>
> "So I went out with the others into the courtyard. The prince said to the others, 'Send this one'—meaning me—'out to pray.' So I entered with them and then I was sent out to pray. It was as if we had been chosen from all the souls on earth. I walked on past the prince's troops and past the Turks, and no one laid a hand on me. I realized then that the prince thought well of me, and that he had assembled all those people for my sake. He had sought out those forty souls only because I would be among them."
>
> "Now you can rest," I said.
>
> "I am saved from myself," you said, and went up to the mosque. I watched you move away, borne above the heads of the people. Then I woke up.

Later she had another dream, this time in Persian.[6] At the end she said, "Then I woke up." Then she was seized by an ardent desire to listen to sermons and to exact obedience from her soul. The first validation of her visions came on the twenty-seventh of the month of Dhū al-Qaʿda, five or six days after her last vision. While sitting in the garden, she heard in her heart the words, "O Light and Guidance to all things! O You Whose light cleaves the darkness!"

She said:

> I felt as if something had entered my breast and wrapped itself about my heart. My chest and throat were full, so full that I felt near to choking, full of something hot that scorched my heart. All things seemed beautiful to me. Everything I looked at—the earth, the sky, the creatures—had taken on a new and different shape, a shape lovely, glorious and sweet. There came to me then words in Persian: "We have given you a seal-ring." I was filled with joy, contentment and cheer.

She told me of this experience and the next day she told me of another:

> I heard the words, "We have given you three things"—in Persian—"My glory, My greatness, and My majesty." A light appeared above me, and remained

> there above my head, as I had seen once before in a dream. And in the light appeared the mark of glory, the mark of greatness, and the light of majesty. Of this glory, I saw a house that moved [in Persian] with something in it, with all of mankind moving along in it, and the greatness of the kingdom and of all things, and the majesty of all things, and their grandeur, were in it. I saw clearly a flame spreading through the heavens . . . and then downwards.

Then on the third day she heard in her heart: "I have bestowed upon you the knowledge of those who have gone before and those who are to come." And in this state, she spoke the knowledge of the [99] Names of God. Every day, names were revealed to her. A light would shine upon her heart and reveal the hidden meaning of the Names to her. This continued until, on Friday, the tenth of the month, she attended our gathering and told us that God's Beneficent [100th] Name had been revealed to her.

Notes

1. See Leah Kinberg's series of articles on this topic: "The Legitimization of *Madhāhib* through Dreams," *Arabica 32* (1985): 47–79; "The Standardization of Qur'ān Readings: The Testimonial Value of Dreams," *The Arabist: Budapest Studies in Arabic* 3–4 (1991):223–38; and "Literal Dreams and Prophetic *Ḥadīth* in Classical Islam—A Comparison of Two Ways of Legitimization," *Der Islam* 70 (1993): 279–300.

2. The present translation was completed before the appearance of another, more fully annotated English translation in Bernd Radtke and John O'Kane, *The Concept of Sainthood in Early Islamic Mysticism: Two Works by al-Ḥakīm al-Tirmidhī* (Richmond, Surrey: Curzon Press, 1996), to which the reader is referred for a detailed study of al-Tirmidhī. The authors would like to thank Professor Radtke for making his German translation available to them at an early stage of their work. Unlike Radtke's, however, the present translation follows ʿUthmān Yaḥyā's reconstruction (in the *Khatm*) of the Persian passages in the text.

3. *Shaykhī:* possibly "my teacher" or "my master," but the possessive form without a name suggests that he means his father; see Radtke and O'Kane, *Concept of Sainthood,* 15.

4. *Furuzd* is a Persian word; eating grass appears to have been a practice of ascetics (Radtke and O'Kane, *Concept of Sainthood,* 140–41).

5. The names Muḥammad and Aḥmad both refer to the Prophet.

6. The Persian text was apparently omitted by the copyist.

The Autobiography of al-Mu'ayyad fī al-Dīn Hibat Allāh al-Shīrāzī

(ca. 1000–1077)

Introduction

Al-Mu'ayyad fī al-Dīn Hibat Allāh al-Shīrāzī was born in the city of Shiraz in southern Iran. During his lifetime the rivalry between various Sunnī and Shiʿite sects of Islam took the form of competing political states as well as competing religious doctrines. He, like his father before him, became a "missionary" [*dāʿī*] for a sect of Shiʿite Islam known as Ismāʿīlism, most notably championed by the Fatimid dynasty of Egypt from the tenth through the twelfth century. As a *dāʿī,* al-Mu'ayyad acted equally as a local religious leader and as an agent provocateur for the Fatimids in their struggles with rival states in Syria and Iran. Al-Mu'ayyad held many different posts during his career: religious teacher, political agitator, missionary, senior court official, and military commander. The language of his writing reveals him to be a highly educated and accomplished rhetorician, and certainly bilingual in Arabic and Persian. He was also a poet. Al-Mu'ayyad's autobiography is a gripping story of high-stakes political intrigue, military adventure, and espionage.

Al-Mu'ayyad's account of his life proceeds chronologically, with occasional flashbacks and foreshadowing, and focuses on three main periods of his career. The first section details his activities in Shiraz, his attempts to win the sultan Abū Kālījār over to Ismāʿīlism, and the enmity he provoked among the local clergy who on one occasion forced him to flee for his life in disguise in a dramatic escape from the city. Later sections of the autobiography recount al-Mu'ayyad's tenure at the Fatimid court in Cairo, providing a valuable depiction of the functioning of the court during the reign of al-Mustanṣir (r. 1036–94), and offer a detailed account of his military expedition against the Seljuq Turks and the brief capture of Baghdad by a fragile coalition he had forged among Arab tribes and Turkic mercenaries in 1058.

In the excerpts translated here, taken from the first section of the text, al-Mu'ayyad is in residence in the city of Shiraz, then governed by the Būyid sultan Abū Kālījār (d. 1048).[1] When we enter the story, he has already converted many soldiers from the region of Daylam in north-central Iran (who constituted a major part of the sultan's army) to Ismāʿīlism. Al-Mu'ayyad is thus engaged in activities just short of outright sedition but has sufficient popular support to make him both dangerous and difficult to eliminate openly. The story opens at the end of Ramadan, 1037, as al-Mu'ayyad and his converted followers are about to break the monthlong fast two days earlier than the Sunnī majority because of their different method of calculating the lunar month, an incident that leads to civil unrest. In the first excerpt, al-Mu'ayyad manages to avoid both being assassinated and being exiled through his astute political instincts and powerful eloquence. His dramatic escape from Shiraz in the second excerpt is but the first of many such adventures recounted in the remainder of the text.

Al-Mu'ayyad's prose style is ornate, rhymed, and filled with parallelisms, a common embellishment in Arabic and Persian prose: ". . . their determination and resolve to oppose and prohibit my activities . . ." or "People in the marketplaces began to whisper, and in their gatherings and households they began to talk." Although such doubled phrases can be awkward in English, many of them have been retained in the current translation to communicate something of the feel of the original. Another important element of his style lies in the rhetorical dimension, particularly the way in which he attributes to himself lengthy and flowery argumentation whenever he is speaking publicly, while his opponents are either left anonymous and silent or depicted as giving only terse, simple responses. Despite the brash rhetoric of his speeches, al-Mu'ayyad often confides to the reader his deep fear and even terror during his adventures, typically at moments when he is alone, such as at home at night or cowering in hiding.

Bibliography

Daftary, Farhad. *The Ismailis: Their History and Doctrines.* Cambridge: Cambridge University Press, 1990, 213–15, and index, 779, s.v. "al-Mu'ayyad fī al-Dīn al-Shīrāzī."

Klemm, Verena. *Die Mission des faṭimidischen Agenten al-Mu'ayyad fī d-dīn in Širaz.* Frankfurt: Peter Lang, 1989.

al-Mu'ayyad al-Shīrāzī. *Sīrat al-Mu'ayyad fī al-Dīn dāʿī al-duʿāt* . Ed. M. K. Ḥusayn. Cairo: Dār al-Kutub, 1949.

Muscati, J., and K. Moulvi. *The Life and Lectures of the Grand Missionary Al-*

Mu'ayyad-fid-din Al-Shirazi. Karachi: Ismailia Association of West Pakistan, 1950 [contains long paraphrased passages from the *Sīra*].
Poonawalla, Ismail. "Al-Mu'aiyad fī 'l-dīn al-Shīrāzī." *EI*[2] 5:270.

The End of Ramadan
[*Sīrat al-Mu'ayyad,* pp. 5–11]

On the day before the feast at the end of Ramadan 428 A.H. [1037 C.E.], I was preparing for the holiday by obtaining carpets, furnishings, and the rugs necessary for the worshipers to pray on. News spread that I was gathering a great crowd the following day for the prayer and sermon and was setting up tents and pavilions in the courtyard of my house in an overt display of defiance and provocation. An extremely dim view was taken of this [by the authorities], which led to their determination and resolve to oppose and prohibit my activities. Talk of this spread quickly through town. People in the marketplaces began to whisper, and in their gatherings and households they began to talk. This soon reached the ears of Shiʿites even in the farthest reaches of the city. Every so often, one of them would rush over to my house to reassure himself about my safety and to inquire whether anything had happened to me, only to find me safe and sound and still in one piece.

The next day, which was the holiday, a great mass of people from Daylam gathered together to pray and I led them in prayer. When I had finished, I addressed them vigorously in my sermon with admonitions and warnings, saying: "As must be clear to you, times are tense, and our enemies are showing themselves openly and in great numbers. They aim to besmirch our good works and attribute great sins to us, even though we are the ones who are diligent in bearing the charge of worship and the performance of prescribed religious duties and time-worn rites! You must rein yourselves in, make an effort to see the good in their deeds, and fear God as is His due! Take care that not one of you is linked to any form of transgression—let no loose tongue find room to fault you. Patience! Prayer! God is with the steadfast!"

In the evening of that same day, the Sunnīs sought the crescent moon in accordance with their custom [i.e., by visual sighting], but it was hidden from them for a while.[2] So they rejoiced thinking that having fasted for twenty-nine days they would complete the fast on the next day, the thirtieth. They lashed out at us with words and deeds for breaking the fast two days before them, so that this might be more damning and more effective in venting their anger on us. But shortly thereafter the moon appeared and their tongues dried up in their mouths and their hearts died in their bodies from the intensity of their rage and wrath. The next day they went to their place of worship, prayed, and returned. They were filled with talk against us and schemes to ensnare us, but nothing happened that day.

The following day, however, I was summoned by the minister of state, Bahrām ibn Māfina ibn Shahl, who had been given the title “the Just”—may God have mercy upon him—to his court. A man of great intelligence, of noteworthy erudition, conciliatory in all situations, and refined in words and deeds, he bade me approach and draw near, and then he welcomed me. He disliked having to address me with such harshness, knowing that it was not proper to do so, nor even the necessary place to do so, but he was acting under orders from a master whose commands could not be disobeyed and whose decrees could not be opposed [i.e., the sultan].

“You know,” he began, “of my deep regard and fondness for you, and that I would not ask you to do something were it not in your own best interest, but I am of the view that your activities have crossed over the boundary of wrongdoing and reached their limit. Yesterday, the sultan, on his way riding through the street from his palace to the mosque and back again, spoke of you the whole time, filled with wrath against you. He said, in short, that if you do not take your leave of this country and depart, he will order someone to do such-and-such to you, indicating that you would be killed, though he avoided saying so outright. So consider whether there is any point or sense in remaining here after that. Moreover, this morning, the chief judge was here and said that the religious storytellers and other mosque officials had come to him to say that they were losing patience with what that person—meaning you—was doing to spread heresy and the rejection of the Prophet’s *sunna* [and saying]: “We should gather en masse and head for the sultan’s gate to seek assistance with this situation, and demand some sort of permission so that we can attack his house, tear it down, burn it, kill him, and cause whatever other damage we can.”

The minister continued, “I responded by telling him that this would be no simple matter, since it would confirm the suspicions of the Daylamī soldiers [Mu’ayyad’s staunchest supporters] and should anything rouse them from their current peaceful state, it would surely lead to sedition, bloodshed, rape, and terrible deeds. The judge answered me,” said the minister, “that if al-Mu’ayyad turns to them for help—meaning the Daylamīs—then their enemies will turn to others—meaning the Turks.”

Then the minister said to me, “Setting aside for the moment the sultan’s enmity, which is in any case neither settled nor fixed, if there were nothing to this talk but the talk of the masses and their unrest, then our assumption about you, with your understanding, would be that you do not choose to be a source of sedition and unrest. But it is better that you seek guidance from Almighty God and leave the country immediately. I can send a number of riders with you to protect you as far as whichever lands you choose as your destination.”

I answered, "This is yours to command for it is your kingdom. To every statement there is a reply except to him who in his own house says, 'Leave my house!' To him there is no reply. But as I think about your telling me, 'Leave our lands!' I do not know whether you should be saying this or I, whether it is your right or mine. For I do not see that I am any toil or trouble as far as you are concerned: I receive no share of your generosity, no mention of me appears in your register of royal gifts, nor have I received any kindnesses from you under any circumstances. And yet I see that all who creep and crawl—judges and jurists and scholars and scribes, people from every walk of life—gain entry into your hall and your council meetings, and are well rewarded by you either with what they receive directly as presents or indirectly as a living allowance or some other favor by means of your signature. My page is bare of such things. Moreover, you know better than anybody how your judges and notaries and the religious scholars of your mosques are marked by deficiencies and marred by shortcomings and objectionable faults; and you know that I am not marked with the characteristics of their deficiencies, nor am I marred by any of their shortcomings or defects. On the contrary, I remain a paragon of propriety and thoughtful integrity, and am the foremost of those known for their piety and their fear of God. Were it not for my open display of Shiʿism, the masses would take the dust from my sandals as medicine for their eyes and the water from my ablutions as a cure for their ailments!

"Furthermore, your officials seek nothing but to acquire property, to procure income, and to add dirham to dirham; but the person has yet to meet me whom I have troubled for anything or to whom I have begrudged a day of my life. Indeed, worldly goods have always been insignificant in my eyes—my desire for them ceased long ago. So, is your expulsion of someone whose conduct is such, without having proven that any fault blemishes him or that the trouble of supporting him burdens you, what I deserve (when I am blameless of either of these faults) or what you deserve? Nay, you do not merit my presence here! It is well known that, because I require no such support, every destination would welcome me and every land tolerate me. I only reside among you out of my passion for the religion with which I worship God and in order to protect it from an infirmity which afflicts it. If not for that, then the one agitating most for departure from among you would be myself, and the voice calling loudest for leaving you would be that of my own heart, so that I could have a rest from this constant humiliation. Especially since, as is known, I have my own master [i.e., the Fatimid caliph of Egypt]. Whenever a messenger seeks him out with a few lines of my composition or dictation, [the caliph] lavishes him with handsome accommodations and relieves him of worldly cares. If I sought him out myself, would he do less for me or make my share less than that of those who seek him out with my missives?

"Departure does not frighten me. Indeed, nothing save what I have mentioned [about my religious devotion] keeps me from leaving. I shall, God willing, do everything in my power to relieve you of the burden of my presence and turn my back on those favors due me in your lands, so that your hearts are not weighed down.

As for the chief judge and his resolve to wage war on us, would that I were speaking to him and to the masses with whom he tries to frighten us. Then he would see a wonder or two. But the sultan's intervention weakens his power, and his intention undermines the pillars of stability and solidarity. And the chief judge, if he does not fear for his ample property, his fabulous estates, and his own combativeness, though his religion be to him a blindness[3]—why do none of those who own not a handful of this world, and have only miserable scraps and tatters actually support him while he is in full view of his Lord?[4] Would that you had left us at each other so that each of us could try his luck. Peace be upon you!"

With that I stood up, left the meeting, and returned to my house, intent on rectifying this state of affairs. I searched high and low for a possible destination, but the escape routes were all laden with enemies—especially should the fact that I was fleeing as a result of the sultan's hatred and scheme become known. I spent a sleepless night trying to think of how to further my cause and whither to take my affairs, but no reliable course of action occurred to me, nor any good ideas upon which I could act.

The next day I returned for an audience at the ministry, knowing neither why I had returned to him nor what I would say. Thus it was through God's inspiration—praise be unto Him—that when I met the minister I said, "I have returned to tell you of something that suggested itself to me after I left yesterday. Namely, you enjoined me to leave the country once and for all and I replied that I would try. Then I thought about the consequences of my leaving, and concluded that it would propel me toward something worse and even more injurious than what I am fleeing and would put me into a vile situation from which I fear an ignominious end. I am, after all, fleeing from the sultan's threat against me—he exalted and in a position of great power—and from nothing else. Yet I am not safe from the occurrence of that same thing at the hands of the most humble and obscure of persons. Accordingly, if I stay in place and hold my ground against the inevitable, that is better; I will at least know my killer. People will say, 'So-and-so has been killed unjustly,' and 'So-and-so has killed him wrongly,' and each of us will gain, respectively for better and for worse, a lasting reputation. Thus, I shall stay where I am, neither departing nor leaving the known for the unknown. But if expelled I must be, then you are certainly able to put me in fetters, bind me with chains, set me upon a riding beast and let it carry me away so that I will be blameless in my own eyes. As for leaving on my own two feet, I will not, unless, by God, you grant me a postponement of several days to return home and put my affairs in order, sell my home, gain some small sum for the journey, and then depart, secretly, safe from any situation that might confront me, until I leave your lands and cross your borders."

The minister lowered his head in thought, stared at the ground for a while, then replied, "I grant you approval to leave in this manner. So return and organize your affairs as you see fit, but you may stay no more than one week." I replied, "I hear and obey. I will do as has been described and strive to make ready to depart. Still, there is one issue that I cannot fail to mention, and which I must raise." He asked, "What is that?" I said, "The good relations and close ties between the Daylamīs and myself are well known. If one of them has an argument with his wife in the evening, he comes to me with the problem in the morning, laying out the whole matter in all of its details. There is no doubt that, if they knew the truth of this affair, they would clamor and shout, and become greatly agitated. Let that not be attributed to me, nor be reckoned against me as my crime." "You must prevent them from seeing you for the period of your stay," he said, "and you must interpose between them and yourself the excuse that you have been prescribed medical treatment for a week." I said, "They have never known me to conceal myself from them for an hour of the day, nor even to cut myself off from them for a shorter period of time, but I shall do as you decree, God willing."

I left to do as he had described and to prepare to depart. I locked the door behind me, forbade the people from seeing me, and spared myself in neither supplication nor prayer to God to remove this calamity. But talk of the situation I faced erupted and spread, and the hearts of the Daylamīs grew heavy. They could not meet for any funeral or festivity without whispering among themselves about annoyance after annoyance that came their way. Things reached a point where they were constrained in the exercise of their religion and forbidden from holding fast to their creed, even though the Christians and the Jews were kept neither from practicing their religion nor from their churches and synagogues. They determined to gather because of their miserable state. A great number of them congregated in the livestock market in Shiraz—that being where they usually went when agitated—and selected delegates to carry their messages and lodge their grievances. The delegates went to one of the minister's deputies and delivered their message. They painted a grim picture, mixing sweet words with bitter, gentle words with forceful. They claimed that if things continued thus, all hope would be lost and they would be forced to protect themselves from having to suffer being abased and stigmatized due to their weakness and their small number. News of this spread everywhere and it became known that uncontrollable evil would result and sparks would fly. So the sultan decreed that the minister should settle the matter and extinguish the flames. It was due to the minister's good grace, excellent administration, and fine patience that he sought to remedy the situation and set things right.

On the day of the large gathering in the square, the minister arrived before the Daylamīs and spoke of rectifying the situation. He ordered that the judges, the religious storytellers, and the Sufi mystics be brought to him, every last one of them. They arrived, cutting through the ranks of the Daylamīs right and left. The Daylamīs' tongues lashed out at them, uttering all manner of foul speech and revilement right to their faces, until they had entered the building, frightened to death by what they had just suffered at the hands of the Daylamīs and by what had caused them to be summoned to the sultan's palace.

When they stood before the minister's court, they were set upon with every kind of reproach, chiding and reprimand [by the minister]: "You have squandered our grace, and our gifts have made you ungrateful for the protective shade of security and justice that has been extended over you. You have become bent on stirring up sedition, and your talk has become an incitement to riot between the Shiʿites and the Sunnīs. If it reaches me that any of you entertains mention of this or that it even crosses the tongues in your mouths, you will have brought death and destruction upon yourselves. And whoever survives thereafter will have his property confiscated and be dragged off in chains. So be heedful and watch where you tread. Peace be upon you!" Thus they [the judges, storytellers, and Sufis] departed heavyhearted after having entered lighthearted.[5]

Then the Daylamīs were asked what had gathered them, young and old, in the square. He ordered that they select a number of them to enter and to represent the rest. They were chosen, they entered, and the minister then asked them the reason for their gathering. They responded that the Daylamīs held to a faith whose truth had settled firmly in their souls and that the religious obligations of this faith were incumbent upon them due to the oaths and convenants they had accepted. Morever, they had adopted that man [= al-Mu'ayyad] to be in charge of this faith, as a father unto them, and as a brother and a friend, a repository for every secret, a refuge in good times and bad.

[They said:] "Yet for days he has been locked in! It is rumored that he is to be exiled from the country, mistreated, and is being plotted against! That is what has brought us together and moved us to action!" "No mention of exile in any form has occurred—God forbid!" replied the minister. "He is too greatly esteemed and too modest and decent for such a thing to befall him. Rather I have asked him to stay in his house and to prohibit people from meeting with him for a few days because of the unrest which has occurred among the masses on his account, until I can untangle the knot and douse the flames. This very hour I have summoned the chief instigators and agitators responsible for this misguidedness and given them a taste of their own medicine. I warned them of a terrible punishment if they begin once again to do as has been forbidden them, namely to speak of [the schism between] Shiʿism and Sunnism and to foment sedition. So you should now return to your dwellings and breathe a sigh of relief. You need no longer worry about your friend."

They left pleased and thankful. A day or two later the minister wrote me a letter in which he granted me permission to open my door and to return to things as they had been before, and hold my sessions as usual. So I opened it, rejoicing in God's benevolence—may He be exalted!—for what He had saved me from in the short term and fearful of the doubled wrath toward which He was propelling me in the long term. I said:

God has been generous in all that has passed,
May He continue to be generous in that which comes.

Fleeing Shiraz [pp. 68–72] sometime between 1042 and 1044/45:

The king [= Sultan Abū Kālījār] was on the point of traveling to Ahwaz with his troops. I concluded that if I remained in Shiraz, I would not be safe from whatever trickery or subterfuge might be used to fulfill the desires of [my enemies]. Accordingly, I told myself that it would be most prudent to remain with the group and not to separate from the collective.[6] Thus, I sought permission to travel with them but was refused. This refusal only increased my forebodings. I continued to send written requests for permission, but I met with no approval, and in spite of more urgent requests, I met with nothing but more obstinate refusal. I therefore undertook the difficult course of clandestine flight. It had not occurred to me, and certainly not to anyone else, that I was capable of such a thing. I gave my followers and companions in Shiraz to understand that I had received approval for my request to join the troops but would be traveling in the entourage incognito, while I gave those traveling in the entourage to understand that I would be remaining in Shiraz, in hiding, but that I would be sending along with them some of my baggage, riding beasts, and servants. I then donned a disguise and assumed an unfamiliar demeanor, wearing old and ragged clothes. I acquired two new servants, unknown to anyone, and set off on back roads, hiring at each way station an ass to ride, or a camel, or a steer, as circumstances dictated.

The travails of journeying that I endured during that time—descending into ravines and mires, bearing the freezing cold, alighting in filthy places—was something for which, had it been a disease, death would have seemed a cure! The most difficult thing I had to bear was that every time I hired an ass to ride, I wanted to go down the road alone so no one would see me. Its owner, however, would want to accompany us to keep an eye on his animals, squarely defeating the entire purpose. He would ask what caused me to prefer traveling alone when the custom among travelers was to prefer the opposite, namely, that they would ask to be accompanied. I was tongue-tied, unable to give a reasonable excuse for this. Along the way I would alight with people from the countryside and backcountry. I listened as they mentioned me in very unflattering terms and I realized that if they recognized me, they would have performed ritual ablutions in my blood and gone to prayer! May you never have to go down such roads and hear with your own ears such horrible things about yourself!

Among the places in which I wished neither to be, nor to be apprehended, and in which my safety was preserved only through the subtle graces of Almighty God, was a place called Jannāba. [. . .] I felt this way because I arrived there on a rainy day, and my search for some shelter from the rain led me to the congregational mosque. The town market was next to it, and someone came in to pray who knew my name, ancestry, and everything else about me. When his gaze fell upon me, he came closer, approaching as you would approach someone who enjoys an elevated station in life. Then he saw my demeanor, my state, my clothes and what I was doing, and he realized right away that I was fleeing. He offered himself and his money to me, saying, "If there is anything you need, I can help you, or, if you need a little extra money to take with you, I have some and cannot think of a better use for it than you." "God bless you and your money," I replied. "I have no need more pressing than that you have not seen me, nor I you."

Then a second person came over to me, an ʿAlid [i.e., a Shiʿite], and asked one of my servants about me. My servant replied that I was a *sharīf* [i.e., a descendant of the Prophet Muhammad through ʿAlī and the Prophet's daughter, Fāṭima] traveling from Kirman to Baghdad. He said that this was not what people were saying about me. He approached and greeted me, and I greeted him politely and welcomed him. He said, "It seems as if I know you, sir—may God protect you." "Perhaps that is the case," I said. He said, "I met you in Ahwaz." I replied, "I have indeed been there." "In the place known as the Palace of al-Ma'mūn, I remember that you were building a building there," and in saying this alluded to the shrine that was the cause of the current misery afflicting me.[7] "I do not know that place; I have only gone to Ahwaz when passing through. Anyway, where would I get the means to build something? I am too busy looking out for myself to pay attention to such a thing." "Well, what have I been doing trying to cover for you then? They said you were so-and-so and spoke of you with terms of great honor and respect." "I have on occasion heard of that man," I said. "He is a man of important affairs, the leader of the Daylamīs, a powerful position. Still I have never seen him, but some people resemble others and perhaps someone would liken me to him." He continued, "Some people said to the local governor, 'You should take him into custody, perhaps he is fleeing the sultan. If you capture him you may gain favor with the court.' He was about to detain you until I pointed out to him that he should really ignore that sort of talk completely. I said to him, 'You are neither commanded nor required to do so. He may be the man they mean and he may not. If he is the one they mean, exposing yourself to his enmity together with the enmity of all of the Daylamīs would outweigh whatever reward you might earn by seizing him. And if he is someone else, then you have frightened a stranger, detained him on his way to some place or another, and earned yourself the embarrassment of it.' 'You are right,' replied the governor, and he accepted my counsel regarding you. But now I would like for you to take as much money from me as you want and let it help you along your way. You would both honor me and favor me by doing so." I thanked him profusely.

Then a third person approached me carrying himself differently than had the other two. He greeted me, came up to me, and said, "There has been much talk of you in this town. Some say that you are Ẓahīr al-Dīn, lord of Basra, escaped from prison and making your way back to Basra. Another says you are so-and-so," and he called me by a name which only a passionate and ardent devotee would use, showing himself to be a fervent adherent of Shiʿism and its doctrines. I said, "Sir, I am neither the one nor the other of these two men, but rather merely an ʿAlid passing through." The man replied, "Then I would ask something of you." "What is it?" I asked. "That you write for me, in your own hand, a prayer from which I might receive some blessing." "As for writing the prayer," I replied, "there is nothing which could keep me from doing that, but as for your taking it as a blessing because it is written in the hand of the man to whom you referred, I am not he, and there is no blessing in my hand or in his, in my opinion and according to my creed." "That would be fine," he said, "please write it." I said to him, "Then I have a favor to ask of you, too, so please do it, one favor for another." "What is that?" he inquired. "I would like you to rent a riding ass for me, so that I can leave this place." "I hear and obey," he replied.

So the man left in search of a riding ass to rent, and I busied myself with writing what he had asked for. He returned after a while with the muleteer, having agreed with him on a price, and so he was paid. I said, "Where is the ass for me to ride so that we can travel?" "I will bring it to you shortly," he said, "it is in an outlying village." He then left me while it was still morning. The time came for the first afternoon prayer and he had not yet returned. Dusk approached and he had still not returned. I had no doubt that I had been delayed by the local governor and that he would arrest me, having forbidden the muleteer from returning and sent spies to follow me if I left the place. I was in no position to run and escape my pursuers had I wished to flee. This gave me a fright of apocalyptic proportions, so I sent for the man who had brought the muleteer and said to him, "That man has left me high and dry, for he has not returned, despite the fact that it was settled that he would do so within a short time. So, if you please, could you track him down and bring him back with the riding ass? If you would, it would be most kind and I would not be able to thank you enough." "I hear and obey," he said. He set off at once, and suddenly there he was approaching with the muleteer and the ass, shortly before sunset. So we set off, I not believing that I had escaped from that predicament, and looking back to see if anyone was following us. We traveled and stopped overnight in a ruined palace on the riverside. It was in fact haunted by demons, but when I entered it, I felt as though I had been plucked out of Hellfire and dropped into Heaven.

When we awoke, we traveled wherever God in His munificence led us. Such was my wont for an entire month, experiencing all of life's hardships, wrapped in the garments of terror, undergoing every genus and type of torment and travail, until I entered my home in Ahwaz one evening, prior to the sultan's return. For he had remained en route between Shiraz and Ahwaz for some time, engaged in diversions and pastimes, until he encamped for a month in a town called Sābūr, three days' march from Shiraz. During his stay there, a letter from the intelligence network reached him informing him that I had disappeared, and that, since the time his entourage had departed, no trace of me had been seen, but that there was a rumor that I was traveling in his company in disguise. He was shaken by these rumors and I heard that he placed spies and agents in the tents of the Daylamīs and in their camps to ascertain my whereabouts. He stepped up his efforts to narrow the search, examining the cavalry and the infantry man by man, and in a number of cases laid bare the faces of some who had disguised themselves. But all that was lost effort, for I was tucked away in my hiding place and not among them, kept safe by God in His mercy.

Notes

1. The Būyids were Shiʿites of a different sect; the region they ruled, large parts of present-day Iraq and Iran, was populated by both Shiʿites and Sunnīs.

2. The Sunnīs, failing to see the moon, assumed that the month had not yet ended (the new moon marking the beginning of the next lunar month), and they would therefore break the fast after the thirtieth day. The new moon was only temporarily obscured, however, and when it was sighted, this proved that Ramadan had in fact ended. The Ismāʿīlīs fast a set number of days and had ended their fast accordingly, without having to wait for a sighting of the new moon.

3. See Qurʾān 41:44: "To the believers it [the Qurʾān] is a guidance and a healing; but to those who believe not . . . to them it is a blindness" (trans. Arberry).

4. See Qur'ān 84:15: "Nay, but lo! His Lord is ever looking on him" (trans. Arberry).

5. See Qur'ān 9:41: "Go forth light and heavy!" (trans. Arberry).

6. Al-Mu'ayyad adds a touch of humor and irony here by using a phrase at the end of this sentence that is a slogan of Sunnī Islam. The Prophet Muhammad is reported to have said, "Do not separate from the collective," commonly understood by Sunnī Muslims as a condemnation of all non-Sunnī sectarianism. But al-Mu'ayyad, who is fleeing Sunnī enemies and seeking safety by hiding among a group of Sunnīs, wryly quips that he is doing so according to the Sunnī teaching not to separate from the collective!

7. Al-Mu'ayyad had restored a mosque, an act that caused him difficulties with the sultan Abū Kālījār.

The Autobiography of al-ʿImād al-Dīn al-Kātib al-Iṣfahānī

(1125–1201)

Introduction

ʿImād al-Dīn's memoirs of his life with Saladin are titled *The Syrian Thunderbolt* (al-Barq al-shāmī), which refers to the brief but glorious reigns of Nūr al-Dīn and Ṣalāḥ al-Dīn [= Saladin] that saw the unification of Syria, Palestine, and Egypt into a single kingdom and the recapture of Jerusalem from the hands of the Crusaders who had held it for eighty-eight years (1099–1187). After Saladin's death, the kingdom was divided among his three sons and one of his brothers, who soon began to vie with one another for control of the region, leading rapidly to a period of political instability.

Although ʿImād al-Dīn's work is framed as a life of Saladin, the narrative focus slips away again and again to highlight the role of ʿImad al-Dīn himself, so much so that later Arab autobiographers such as al-Suyūṭī and al-Shaʿrānī regarded the work as autobiographical, one in which the author had "portrayed himself" (*tarjama nafsah*). Reading ʿImād al-Dīn's work, one might well wonder whether a single work can portray two lives and therefore function simultaneously as both biography and autobiography. The text could in any case easily be titled "My Life with Saladin." We view Saladin's reign and his deeds through the eyes and opinions of his faithful, though none too modest, personal secretary and assistant, ʿImād al-Dīn. One of the constant motifs within the narrative is the contrast between "the pen" and "the sword" and the interdependence of the men who wield them. This is a relationship that is depicted as being complementary and necessary to both groups.

ʿImād al-Dīn gives us a wonderfully detailed account of the day-to-day activities of a high-ranking administrative secretary: drafting reports, writing elaborately euphuistic proclamations, composing verses to be used as embellishments in the ruler's personal correspondence, buying books, attending public readings of poetry and lectures on religious topics, and even helping the ruler to organize public disputations over religious law in celebration of the holy month of Ramadan. The following selected passages demonstrate two of the author's favorite themes: his personal role during the reign of Saladin and his own social commentaries regarding the "men of the pen" and the "men of the sword." The final passage translated here constitutes one of ʿImād al-Dīn's true moments of personal glory, when he is selected by Saladin to draft the official proclamations sent out to all the cities of the realm announcing the reconquest of Jerusalem from the Crusaders. Only two volumes of ʿImād al-Dīn's original work have survived, but an abridgment by al-Bundarī, *Sanā al-barq al-shāmī,* gives a sense of the whole. The following passages are translated from al-Bundarī (as marked).

Bibliography

al-Barq al-shāmī, vol. 3, ed. Muṣṭafā al-Ḥayarī; vol. 5, ed. Fāliḥ Ḥusayn. Amman: Mu'assasat ʿAbd al-Ḥamīd Shūmān, 1987.

al-Bundarī, al-Fatḥ ibn ʿAlī. *Sanā al-barq al-shāmī.* Ed. Ramazan Şeşen. Beirut: Dār al-Kitāb al-Jadīd, 1971.

Gibb, H. A. R. "The Arabic Sources for the Life of Saladin." *Speculum* 25 (1950): 58–72.

———. "Al-Barq al-Shami: The History of Saladin by the Kātib ʿImād ad-Dīn al-Iṣfahānī." *Wiener Zeitschrift für die Kunde des Morgenlandes* 52 (1953): 93–115.

Massé, Henri. "ʿImād al-Dīn." *EI*² 4:1157–58.

Richter-Bernburg, Lutz. "Observations on ʿImād al-Dīn's *al-Fatḥ al-qussī fī-al-fatḥ al-qudsī.*" In *Studia Arabica et Islamica: Festschrift for Iḥsān ʿAbbās on His Sixtieth Birthday,* ed. Wadad al-Qadi, 373–79. Beirut: American University of Beirut, 1981.

The Pen and the Sword

Prologue [*Sanā al-barq,* pp. 13–14]

Thoughtful is the person who recognizes the value, and acknowledges the generosity, of the one who fostered and promoted him. If he is appointed to the service of a master, he should return this benevolence by praising him even after his death. As for me, the one who provided me with my livelihood and selected me as his secretary during his lifetime, then left me to write his praises after his death, was the Victorious King Ṣalāḥ al-Dunyā wa-l-Dīn Abū Muẓaffar Yūsuf ibn Ayyūb [= Saladin]—may God's mercy be bestowed upon him. I worked alongside him and found him to be the best of company. Now that his epoch and his life have ended, I fear lest his memory fade, so I am writing this book and endowing it with the finest of rhyming prose. After pondering and considering the completed work, I decided to call it *The Syrian Thunderbolt* [al-Barq al-shāmī], because I arrived in Damascus in the month of Shaʿbān 562 [1166 C.E.], during the reign of the Just King Nūr al-Dīn Maḥmūd ibn Zankī—may God bless his era with the best of mercy—and I found the state well structured and stable, its reputation strong, and its leadership benevolent under his rule and likewise during the reign of Saladin up until the twenty-seventh of the month of Safar in 589 [March 3, 1193—the date of Saladin's death]. I then saw that regime vanish as if in a sudden flash or the blink of an eye. All was over. Gone were the days, the nights, the months, and the years as if they had all been nothing but a dream.

In this book I present some recollections of my days with Sultan Saladin. I start by reporting how and when I first met him and by describing my service to him. I describe the beginning of his rule and the circumstances of his arrival in Syria where I joined his administration. Then I chronicle every year of his reign and list all of his good deeds.

My pen accompanied his sword and helped his dominion: the former providing endorsement, the latter causing death; the former sustaining security, the latter inducing fear. The sultan depended upon my penmanship and used to say, "Thank God, for He did not cause me to be disappointed by al-ʿImād and He coupled my success with his." Then, after his passing, I showed my loyalty's endurance and sang his praise in my writing. I revived his memory with my accounts and immortalized his deeds in my books. I have in truth offered him a second life after his death. After the Almighty chose to call him to His side, and his kingdom was divided between his sons, I told myself they would follow their father's example and acknowledge my value and elevate my rank further and grant me my due. But instead, they withheld my salary and caused me such distress that I had to write a lengthy letter to the master al-Qāḍī al-Fāḍil to complain.

How I arrived in Damascus [pp. 17–21]

I left Baghdad and came to Damascus not because I aspired to join the service of any of its nobility, but because I felt alienated in Baghdad after the death of my patron the vizier ʿAwn al-Dīn Yaḥyā b. Muḥammad b. Habira. He had favored me, selected me for his service, and appointed me his deputy in Basra and Wasit many times, so that I became known as his client. After his death in 560 [1164], I stayed in Baghdad where all those who were associated with him were oppressed. I was not directly targeted and was left to go about on my own. I started frequenting the circles of scholars and jurists, learning from them and debating with them. One of these scholars was from Damascus and always extolled his city's excellence and described the beauty of its orchards, the purity of its air, and the scarcity of its illnesses. I enjoyed his company and was enticed by his description of his city, so I decided to go to Damascus as a distraction from my malaise. He escorted me until we got close to Damascus. Then suddenly he changed his friendly attitude and left me there. Alone, disappointed, and frustrated, I told my companions, "Pitch my tent here and let us wait, maybe someone will help us." By that time, one of the Sufis who recognized me had gone to the judge of Damascus, Kamāl al-Dīn Muḥammad b. ʿAbd Allāh b. al-Qāsim al-Shahrazūrī, and informed him of my presence in the vicinity of the city.

Soon afterward, still wallowing in incertitude, we were surprised by the arrival of a group of the judge's pages, deputies, and servants who offered me his apologies for not being able to come personally and extended his invitation to lodge anywhere I chose. I opted for the *madrasa* [college of law] of which I am now the rector. I started to visit the judge regularly and to attend his sessions and lessons. I distinguished myself by participating in the discussions and by quoting from original sources in my debates in both basic and advanced fields of learning. At that time, news of my arrival reached Prince Najm al-Dīn who was curious to meet me because of his prior acquaintance with my uncle. He came personally to my home to show me his respect and to satisfy my expectations. I welcomed him and hurried to offer him reverence. At the end of the month of Shawwāl 562 [1167], I composed a poem in his honor in which I extolled his virtues and predicted the conquest of Egypt at the hands of his brother Asad al-Dīn and his son, Saladin, who had gone there on campaign for the second time.

When Asad al-Dīn came back to Damascus, he was informed of my presence. He used to sit every night with the notables, so I went to him to pay him homage. He received me with all the signs of respect and friendship. He spent a long time with me remembering my uncle al-ʿAzīz and praising his memory, and showered me with generous offers and gifts. I, in return, presented him with a panegyric poem on the night of Friday, the twenty-seventh of the month of Dhū al-Qaʿda 562 [Sept. 14, 1167]. I also met Saladin and we soon became close friends. He often asked me to offer him some of my poetry or my prose.

How I entered the service of Nūr al-Dīn and changed the secretariat [pp. 22–23]

The judge Kamāl al-Dīn al-Shahrazūrī told me, "It would be in your interest to write a poem praising Nūr al-Dīn; we hope you will attain a good position in his administration." So I composed a poem which was delivered to Nūr al-Dīn by the judge, of which these are the opening verses:

If she had kept her oaths on the day of departure,
her promises of meeting would not have delayed our meeting.
What [wrongs] have my heart committed that it,
in burning fire, must ever yearn for you?
I have not forgotten how her tears were scattered
o'er her cheeks, like the pearls of her necklace unstrung.
As she drew near to bid me farewell,
in her closeness her distance grew clear.
As when the archer pulls his arrow tight,
drawing near was but the first step of her flight.

Then Nūr al-Dīn appointed me to his secretariat as a scribe in the beginning of the year 563 [1167]. Soon afterward he left for the city of Ḥimṣ where he stayed for a few days to review a number of matters and solve a few problems. I went after him and then followed him to the city of Ḥamāh where I was lodged by Asad al-Dīn Shirkuh in a tent next to his own tent. Early every day, I used to go to work engrossed in my worries about my performance in a job to which I was unaccustomed. I thought that the other secretaries and scribes looked down on me and considered my talents lacking. I also thought a career in the secretariat a difficult one, especially with regard to the redaction of reports, until I read the notes and letters which came in from different regions and provinces and found them very weak in language and style.

I felt strong enough to undertake the task of changing the mediocre state of affairs and introduced a new style of writing that was unknown to my colleagues. In it I fulfilled the requirements of high prose and eliminated the distortion of language that dominated the old style. I wrote in this new style to the provinces while the other scribes mocked and slandered me. I ignored them and all the while I tried to show them the right way and did my best to advise them. Soon afterward, my pen spoke for the excellence of my style and my knowledge elevated my status. My colleagues gathered around me and acknowledged my skills. My prestige rose constantly and Nūr al-Dīn endowed me with further honor by appointing me to a position closer to him. I, in return, improved the quality of his statements by my prose. Nūr al-Dīn liked me all the more and rewarded me correspondingly.

When Nūr al-Dīn decided to go to Aleppo, Asad al-Dīn was sent a few days ahead of him. Before leaving, he entrusted me to his nephew, Saladin, and left me the tent that he had ordered pitched for me with all its accoutrements. I stayed behind and spent the time in the company of Saladin day and night until Nūr al-Dīn ordered us to proceed to Aleppo. There he resided in the citadel throughout the winter and I stayed in the *madrasa* of Ibn al-ʿAjamī. That winter was very cold and gray and I used to visit Saladin frequently in his home. He asked me to compose a few verses for him on yearning so that he could insert them in his letters to those he missed and was longing to see.

[. . .] On Monday the fourth of the month of Ramadan [569/1174], Nūr al-Dīn went on horseback for his tour as usual. We [the scribes] were left in his office to do our work. Someone came and informed me that Nūr al-Dīn had visited the *madrasa* of which I was in charge, spread his carpet, and prayed in its *qibla.* I immediately went there and met Nūr al-Dīn in its vestibule when he was leaving. He stopped when he saw me and I said, "You have honored this place with your presence, but have you noticed how it was affected by the last earthquake?" [June 29, 1170] "We shall restore it to its original form," he replied. I then sent him sweet confections, an item of clothing, some incense, and some camphor, and to accompany them composed three verses:

For Solomon with all his might
a present from an ant sufficed.
Kings are no greater than a small nuisance
for you, and they always hope for your goodness.
I am a slave to our master, all I own is his,
my heart is filled with gratitude toward him.

He noticed that the prayer niche of the *madrasa* was not covered with gold mosaics, so he sent for gilded tesserae and gold, but he died before the mosaic could be applied. I then traveled to Mosul, where he appeared to me in my sleep. In the dream he said to me, "The *madrasa* needs what belongs to it." I explained to him, "I have appointed someone to take care of it for me." He retorted, "The prayer [niche]!" And when I woke up, I understood his reference to the prayer niche and that it was now in a ruinous state. So I wrote to the jurist who had taken my place and who had the gold in storage with him, and told him to use it immediately for the finishing of the prayer niche. When I came back to Damascus in the days of Saladin, I entered the city on the day of the completion of the prayer niche's gilding and thus fulfilled the wish of my late patron.

How I departed from Damascus and returned to Cairo [pp. 114–18]

Saladin decided to leave Damascus and go back to Cairo. He left in the morning of Friday the fourth of the month of Rabīʿ al-Awwal. I waited until I performed the Friday prayer and then headed toward the royal encampment, reaching it after nightfall. I missed my family dreadfully and expressed my feelings in verse at every stop on the road.

After we arrived in Cairo, I was assigned the editing of the letters sent to Syria, which did not take up all of my time, so I was able to take the opportunity to spend my free time attending poetry readings in Giza and al-Jazīra [Rawḍa island], participating in sessions in the *madrasas* and study circles, and investigating literary and legal topics. At night, I used to go to the sultan [Saladin] for consultation and for study, for literary discussions and ascetic readings. The sultan used to spend some time with me after evening prayers whenever he needed to send some communications or to consult me on some state secret. He would dictate what he wanted to me. I would then go back home to compose the letters and come back to him early in the morning to show him the final drafts and add whatever corrections he deemed necessary.

[. . .] Book sales used to be held in the Fatimid palace twice weekly. Books were sold for very low prices. I did like everyone else and took advantage of the situation by buying a number of precious books. When I informed the sultan of what I had bought, he granted me their price as a gift and added to it by giving me more books from the palace's shelves than I had selected. I once entered into his presence and found him examining a large number of folios from the palace's collection. He asked me, "Aren't some of these among the books you have selected?" "All of them," I replied, "and I would not let go of a single one." So he ordered a porter to carry them all to my house. This was but one example of his generosity; it was his custom to give without making one ask for what one needed.

[. . .] We suggested to the judge Ḍiyā' al-Dīn al-Shahrazūrī that he take us to the pyramids and his face lit up in appreciation. He owned the island of al-Dhahab on the the way to the pyramids, so we crossed over to it and spent the night there in the best of company with all the pleasant things necessary for a party.

The next day, we crossed to Giza and passed by a number of people seated in circles and dressed in mantles like those of our Syrian or Iraqi jurists. When we approached them, they fled the place in a hurry. I thought they were students, but I was told that they were drinkers of ale. I said, "Why are they wrapped in mantles?" I was told, "This is the habit in this country. You cannot expect people to be alike everywhere."

When we finally got to the pyramids, we were greeted by our slaves, who had preceded us and prepared the tents for us. We circled around the pyramids a few times. The scene left us in utter awe. We were intensely dazzled by the Sphinx, and we were at a loss for words to describe our impressions. We spent the evening in conversation about the monumentality of these pyramids and their builders and how they eclipse everything else in their grandeur.

How I was saved from the Battle of Ramla [p. 128]

On the evening of Friday the third of the month of Jumāda al-ʾŪlā [573/1177], Saladin left Cairo with the intention of going on campaign against Gaza, Asqalan, and Ramla. I accompanied the army and it was announced that people should procure provisions for at least ten days. I was feeling uneasy about this campaign and told my servant, "I think I should go back to Cairo. I am a man of the pen, not of the sword, and I have an ominous feeling about this campaign. The road is long, the dangers are many, and the route is all in sandy desert. My beasts cannot endure such an ordeal. This is a task for fighters, not for writers, and everyone should focus on his work without infringing on the other's duties. Besides, all the other scribes and secretaries have requested the sultan's permission to go back." I informed al-Qāḍī al-Fāḍil of my worries and my desire, but he kept them secret to protect me.

The sultan, though, was willing to let me do what I chose. He asked me, "Are you coming along or would you rather go back?" I said, "The choice is my lord's, whatever you decide for me shall be." He replied, "You had better go back and pray for us so that God may grant us victory." I had already written a few verses to the master al-Fāḍil as a joke:

I was asked to go on campaign
    Tell me, what would my efforts at jihād achieve?
I do not feel audacious amidst men of the army,
    My bow is not tight enough to loose arrows.

This was the only time I failed to accompany the sultan on his campaigns, and God thus saved me from being present at the defeat [at the Battle of Ramla, November 25, 1177].

How I avoided wielding the Sword [pp. 155–56]

A group of Frankish Crusaders and their wolfish infidel allies [eastern Christians] had been raiding the environs of the city of Ḥamāh for some time. Prince Nāṣir al-Dīn Mankurus, the governor of the city, attacked them with a hundred of his warriors and defeated them. He captured great numbers of infidels and brought them to the camp of the sultan.

On the morning of the eleventh of the month of Rabīʿ al-Ākhir [574/1178], the sultan was mounted on his horse with all the army around him when Prince Mankurus approached him, came down from his horse, kissed the ground, greeted the sultan, and kissed his right hand after having pressed his forehead to his foot. He had the captives—"who looked drunk without having drunk anything" [Q 22:2]—brought before the sultan who ordered that they be beheaded by men of religion. Al-Ḍiyāʾ al-Ṭabarī was the first to execute a captive, followed by Shaykh Sulaymān al-Dīrī al-Maghribī, and then many others. Prince Aqtafan b. Yarūq was present and he also executed an enemy of God.

At this moment I was summoned into the presence of Saladin, and I thought I was needed for something important that could not be carried out by anyone else. Instead, when I presented myself, the sultan asked me to draw my sword and to kill one of the infidels. I told him, "I am a man of the pen and do not compete with swords. I announce victories but do not cause deaths. Please grant me this boy as a slave and let some warrior kill the captive you have designated for me." The sultan laughed and released me from the task and said, "We will use this boy in exchange for one of the Muslim captives held by the Franks. Instead, we will give you a slave from among the prisoners brought in by the Egyptian fleet."

I instantly took advantage of the sultan's offer and brought my pen and inkwell and asked the prince ʿAḍud al-Dīn Murhaf b. Mu'ayyad al-Dawla Usāma b. Munqidh [son of the autobiographer Usāma ibn Munqidh] to write me a decree. He then asked the sultan for his signature on it. Later I drafted a letter to the master al-Fāḍil asking him for what the sultan had granted me. I described the slave I wanted and exaggerated somewhat the qualities I was seeking. Al-Fāḍil sent me a hundred dinars instead of a slave and wrote, "I realized that what you are requesting is impossible to find, and the slaves brought in by the fleet are of inferior quality. The best among them is not worth more than thirty dinars. Therefore, I decided to send you these hundred dinars as compensation. I have taken from the state purse fifty dinars instead of the slave, added to it thirty from the privy purse of al-ʿĀdil [Saladin's brother], and twenty from my own."

My heart was delighted by this turn of events. After my sword had turned against killing, I did not lose anything by my decision not to spill blood. I turned from that deed for fear the company would laugh at me as they had at the others.

A successful debate and how I came to have a residence in Damascus [pp. 286–88]

The sultan decided to distribute turbans and robes to the preachers and Qur'ān-reciters during the month of Ramadan [582/1186]. He spent the first two weeks of the month listening to preachers in the citadel and giving away turbans. When he had done enough, I told him, "We have satisfied the reciters, preachers, and poets. There remain only the jurists to invite for disputations and to reward, for they are the bearers of law and the interpreters of rules." He replied, "I fear their polemics and the results of their debates, which usually end in quarrels." I said, "I personally shall guarantee their behavior and shall invite only those known for their patience and good manners." He said, "You promote them because of your respect for them; if you bring them, do not allow them to indulge in fights."

So it happened, and the first day of disputation a number of the most famous jurists were present. A brilliant discourse and a beneficial argument took place. Then the sultan asked Burhān al-Dīn Masʿūd, the Ḥanafī law professor of the Madrasa al-Nūriyya, to argue a case and deduce the conclusion. He hesitated and was about to refuse for fear of abusive reactions. I told him to begin without fear for he was the most persuasive of the discussants. He said, "If you are going to object, I will acquiesce to your judgment." I appeased him and assured him of my support. He started his presentation, furnished his argument, and satisfied the questions of all those present.

The sultan next chose me to develop the counterargument. I started by presenting my view and refuting the argument, correcting the mistakes and misinterpretations, providing the evidence, and solving the problem. I pressed Burhān al-Dīn to carry the debate further and he responded well and provided a good argument. The session ended up being very beneficial for all present. The same was repeated the next day, and the day after, until the holidays. The sultan sat through all the sessions and before the Feast he ordered the preparation of robes of honor to be distributed to the jurists. There were more than two hundred jurists, and the sultan offered them all robes and turbans. I accompanied the jurists in my robe of honor when they all entered the hall on the first day of the Feast.

In that year, 582 [1186–87], I also built my house in Damascus across from the citadel. The sultan was usually on the move to check on his dominions, wage war against the enemy, or force the client kings to do his bidding. So when he decided to spend most of this year in Damascus residing in the citadel, I decided to build my house near his residence so that I could attend him whenever he needed me and return home whenever I left him. This house is now my dwelling and my resting place. In it my children reside and in it I compose my poetry and prose.

How I wrote the proclamations of the reconquest of Jerusalem [pp. 305, 313]

I had left the sultan when the army was besieging Beirut because of an illness that could not be cured there and for which I needed to go back to Damascus. When the sultan wanted to write a pledge of safe passage for the besieged, he asked for me, but I asked to be excused from this task because of my illness. The sultan brought all the other scribes and asked each of them to draft the document. He was dissatisfied with all of them and realized my talents and my superiority in composition. An envoy came to me and saw me in pain. He said, "Write this pledge of safe passage, for you are the best of scribes." I replied, "I do not feel well and I doubt I will be able to comply." Then I asked that God guide me to write the appropriate text and I did. I left for Damascus afterward and rejoined the sultan after the conquest of Jerusalem.

• • •

I arrived in Jerusalem on Saturday, the second day after the conquest [October 3, 1187]. The sultan's companions were pressuring him to order letters of proclamation to be carried to all the regions to announce the conquest. The sultan was reluctant to do so and told them, "For this task there is but one person; if only he could join us now that we need his writing talents." His scribes had gathered together to compose a letter, and were busy drafting it when I arrived. They all greeted me enthusiastically, especially the sultan, who said, "Your arrival today is another proof of the good omen of this conquest. This is your day! Prepare your pens and paper and draft me all the letters of proclamation, for all the provinces and regions are awaiting this great news!" In the course of that day I penned seventy letters, each more intricate and ornate than the last. Then I followed them that night with a number of letters in which I included all the details of the conquest, and I prefaced each with great praise for the conquest and the conqueror.

The Autobiography of ʿAbd al-Laṭīf al-Baghdādī

(1162–1231)

Introduction

Muwaffaq al-Dīn Abū Muḥammad ʿAbd al-Laṭīf ibn Yūsuf al-Baghdādī was a man of great learning who became well known for his expertise in many fields: grammar, lexicography, law, natural sciences, alchemy, philosophy, and, most notably, medicine. He was born in Baghdad in 1162 and died there in 1231 after an absence of forty-five years during which he traveled widely in the Islamic world. He had a succession of patrons and came into contact with a number of prominent military leaders, scholars, philosophers, and physicians, including Saladin, Maimonides, ʿImād al-Dīn al-Kātib al-Iṣfahānī (Saladin's personal secretary and a fellow autobiographer), and Ibn Sanāʾ al-Mulk.[1]

The *sīra,* or life narrative, of ʿAbd al-Laṭīf seems to have formed part of a larger work, no longer extant, entitled simply *taʾrīkh* (history or diary), which he wrote for his son.[2] Although it does not seem to have survived in toto, the *sīra* was used by Ibn Abī Uṣaybiʿa (d. 1270) in compiling his biographical dictionary of physicians. Similar to the autobiography of Ibn al-ʿAdīm as recorded by Yāqūt, the autobiography of ʿAbd al-Laṭīf survives as a composite of first-person extracts from his original text, interwoven with paraphrases and additional firsthand knowledge supplied by Ibn Abī Uṣaybiʿa, for ʿAbd al-Laṭīf was a close friend of his grandfather and a teacher of both his father and paternal uncle. In spite of conforming somewhat to the standard curriculum vitae model, it is clear from these fragments and those preserved in other works that ʿAbd al-Laṭīf's *sīra* was replete with insights and judgments about the places he lived and visited, the people he encountered, and the intellectual currents of his day. He notes, for example, that many of the best scholars of his era, including himself, were unduly preoccupied with alchemy (which he finally denounces toward the end of his autobiography); that were it not for the ineptitude of the attending physician, Saladin's death might have been averted; and that Maimonides, though extremely knowledgeable, was misguided and overly concerned about currying favor with his "worldly lords."

ʿAbd al-Laṭīf is a towering figure in the intellectual and scientific history of the Islamic Middle Ages. His autobiography, besides providing glimpses into the ingredients that make a scholar, is a record of the triumph of knowledge and learning even in times of turmoil, upheaval, and shifting alliances. The translation below contains most of the first-person passages preserved in the entry on ʿAbd al-Laṭīf in Ibn Abī Uṣaybiʿa's compendium.

Bibliography

Cahen, Claude. "ʿAbdallaṭīf al-Baghdādī, portraitiste et historien de son temps: Extraits inédits de ses Mémoires." *Bulletin d'Études Orientales* 23 (1970): 101–28.

Ibn Abī Uṣaybiʿa. *ʿUyūn al-anbāʾ fī ṭabaqāt al-aṭibbāʾ*. Ed. Nizār Riḍā. Beirut: Dār Maktabat al-Ḥayāt, 1965. 683–96.

Toorawa, Shawkat. "The Educational Background of ʿAbd al-Laṭīf al-Baghdādī." *Muslim Education Quarterly* 13, no. 3 (1996): 35–53.

———. "Language and Male Homosocial Desire in the Autobiography of ʿAbd al-Laṭīf al-Baghdādī." *Edebiyât: Special Issue—Arabic Autobiography*, N.S. 7, no. 2 (1997): 251–65.

Selections from the Autograph Notes of ʿAbd al-Laṭīf al-Baghdādī

[*ʿUyūn*, pp. 683–96]

[Ibn Abī Uṣaybiʿa writes]:

The learned master Muwaffaq al-Dīn Abū Muḥammad ʿAbd al-Laṭīf ibn Yūsuf ibn Muḥammad ibn ʿAlī ibn Abī Saʿd, known as Ibn Labbād. Town of family origin: Mosul. Birthplace: Baghdad.

Renowned for his polymathy and blessed with moral excellence, he was eloquent and prolific. He was distinguished in grammar and lexicography, and very knowledgeable in speculative theology and medicine. He devoted a great deal of attention to the craft of medicine when he was in Damascus and became famous as a result of this. A group of students and student physicians used to visit him frequently in order to study medical texts under his direction.

[Here follows a passage by Ibn Abī Uṣaybiʿa on ʿAbd al-Laṭīf's father and paternal uncle, their education, and their writings.]

He was a friend of my grandfather's: a strong friendship had developed between them when we lived in Egypt. My father and my uncle both studied the literary arts under his direction. My uncle also studied the books of Aristotle with him. ʿAbd al-Laṭīf himself was much interested in the works of Aristotle and their import. He came to Damascus from Egypt and stayed there for some time; his students learned a great deal from him. I saw him when he was living in Damascus the last time he was there: a thin, elderly man, of medium height, sweet voiced and expressive, whose writing was more eloquent than his tongue. Perhaps it was because he thought so highly of himself that he said inappropriate things—may God show him mercy! He found the men of learning of his time, and those of earlier times too, deficient in their scholarship, and he greatly disparaged many of the Persian scholars and their works, especially the Master, Avicenna, and others of his caliber.

I have copied the following verbatim from a manuscript, in his own hand, of the autobiography [*sīra*] he composed.

• • •

I was born in 557 [1162 C.E.] in a house that belonged to my grandfather on Falūdhaj Lane, and was raised and instructed under the care of Shaykh Abū al-Najīb. I knew neither pleasure nor leisure, and spent most of my time learning *ḥadīth*. Certificates of *ḥadīth* audition were obtained for me from professors in Baghdad, Khurasan, Syria, and Egypt. One day my father [proudly] declared: "I have given you the opportunity to learn *ḥadīth* directly from the top scholars of Baghdad and I have even had you included in the chains of transmission of the older Masters." I was learning calligraphic writing at that time and also memorizing the Qurʾān, the *Faṣīḥ* [a treatise on Arabic linguistics by Thaʿlab, d. 904], the *Maqāmāt* [picaresque tales by al-Ḥarīrī, d. 1122], the collected poems of al-Mutanabbī, an epitome on jurisprudence, another on grammar, and other works of this kind.

When I was old enough, my father took me to Kamāl al-Dīn ʿAbd al-Raḥmān al-Anbārī, who was, in those days, the Master of Masters in Baghdad. He was an old classmate of my father's from their days at the Niẓāmiyya law college, where they had studied law together. It was under his direction that I was to study the introduction to the *Faṣīḥ,* but I couldn't understand one bit of his continuous and considerable jabbering, even though his students seem pleased enough with it. So he said, "I avoid teaching younger boys and instead pass them on to my protégé al-Wajīh al-Wāsiṭī to study under his direction. If and when their situation improves, I then allow them to study with me."

Al-Wajīh, a blind man from a wealthy and virtuous family, was employed by some of the children of the Chief Master.[3] He welcomed me with open arms and taught me all day long, showing me kindness in many ways. I attended his study circle at the Ẓafariyya mosque, and he would teach me the commentaries and discuss them with me. Then he would read my lesson and favor me with his own comments. We would then leave the mosque and he would even help me memorize on the road home. When we reached his house, he would take out the books he himself was studying and I would memorize with him and help him memorize as well. We would then go to Kamāl al-Dīn, to whom he would recite and who would then comment on the lesson, while I listened. I trained in this way until I surpassed al-Wajīh in both memorization and comprehension, for I used to spend most of the night memorizing and reviewing. We continued in this way for a long time, with me affiliated to both the Master and the Master's Master. My memorizing got better, my recall improved, my understanding grew, my insights became more acute, and my mind became keener and more reliable.

The first thing I memorized was the *Lumaʿ* [a grammar by Ibn Jinnī, d. 1002], which I completed in eight months. I listened to a commentary on most of it, read by another, every day, and returned home to peruse the commentaries of al-Thamānīnī, al-Sharīf ʿUmar ibn Ḥamza, Ibn Barhān, and any others I could find. I explained the *Lumaʿ* to those pupils who preferred my instruction till I reached the point where I began to use up a whole notebook on each chapter without even completing a fraction of what I had to say.

[Here follows a description of ʿAbd al-Laṭīf's studies including references to more than twenty specific works, the time it took to memorize each, and the teacher with whom he studied that work, as well as more general references to various authors and disciplines.]

In the year 585 [1189], when there no longer remained in Baghdad anyone to win my heart or to satisfy my desires, or to help me resolve what was perplexing me, I went on to Mosul. I was disappointed there, but I did chance upon al-Kamāl Ibn Yūnus, who was an expert in mathematics and law, but only partially learned in the remaining fields of science. His love of alchemy and its practice had so drowned his intellect and his time that he dismissed and disdained everything else.

Large numbers of students flocked to me, and a number of teaching posts were offered to me. I chose the second-story law college of Ibn Muhājir and the Dār al-Ḥadīth located beneath it. I remained in Mosul for a year in continuous and uninterrupted independent study, day and night. The people of Mosul claimed they had never seen anyone before with such an expansive and rapid memory and possessed of such grave demeanor. [. . .]

When I got to Damascus I came upon a large group of scholars, gathered together through the generous patronage of Saladin, consisting of notables of Baghdad and the whole region. Among them were Jamāl al-Dīn ʿAbd al-Laṭīf, son of my former teacher Abū al-Najīb; a group from the Chief Master's family; Ibn Ṭalḥa, the secretary; members of the house of Ibn Juhayr; Ibn al-ʿAṭṭār, the vizier who was later executed; and Ibn Hubayra, the vizier. I also met al-Kindī al-Baghdādī, the grammarian, with whom I had many debates. He was an intelligent, sharp-witted, and wealthy professor, with a certain amount of influence, but who was quite taken with himself and offensive to his company. We had many debates and God—may He be exalted—permitted me to surpass him on many topics. I soon left his side, and my neglect offended him, even more so than people were offended by him!

In Damascus I produced a number of works. [Here follows an annotated list of six works with brief descriptions.]

In Damascus I again came across Professor ʿAbd Allāh Ibn Nāʾilī who had taken up residence at the western minaret. Gathered round him was a group of followers obsessed with him. People were divided into two camps, one for him and one against. Al-Khaṭīb al-Dawlaʿī, a notable of standing and principle, was against him. It was not long, however, before Ibn Nāʾilī had himself in quite a mess, at which time his enemies prevailed. He would lecture defending alchemy and philosophy, and talk against him soon increased. I used to get together with him and he would ask me to describe certain procedures so that he could record them, procedures I thought contemptible and trivial, but to which he attached great importance and to which he gave himself over completely. I saw through him, though. He was not at all what I had expected. I was thoroughly unimpressed by him and his methods. When I debated science with him, I found that he only had scraps of knowledge. One day I said to him, "If you had devoted the time you have wasted in the pursuit of the Craft to some of the Islamic or rational sciences, you would today be without equal, waited on hand and foot. This alchemy nonsense simply does not have the answers you seek."

I learned from his example and kept my distance from the evils of what befell him: "Contented is he who learns from others." So I pulled myself away, but not entirely. He set off to see Saladin on the outskirts of Acre to complain about al-Dawlaʿī. He returned sick and was taken to hospital, where he then died. Al-Muʿtamid, [Saladin's] marshal of Damascus, who was himself infatuated with alchemy, confiscated his books.

Then I myself set off on a journey, first to Jerusalem and then to the outskirts of Acre to see Saladin. I also met Bahāʾ al-Dīn Ibn Shaddād, [Saladin's] military judge at the time. My fame had reached him in Mosul, so he was most pleased to meet me and was quite attentive. "Let's go and meet ʿImād al-Dīn al-Kātib," he suggested, so we did. His tent was near Bahāʾ al-Dīn's.

ʿImād al-Dīn was writing a letter to the chancery of al-ʿAzīz in [the ornate] *thuluth* script, without so much as a rough draft! "This is a letter to your hometown," he said, and then proceeded to test me on some matters of speculative theology. Then he said: "Come with us to see al-Qāḍī al-Fāḍil," so we entered his presence. What I saw was a slight man, all skin and bones, simultaneously writing and dictating, the various shapes of the words playing upon his face and lips, mouthed from the force of his effort to produce them, as if he were writing with his whole body. Al-Qāḍī al-Fāḍil interrogated me about some of the Almighty's words: "Where is the apodosis of the particle 'when/if' in the Qur'ānic verse—'Until, when they arrive there, its gates will be opened and its keepers will say . . . ' [Q 39:71]? And where is the apodosis of 'if' in the verse—'If there were a Qur'ān with which mountains were moved . . . [Q 13:31]?'" He asked me about many other matters and yet, in spite of this, never once interrupted the flow of his writing or of his dictation. "Return to Damascus," he said, "and you will be provided for." I said that I preferred Egypt, upon which he replied: "The sultan is anxious about the Franks' capture of Acre and the slaying of Muslims there . . ." "But it simply must be Egypt," I insisted, so he wrote me a short note to his agent there.

When I entered Cairo, I was met by his agent, Ibn Sanā' al-Mulk. He was a most honorable man, of lofty status, powerful, whose commands were obeyed. He secured a renovated house for me, the defects all repaired, and supplied me with money and with a grain allowance. He then called in some government officials and introduced me as the guest of al-Qāḍī al-Fāḍil. I received gifts and kindnesses from people in every quarter. Every ten days or so a memorandum would come to the Egyptian chancery from al-Qāḍī al-Fāḍil outlining the requirements of state. In it would be a paragraph certifying the stipend earmarked for me. I taught and was resident at the mosque of the Chamberlain Lu'lu'—may he rest in peace.

My purpose in going to Egypt was to seek out three people: Yāsīn 'the Magician,' Maimonides the Jew, and Abū al-Qāsim al-Shāriʿī. As it turned out, all three came to me. Yāsīn I found to be absurd, a liar, and a conjuring cheat. He swore to al-Shāqānī's expertise in alchemy just as al-Shāqānī would swear to his. It was said of him that he could do things even the Prophet Moses was unable to do, that he could produce minted gold whenever he wished, of any quantity he wished, and of any minting he wished, and that he could turn the waters of the Nile into a tent in which he would then sit with his friends. He was most churlish.

When Maimonides came to see me, I found him to be tremendously learned, but overcome with the love of leadership and of service to worldly lords. One of his works was on medicine, based on the sixteen books of Galen and on five books by others. He took it upon himself not to alter a single word unless it was an "and" or a "so," and, in point of fact, copied sections in their entirety. He also wrote a work for the Jews titled *Kitāb al-*

Dalāla [Guide for the Perplexed] and cursed anyone who transcribed it into anything but Hebrew script.[4] I looked through it and found it to be an evil book that corrupted the articles of Law and Faith with elements he thought would reform them.

One day, when I was in the mosque with a number of people gathered around me, a master in ragged clothing entered. His face shone and his appearance was pleasing. The people in the gathering were in awe of him and showed him reverence. I finished what I had to say, and when the lecture was over, the imam of the mosque came up to me and said, "Do you know this master? This is Abū al-Qāsim al-Shāriʿī." I embraced him and said, "It is you I seek!" I took him to my house where we had food and spoke at length. I found him to be as excellent as one could wish and a sight to behold. His conduct was that of the wise and learned, his bearing likewise. He took little pleasure from the world, not involving himself with anything that would distract him from moral excellence. He became my constant companion and I found him to be learned in the books of the Ancients and of Abū Naṣr al-Fārābī. I did not trust any of those authors because I used to think that Avicenna had gained access to all philosophy and stuffed it all into his own books! When we engaged in debate, I would surpass him in disputation and the use of language, and he would surpass me in producing proofs and in the strength of his arguments. I was inflexible in not submitting to his enticements and did not abandon my stubborn and passionate resistance to his theorizing. But he began to present me with work after work by al-Fārābī and by Alexander Themistius to tame my aversions and to soften the tenor of my intransigence, until I began to incline toward him, hesitant, unsure which step to take next.

News spread that Saladin had concluded a treaty with the Franks and had returned to Jerusalem. I was driven by a need to see him, so I took what I could carry of the books of the Ancients and headed for Jerusalem. There I saw a great sovereign, generous, affectionate, and awesome to behold, who filled the hearts of those near and far with love. The members of his entourage emulated him, competing for acknowledgment. As the Almighty says: "And we shall remove from their hearts any lurking sense of injury" [Q 7:43]. The first night I entered his presence I found an assembly filled with men of learning, discussing numerous fields of knowledge. He listened attentively, contributed his opinion, and discussed how to build walls and dig trenches. He was well versed in this, and suggested innovations for every scheme. He was concerned about the rebuilding of Jerusalem's walls and about the digging of its trenches. He took this upon himself and personally carried stones on his shoulders. The majority of the populace, rich and poor, strong and weak alike, even ʿImād al-Kātib and al-Qāḍī al-Fāḍil, followed his example. He devoted himself to this from before sunrise to noon, then he returned to his tent, had his meal and rested. He would carry stones all afternoon and return in the evening, then spend most of the night planning what he would do the next day. Saladin granted me a stipend of thirty dinars a month from the Friday mosque treasury and his sons gave me stipends, as well, so that my monthly income amounted to one hundred dinars.

I returned to Damascus and devoted myself eagerly to my studies and my lecturing in the Friday mosque. The more assiduously I studied the books of the Ancients the more my desire for them increased, whereas my desire for the books of Avicenna waned. I came to realize the falsity of alchemy and to know the truth of the matter with regard to its concoctions, its lying inventors, the falsehoods they spread, and their deluding motivations. I was thus saved from two great, terribly ruinous and humiliating errors. My thanks to the Almighty for this redoubled, for many have been destroyed by the books of Avicenna and by alchemy!

Saladin entered Damascus, accompanied the pilgrimage caravan out of the city to bid it farewell, returned, and contracted a fever. He was bled by a man without any skill, so his strength gave out and he died before the fourteenth. Upon his body people found such signs as are found on prophets. I have never seen a ruler whose death so saddened the people. This was because he was loved by pious and profligate alike, by Muslim and non-Muslim.

His sons and associates scattered to the four winds and tore the realm to bits. Most of them left for Egypt, because of its great fertility and the sheer extent of its dominion. I stayed in Damascus, which was then under the rule of al-Malik al-Afḍal, Saladin's oldest son, until al-Malik al-ʿAzīz beseiged him with the help of the Egyptian army. But al-ʿAzīz was unable to get what he wanted from his brother, al-Afḍal. He was late leaving for Marj al-Ṣafar because of a colic that had overcome him. I went to see him after he had gotten over it and he allowed me to travel with him, providing for my needs, and more besides, from the treasury.

I stayed with Abū Qāsim [al-Shāriʿī]; we were inseparable morning till night, until he passed away. When his illness grew worse, and his head cold turned to pneumonia, I advised him to take medication, but he recited the following:

> I do not chase away the birds from trees
> whose fruit I know from experience is bitter.

Then I asked him about his pain and he said:

> More pain cannot be caused
> than that of the wound of a dying man.

My daily routine at that time was as follows: I taught Islamic sciences in the al-Azhar mosque from the break of day until the fourth hour. Midday, those who wished to study medicine and other subjects would come to me. And then at the end of the day, I would return to the al-Azhar mosque and teach other students. At night I would do my own studying. I did this until the death of al-Malik al-ʿAzīz. He was a generous young man, valorous, modest, and unable to say no. And he was, in spite of the tenderness of his years and being in the prime of his youth, wholly abstinent from worldly possessions and women.

• • •

[Ibn Abī Uṣaybiʿa completes his entry on ʿAbd al-Laṭīf al-Baghdādī in his own voice with the exception of one short passage that gives the precise dates for some of ʿAbd al-Laṭīf's travels. He notes that throughout these remaining years ʿAbd al-Laṭīf stayed in contact with Ibn Abī Uṣaybiʿa, sending him copies of each of his new books.

According to Ibn Abī ʿUṣaybiʿ, ʿAbd al-Laṭīf al-Baghdādī remained in Egypt until it was struck by a plague the likes of which he had never seen and about which he then wrote a book. In the political turmoil that ensued after Saladin's death, he left for Jerusalem, where he resided, taught, and wrote a number of books. He later traveled to Damascus, where he practiced as a physician and wrote his most famous books on medicine. Previous to this, Ibn Abī Uṣaybiʿa informs us, he had been known primarily as a grammarian. He then traveled to Aleppo and to Turkey, where he enjoyed the patronage of King ʿAlāʾ al-Dīn Dāwūd ibn Bahrām of Erzinjān for a number of years. He traveled for several months in central Turkey, returned one last time to Aleppo, and finally died in Baghdad after an absence of forty-five years and was buried in his father's grave.]

Notes

1. Author of *Dār al-ṭirāz,* the most important medieval treatise on the *muwashshaḥ* poetry of Islamic Spain.

2. Ibn Abī ʿUṣaybiʿa's work has been edited numerous times. The most recent complete edition is *ʿUyūn al-anbāʾ fī ṭabaqāt al-aṭibbāʾ,* ed. Muḥammad Bāsil ʿUyūn al-Sūd (Beirut: Dār al-Kutub al-ʿIlmiyya, 1998). ʿAbd al-Laṭīf's autobiography is found at pp. 634–48. Another version of the autobiography is currently being edited and translated by Dimitri Gutas and corresponds in part to the entry on ʿAbd al-Laṭīf in *ʿUyūn al-anbāʾ.* Pers. comm. April 5, 1998, and February 13, 2000.

3. *Raʾīs al-ruʾasāʾ;* on the nuances of the term, see Roy Mottahedeh, *Loyalty and Leadership in an Early Islamic Society* (Princeton: Princeton University Press, 1980), 130–35; and Makdisi, *The Rise of Colleges,* 130–31.

4. Maimonides, *A Guide for the Perplexed,* trans. E. F. Schumacher (New York: Harper and Row, 1977).

The Autobiography of Ibn al-ʿAdīm

(1192/93–1262)

Introduction

When Yāqūt—the most prolific compiler of biographies of his age—set out to write the biographical notice for his close friend Ibn al-ʿAdīm, he first asked Ibn al-ʿAdīm to write out a history of his family and of himself. Ibn al-ʿAdīm assented to his friend's request and in the space of a week wrote a book of ten fascicles; it is probable that he drew on other previously written texts as sources for this work. The final section of this family history was an account of his own life. Yāqūt read the book written for him by Ibn al-ʿAdīm and questioned him further on several points in person. He also gathered supplementary material from various members of the family and other persons in Aleppo. After drafting his "biography" of Ibn al-ʿAdīm—using many verbatim passages from Ibn al-ʿAdīm's autobiography—he had Ibn al-ʿAdīm review the text personally and give his explicit approval of the final product.

The text as it has come down to us is thus an autobiography by Ibn al-ʿAdīm *as told to* Yāqūt, with a mixture of many different voices, the result of an active collaboration between autobiographer and biographer. It is a complex text but one that is fascinating not only for the life that is portrayed therein but also for the light it sheds on the processes of biography and autobiography at the eve of the Mongol invasions. Both Yāqūt the biographer and Ibn al-ʿAdīm the autobiographer demonstrate clear concern with establishing the historical facts and documenting the authority by which those facts have been transmitted. Although Ibn al-ʿAdīm's own writing forms the foundation of the text, Yāqūt seeks out and quotes external sources for critical points, such as the statement that every male in Ibn al-ʿAdīm's family for many generations had memorized the entire

Qur'ān. Ibn al-ʿAdīm reports this on the authority of his paternal uncle, who reported it from his father (Ibn al-ʿAdīm's grandfather), who reported it from his own father (Ibn al-ʿAdīm's great-grandfather); Yāqūt then verifies this claim by checking various reputable sources in Aleppo, one of whom he then quotes. Ibn al-ʿAdīm shows equal concern with historical accuracy and authority when, for example, he carefully cites two slightly different accounts of how the family originally came to move from Basra to Aleppo.

Yāqūt also seeks out sources for material that Ibn al-ʿAdīm was not in a position to report. Thus we are presented with portions of an oral interview conducted with the tutor of Ibn al-ʿAdīm's children who had also been a close companion of Ibn al-ʿAdīm's deceased father. It is through his voice that we hear of the tragic early death of Ibn al-ʿAdīm's brother, of the dramatic cemetery scene in which the father—driven nearly mad with grief—digs up the grave of his son with his bare hands in an attempt to hold the boy's body in his arms one final time, and, finally, of the vision that foretells the birth of Ibn al-ʿAdīm and his future success.

Reflections of the uncertain fate of young children are found at several points in the text: the early death of Ibn al-ʿAdīm's brother, the father's statement that at first he was not attached to Ibn al-ʿAdīm because he was so skinny (i.e., not likely to survive), and the teacher's conditional prediction about Ibn al-ʿAdīm on his first day at school ("*If this child lives,* no one will be able to compete with his [calligraphic] writing").

Ibn al-ʿAdīm eventually achieved the success foretold in his father's vision. He became a well-known historian and wrote not only a history of Aleppo but also a forty-volume biographical dictionary of people associated with Aleppo. (Both Ibn al-ʿAdīm and Yāqūt were historians, biographers, and autobiographers, though Yāqūt's autobiography has not survived.) Ibn al-ʿAdīm also rose to become a ranking diplomat and served as an emissary to the ʿAbbāsid court in Baghdad in 1257, one year before it was sacked by the Mongols, and then to the Mamluk court in Cairo to seek help in fending off the Mongol invasion that then threatened Aleppo. Following the Mamluk defeat of the Mongol forces at ʿAyn Jālūt in 1260, he visited Aleppo one last time and composed a long poem describing its devastation. Unable to bear living among the wasted ruins of his hometown, he moved to Egypt, where he died a year later, in 1262. These intellectual and diplomatic achievements, however, are not found in Yāqūt's text, for it was written when Ibn al-ʿAdīm was only thirty-one years old and Yāqūt died before Ibn al-ʿAdīm achieved his most prominent accomplishments. Ibn al-ʿAdīm is therefore portrayed here primarily as a promising young scholar from a prestigious family, a prolific author, and an accomplished calligrapher.[1]

Several points of personal detail in the autobiographical passages communicate a more intimate tone than most of the biographical entries in Yāqūt's compendium; the childhood memories of school, the story of how Ibn al-ʿAdīm's father offered him money to memorize more books, the portrayal of his close relationship with his father, and the reference to his failed first marriage all would probably not have been included in a purely biographical entry. Otherwise, however, the account of his youth reflects standard educational practices of the day, a childhood devoted to memorizing works and reciting them back to reputable teachers, an adolescence spent furthering his education and his skill in calligraphic writing [*khaṭṭ*], and a young adulthood spent producing his first publications. At the close of the entry, Yāqūt shifts to his own voice to recount Ibn al-ʿAdīm's appointment to the Shādhbakht academy at a surprisingly young age, to list Ibn al-ʿAdīm's writings, and finally to cite a poem by Ibn al-ʿAdīm followed by a responding poem by himself praising his friend. It is this final poem that indicates that Ibn al-ʿAdīm was thirty-one years old at the time this entry was being compiled.

Along with intimate details of Ibn al-ʿAdīm's life, Yāqūt includes a number of poems composed by Ibn al-ʿAdīm that shed additional light on his life and personality. These poems, the contents of which evolve over the course of the text from externalized referents to ones of a more personal and emotional nature, imbue the auto/biography with additional psychological impact. The interplay between the two roots *N-ʿ-M* (blessings, bounty) and *ʿ-D-M* (destitution, deprivation) is a motif that recurs in both the poetry and the prose of the text, demonstrating that the poetry is integral to the text as a whole. It is also closely tied to Yāqūt's curious opening question regarding the family's name, the Banū ʿAdīm (Sons of the Destitute). Ibn al-ʿAdīm's denial that the name was ancestral makes clear that the issue carried immediate and personal import; indeed, it seems clear that there was no Banū ʿAdīm family, as modern scholars have assumed, but rather a single Ibn al-ʿAdīm (Son of the Destitute). The text lingers over Ibn al-ʿAdīm's father and in many ways is devoted to the psychological portrayal of a son determined to rise above the tribulations and trials suffered by his father (the losses of the judgeship of Aleppo and of his firstborn son) and to continue the older, more august strain of the family's history.

In this translation, all passages reported in Ibn al-ʿAdīm's voice appear in boldface. The text opens with a list of the generations of Ibn al-ʿAdīm's family back to ʿAdnān, legendary progenitor of the northern Arabs. The following chart shows the fourteen most recent generations of Ibn al-ʿAdīm's family.

Abū Jarāda
[Eponymous ancestor of the clan and companion
to the fourth caliph, ʿAlī ibn Abī Ṭālib]
|
Muḥammad
|
ʿAbd Allāh
|
ʿĪsā
|
Mūsā
[ancestor who first moves from Basra to Aleppo]
|
Muḥammad—Hārūn—ʿAbd Allāh
|
Zuhayr
|
Yaḥyā
|
Aḥmad
|
Hibat Allāh
|
Muḥammad
|
Hibat Allāh
|
Aḥmad
|
Kamāl al-Dīn Abū al-Qāsim ʿUmar, known as Ibn al-ʿAdīm

Bibliography

Khoury, Nuha N. N. "The Autobiography of Ibn al-ʿAdīm as Told to Yāqūt al- Rūmī." *Edebiyât: Special Issue—Arabic Autobiography,* N.S. 7, no. 2 (1997): 289–311.

Lewis, Bernard. "Ibn al-ʿAdīm." *EI²* 3:695–96.

Morray, David. *An Ayyubid Notable and His World: Ibn al-ʿAdīm and Aleppo as Portrayed in His Biographical Dictionary of People Associated with the City.* Leiden: E. J. Brill, 1994.

Yāqūt al-Rūmī. *Irshād al-arīb ilā maʿrifat al-adīb (Muʿjam al-udabāʾ).* Ed. D. S. Margoliouth. 7 vols. Cairo: Hindiyya Press, 1907–26.

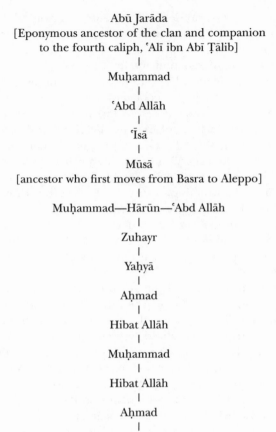

ʿUmar ibn Aḥmad ibn Abī Jarāda, known as Ibn al-ʿAdīm
[*Irshād,* pp. 18–46]

From the ʿUqaylī tribe. His agnomen is Abū al-Qāsim and his surname is Kamāl al-Dīn. He is one of the notables and elite of Aleppo. His full name is ʿUmar, son of Aḥmad, son of Hibat Allāh, son of Muḥammad, son of Hibat Allāh, son of Aḥmad, son of Yaḥyā, son of Zuhayr, son of Hārūn, son of Mūsā, son of ʿĪsā, son of ʿAbū Allāh, son of Muḥammad, son of Abū Jarāda, one of the companions of the caliph ʿAlī ibn Abī Ṭālib—may God's blessings be upon him. Abū Jarāda's full name was ʿĀmir, son of Rabīʿa, son of Khuwaylid, son of ʿAwf, son of ʿĀmir, son of ʿUqayl (father of the tribe of the Ibn Kaʿb), son of ʿĀmir, son of Ṣaʿṣaʿa, son of Muʿāwiya, son of Bakr, son of Hawāzin, son of Manṣūr, son of ʿIkrima, son of Ḥafsa, son of Qays, son of ʿAylān Muḍar, son of Nizār, son of Maʿadd, son of ʿAdnān.

The Banū Jarāda house is a famous Aleppan family of literati, poets, jurists, pious worshipers, and judges who inherit nobility and virtue from earlier generations and pass them on to later ones. Before I begin my account of Ibn al-ʿAdīm, I will first report on the history of his family and some of its most famous members, after which I will give an account of him, copying the information from a book Ibn al-ʿAdīm composed—may God extend his life—that he titled *al-Akhbār al-mustafāda fī dhikr Banī Jarāda* [A Useful History of the Banī Jarāda Family]. I have read this [account of his life] back to him and he has approved it.

First I asked him: Why is your family called the Banū al-ʿAdīm [lit. "Sons of the Destitute"]?

Ibn al-ʿAdīm replied: **I have inquired among my family about that and they do not know. It is a recent name, not an ancestral one. My best guess is that my great-grandfather, the judge Abū al-Faḍl Hibat Allāh, son of Aḥmad, son of Yaḥyā, son of Zuhayr, son of Abū Jarāda, though he had great wealth and lived in complete contentment [*niʿma shāmila*], often spoke of destitution [Ar. ʿ*adam*] and complained of the tribulations of time in his poetry, and so was named accordingly. I can think of no reason other than this.**[2]

Ibn al-ʿAdīm said to me: **My uncle Jamāl al-Dīn Abū Ghānim Muḥammad, son of Hibat Allāh, told me, "When I had memorized the Qurʾān, my father—may he rest in peace—kissed me between the eyes, wept, and said, 'Thanks be to God, my son. This is exactly what I had hoped for and expected from you. Your grandfather told me that among our forefathers, going all the way back to the Prophet—upon whom be peace—there was no one among us who did not memorize the entire Qurʾān.' "**

The author [Yāqūt] says: This is an honorable trait the like of which I do not know of among other men. I inquired about its veracity among the people of Aleppo and they assured me that it is true. Zayn al-Dīn Muḥammad, son of ʿAbd al-Qāhir al-Niṣṣībī, told me: "Forget about the past and look to the present for proof. For I can count for you each living member of the Banū Jarāda family, and there is not one among them who has not completely memorized the Qur'ān." He started listing them one by one, and not a single one among them broke this rule.

Ibn al-ʿAdīm—may God extend his life—told me: **The descendants of the Banū Abī Jarāda used to live in Basra, in the Banū ʿUqayl quarter there. The first [of our family] to move away from Basra was Mūsā, son of ʿĪsā, son of ʿAbd Allāh, son of Muḥammad son of ʿĀmir, who, after the year 200 [815], came to Aleppo for trade.**

Ibn al-ʿAdīm told me: **My uncle Abū Ghānim Muḥammad, son of Hibat Allāh, son of Muḥammad, descendant of Abū Jarāda, also told me, "I heard my father mention, based on information he received from his forefathers, that our ancestor had come from Basra to Syria on business and settled in Aleppo." [My uncle also] said, "I heard my father say that he heard that when Basra was visited by the plague, a group of the Banū ʿUqayl left it and went to Syria, and our ancestor settled in Aleppo." [My uncle also] said, "The sons of Mūsā[3] were Muḥammad, Hārūn and ʿAbd Allāh. Muḥammad had a son named ʿAbd Allāh, and I do not know whether or not this ʿAbd Allāh had any progeny. Those who are alive today are the descendants of Hārūn, our own ancestor, and of ʿAbd Allāh, and these latter are our uncles."**

[Here follow several pages on the individual descendants of both ʿAbd Allāh and Hārūn, all extracted from Ibn al-ʿAdīm's *Useful History*. Yāqūt closes the account of the family with a notice on the life of Ibn al-ʿAdīm's father and then turns his attention to Ibn al-ʿAdīm himself.][4]

This is what I [Yāqūt] copied in summary form from the book I mentioned earlier, and these are but a sampling of this family's many virtues. Now I will mention my subject, Kamāl al-Dīn Abū al-Qāsim ʿUmar, son of the Judge Abū al-Ḥasan Aḥmad, son of the Judge Abū al-Faḍl Hibat Allāh, son of the Judge Abū Ghānim Muḥammad, son of the Judge Abū Saʿīd Hibat Allāh, son of the Judge Abū al-Ḥasan Aḥmad descendant of Abū Jarāda. All of these ancestors of his were judges of the Ḥanafī school of law in Aleppo and its dependencies, and he is our current subject.

[Passage in rhymed prose praising Ibn al-ʿAdīm][5]

I asked Ibn al-ʿAdīm—may God preserve his exalted state—about his birth and he told me: **I was born in the month of Dhū al-Ḥijja in the year**

588 [= December 1192]. When I was seven years old I was taken to [Qur'ān] school and seated in front of the teacher who began instructing me as one would instruct a little child, drawing a line and placing three [letter] *S*'s upon it. I took the pen from him and, having seen him write the word *bism* and extend it, I did the same so that my writing resembled his own.[6] Surprised, the teacher turned to those around him and said, "If this child lives, no one will be able to compete with his writing."

[Yāqūt notes]: By my life, the teacher's prophecy has come true, for his writing is certainly better than that of all those who came before him as far back as Ibn al-Bawwāb.[7]

Ibn al-ʿAdīm said: **I finished memorizing the Qur'ān when I was nine years old, and could recite the Qur'ān in all ten variant readings when I was ten. Penmanship and calligraphy [*khaṭṭ*] appealed to me and my father encouraged me to pursue this.**

The teacher of Ibn al-ʿAdīm's son, Shaykh Yūsuf, son of ʿAlī, son of Zayd al-Zuhrī al-Maghribī al-Adīb, told me in Ibn al-ʿAdīm's presence: This man's father (and he pointed to Ibn al-ʿAdīm) told me, "A number of girls had been born to me, but I had only one son. This son was extremely good-looking, handsome, intelligent, and bright, and he had memorized a good portion of the Qur'ān by the time he was five. One day I happened to be sitting in a room of ours that overlooked the street when a funeral procession passed by. That child watched the procession, then turned to me and said: 'Father, if I were to die, what would you cover my coffin with?' I scolded him, but felt extremely worried about him at that moment.

"No more than a few days passed before he fell ill and passed on to God's mercy and joined his Lord. I was stricken with grief over his death as no father has ever been stricken for the death of a child. I stopped eating and drinking, and sat in a darkened room enjoining myself to be steadfast, but I could not endure his loss. In my extreme grief, I went to his grave and dug it up myself, and I intended to take him out and console myself by seeing him again. It was due to God's will and His kindness, to either the child or to me—lest I see what I would not like—that I encountered a large rock that I could not remove no matter how hard I tried despite the strength for which I was well known. When I noted that moving the rock was beyond me, I realized that this was from God's pity on the child or on me. So I chided myself and, after returning his grave to its previous state, I went home filled with feelings of loss and longing.

"Afterward I saw the child in a dream, and he was saying, 'Father, let my mother know that I want to come to you.' I awoke startled and informed his mother of what I had seen. We cried and invoked God's mercy and said, 'We are God's and to Him we shall return.' Then, in my sleep, I had a vision of a [shaft of] light that appeared to come out of my male member and hang above our houses and the entire quarter, rising up to a great height. When I woke up, I had the vision interpreted and I was told, 'Rejoice, for this is news of a newborn who will be of prodigious worth and great importance, whose renown will be as great among people as the greatness of the light that appeared to you.' So I rejoiced in God, Almighty and Exalted, and I invoked and thanked Him. I fortified myself after my despair, for I had exceeded the age of forty.

"A short time later, the mother of this boy—my son (and he pointed to Ibn al-ʿAdīm—may God always support him)—completed her term and gave birth to him on the aforementioned date. But he was at first not as sweet to my heart as my first son had been, for he was very skinny. As he grew older, however, he grew in stature and worth, and I invoked God many times regarding him. I asked God for many things for him, and—thanks be to God—I have seen most of these requests realized in him."

[The teacher added]: One day in my presence a man said to [Ibn al-ʿAdīm's father], as people are wont to say, "May God give you the pleasure of seeing him a judge like his forefathers before him!" He said, "I do not want that for him. My desire is that he should become a teacher." [Yāqūt notes]: God fulfilled that wish after his [i.e., Ibn al-ʿAdīm's father's] death.

[Yāqūt, summarizing from the *Useful History,* writes:] He heard *ḥadīth* from a number of people in Aleppo, some who are settled there and others who were passing through. He also heard much from al-Shaykh al-Sharīf Iftikhār al-Dīn ʿAbd al-Muṭṭalib al-Hāshimī. Twice, in 603 [1206/7] and 608 [1211/12], his father took him to Jerusalem, where he met a number of shaykhs, and he also met shaykhs in Damascus. On both trips he read much of what one now hears from him with Tāj al-Dīn Abī al-Yumn.

Ibn al-ʿAdīm—may God preserve his high worth—told me: **My father told me, "If you memorize the *Lumaʿ*, I will give you such and such." I memorized it and read it to the Aleppan shaykh of the day who was al-Ḍiyāʾ ibn Duhn al-Ḥaṣā. Then he told me, "If you memorize al-Qudūrī, I will give you a good amount of money as well." I memorized it quickly.**[8]

During that time I used to practice calligraphic writing. My father—may he rest in peace—used to encourage me in that, polishing the paper for me himself. I remember one time when we were out at a village of ours and he ordered me to write, whereby I said, "There is no good paper here." So he took some low-quality paper that we had and some ceruse mixture we had with us, and polished the paper with it himself, saying to me, "Write!" His own handwriting was not particularly good, but he knew the principles of calligraphy and used to tell me, "This is good, and this is bad."

He had samples in the hand of Ibn Bawwāb in his possession and used to point out its principles and rules to me until I perfected it to my satisfaction. I did not study calligraphic writing with any renowned teacher, but Tāj al-Dīn Muḥammad, son of Aḥmad, son of al-Birfatī al-Baghdādī, came

to visit us in Aleppo and I wrote under his direction for a few days, but got no additional benefit from him.

Later on, my father—may he rest in peace—got me engaged and married me to a woman from the elite of Aleppo, and he took the family the gifts customary on such occasions. But things happened between us [i.e., the woman and Ibn al-ʿAdīm] that caused constraint to my heart. So my father let them keep those gifts and I got divorced. After that, he got me married to the daughter of the great shaykh Bahāʾ al-Dīn Abū al-Qāsim ʿAbd al-Majīd, son of al-Ḥasan, son of ʿAbd Allāh, known as al-ʿAjamī ["the Persian"], who is the head of the Shafiʿite community and among the wealthiest, most prestigious, and highest-ranking people in Aleppo. My father sent them the bridal gift and was exceedingly generous and kind.

My father—may he rest in peace—was extremely kind and generous to me. He enjoyed nothing more in the world than seeing to my affairs, and he used to say, "My wish is [to live long enough] to see you with a son and to see him [old enough to] walk." My son Aḥmad was born and my father saw him. My father lived to a ripe old age and then fell ill with his final illness. The day he died, the child walked [for the first time] and fell upon his breast, and then my father died, on the aforementioned date.

Al-Malik al-Ẓāhir Ghāzī, son of Saladin, ruler of Aleppo—may he rest in peace—used to show me great honor. Whenever I was at his court, he never treated anyone better than he treated me, despite my youth.

In the year 618 [1220/21], I happened to fall ill, and people despaired for my life. But during that illness it occurred to me that God Almighty would no doubt restore my health, for I had confidence in the vision my father had seen; I would say, "I have not yet achieved a position that would fulfill that vision." When God—thanks be to Him—generously restored my health, I forgot all about those imaginings, and I no longer think about them, for God's blessings enfold me and His hand continuously supports my rights.

[At this point there appears to be a conflation between Yāqūt's voice and that of Ibn al-ʿAdīm, perhaps as a result of summarizing from the autobiographical section of the *Useful History;* the passage starts in the first-person voice but soon shifts to the third person, possibly so that Yāqūt could add the passages of praise that could not, for modesty's sake, be included in Ibn al-ʿAdīm's own voice.]

I say: Some time after my father died, the Shādhbakht academy's professor of law passed away as well, the Shādhbakht being the most esteemed and important of Aleppo's academies. He [i.e., Ibn al-ʿAdīm] was then appointed professor there in the month of Dhū al-Ḥijja 615 [1219], at the age of twenty-eight. Even though Aleppo was teeming with jurists, scholars, shaykhs, and other learned persons, he alone was considered capable enough and deserving enough of that position. He achieved prominence and lectured with a strong heart and sharp tongue, and he mesmerized the audience and pleased them.

Despite his youth, he has written many books, among which is the *Kitāb al-Darārī fī dhikr al-dharārī* [The Book of Pearls on the Mentioning of Offspring] that he compiled for [the above-mentioned ruler] al-Malik al-Ẓāhir and which he presented to him on the day his son, al-Malik al-ʿAzīz, Aleppo's current sultan, was born. He had also compiled the *Kitāb Ḍawʾ al-ṣabāḥ fī al-ḥathth ʿalā al-samāḥ* [The Book of Morning Light on Provoking Generosity] for al-Malik al-Ashraf who had sent for him from Harran; after he saw a sample of Ibn al-ʿAdīm's writing, he desired to meet him. Ibn al-ʿAdīm went to him and al-Malik al-Ashraf treated him well and honored him, and bestowed a robe of honor upon him.

He also compiled the *al-Akhbār al-mustafāda fī dhikr Banī Jarāda* [Useful History of the Abī Jarāda Family]. I asked him to do this, and in the space of a week he did so. It is ten fascicles in length. He also has a book on calligraphy concerning its principles, requirements, rules, pens and papers, as well as the *ḥadīth* and bons mots that have been said about it. It is still incomplete at this time.

[Also] *Kitāb Taʾrīkh Ḥalab* [History of Aleppo], a history of Aleppo's kings and rulers, its founding, and an account of the scholars who lived in it and those scholars of *ḥadīth* and religious knowledge who came to it, as well as its kings, princes, and authors.

[Here follows a passage in rhymed prose by Yāqūt in praise of Ibn al-ʿAdīm and his writing, followed by his account of the monetary worth of the latter.]

He became renowned throughout the land, and his calligraphy was famed among those near and far. It became a gift among kings, like precious pearls strung on strings. In his own lifetime he is considered an exemplar, an ideal for all his contemporaries.

One reason people seek samples of his calligraphic writing is that one day he bought a single sheet of Ibn al-Bawwāb's writing for forty dirhams. He copied it on a piece of antique paper and gave it as a gift to [the bookseller] Ḥaydar al-Kutubī, who claimed that it was in the hand of Ibn al-Bawwāb himself and later sold it for sixty dirhams, twenty dirhams more than the price of the authentic sample of Ibn al-Bawwāb!

Ibn al-ʿAdīm wrote this text for me in his own hand, and contemporary scribes have offered me an Egyptian dinar for it, knowing that it is in his hand, but I cannot bring myself to sell it. He also wrote a piece in thirteen columns for me that he had copied from a sample by Ibn al-Bawwāb. I was offered forty Nāṣirī dirhams for it—the equivalent of four gold dinars—but I did not sell it. I know for a fact that Ibn al-Bawwāb's writing was never so highly valued during his own lifetime, nor did anyone pay such prices for it.

[Here follows another section concerning Ibn al-ʿAdīm's calligraphic writing, followed by several samples of his poetry translated below.]

[Yāqūt writes]: [Ibn al-ʿAdīm]—may God cause his high status to endure—recited for me a love poem in which he used a curious motif:

Slender and honey-lipped, I imagined that
  in his cheeks was a press [*ʿāṣir*] for wine,
That causes the most delicious of wines to flow to his mouth,
  a nectar that over years [*aʿāṣir*] has been aged.
From this his figure grows drunk and unsteady,
  he sways haughtily, with languid eyes,
As if the prince of sleep were lowering his eyelids,
  when he attempts to raise them, his eyes decline.
I was alone with him after all his people had retired,
  the stars of Gemini slipped away and the night protected us.
My palm was his pillow and he slept in my embrace,
  until the morning's pure light first appeared.
Then he arose, casting off the night's chill, untouched,
  and I rose as well, having given no cause for rebuke.
This is the sweetest form of love, for its ending was
  blameless, a tryst unsullied by guilt.

[Ibn al-ʿAdīm] himself recited for me in his home in Aleppo [these verses] in the month of Dhū al-Ḥijja, 619 [1222], and he dictated [them to me]:

She of bewitching eyes and honeyed deep-red lips,
  Her mouth bestows a cure for every thirst.
She arched her brows at me and loosed
  arrows from her eyes into my soul.
A wonder is her [sweet] saliva, so pure
  and permitted, yet now it is forbidden to me.
If it were wine, what wine could possess its color
  and its flavor? Though I have never tasted either.
She has a residence in the district of my heart, its place
  is well-guarded there, ever since she made it her own.
Her love's course is the flow of my life, intermixed
  is her love with my soul, my flesh, and my blood.
"How long will you live so unhappy," she says to me,
  "content in not becoming whole, resigned?

Go seek your fortune in God's [wide] lands,
perchance you will find a rescuer if you wish, or, if you wish, an accuser."
I said to her, "He who created Mankind
has graciously blessed and secured for me sustenance.
It does me no harm to be lord only of virtues
and knowledge, strong-willed, free and respected.
If I am made destitute [*ʿudimat kifāya*] of wealth and fortune,
my soul is safeguarded from humiliation and deprivation.
I have not dedicated my life to serving knowledge
in order to serve those I meet, but in order to be served."

[Yāqūt comments:] Whoever reads these lines should not be deluded into thinking that the author of these verses is of poor or modest means; quite the reverse, for he—may God protect him!—is the owner of extensive villages and many estates; he possesses great wealth, many slaves and serving women, horses and livestock, fine clothes and robes. Take for example the fact that following his father's death he paid thirty thousand dirhams for a house that had once belonged to his family. But he is expansive of spirit and a man with high ambitions; verily, the desires of this world are in proportion to those who crave them, and the yearnings for them are in proportion to those who seek them. [Ibn al-ʿAdīm] also recited for me at his home on the same date [the following verses]:

Beware your paternal cousin, for he is [as two-faced] as a book [*muṣaḥḥaf*]
and your close relative, for he is as crooked [*aḥraf*] as letters [*uḥruf*].
The letter *qaf* is for the grave [*qabr*] he digs for you,
the letter *rāʾ* is the death [*radā*] he plots for you.
The letter *yāʾ* is your perpetual despair [*yaʾs*] that any good might come of him,
the letter *bāʾ* is the ever-present hatred [*baghd*] you get from him.
Accept this advice as a gift from me,
for when it comes to cousins, I know best![9]

[Ibn al-ʿAdīm] also recited for me in his home, emulating others of his relatives in their family pride:

I shall force myself to pardon all wrongs committed against me
and shall forgive them as an act of nobility and generosity.
I shall use my wealth, as well as my honor, as a protective safeguard,
even if this does not leave me with a single dirham.
I shall follow the paths of the most righteous, those who earned their high rank
and attained it from whomsoever approached through their good deeds.
These are my people, great benefactors, men of power,
the Banū ʿĀmir—so ask about them so that you may learn [of them].
Whenever they are called during times of trouble, when the situation is grim,
with their speech they cast light upon what was in darkness.

Whenever they sit in the gathering to make judgment they are like
full moons in the darkness and the others around them like stars.
Whenever they ascend the pulpit to deliver a sermon,
they are more eloquent than any who ever in preaching spoke.
Whenever they pick up their pens to write,
they are better than any who ever ornamented a page.
Their words clarify their excellence
and their judgments have made the religious law secure.
Their invocations [to God] remove tribulations when they occur,
and bring down drops of water from the heavens' horizons.
A woman [wife?] says to me: "O Ibn al-ʿAdīm [Son of the Destitute] how long
shall you be so generous with all you possess? You'll be destitute [*muʿdam*]!"
So I said to her: "Leave me be!
for I believe that the best of people are the generous [*munʿim*].
I reject meanness, [for] I am of noble origin, from a family
of the ʿUqayla tribe, who radiate with generosity and munificence.

Ibn al-ʿAdīm recited to me the following verses that he had composed when he noted his first gray hairs, at the age of thirty-one:

Dawn on the horizon is but a sign or mark
of the passage of night and its period of dark,
So also does youthful growth come close to dryness
when in its [dark] field there first appears brightness.

One day I went to [Ibn al-ʿAdīm] and he said to me, "Do you not see, I am now but thirty-one years old, and I have just found some white hairs in my beard." So I said of him:

Congratulations, [Ibn al-ʿAdīm], for a virtue that you like
and a blessing of which no one before you has received the like,
Your forehead is busy its youth to assure
while the attainment of noble goals remains your cynosure,
At this decade of your life you have become complete
in glory with which your elders cannot compete,
When with wisdom and understanding you matured
your beneficence was perfected with white hair, premature.[10]

Notes

1. The terms *kataba* and *kitāba* ("to write" and "writing"), often used with reference to the quality of Ibn al-ʿAdīm's handwriting, also emphasize the fact that he was a prolific author, another possible interpretation of his teacher's statement: "If this child lives, no one will be able to compete with his writing" (*la yakūn fī al-ʿālam aktab minhu*). Other terms used in the text in reference to his writing are *khaṭṭ* (tracing, inscribing) and *tajwīd* (perfecting, beautifying).

2. In fact, no other member of the family is known by this name, whether in

Yāqūt's biographical compendium or elsewhere. This suggests that the name was even more recent than Ibn al-ʿAdīm implies and that it was attached primarily to him because of his father who had suffered great losses in his life and career. This explains why Ibn al-ʿAdīm could not find any explanation for it. It also explains why the issue was considered important enough to be raised and included in the account. From the outset, Yāqūt allows his subject to rationalize a name that is the antithesis of *niʿma,* the blessings that autobiographers often cite as a reason for writing accounts of their lives.

3. Ibn al-ʿAdīm's great-great-great-great-great-great-great-grandfather.

4. Yāqūt al-Rūmī, *Irshād al-arīb ilā maʿrifat al-adīb (Muʿjam al-udabāʾ,* ed. D. S. Margoliouth (Cairo: Hindiyya Press, 1907–26), 6:20–35.

5. Ibid., 35–36.

6. *Bism* means "in the name of" and is the first word of the *basmalah* [*bism Allāh al-raḥmān al-raḥīm*], "In the name of God the All-Merciful, the All-Compassionate," a favorite subject for calligraphic art and commonly placed at the top of the opening page of any piece of writing.

7. Ibn Bawwāb (d. 1022) is the copyist of the first known cursive-script Qurʾān manuscript (Chester Beatty Library, 1431, dated A.H. 391/1000–1 C.E.). His achievement, according to the medieval commentators, was to refine the methods invented by Ibn Muqla, investing the script with "elegance and splendor." Ibn Muqla (d. 940), who also appears in Yāqūt's entry on Ibn al-ʿAdīm, is the ʿAbbāsid minister who reformed Qurʾānic scripts through the invention of the "six pens," or types of writing. This reform replaced the older Qurʾānic scripts with new ones whose primary qualities were clarity and precision. An important study of these reforms, which places them within the context of ʿAbbāsid-Fatimid polemics, is Yasser Tabbaa, "The Transformation of Arabic Writing: Part I, Qurʾānic Calligraphy," *Ars Orientalis* 21 (1991): 119–48. Nuha N. N. Khoury is currently preparing a study on the implications of the text for the aesthetics and meaning of Ibn al-ʿAdīm's writing.

8. Al-Qudūrī (d. 1037) is the author of *al-Mukhtaṣar,* one of two foundational texts on *Ḥanafī* jurisprudence (the other being the *Mabsūṭ* of Sarakhsī, d. 1090). The *Lumaʿ,* the author of which is not mentioned, is probably Ibn Jinnī's work on Arabic language and grammar or another short treatise on law. This "curriculum" implies that Ibn alʿAdīm was being groomed by his father for a career in law.

9. The letters cited in the poem (*q-r-y-b*) spell out the Arabic word "relative," *qarīb.*

10. The early appearance of gray hair plays a similarly prominent role in the autobiography of Ibn al-ʿAdīm's contemporary, Abū Shāma (translated in this volume).

The Autobiography of Abū Shāma

(1203–1268)

Introduction

Abū Shāma was born in 1203 in Damascus to a family of religious scholars. He is best known today as the author of *The Book of the Two Gardens on the History of the Two Reigns* (Kitāb al-Rawḍatayn fī akhbār al-dawlatayn), a chronologically arranged history of the reigns of Nūr al-Dīn Zangī (d. 1174) and Saladin (d. 1193), regarded as one of the most important Arabic sources for the period of the Crusades.[1] Abū Shāma's autobiography is found listed under the year of his birth in his continuation of the original work, the *Sequel to the Book of the Two Gardens* (Dhayl kitāb al-rawḍatayn), which covers the years from Saladin's death to Abū Shāma's. The *Sequel* is also arranged chronologically and includes biographical notices of prominent figures listed under the years of their deaths. The final scene of the *Sequel,* in fact, describes how the author was beaten up by thugs, an incident that apparently led to his death soon afterward.

Although Abū Shāma is today remembered primarily as a historian, his self-portrayal in his autobiography, translated here in full, shows that he considered himself first and foremost a scholar of Islamic religious sciences, particularly of Islamic law. His account of his life begins with a list of his forebears—all men distinguished by their religious learning—and then sketches the broad outlines of his education. The turning point in Abū Shāma's life is depicted as the year 624 (1227), when he traveled to Jerusalem with his most important teacher and his hair suddenly turned gray though he was only twenty-five years old. He interprets this event, in conjunction with the trip to Jerusalem and some dreams from that same year, to mean that he had "arrived" as a mature religious scholar. As he puts it in the short poem that appears in his autobiography—a poem he conventionally attributes to "some good person or other" but which he himself wrote—God marked him with the outward signs of intellectual maturity to reflect his inner intellectual growth.

Abū Shāma's autobiography poses some intriguing problems concerning the nature and function of the self-*tarjama* in the Arabic tradition. Throughout the larger historical text, the *Sequel,* Abū Shāma refers to himself exclusively in the first person, which communicates to the reader a clear sense of the author as a person beyond the text. In addition, in the larger text, he provides information of a rather personal nature (at least, in the modern sense), noting, for example, his reactions to the tragic deaths of several of his children (e.g., *Dhayl,* 176), expressing his love and affection for his wife in a lengthy poem (*Dhayl,* 196–98), and giving other intimate details of his life. He intermingles many of these with the major historical occurrences of the realm, thus placing the events of his own life on par with those of the kingdoms and reigns he chronicled:

> In this year Ibn Abī Firās led the people from Iraq on the pilgrimage, and Sharaf al-Dīn, the ruler of Sarkas, those from Syria.
>
> Also in this year, my mother passed away—May God have mercy on her! I buried her in the foothills on the road near al-Imāj and al-Maghar, next to the wadi. I hope to be buried next to her. Her death occurred on Saturday, the sixth of the month of Rajab. She was pious and virtuous—May God be pleased with her!
>
> Also in this year, the Amīr Mubāriz al-Dīn Sunqur of Aleppo died, one of Saladin's contingent. (*Dhayl,* 134)

Because of the many references to Abū Shāma's own life that are woven into the larger historical flow, some scholars have suggested that the overall work should be considered a memoir.[2] In any case, in his work of history, Abū Shāma inserts the kind of information a modern reader might expect to find in an autobiography.

In the autobiography itself, however, Abū Shāma curiously shifts to the third person and changes the tone of his self-representation drastically. Here, little of Abū Shāma's "personal" life (again, in modern terms) is portrayed, while materials such as dreams and visions occupy a prominent place alongside details of Abū Shāma's education and career. Although the critical historical facts of Abū Shāma's life are presented here, the sense of "person" that is communicated interstitially in his historical writing is replaced with an entirely different self-representation.

By Abū Shāma's time there were a substantial number of first-person autobiographical texts in wide circulation, several of them written by famous figures of the period of Saladin's reign and therefore almost certainly known to him. Yet Abū Shāma chose to present information about his life in the standard third-person format of scholarly biography; he probably composed it specifically as a "camera-ready" text to be quoted by later historians and biographers. Arabic autobiographers clearly had a choice between first-person and third-person portrayal; Abū Shāma, however, is the only Arabic autobiographer to have couched a third-person autobiography in a larger framing text in the first person (cf. the texts by ʿImād al-Dīn al-Kātib al-Iṣfahānī, ʿAbd al-Laṭīf al-Baghdādī, and Ibn al-ʿAdīm, all translated in this volume, as well as the famous autobiographies of ʿUmāra al-Ḥakamī al-Yamanī and Usāma ibn Munqidh, available in French and English translations respectively). In some sense, a complete reading of Abū Shāma's text can only be accomplished alongside the numerous passages of the *Sequel to the Two Gardens* that provide other autobiographical glimpses of the author.

Abū Shāma does not fully subordinate his account to the scholarly *tarjama* genre, however; he includes dimensions not commonly found in those texts, such as a large number of dream narratives (cf. al-Tirmidhī, translated in this volume), and his account of his hair turning gray (cf. Ibn al-ʿAdīm, translated in this volume), marking this event even further with the inclusion of a poem (the only one in the text). His text is also lacking many of the standard components of the scholarly *tarjama,* such as a detailed list of his teachers and writings and extracts from his poetry. Abū Shāma's text shares much with other Arabic autobiographies and differs significantly from standard scholarly biographies. In fact, a later hand, probably that of one of his students, has attempted to rectify this situation by adding a list of teachers, some information about his writings, and a collection of extracts from his poetry.

If Abū Shāma wrote this text to be cited by later writers, his strategy failed. None of his main biographers quote it, although Ibn Kathīr (d. 1373) at least mentions its existence. On the other hand, al-Sakhāwī (d. 1497) notes Abū Shāma's sharp tongue and makes reference to his high opinion of himself,[3] despite the approbative tone of other biographies of Abū Shāma; this may in fact be a veiled reference to Abū Shāma's autobiography, for Abū Shāma's text was cited as a respectable precedent for writing an autobiography by al-Sakhāwī's chief rival, Jalāl al-Dīn al-Suyūṭī (d. 1505).

Bibliography

Abū Shāma. *al-Dhayl ʿalā al-rawḍatayn.* Ed. M Kawtharī [under the title *Tarājim rijāl al-qarnayn al-sādis wa-l-sābiʿ*]. Cairo: al-Ḥusaynī, 1948. 37–39.

Barbier de Meynard, C. *Recueil des historiens des Croisades, historiens orientaux.* Paris: Imprimerie National, 1872–1906. Vol. 5:207–16. [Arabic text and French translation of Abū Shāma's autobiography]

Gabrieli, F. *Arab Historians of the Crusades.* Trans. E. J. Costello. Berkeley: University of California Press, 1969.

Ibn Kathīr, Ismāʿīl ibn ʿUmar. *al-Bidāya wa-l-nihāya.* 14 vols. Cairo: al-Maṭbaʿa al-Salafiyya, 1932. Vol. 8: 250–51.

Lowry, Joseph E. "Time, Form, and Self: The Autobiography of Abū Shāma." *Edebiyât: Special Issue—Arabic Autobiography,* N.S. 7, no. 2 (1997): 313–25.

Pouzet, Louis. "Maẓāhir al-sīra al-dhātiyya fī kitāb *Tarājim al-qarnayn al-sādis wa-l-sābiʿ* li-Shihāb al-Dīn Abī Shāma al-Maqdisī al-Dimashqī [Autobiographical Passages in the *Biographies of the Sixth and Seventh Centuries* by Shihāb al-Dīn Abū Shāma al-Maqdisī al-Dimashqī]." *Annales de Départment des Lettres Arabes, Institut de Lettres Orientales, Université Saint-Joseph* 1 (1981): 25–35.

Rosenthal, Franz. *A History of Muslim Historiography.* 2d rev. ed. Leiden: E. J. Brill, 1968.

al-Sakhāwī, Shams al-Dīn Muḥammad. *Iʿlān bi-l-tawbīkh li-man dhamma al-taʾrīkh.* Damascus: al-Qudsī, 1930.

The Life of Abū Shāma
[*al-Dhayl,* pp. 37–39]

Also in the year 599 [1203 C.E.], the compiler of this book was born, God's supplicant, ʿAbd al-Raḥmān ibn Ismāʿīl ibn Ibrāhīm ibn ʿUthmān ibn Abī Bakr ibn Ibrāhīm ibn Muḥammad of Jerusalem, of the Shafiʿite school of law, on the evening of Friday, the twenty-third of the month of Rabīʿ II—may God pardon him. He was known as Abū Shāma, "possessor of the mole," due to a large mole over his right eyebrow; he was also named Abū al-Qāsim Muḥammad. He was born in this year at the head of al-Fawākhīr Street in Damascus, just inside the city's East Gate.

His distant ancestor Abū Bakr was originally from Jerusalem and Abū Bakr's father, Ibrāhīm, was a notable there. Perhaps Muḥammad, which is as far back as the family tree goes, was Abū Bakr Muḥammad ibn Aḥmad ibn Abī al-Qāsim ʿAlī of the city of Ṭūs, a Qurʾān reciter and Sufi, as well as Imam of the Dome of the Rock in Jerusalem. This Muḥammad is mentioned by the scholar Abū al-Qāsim in his *History of Damascus.*[4] Ibn al-Akfānī[5] relates as follows: "The Franks—may God forsake them—killed Muḥammad when they entered Jerusalem in the month of Shaʿbān, 492 [1099]. He is one of the martyrs whose heads are in the cave people visit in the cemetery of Mamella in Noble Jerusalem."[6]

His descendant Abū Bakr later moved to Damascus and resided there where there were born to him two sons, ʿUthmān and ʿAbd al-Raḥmān; the latter was a teacher near the Damascus Mosque Gate—his story will be told below.[7] God increased their progeny in Damascus, and their dwellings in the districts around the East Gate, and, by and by, ʿUthmān fathered Ibrāhīm, the author's grandfather, who passed away in the month of Shaʿbān in 575 [1180], and was buried in the cemetery at Paradise Gate.[8] Ibrāhīm sired two sons, Abū al-Qāsim, who passed away on Friday, the ninth of

Ramaḍān, in 604 [1208] and was buried in a cemetery between the East Gate and the Gate of Thomas, and Ismāʿīl, who passed away on the thirteenth of the month of Rabīʿ I in 638 [1240]. Ismāʿīl also had two sons, Ibrāhīm, whose birthday was on the night of Monday, the twenty-fifth of the month of Muḥarram 591 [1194], and the compiler of this book, ʿAbd al-Raḥmān.[9]

God—may He be exalted—instilled in him even in his youth a love for memorizing the Precious Scripture and for the pursuit of knowledge, making that his ambition. He did not let his father know of this until he said to him, "I have finished memorizing the Qurʾān!" Then he took up the study of the seven variant readings of the Qurʾān, law, Arabic grammar, the *ḥadīth* of the Prophet, history, the biographies of the transmitters of the Prophet's *ḥadīth* and other fields, and he wrote many works on these subjects that will be mentioned below [= later in the book, not in the autobiography]. He made the pilgrimage to Mecca with his father in the year 621 [1224–25], and then again in the following year. He visited Jerusalem in 624 [1226–27] and Egypt in 628 [1230–31], studying in various places in Egypt, then in Cairo, Damietta, and Alexandria. Thereafter, he continued to reside in Damascus, engaged in the task at hand, namely, his pursuit of knowledge. He assembled it in his writings and in the legal opinions he issued on the the rules of law and other such matters.

In his youth he used to recite the Qurʾān in the Damascus mosque while observing the learned professors such as Fakhr al-Dīn Abū Manṣūr Ibn ʿAsākir.[10] He noted how the latter related his legal methodology and conclusions when giving legal opinions for Muslims, how people sought him out and studied the Prophet's *ḥadīth* with him all while he made his way from the *maqṣūra* [the enclosed area in a mosque] named after the Prophet's Companions beneath the Eagle Dome, where he taught *ḥadīth*, to the Taqwiyya law school where he gave lectures in jurisprudence. He noted how people turned to him and resorted to him time and again, as well as his good reputation and his moderation in dress. He found that he liked these ways of Ibn ʿAsākir, and therefore desired to attain the same rank in learning, to be equally well known, and to have people derive benefit from his own legal opinions. God granted him this beyond his most fervent hopes. Gray appeared in his beard and in his hair when he was but twenty-five years old. God—may He be exalted—brought old age to him prematurely, both in outward appearance and in inward demeanor. About this, some good person or other has composed the following:

If he grew gray upon reaching his twenty-fifth year,
still, the grayness in him was not uncouth.
People knew not the full maturity of his learning,
though his lights shone bright even in his youth.

God illuminated the very heart of him;
truly he embodied guidance for those unsure of truth.
A shaykh in the true meaning; grayness came early to him,
dignifying him above his fellow youths.
He comprised excellence as a boy and old man;
a station near to God and a fair resting place are his both.[11]

People had auspicious visions in their sleep which foretold of the good fortune in learning that was to come his way, and of the good things for which he had hoped. For example, while he was still quite young, going to and from grammar school, and his father was marveling at his enthusiasm for school and his ardor in reading, contrary to the fashion of most young boys, his mother—may God rest her soul—told his father: "You shouldn't be surprised! For when I was pregnant, I dreamt that I was at the very highest spot on a minaret, at the crescent moon on its top, and I was giving the call to prayer. I later recounted this to a dream-interpreter who said, 'You will give birth to a boy whose fame in learning and goodness will spread throughout the earth.' "

He himself [= Abū Shāma], in the month of Ṣafar 624 [1227], dreamt that ʿUmar ibn al-Khattāb [the second caliph, renowned for his piety and righteousness]—may God rest his soul—had come to Syria to aid its people against the Franks—may God abandon them. He had a special relationship with ʿUmar such that ʿUmar would delegate things to him and talk with him concerning the affairs of Muslims while he walked at ʿUmar's side, touching his shoulder. This continued until people began to ask him about ʿUmar and what ʿUmar intended to do. He would inform them and it was as though he were the medium between ʿUmar and the people.

In this year, he also dreamt that he and the legal scholar ʿAbd al-ʿAzīz ibn ʿAbd al-Salām[12]—may God grant him peace—were inside the Gate of Mercy in Jerusalem. He wanted to open it, but there was someone preventing him from doing so, pushing on it so that it stayed closed. The two of them, however, continued to apply themselves to the matter until they opened its two halves completely, such that each half of the door ended up leaning against the wall behind it.

He also dreamt in the month of Jumādā II of that year that some Muslims were performing their Friday prayers in severe heat. He grew afraid that they might become dehydrated since there was no water there, so far as anyone knew. Then he saw an ancient well near him and a trough, and it occurred to him to draw water from the well and to pour it into the trough so people could drink from it when they finished their prayers. Someone in front of him whom he did not know drew a bucket or two, then he took the bucket from him and drew a great number of buckets, so many he could not count them all, pouring them into the basin.

Then al-Muhtār Hilāl ibn Māzin ibn al-Ḥarrābī dreamt that he saw Abū Shāma bearing the weight of a great edifice and al-Muhtār exclaimed: "See how so-and-so assumes the burden of the Word of God!"

An old woman dreamt that a group of the pious had gathered in the mosque of the village of Bayt Sawā, one of the villages in Ghūṭa, outside Damascus. They were asked what they were doing and replied, "We are waiting for the Prophet—may God bless him and grant him peace—to pray with us." She said that he—that is, the author of this book—arrived and prayed with them.

Also, there was once a man who had come seeking a legal opinion while he was in the great lecture area reserved for books, in the uppermost part of the lecture hall in the ʿĀdiliyya law college—this is the place where he sits most of the time giving out legal opinions and so on—and at that point [Abū Shāma] passed by on his way to pray in the law college. The man was astonished and was asked, "What do you find so astonishing?" "I have never seen this place before," he said, "but I dreamt in my sleep that I was in this, the ʿĀdiliyya law college, and there was a huge group of people in it. Someone said to the people, 'Stand aside, for the Prophet—may God bless him and grant him peace—is passing by.' So I looked up and he came out to us from the great lecture area reserved for books and passed by, exactly as [Abū Shāma] just did, on his way to the prayer niche."

Also, al-Ṣalāḥ the Sufi dreamt, on the first night of the month of Jumādā II in 665 [1267], that the compiler of this book was setting out on the pilgrimage so well outfitted that he had provisions for everything that he could possibly need, such that the one dreaming was astonished.

Ḥasan al-Ḥijāzī, in the month of Ramaḍān 657 [1259], dreamt that someone from the occult world, unseen by him, but whose voice he could hear, said, "Shaykh Abū Shāma is the Prophet of this era," or something to that effect. He also said that he saw him another time on a lofty bridge and under the bridge was abundant wheat.

Among these auspicious dreams were those of his brother, Shaykh Burhān al-Dīn Abū Isḥāq Ibrāhīm ibn Ismāʿīl, older than him by about nine years and one of the pious. He dreamt that their father—may God rest his soul—was saying to him, "Occupy yourself with learning; look at the station of your brother." So he looked up and suddenly his brother was on top of a mountain and his father and the one dreaming were walking at its base. He also dreamt in the month of Ṣafar in 657 [1258] that the author was holding fast to a rope that was hanging down from the heavens, leading up to them. So he asked someone in the dream about that and suddenly there appeared to the two of them the Dome of the Rock and the Aqsa mosque [of Jerusalem], whereupon that person asked, "Who built that mosque?"

"Solomon, son of David," he replied.

"Your brother has been given the like of that which Solomon was given," he said.

"How is that?"

"Was not Solomon brought so many things that he had no need of anyone thereafter? Was he not given this and that and brought a great number of different types of things?"

"Indeed, yes he was."

"And so too your brother has been brought many different kinds of knowledge," or something to that effect.

Also, al-Sharaf al-Ṣarkhadī dreamt that the author was above the roof of an isolated house giving the call to prayer, and that he then recited from the Qur'ān: "And listen for the Day when the Caller will call out from a place quite near . . ."[13] He also dreamt that the Day of Resurrection had come and that the author of this book was riding a donkey, making great haste. He was asked about this and replied, "I am seeking out the Prophet—may God bless him and grant him peace—for the sake of the pool from which his people will be given to drink."[14]

And finally, al-Sharaf ibn Ra'īs also dreamt that he saw the Day of Resurrection and described some of it terrors. He said, "I saw so-and-so—that is, the compiler of this book—and so I asked how he was, saying to him, 'How were you met?' 'I was well met,' he replied."

But these dreams and other things have only been recorded here to testify to the grace of God—may He be exalted—just as He commended in His words—may He be exalted: "And as for the bounty of your Lord, speak!" [Q 93:11]. Moreover, the Prophet said—may God bless him and grant him peace—"All that will remain of the glad tidings is a true vision which the faithful person will view, or which will be shown to him."

O God, give us thanks that we might thank You for these blessings, seal them with goodness, protect us in this life and in the next, help us to have faith in Your well-conceived plan, and let us not forget Your mention.[15]

Notes

1. Excerpts in English translation are found in F. Gabrieli, *Arab Historians of the Crusades* (Berkeley: University of California Press, 1969).

2. Louis Pouzet, "Maẓāhir al-sīra al-dhātiyya fī kitāb *Tarājim al-qarnayn al-sādis wa-l-sābi'* li-Shihāb al-Dīn Abī Shāma al-Maqdisī al-Dimashqī [Autobiographical Passages in the *Biographies of the Sixth and Seventh Centuries* by Shihāb al-Dīn Abī Shāma al-Maqdisī al-Dimashqī]," *Annales de Départment des Lettres Arabes, Institut de Lettres Orientales, Université Saint-Joseph* 1 (1981): 25–35.

3. Franz Rosenthal, *A History of Muslim Historiography,* 2d rev. ed. (Leiden: E. J. Brill, 1968); Shams al-Dīn Muḥammad al-Sakhāwī, *I'lān bi-l-tawbīkh li-man dhamma al-ta'rīkh* (Damascus: al-Qudsī, 1930).

4. That is, Ibn ʿAsākir (d. 1176), author of *Tarīkh madīnat dimashq* .

5. A Damascene historian (d. 1129); the quote may be from his now lost *Jāmiʿ al-wafāyāt.*

6. Cf. "Jerusalem was taken from the north on the morning of Friday, July 15, 1099. The population was put to the sword by the Franks, who pillaged the area for a week. . . . In the al-Aqsa Mosque, the Franks slaughtered more than 70,000 people, among them a large number of Imams and Muslim scholars, devout ascetic men who had left behind their homelands to live lives of pious seclusion in the Holy Place." Ibn al-Athīr (d. 1233), quoted in Gabrieli, *Arab Historians of the Crusades,* 10–11.

7. The biographical notice of ʿAbd al-Raḥmān ibn Abī Bakr, Abū Shāma's grandfather's uncle, appears later in the *Dhayl.*

8. Reading *fa-awlada ʿUthmān Ibrāhim ibn ʿUthmān* (the Arabic edition contains an extra *ibn* that does not accord with Abū Shāma's full name given at the beginning of the text).

9. Only first names have been used in this passage; the original Arabic includes two or more generations for each individual cited.

10. Nephew of the above-mentioned and far better known historian of the same last name.

11. A reference to Qur'ān 38:40, where this phrase is said of Solomon.

12. Abū Shāma's most important teacher with whom he twice made the journey to Jerusalem.

13. Qur'ān 50:41; trans. Yusuf Ali.

14. Reference to the pool [*ḥawḍ*] from which the faithful will be given to drink on the Day of Resurrection.

15. Two editions contain additional text after this point that has not been translated here. They appear to be additions made by one of Abū Shāma's students. This is the opinion of the Egyptian editor and appears reasonable on internal grounds as well; at this point, for example, all references to the author shift from "the compiler of this book" [*muṣannif al-kitāb*] to "the aforementioned one" [*al-madhkūr*].

The Autobiography of ʿAlāʾ al-Dawla al-Simnānī

(1261–1336)

Introduction

Abū al-Makārim Rukn al-Dīn Aḥmad ibn Muḥammad ibn Aḥmad ʿAlāʾ al-Dawla al-Biyābānakī al-Simnānī was an important Sufi master and writer under the Mongol Īlkhānid dynasty that ruled Iran from 1256 to 1335. Born into a family of wealthy landlords in Simnān, in north central Iran, al-Simnānī joined his father in the service of the Īlkhānid prince Arghūn. Arghūn, like others of his dynasty, displayed great tolerance toward Christianity but is himself said to have a been a follower of Buddhism; Buddhist priests were in any case among his closest advisers. Al-Simnānī was raised for a life at court: both his mother's and his father's lineages included courtiers of the Khwārazmshāhs, the dynasty that had come to an end with the arrival of the Īlkhānids; his maternal uncle served as chief judge under the Īlkhānids until his execution in 1301; his paternal uncle rose to the rank of chief minister of Iran before falling from favor and being executed in 1299; and his father served intermittently as master of the guards, master of the treasury of Iraq, and governor of Baghdad until his execution in 1295/96. Al-Simnānī served as a companion of Prince Arghūn, who was six to ten years older, from the time they were both children.

Al-Simnānī appears to have been increasingly dissatisfied with court life as he entered young adulthood and began to be drawn to a mystical career, but he was strongly dissuaded by his family from giving up royal service. Following a dramatic mystical experience on the battlefield, however, al-Simnānī abruptly left the court in 1286 and thereafter devoted himself to a life of seclusion in his hometown, Biyābānak. He devoted himself entirely to mystical endeavors and experienced a great deal of success; by the time of his death in 1336, he had become one of the most respected religious scholars of the Īlkhānid empire. He used his considerable wealth to construct a large Sufi complex called Ṣūfiyābād-i Khudādād, where he instructed a large group of disciples including several Īlkhānid princes and courtiers.

Al-Simnānī had a keen sense of the narratability of his life and wrote several autobiographical tracts, some of which constitute complete treatises; others take the form of subsections in larger works. The bulk of his autobiographical writings are in Persian, but a number of Arabic texts exist that range from highly structured *apologiae pro vita sua* to detailed anecdotes of his life at court and the process by which he secured permission to retire to Simnān and devote himself to Sufism. The selection translated here is taken from one of his two most important works, *al-ʿUrwa li-ahl al-khalwa wa-l-jalwa* (The Bond for the People of Reclusion and Unveiling), written in 1320–21, which contains the longest of his Arabic autobiographical writings. This selection describes al-Simnānī's conversion experience, his establishment of a large endowment to support Sufi teaching establishments—*khānqāhs*—and a confrontation with Satan in which al-Simnānī is almost tempted to abandon his ascetic life and return to the pursuit of wealth and position.

There are several references in the text to the creation and preservation of charitable endowments (sing. *waqf,* pl. *awqāf*). This singular development of Islamic culture allowed a benefactor to endow an institution, such as a school or a hospital, with the income from a specific source, such as a parcel of land or the rent from a building, in perpetuity. Such endowments often included provisions for the salary of one or more employees: the endowment's executor, teachers, bookkeeper, cleaning staff, and the like. In al-Simnānī's time, these salaries were often transformed into sinecures from which family members or descendants of the benefactor could derive a tax-free income, and were even bought and sold, though this was a clear abuse of their original purpose. The detailed account al-Simnānī gives of the care with which he set up his religious endowments, prohibiting relatives, descendants, and political figures from being involved and preventing the executorship of the endowment from passing down within one family, contrasts sharply with the young al-Simnānī he describes earlier whose only concern was the accumulation of wealth and power. His chagrin at the hereditary executorship of religious endowments in his day perhaps echoes his wealthy landowning roots and an alienation from his family.

By his own account, al-Simnānī's many short autobiographical pieces are intended to serve the didactic function of illustrating his teachings through examples from his personal experience and demonstrating the way to the True Path: "for it [is] impossible for anyone to understand [how I came to know the True Path] without hearing the account of my life from beginning to end."[1]

Bibliography

Al-ʿUrwa li-ahl al-khalwa wa-l-jalwa. Ed. Najīb Māyil-i Hirāwī. Teheran: Mawla, 1983. 396–400.

Elias, Jamal J. *The Throne Carrier of God: The Life and Thought of ʿAlāʾ al-Dawla al-Simnānī.* Albany: SUNY Press, 1995.

Finding the Straight Path

[*al-ʿUrwa,* pp. 396–400]

On how I came to know the Straight Path from among the various paths, and the group deserving of salvation from among the various schismatic sects, it being impossible for anyone to understand this without hearing the account of my life from beginning to end

O eager student and traveler on the right path! If you have acquired a new awareness and possess a receptive heart and if you seek hidden knowledge and guidance to the Righteous Path, then know that from childhood to adulthood I sought privileges, thinking little of other matters, loving only noble things and despising the trivial, such that I could not content myself with being the companion of anyone other than the sultan of my time [i.e., Arghūn], and I was not satisfied until I had displaced all of my contemporaries in the role of his servant and companion. I served him for ten years after leaving the *madrasa* when I was a boy of fifteen, trained in the arts and letters, but completely ignorant of the rational and religious sciences. I surpassed all other youths of my kind in my service to him, and he favored me and kept me by his side to the point that I became the object of envy for the highest princes and ministers in his state because I served him in love and companionship. He was proverbial in his generosity and unanimously acclaimed for it everywhere. My purpose in serving him was only companionship and the desire to please him, not wealth and property. I ignored offering my prayers and was so engrossed in his company and occupied in his service that I did not have time for study or the subtleties of what I had read and memorized until I entered my twenty-fourth year.

Then a rebuking Voice summoned me during the combat that transpired between Arghūn and the army of his uncle, Sultan Aḥmad, just below Qazvīn in the year 683 [1284]. The moment I uttered the phrase "God is Most Great!" and attacked the enemy, the veils were lifted by the strength of this Rebuker and I saw the Afterlife and all that is in it, just as it is mentioned in the Qurʾān and the sayings of the Prophet. This powerful condition stayed with me all that night until the next morning. When I sat down to eat, the condition subsided, but its effect remained in my soul. In my heart there arose a beckoning to withdraw from humanity and, at the same time, a command to make up for all of my forfeited prayers. However, I was unable to leave the sultan's service. I did not seek any companionship after that experience, and I forced myself to offer ten days' worth of prayers every night and to memorize five verses of the Praiseworthy Qur'ān, for until then I did not know any of it by heart save the five short chapters, the four which begin with the command "Recite!" [*al-qalāqil*], and the Opening Chapter.

Matters remained thus until the middle of the month of Shaʿbān in the year 685 [October 1286], when I was struck by a malady so grave that the sultan's physicians proved incapable of finding a cure. I therefore asked his permission to return to Simnān for treatment. I departed Tabriz on the sixteenth of Shaʿbān 685 [October 7, 1286] heading toward Simnān. When I reached Ūjān in the region of Arrān, I realized that I had been restored to perfect health without any medication, and I understood that this was because of the blessing of abandoning the court's company, turning away from wrongdoers and their wrongful deeds, and moving toward truth and its devotees. My desire to abandon the world, to strive in obedience to God, and to eliminate any pretext for falling short in the service of my Lord and Creator, all increased while I sought forgiveness for having spent time in the service of one who worshiped idols.[2]

When I reached Simnān, in the month of Ramadan, I occupied myself with learning what I had to of religious obligations, for I knew nothing at all of them, nor, in fact, anything of the legal sciences. I worked hard and succeeded in learning what I had to that winter. I established my spiritual practice on the basis of what is written in the book *Food for Hearts* [Qūt al-qulūb] of Abū Ṭālib al-Makkī—may God sanctify his secret. I yearned to dissociate myself from the world, so I distributed my wealth, freed my slaves, provided my wife with her due, and gave my son more than my father had given me. Then I began to live at the *khānqāh* [Sufi lodge] named after the great master al-Ḥasan al-Sakkākī al-Simnānī, who was an associate of Shaykh Abū Saʿīd ibn Abī al-Khayr and Shaykh al-Ḥasan al-Kharaqānī and the Shaykh of Shaykhs Abū ʿAbd Allāh al-Dāstānī from whom many chains of authoritative transmission derive. He was a disciple of Shaykh Abū al-Ḥasan al-Bustī who was his master, and Shaykh Muḥammad al-Ḥamawī al-Juwaynī, and had studied with and benefited from the great Shaykh Abū al-ʿAbbās al-Qaṣṣāb al-Āmulī—may God sanctify their spirits. Shaykh al-Ḥasan al-Sakkākī was honorable and diligent, devoted to and accepted by the saints of his age, standing firmly in body, words, and deeds upon the path of the Prophet, his heart illuminated by the light of mysteries of the pure path attributed to the Sufis.

I constructed other *khānqāhs* and conferred upon them *waqf* endowments of my remaining property, double what I had given to my son and his mother. I stipulated that my descendants not serve as executors, employees, or supervisors of the endowments I created. I composed a registered endowment document and forbade the sultan's judges, scholars, and courtiers from being appointed to manage the endowments, audit their expenses, record them into the registers, or enter them for the purpose of residing, seeking temporary lodging, or eating at the table of our disciples. May God destroy them, for they are the vilest of men in character, lowest in resolve, most loathsome in beliefs, most repulsive in character, most disgusting as companions, and most vulgar in speech.

I entrusted the position of executor after me to one of my disciples who had traveled the Sufi path to the point of becoming a mystical guide, expansive by nature, generous, mindful of being neither prodigal nor miserly, possessing patience, fortitude, and benificence, pure of heart and body, of complete reliance on God, sincerely repentant and just in word and deed in all matters. And I entrusted the position after him to one like him from among the disciples, not to one of his children. I forbade executorship, supervision, and employment to the children of any executor, supervisor, or employee, even if they be ascetic, worshiping mystics, lest they confuse it with their inheritance. For we have seen in this age the making of hereditary charitable endowments and the appointment of heirs as executors, supervisors, and employees, thereby mixing up property. God will repay these people for coveting these properties—great is His power! Strangest of all is that the owners of charities like to buy them, despite being fully cognizant of the fact that they are charitable endowments! May God guide them away from this heedless behavior!

Satan came whispering in my breast and tempted my soul, saying: "You have chosen a momentous thing arbitrarily, without being certain. A sensible person cannot just abandon the delights of the world—the highest of which is being close to the sultan and the clearest of which is the fulfillment of the soul's desire and heart's delight in keeping to one's goal from the days of his youth—without giving it any serious consideration. There is nothing more delightful than being alive and the best part of a person's life is passing one's youth without a care in whatever one's soul desires. You are ruining the joy in your life by wearing coarse cloth, eating chaff, keeping constant night vigils, eating too little, and fasting all the time. If perchance after a while you realize the futility of your behavior, and wish to return to what you once had, then even if it were easy for you to reacquire all the money and property you have given away, and simple for you to again grow close to the sultan, how will you regain the lost days of your youth? Remorse over the loss of your sweet, fresh life will only gain you weariness and sorrow!"

But I said that all the prophets and saints have urged people to abandon the world and turn away form their base desires toward obedience to God—

may He be exalted—and toward building a place for themselves in the Afterlife. He said, "How do you know that what they said is true in the specific context of lifting the mystical veil [*kashf al-ḥijāb*]?" I replied, "Indeed, I sought the world and its delights and I attained its highest stations; but then my soul turned away from it and its devotees in revulsion. I abandoned it voluntarily, not because I had to. I will not return to what I have abandoned out of weariness, boredom, or complacency. Indeed, from these practices and acts of worship I find such nonwearying delights that in each hour I long to experience what I had in the previous hour. True delight is that which does not tire the one who has it."

He said: "These are rhetorical and persuasive words, but a seeker of truth must not heed that which is not demonstratively proven. Do we not hear how God—may He be exalted—commands His prophet to demand proof from his adversary in His Book: 'Say: Bring forth your argument!' [Q 27:64]." His words stirred my soul, even though it was not disposed to heed them, being occupied with delightful religious exercises and acts of worship, striving to change its despicable characteristics and past habits into noble and praiseworthy attributes. So my soul cried out to God and said beseechingly: "O Lord! You have spoken and Your words are true: 'Or, who listens to the distressed when he calls on Him' [Q 27:62], and You have commanded us to pray with Your words: 'Call on me. I will answer your prayer' [Q. 40:60]. I am calling on You with the prayer of the destitute and requesting You as one who has no recourse but to beseech You, certain that he has no way out except Your door! So hear my request, answer my prayers even if You do not fulfill my desires, and reveal to me a retort to my enemies so that Satan and his arguments will be silenced by incontrovertible proof!"

An unseen voice called to me: "Do not be in haste! Follow in the footsteps of the Beloved of God and persevere in the worship of God. He will open unto you the gates to that which you seek!"

After this I strove to establish a daily regimen of meditation and prayer, as stipulated in the *Food for Hearts,* and of Qur'ānic recitation. I was careful that not a single breath be wasted in something that did not assist me in my faith. And my time became completely consumed in my religious exercises so that not a moment was left for me to spend on any of my associates.

Notes

1. For further information on al-Simnānī's life and thought, see Jamal J. Elias, *The Throne Carrier of God: The Life and Thought of ʿAlā' al-Dawla al-Simnānī* (Albany: SUNY Press, 1995).

2. Arghūn was not a Muslim; the idols in question were probably figures of Buddha.

The Autobiography of Fray Anselmo Turmeda, ʿAbd Allāh al-Turjumān

(1352–1432?)

Introduction

Conversion narratives constitute a significant subcategory of autobiographical writing in both the Arabo-Islamic and European traditions. Among Arabic texts we find conversions to Islam from Christianity (Turmeda), from Judaism (Samawʾal al-Maghribī), from a less committed sense of Islam to a more pious lifestyle (al-Tirmidhī), and from more traditionalist versions of Islam to Islamic mysticism via rational study (al-Ghazālī) or through visionary experience (al-Simnānī). Many of these texts are attached to polemical works that reaffirm in different rhetorical terms the transformation undergone by the author in the conversion narrative itself. Conversion autobiographies have a very intimate engagement both with convincing the reader that the story told is true and with persuading the reader that the path taken is the path of truth.

The autobiography of Fray Anselmo Turmeda/ʿAbd Allāh al-Turjumān (lit. ʿAbd Allāh "the Interpreter") constitutes the first chapter in a work that is aimed at refuting Christianity's claim to be the true faith and convincing other Christians to convert to Islam as did the author in approximately 1387. A native of Mallorca, ʿAbd Allāh recounts a straightforward chronological narrative of his early life and religious studies. Perhaps most striking are his recollections of the unusual characteristics of the cities in which he lived and studied. Of Mallorca, he notes the prodigious local production of olives and figs; concerning Lérida, Spain, he tells of the gold dust found in the nearby river and of how the inhabitants preserved fruits and vegetables by drying them so they could be stored through the winter; of Bologna, Italy, he tells us about the municipal system for overseeing the quality of local brick production. Why are these curious details in his story at all? In part, they may be substantiating evidence that he did indeed live in these regions, evidence that would lend credence to his narrative of sincere conversion to Islam; but they also reflect a world of trading networks in a time when the popularity of travel literature was experiencing dramatic growth in Islamic domains as well as in Europe. ʿAbd Allāh al-Turjumān lived within a century of both the most famous western traveler, Marco Polo (1254–1323), and the most renowned Muslim traveler, Ibn Baṭṭūṭa (1304–77), of the late Middle Ages.

Most fascinating, however, is his forthright account of confusion over the figure of the Paraclete in the New Testament, at best an ambiguous figure in Christian thought. This is the figure whom Jesus promises God will send after him (John 16:07) to teach the world all things (14:26), who will be another counselor and testify about Jesus (15:26), but whom the world will not accept (14:16–17). When the young priest Anselmo Turmeda in his confusion turns to his teacher and mentor, the older priest confesses surprisingly that the Paraclete is none other than the Prophet Muhammad and advises his young student to flee to Muslim lands and save his soul! This ʿAbd Allāh does, and at the age of thirty-five he stands before the sultan of Tunis and a crowd of Christian merchants and gives public witness that Islam is the True Faith and that Muhammad is God's Messenger. We know little of ʿAbd Allāh's later life, but his autobiography leaves him happily married, the father of a young son, and enjoying the personal favor and blessing of the sultan.

Bibliography

ʿAbd Allāh al-Turjumān. *Tuḥfat al-adīb fī al-radd ʿalā ahl al-ṣalīb*. Ed. Maḥmūd ʿAlī Ḥamāya. Cairo: Dār al-Thaqāfa li-l- Ṭibāʿa wa-l-Nashr, 1983. 27–39.

Calvet, Agustín. *Fray Anselmo Turmeda: Heterodoxo español (1352–1423–32?)*. Barcelona: Casa Editorial Estudio, 1914.

de Epalza, Miguel. *Fray Anselm Turmeda (ʿAbdallah al-Taryuman) y su polémica islámo-cristiana: Edición, traducción y estudio de la Tuhfa*. 2d ed. Madrid: Hiperion, 1994.

———. "Nuevas aportaciones a la biografía de Fray Anselmo Turmeda (Abdallah al-Tarchumān)." *Analecta Sacra Tarraconensia: Revista de Ciencias Histórico-Eclesiásticas* 38 (1965): 87–158.

Samsó, Julio. "Turmediana: I. Trasfondo cultural islámico en la obra catalana de Anselmo Turmeda; II. En torno a la "Tuḥfa" y al "Libre de bons amonestaments." *Boletín de la Real Academia de Buenas Letras de Barcelona* 34 (1971–72): 51–85.

A Unique Find for the Intelligent Mind
[*Tuhfat al-adīb*, pp. 27–39]

A Treatise of Riposte to the People of the Cross

Chapter One

Know then—may God have mercy on you—that I am originally from the city of Mallorca (may God Almighty return her to Islam!), a large city on the coast that lies in a small valley between two mountains. It is a city of commerce with two harbors where large ships dock carrying splendid merchandise. The city is known by the name of the island, Mallorca, and its most important agricultural products are olives and figs. In a good year, more than twenty thousand barrels of olive oil are shipped from there to the cities of Cairo and Alexandria. In addition, the island of Mallorca has more than one hundred twenty well-populated walled towns, and many springs of water which emerge in all directions and flow to the sea. My father was considered one of the important people of the city of Mallorca. I was his only son, so when I reached six years of age he sent me to a priest who became my teacher and with whom I studied the Gospels until, in the space of two years, I had memorized more than half of them. I then began a six-year course of study in the language of the Gospels and the science of Logic.

I then left my homeland of Mallorca for the city of Lérida [on the mainland] in the land of Catalonia, the center of learning for Christians in that region, which has a large valley that cuts through it. There I saw gold dust mixed with the valley's sands, but since it is well known among the people of that region that the cost of extracting it is not matched by the price it brings, it is simply ignored. In this city there is a great abundance of fruit, and I have seen the peasants there split peaches, as well as squash and carrots, into quarters and place them in the sun [to dry]; during the winter, whenever they wish to eat these, they place them in water overnight and then cook them as if they were fresh. Christian students seeking knowledge gather in this city and number one thousand or even one thousand five hundred, and no one is in charge of them other than the priest with whom they are studying. The most common plant in its hinterlands is saffron. I studied the natural sciences and astrology there for six years. Then I was charged with teaching the Gospels and the language of the Gospels for four years.

I later traveled to the city of Bologna in the land of Lombardy, a very large city whose buildings are of strong red baked brick due to the lack of stone quarries in the region. Each master brickmaker has a stamp with which all of his bricks are imprinted and there is a supervisor who oversees the quality of the clay in the bricks and of the baking. If any should crack or crumble, the brickmaker is forced to pay the cost and is punished with a beating. This city is known as a city of learning among all the people of that region, and each year more than a thousand men gather there seeking knowledge. They wear nothing but a simple wrap which is the vestment of God [*ṣibāgh Allāh*]; even if a student is a king [*sulṭān*] or the son of a king, they all wear nothing but this, so the students are easily distinguishable from all other [residents of the city]. And no one is in charge of them but the priest with whom they are studying. I lived in that city [for quite a while].

There is a church there with an old priest who was of very high rank, by the name of Nicola Martello. His status among them in knowledge, observance, and asceticism was very high. He was peerless in these characteristics in his time among all the people of Christendom. Questions, particularly those concerning religion, would be brought to him from distant regions from kings and others, accompanied by great gifts which was the point of the matter for they wished to acquire his blessings by doing this. When their gifts were accepted, they deemed themselves greatly honored. With this priest I studied the principles [*uṣūl*] and the details [*aḥkām*] of the Christian religion. I grew closer and closer to him by serving him and taking care of many of his errands until he eventually made me the closest of his retinue, to the point that I ended up being given the keys to his house and his storerooms. I had access to everything with the sole exception of the key to a small room within his house where he would retire by himself that was apparently his storeroom for all the wealth that had been given to him, but God only knows.

I studied with him there and served him, as I have recounted above, for ten years. Then one day he unexpectedly took ill and did not attend his seminar. The students of his class waited for him and passed the time discussing various problems of knowledge. Eventually, their discussion turned to the words of God Almighty as expressed by the Prophet Jesus (upon whom be peace!): "There will come after me a prophet whose name shall be the Paraclete [Bāraqlīṭ: cf. John 14:15, 26; 15:26; 16:7–15]," and they began to discuss the identity of this prophet: Which was he among the Prophets? Each one spoke according to his own knowledge and understanding. Their discussion was lengthy and they debated a great deal, but they left without having reached any conclusion regarding this matter.

I went to the residence of the teacher of the aforementioned class, and he asked me, "What studying did you do today while I was absent?" So I told him of the disagreement among the students concerning the identity of the Paraclete. I reported that so-and-so had answered thus, and so-and-so had answered in this manner, and thus I narrated to him all of their answers. Then he asked me, "And how did you answer?" "I responded with the answer given by such-and-such a religious scholar in his exegesis of the Gospels." He said to me, "Well, that was a good try and you did get close; but so-and-so is mistaken and so-and-so almost got it right, but the truth is not any of these, because the explanation of this holy name is known only by scholars of extraordinary learning, and as of yet, you [students] have achieved only a small amount of knowledge." So I rushed forward to kiss his feet and said to him, "Master, you know that I have come to you from a far-off land and have served you now for ten years. During this time I have received from you an amount of knowledge which I cannot reckon, but could you find it possible, out of your great beneficence, to supplement this with knowledge of this holy name?" The priest then began to weep and said to me, "My son, God knows that you are very dear to me because of your service and devotion to me. Knowledge of this holy name is indeed a great benefit, but I fear that if this knowledge were revealed to you that the Christian masses would kill you immediately." I said to him, "Master, by God Almighty, by the Truth of the Gospels and He Who brought them, I shall never speak of anything you confide to me in secret except at your command!"

Then he said to me, "My son, when you first came to me I asked you about your country: whether it was close to the Muslims and whether your countries raid each other, in order to determine what aversion you might have for Islam. Know, then, my son, that the Paraclete is one of the names of our Prophet Muhammad (may God bless and preserve him!), to whom was revealed the Fourth Book which is mentioned by Daniel (upon whom be peace!) who says that this book shall be revealed, its religion shall be the True Religion, and its followers the True Community [lit. "white community," *al-milla al-bayḍā'*, Dan. 12:10] mentioned in the Gospels." I responded, "But, Master, what then do you say of the religion of the Christians?" He replied, "My son, if the Christians had persisted in the original religion of Jesus, they would indeed belong to the religion of God, for the religion of Jesus and all of the Prophets is that of God."

"But what then is one to do in this matter?" I asked. He said, "My son, enter into the religion of Islam!" I asked, "Does whoever enter Islam achieve salvation?" He responded, "Yes, he is saved in this world and in the Hereafter." I said to him, "Master, an intelligent man chooses for himself the very best of what he knows, so if you know that the religion of Islam is superior, what then keeps you from it?" He said, "My son, God Almighty only revealed to me the truth of what I have disclosed to you about the superiority of Islam and the holiness of the Prophet of Islam in my old age and after the decrepitude of my body—(There is, however, no excuse for him, for the proof of God is clear to all!)—but if God had guided me to this while I was still your age, I would have left everything and entered the True Religion. Love of the material world is at the heart of all sins. You can see my status among the Christians, the dignity I am accorded, the wealth, the honor, and my reputation in this world. If I were to demonstrate any leanings toward the religion of Islam, the masses would kill me at the earliest possible opportunity. Even if I were able to save myself from them and make my way to the Muslims and say to them, 'I have come to you to become a Muslim,' they would say to me, 'You have done yourself a great benefit by entering into the True Religion, but you do not bestow upon us any favor with your entrance into a religion by which you have saved yourself from the punishment of God.' I would remain among them a poor old man, ninety years of age, where I don't understand their language and they do not know my worth, and I would end up dying of starvation. So I remain, thank God, of the religion of Jesus and of Him who brought it. God knows this of me."

So I said to him, "Master, are you indicating to me that I should go to the lands of the Muslims and enter into their religion?" He responded, "If you are intelligent and seek salvation, then rush to do this, thereby gaining for yourself both this world and the next! But, my son, this is a matter which no one is here to witness and which you must conceal to the utmost of your ability, for if any of it were to become known, the masses would kill you instantly, and I would not be able to help you. Nor would it help you to trace this back to me, for I would deny it, and my word about you would be believed, but your statements against me would not be believed. I am innocent of your blood should you utter a word of this."

So I said to him, "Master, I hope to God that I would never even imagine doing such a thing!" I therefore pledged to him [my secrecy] as he desired. Then I began to make provisions for the journey. I said farewell to him and he asked God to protect me and gave me fifty gold dinars. I traveled by sea, heading for my homeland, the city of Mallorca. I remained there for six months, then I traveled on to Sicily and stayed there five months waiting for a ship heading to the lands of the Muslims. Finally a ship came that was heading to the city of Tunis, so I departed Sicily on it. We set sail at dusk and spotted the port of Tunis around noon. When I landed at the customshouse of Tunis, and the Christian men of religion who were there learned of my presence, they came with a boat and took me to their homes. Some of the merchants resident there in Tunis also befriended me. I stayed there as their guest living the most comfortable of lives for four months. After that I asked them if there were anyone in the household of the sultan who spoke the language of the Christians. The sultan at that time was our Lord Abū al-ʿAbbās Aḥmad (may God have mercy on him!). They told me that there was in the household of the aforementioned sultan a good man, one of the highest-ranking servants, by the name of Yūsuf the physician, for the sultan's physician was part of his personal entourage. I rejoiced at this news. I asked about this man's residence and was given directions to it. I met with him and I explained my position: that I had come in order to embrace the religion of Islam. He was overjoyed at this and decided that this news should be delivered [to the sultan] by his own hands.

I mounted his horse with him and he took me to the house of the sultan, entered, and informed the sultan of what I had said. He asked permission for me to enter, and I was granted permission. Thus I appeared before the sultan. He first asked me my age and I told him that I was thirty-five years old. Then he asked me as well what sciences I had studied and I told him. He told me that I had arrived in the most auspicious manner possible and that he wished God Almighty's blessings upon me. Then I said to the translator, that is, the aformentioned physician, "Say to Our Lord the Sultan, that no man leaves his religion without causing his people to speak against him and to slander him, so I ask you in your beneficence to summon the Christian merchants and their men of religion, ask them about me and hear what they have to say of me in my absence, and then, God willing, I will convert to Islam." He replied to me via the translator, "You have requested [from me] what ʿAbd Allāh ibn Salām requested of the Prophet himself (May God Bless and Preserve him!) when he converted to Islam!"[1]

The sultan sent for the Christian men of religion and some of the merchants and he put me in a room near his council chamber. When the Christians entered, he asked them, "What do you have to say about this new priest who arrived on that boat?" They said, "He is a very learned man in our religion and our priests have said, 'We have seen none higher than him in knowledge or faith in our religion.' " Then he said to them, "And what would you say of him if he were to convert to Islam?" They said, "We seek refuge in God from that possibility! He would never do such a thing!"

When he had heard what the Christians had to say, he sent for me and I approached him and gave witness to the true credo in the presence of the Christians and they prostrated themselves and called out, "Nothing but a desire to get married could have driven him to this, for priests of our religion cannot marry!" They left distressed and sorrowful. The sultan—may God have mercy on him!—bestowed on me a salary of four dinars per diem, granted me lodging among his retinue, and married me to the daughter of the Ḥājj Muḥammad al-Ṣaffār.

When I resolved to consummate the marriage, he gave me one hundred gold dinars and a complete new set of clothing. I consummated the union with her and she bore me a son, whom I named Muḥammad by way of a blessing, after Our Prophet Muhammad—may God bless and preserve him!

Note

1. ʿAbd Allāh ibn Salām was a Jew who converted to Islam. He initially concealed the matter from his fellow Jews and went to the Prophet requesting that Muhammad ask about him among the Jews so that Muhammad could see what position he held in their community before they learned of his conversion. The sultan of Tunis is pleased and flattered because Anselmo has placed him in the same position that the Prophet had occupied. See Ibn Hishām, *The Life of Muhammad: A Translation of Isḥāq's Sīrat Rasūl Allāh,* trans. Alfred Guillaume (London: Oxford University Press, 1955), 240–42.

The Autobiography of Jalāl al-Dīn al-Suyūṭī

(1445–1505)

Introduction

Jalāl al-Dīn al-Suyūṭī was born in Cairo in 1445. Judge, legal scholar, and prolific writer, his bibliography of published works, included in his autobiography, lists hundreds of treatises, books, pamphlets, and monographs on subjects ranging from grammar to legal opinions to *ḥadīth* to a history of his hometown of Asyut (al-Suyūṭ). His personality did not make him a popular man among his peers. He himself records in detail a number of the public clashes he got into with contemporaries over various legal questions and interpretations. The editor of his autobiography, Elizabeth Sartain, describes him as "the most controversial figure of his time" (1:72) because of his immodest claim to be the most important religious scholar of his century. His remarkable faith in his own judgments, his mocking rebuttals, and his personal attacks on those who disagreed with him all earned him the ire of his fellow scholars. Sometime after composing the autobiography, al-Suyūṭī retired from public life, embittered at the lack of public recognition he received from the very colleagues he so often disparaged. He died in Cairo in 1505.

His autobiography is organized into thematic chapters rather than into a chronological narrative. Although the larger text is not structured as a single narrative, smaller narratives, such as the one translated here, occur within the chapters, and the entire text is ultimately structured so as to present the author as the "Renewer of the Faith" for the tenth Islamic century. It is clear from contemporary references that al-Suyūṭī wrote several versions of his life; by far the lengthiest, and the only one currently available, is *Speaking of God's Bounty*. Al-Suyūṭī apparently did not finish the work, for the single surviving manuscript contains a number of blank spaces and incomplete sections. Even in this form, at two hundred fifty printed pages, it is one of the longest of all premodern Arabic autobiographies.

This short excerpt from chapter 17, "On How God Blessed Me by Setting Enemies Against Me to Harm Me and Tested Me with the False Accusations of an Ignoramus, as Has Also Happened to our Forefathers," recounts one of a series of incidents that pitted al-Suyūṭī against the anonymous "ignoramus" (*al-jāhil*), a fellow religious scholar in Cairo. The term itself is reminiscent of the "father of ignorance" (*Abū Jahl*) found in the biography of the Prophet Muhammad—a troublesome man who plagued the Prophet, but whose misdeeds were patiently tolerated by Muhammad as a trial sent by God—and, in addition, can carry the connotation of something or someone un-Islamic since the pre-Islamic period as a whole is referred to in Arabic to as the Age of Ignorance (*al-jāhiliyya*). Al-Suyūṭī construes the insults and troubles he endures from the "ignoramus" as a parallel to those endured by Muhammad and other righteous figures in early Islamic history. This particular incident involves a "house of ill repute," a building in which sexual licentiousness, drinking, and music are said to take place, and whether the law allowed such an establishment to be destroyed if these activities did not cease. Al-Suyūṭī, of course, portrays himself as the winner in this battle, but the final resolution comes about in a somewhat surprising and even rather unsatisfying manner.

Bibliography

Brustad, Kristen. "Imposing Order: Reading the Conventions of Representation in al-Suyūṭī's Autobiography." *Edebiyât: Special Issue—Arabic Autobiography,* N.S. 7, no. 2 (1997): 327–44.

Sartain, E. M. *Jalāl al-Dīn al-Suyūṭī:* vol. 1: *Biography and Background*; vol. 2: *al-Taḥadduth bi-niʿmat Allāh.* Cambridge: Cambridge University Press, 1975. 175–80.

Chapter 17

On How God Blessed Me by Setting Enemies Against Me to Harm Me and Tested Me with the False Accusations of an Ignoramus, as Has Also Happened to Our Forefathers

The Incident of the House of Ill Repute [*Jalāl al-Dīn*, 2:175–80]

In the month of Ramadan in the year 886 [1481 C.E.], the aforementioned ignoramus stirred up another controversy involving me over the question of the destruction of property. The story is this: For some years there had been in our quarter a house belonging to a man named Qāsim al-Ḥabbāk, next to which there was a mosque that had a caretaker named Ḥasan al-Masīrī. Now this Ḥasan used to come to see me to complain about the residents of the aforementioned house, saying that men would gather there to engage in such debauchery as adultery, sodomy, drinking, playing musical instruments, and so forth. He told me that this activity had increased and become well known, such that this house was sought out by people from far-off places. Large numbers of people would gather there, so many that one group would enter and begin to engage in adultery and sodomy while another group waited their turn at the door. Some would stand in the street and others would sit at the door of the mosque. It was even said that a man was seen inside that mosque with a youth with whom he was engaged in sodomy. This incident became public knowledge in the quarter and in this way the place became famous for such activities and was sought out by people from far and wide.

The aforementioned Ḥasan would say to me, "What can I do? Shall I complain to the palace guard about them? Shall I complain to the military police about them? Shall I have the place raided?" I would reply, "It is more humane to be gentle in disapproval; limit yourself to verbal threats and take no action."

Now it turned out that the aforementioned ignoramus was among the residents of that house, but by God, I had no inkling of that until after the occurrence of the incident that I will now relate.

Matters continued in this same vein for some years, until Ḥasan mentioned to me at the beginning of the present year [886/1481] that the place was finally rid of all that, and for that I thanked God profusely. But then during the month of Ramadan, he came to see me in a terrible state and said, "This calamity has returned to the way it was!" "How so?" I asked. He told me that a commander named Qānṣūh al-Sharafī had been one of those who used to frequent the place, and that he had gone away on a military detail in the company of the ruler. News had come of the detachment's approach, and a group of people who used to accompany him in his activities had rented the place from Qāsim the owner and had begun to repair it and prepare it so that they could gather there after the commander's return and resume their activities. I told Ḥasan to go to Qāsim and tell him that I said he must not rent to these people, and that if he did, I would issue a legal ruling to have the place razed. I meant this to frighten him so that he would turn them away at the outset, which would be much easier than moving them out once they had taken up residence.

The owner then went to the aforementioned ignoramus and told him the whole story. He said, "That's not the law. What is his legal basis for saying that?" A man then came to me and asked about the legal basis for my threat, and I said, "Many things, which I will mention in a separate publication." He replied, "Mention one of them now." I said, "The story of the al-Ḍirār mosque." So he went back to the ignoramus and reported this to him. The latter responded, "How is that relevant? That was a mosque built by hypocrites." The first man returned to ask me again, and I recited to him the Prophet's words: "I decided to call [the people] to prayer and have them gather to do so, then to command a man to lead the people in prayer, then to set out with men carrying bundles of firewood to find those people who were not observing the prayer and to burn down their houses."

He returned to the other and reported this and the latter responded, "This man doesn't grasp the matter at all. People have disagreed about praying in a group. Some hold that it is a collective obligation, while others claim that is an individual obligation. The people who believe the latter use that saying of the Prophet as evidence; but they do not use it as evidence to prove that house of ill repute should be razed." When this was reported to me, I realized that these were the words of an ignoramus, and that arguing with the ignorant is a waste of time, so I issued no reply.

After that, this ignoramus went to seek legal rulings from some local scholars and they ruled against razing the building. Shaykh al-Bānī,[1] as was his habit, added that whosoever ruled in favor of razing the building would be subject to punishment. I would like to say to that so-called legal scholar: "Master, the judgment to raze the building is correct, according to reports transmitted from ʿUmar ibn al-Khaṭṭāb, ʿUthmān ibn ʿAffān, Ibn Masʿūd, ʿAbd Allāh ibn Zubayr, ʿAbd Allāh ibn ʿAbbās, and ʿUmar ibn ʿAbd al-ʿAzīz.[2] The leaders of the three legal schools—Ḥanafī, Malikī, and Ḥanbalī—have all stipulated it, and the two Shāfiʿī jurists al-Ghazālī and al-Kawāshī have also suggested this interpretation. So who exactly among those great leaders should be subjected to punishment? If you feared your Lord, you would carefully verify what you say. If you recall that your ruling will be held up to you on the Day of Judgment and you will be asked about it letter by letter, then you would pay more attention to what you write! It is as if you had never heard the words:

> Do not write with your own hand anything except
> that which you will be pleased to see on Judgment Day.

I do not deny your knowledge or your schooling, but our situation is like that of Shaykh ʿAbd Allāh al-Minūfī who said to one of his teachers after the latter had spoken rudely against one of his own students: 'You are an educated man, Master, but knowledge has not taught you manners!' "

The aforementioned ignoramus returned overjoyed with al-Bānī's ruling in hand, and sat in his market shop calling out in his loudest voice: "So-and-so has broken the unanimous agreement of jurists with his ruling! This man is speaking recklessly about God's religion! He is a such-and-such!"

and so forth, and he began to curse and use foul language. He went to the residents of that house and told them, "Have no fear! They have decided that he is to be punished; he can no longer confront you." The residents lifted their heads up and puffed out their cheeks, while those who disapproved were humiliated and defeated. The former group prepared to resume their debauchery under the protection of Shaykh Shams al-Dīn al-Bānī.

Ḥasan the caretaker, who had tried to stop them, came to see me in utter humiliation and disappointment, barely able to speak. I said, "Hold on, I am in the right. God says, 'So lose not heart, fall not into despair; for you shall overcome, if you are true believers' [Q 3:138]. I swear by God that if they resume their previous debauchery I will inform the caliph and show him the transmitted opinions of the great Muslim jurists in favor of razing, even if a thousand al-Bānī's rule otherwise."

Then God in His Grace decreed that Qānṣūh, whose arrival they were all awaiting, was instead sent by the ruler to Tripoli. The group disbanded and not one of them was heard from after that. The place became free of debauchery, stood empty and closed up, thanks be to God! I wrote something about this problem and titled it: *Raising the Minaret of Religion and Razing the House of Dissipation.* It is also called, *Bringing the Wineshop Down on the Builder* [= al-Bānī]. As for the aforementioned ignoramus, he flew off on the wings of confoundment, donned the womanly robes of cowardice, and escaped by the skin of his teeth.[3]

They wish to straighten his crookedness;
But can people straighten what God Himself has made bent?

I composed [these verses] about the incident:

Marvel [O reader!] at the builder [al-Bānī] of a house of ill repute,
who is master in all types of immorality.
We forbade sodomy and hashish,
and he called our ruling on it ignorant and unseemly.

I also composed the following:

The house of ill repute says, "No Muslim,
due to what I am prepared for, approves of me.
No one of intelligence can fail to see
the measure of my deficiency.
If someone sees my scales tilting to one side
it is because a lame sodomite is weighing me."
I said, "If the house is not emptied of its contents,
The law stipulates razing this wineshop."
Al-Bānī was asked and he ruled that
the one who rules this way is guilty.

O people, listen to what is steady and true,
  and is neither wavering nor shaky,
Who more justly should be accused of a crime,
  whether by friend or by enemy?
The one who razes a house built to disobey God in,
  or the one who has built it: al-Bānī?

Notes

1. The shaykh's name literally means "Builder."

2. A list of early Muslim figures known for their religious knowledge—ʿUmar ibn al-Khaṭṭāb and ʿUthmān ibn ʿAffān were the second and third caliphs who led the Islamic community after the death of the Prophet Muhammad.

3. Literally, "he took the spear in his forearm" (i.e., he escaped the more serious injury that would have resulted from a direct confrontation with al-Suyūṭī).

The Autobiography of al-ʿAydarūs

(1570–1628)

Introduction

ʿAbd al-Qādir ibn ʿAbd Allāh al-ʿAydarūs was a member of a prominent South Arabian family that claimed descent from the Prophet Muhammad. Al-ʿAydarūs's father moved from South Arabia to Gujarat, India, after which it became customary for members of the family to live or at least travel there. The family's reputation for piety and scholarship appears to have ingratiated them with the ruling families of Gujarat. Ministers and ladies of the court march in and out of al-ʿAydarūs's autobiography, and "princes and merchants" study Sufism under his supervision. Other members of the family held high positions at Indian courts and continued the family tradition of Sufi teaching and writing. One descendant, Ḥusayn al-ʿAydarūs (d. 1798), is revered as a saint in Indonesia.

The author's account of his childhood reveals how his father's attentions instilled self-esteem and boundless optimism in the son. Al-ʿAydarūs's father, unlike al-Tirmidhī's, is not shown urging his son to study; rather, he simply predicts his son's greatness, "using allusions and allegories," as in the dream-tale at the beginning of the autobiography. The author seems never to have doubted that he was destined for a bright future. He nevertheless claims to have been surprised when his books became famous, saying that God then "blessed me with something completely unexpected." In context, this remark appears to signal the author's conviction that salvation after death is sufficient reward for his pious efforts and that good fortune on earth is an unexpected bonus. However, none of this prevents al-ʿAydarūs from recounting the virtues of his own books, or relating the praises colleagues lavished on him.

Al-ʿAydarūs's compilation of character recommendations and positive book reviews may, in its fulsomeness and complacency, irritate the modern reader. However, the text, by its very placement, reveals a certain modesty just as characteristic of the author's milieu as of his pride. The autobiography appears under the year 1570, the year of al-ʿAydarūs's birth, in his biographical and historical catalog of the sixteenth century. He tells his life story, therefore, in the entry corresponding to the year of his birth and not at the beginning or end of his work. The entry also mentions other noteworthy events of 1570, such as: "In this year the reservoirs of Ahmadabad overflowed and then emptied out completely. Also in this year, blood was seen in some of the reservoirs of Ahmadabad."

Al-ʿAydarūs's brief autobiographical entry gives his date of birth and mentions poetry composed in honor of the event. He explains how he was named after spiritual figures who appeared to his father in a dream, and recounts the various signs of his father's confidence in his future greatness. He describes his mother, giving the circumstances of how she entered his father's household, and briefly describes her character. Next comes an account of his education, his rise to fame, and his numerous students. He lists his books and compositions, with accompanying self-congratulatory remarks. His citations of his own poetry are striking: only here does he speak of such matters as sorrow, pain, and love. The verses attest to the nearness of God and the vivid presence of the Islamic past. They also express emotions that appear to have arisen in the course of one or more erotic encounters, including one with a man whose eloquence and slim figure captivated his sentiments. Certain lines, particularly the one in which he declares himself free of any law but love, seem scandalous. Yet al-ʿAydarūs's colleagues found nothing reprehensible in his conduct: as he is careful to tell us, they praised his works and composed poems in his honor.

He concludes by justifying his work in conventional fashion, citing the Qurʾānic injunction to speak of the blessings of God and listing earlier scholars who had written autobiographies. Short and succinct, al-ʿAydarūs's text brings together motifs that distinguish many medieval Arabic autobiographies, such as a more intimate view of childhood and parent-child relations than is typically offered in biographical writings, as well as a glimpse of inner passions expressed in verse rather than in narrative. Evidently, Arabic autobiographical texts and their conventions were well known in seventeenth-century Muslim India.

Bibliography

al-ʿAydarūs, ʿAbd al-Qādir. *al-Nūr al-sāfir ʿan akhbār al-qarn al-ʿāshir.* Ed. Muḥammad Rashīd Afandī al-Ṣaffār. Baghdad: al-Maktaba al-ʿArabiyya, 1934. 334–43.

Löfgren, Oscar. "ʿAydarūs." *EI*[2] 1:780–82.

The Life of al-ʿAydarūs
[*al-Nūr,* pp. 334–43]

On the evening of Thursday, the twentieth of the month of Rabīʿ I, 978 [1570 C.E.], the author of this book was born. May God help him achieve the good things he hopes for and bring all his labors to a happy conclusion.

[Here follows five lines of mnemonic verse composed by the author's father citing the date of the author's birth and a list of family friends who composed similar poems.]

About two weeks before I was born, my father—may God rest his soul—saw in a dream a number of the "friends of God," including ʿAbd al-Qādir al-Jīlānī and Abū Bakr al-ʿAydarūs.[1] ʿAbd al-Qādir had appeared in order to ask something of my father. Because of the dream, my father, convinced that I would become a person of importance, decided to name me ʿAbd al-Qādir Muḥyī al-Dīn after al-Jīlānī and Abū Bakr after al-ʿAydarūs.

None of my father's children had grown up healthy in India, and none of them survived except me. My father loved me very much. Once he said to me, "When your time comes, you may do whatever you want." He would very often hint at things to come, using allusions and allegories which I cannot fully express in words, and which at this point it is better not to try and reproduce. I pray that God bring my father's predictions to fruition.

A reliable source told me the following story: "A certain prominent minister visited your father to ask him to pray for them concerning some business or other. You were very young at the time. You were sitting in front of your father, and at that moment you happened to recite the verse, 'Here is another [blessing] dear to you; a God-given victory and speedy success [Q 61:13].' Your father said to him, 'There is your good omen for you—it is practically a revelation from God!' And, by the leave of God, they got what they wished for."

My mother was an Indian slave given to my father by a charitable woman of the royal family famous for her generosity and the kindness and deference she bore toward my father. This lady gave my mother all the household items and furniture she needed, and placed a number of slave women at her disposal. She regarded my mother as one of her own daughters and used to visit her several times a month.

My mother was a virgin when she entered my father's house, and she bore him no children except me. She was a worthy woman, humble, kind, upright, and generous. She died before noon on Friday, the twentieth of the month of Ramadan, 1010 [1602]. Her last words were, "There is no god but God." Her grave is next to my father's, just outside his mausoleum. May God rest her soul!

I studied the Qur'ān with a pious holy man, and finished memorizing the whole text while my father was still alive. After memorizing the Qur'ān, I took up other studies, and read a number of standard introductory texts with prominent scholars. I devoted myself to teaching and—by God's grace—kept company in learned circles, so that I could learn and benefit from scholarly men. I applied myself to finding out what made them great, and I revered them, showing deference to them in my speech and endeavoring to imitate their behavior, striving to gain their affection.

I explored various disciplines and gave myself over entirely to the useful branches of learning, for the sake of God. I resolved to acquire good books, and I traveled far and wide to find them. These, combined with the books I received from my father, added up to a large collection.

When I found out that my ancestor, ʿAbd Allāh al-ʿAydarūs, had said: "Whoever obtains the *Revival of the Religious Sciences* and makes a fair copy of it in forty volumes is guaranteed a place in heaven," I went ahead and—praise the Lord—copied it with that aim in mind.[2]

I devoted myself to hearing lectures on the Prophetic traditions, and I spent my time studying them diligently. With God's help, I read a great many books. I picked up many strange and recondite things in these books, and in the lectures of the outstanding authorities and prominent erudites of the day. By the grace of God Almighty, I was able to catch all the mystical allusions and understand all the scholarly debates and literary references I came across. Nevertheless, I feigned ignorance of these matters. No one should speak of mystical allegories and states of mystical consciousness unless he has understood and experienced them himself. Even then, he should only discuss them with people who already know about them, because these are matters of felt experience which neither tongue nor pen can truly tell. As for literary matters, it does not befit a man of intellect to appear to know too much about them.

I ask God to make my learning a means of approaching Him more closely, and a force that will draw me inexorably nearer to Him. I ask Him to make my happiness complete by letting me die well and enter the Best Place and remain there with my parents, my dear friends, my teachers, my students, and my children. He is the One best asked: He is near and He answers, none guides to success but He. I place my trust entirely in Him and turn to Him repentantly.

Then God blessed me with something unexpected—Glory be to the Bounteous, Most Generous, and Giving One, the Bestower of Gifts! My associates spread knowledge of my writings, and scholars far and wide spoke highly of my work. I thus gained the affection and prayers of many a spiritual guide and exemplar. Learned men east and west made much of me. Dignitaries deferred to me, some willingly and others not. Rulers of distant places wrote to me and sent me stupendous gifts and emoluments. Praises reached me from the ends of the earth, including Egypt, remote Yemen, and other distant lands. More than one notable scholar studied with me, and many people learned from me.

Among the prominent men whom I inducted into Sufism were Jamāl al-Dīn Muḥammad ibn Yaḥyā al-Shāmī al-Makkī, the learned Badr al-Dīn Ḥasan ibn Dāwūd al-Hindī, Aḥmad ibn Muḥammad ibn ʿAbd al-Raḥīm Bā Jābir al-Ḥaḍramī, Shihāb al-Dīn Aḥmad b. Rabīʿ b. al-Shaykh al-Kabīr b. Aḥmad b. ʿAbd al-Ḥaqq al-Sinbāṭī al-Makkī al-Miṣrī, and others. The number of princes, merchants, and people of other classes whom I inducted into Sufism is so great that I cannot possibly enumerate them.

I have written a number of well-loved and appreciated books. These have been greeted with unanimous acclaim, practically the only dissenters being enemies or jealous rivals of mine. My books constitute the most conspicuous testimony of the blessings with which God has favored me.

[Here follows an annotated list of twenty-four books by the author, including biographies of the Prophet, an account of the martyrs at the battle of Badr, expositions on the fundamentals of the Islamic faith and Sufi practice, a commentary on a Qurʾānic verse, commentaries on poems, his work on history ("this book here"), and a collection of his own poetry from which he cites the following nine short examples.]

[The power of prayer]

In my darkest nights of sorrow
  I recall the martyrs of Badr-day,
God will heed my supplication
  if in their name I pray.

[A conceit]

With the beauty of his figure
  And the figures of his speech,
His tropes have all enslaved me
  With the secrets that they teach.

His logic made me languish
  And his waistline made me pine,
When I sentenced us to parting
  I saw his heart decline.

[A punning poem in praise of Aḥmad ibn Ḥanbal, the founder of the author's school of law]

Aḥmad is a *Shāfiʿī,* that is, my intercessor,
  Before *Mālikī,* that is, my Lord and All-Possessor,

God my sins will surely pardon, just for Aḥmad's sake,
And lift my soul to Paradise when I from death awake![3]

[The law of love]

Who would berate me, rebuke me no more;
The sweet pain of passion is what I adore,
The only law I obey is the scripture of love
Which I bear like a prophet sent down from above.

[A request]

Go and seek my love
Pass by his abode
Speak my name in passing
And tell him of my woe

[Advice to a seeker]

Searching for thy Master, thou cam'st to me,
But the One you seek is nearer to thee!
Leave me, and upon thyself reflect!
The Lord is no further than the vein in thy neck.

[On the Prophet]

True, my love was born to a noble line,
But he reached a perfection they could not know:
He brought the last revelation from God above
And ennobled, at last, the world below.

[Parting]

"You can part with beauty," he said.
I cried, "I cannot, I cannot!"

[On being a "Shiʿite"]

I love the Prophet Muhammad and his family:
If that makes me a Shiʿite, that's fine with me.

The majority of these books have met with the approval of learned and upright men whose fame is such that they have no need of further praise from me.

[Here follows a list of four scholars, cited with all of their honorific titles, who complimented the author's work.]

The last of these, Jamāl al-Dīn al-Maghribī, traveled to Yemen and visited ʿAbd al-Malik al-Yamanī. While looking at one of ʿAbd al-Malik's books,

Jamāl al-Dīn came across something I had written and was much impressed. "This writer," he said, "has no living rival! I pray for his long life, so he can keep producing these wonderfully useful compositions, which are so much help to those fortunate people whom God wishes to guide aright."

Important men copied my books in their own handwriting. My brother ʿAbd Allāh, the great holy man and famous theosophist, delighted in them to no end, and spared no effort in acquiring them. He used to insist that I send him every new book I wrote, and would tell me how much he liked their style, and how no one was as good a stylist as I was. I saw in a letter of his to his servant Sālim ibn ʿAlī Bā Mawja some remarks about me, among them that he thought me of the same rank as my father.

Muḥammad ibn ʿAbd al-Raḥīm Bā Jābir wrote to me asking a favor which entailed some difficulty. "Don't think this is too hard for you, Shaykh ʿAbd al-Qādir. You are one of those people who can exert their will freely in this world, and to whom, by God's will, all things respond."

[Here follows a twenty-three verse poem by the jurist ʿAbd al-Malik al-Yamanī expressing his longing to meet the author and praising his scholarship and noble descent.]

I mention these things only as a way of speaking of God's bounty [Q 93: 11]. I have cited men of piety and integrity in order to gain blessings from their words. At any rate, I have said much less than I could have, and the number of kindnesses they have shown me that I have mentioned here is much less than the number I have passed over in silence. May God reward them on my behalf with the best reward that a master can obtain on account of his disciple! Other than making me a Muslim and a descendant of the Prophet, God has conferred upon me no blessing which I treasure more than this [i.e., the approbation of his teachers]. This is why I have mentioned it in this book. I believe that this memory should remain with me, my descendants, and my students until the last day of recorded time. Countless exemplary scholars have preceded me in this, among them Ibn Ḥajar al-ʿAsqalānī, al-Sakhāwī, al-Suyūṭī, Sharaf al-Dīn Ismāʿīl al-Muqrī al-Yamanī (author of the *Irshād*), al-Daybaʿ, al-Fāsī, Ibn Ḥajar al-Haytamī, and others.

Notes

1. Al-Jīlānī (d. 1166) championed the Sufi path but within the strict confines of the Ḥanbalī school of law; he is often portrayed as a saintly figure with miraculous powers. Abū Bakr al-ʿAydarūs is apparently the author's great-grandfather, Abū Bakr ibn ʿAbd al-Raḥmān al-Saqqāf.

2. *The Revival of the Religious Sciences* (Iḥyāʾ ʿulūm al-dīn) is the most famous work

of the religious thinker Abū Ḥāmid Muḥammad al-Ghazālī (d. 1111). The book is a guide to Muslim conduct and ethics, informed by the mystical impulse.

3. The words *shāfiʿī* and *mālikī* mean "my intercessor" and "my possessor" respectively; the words coincide with the adjectival forms of two prominent Sunnī legal schools founded by al-Shāfiʿī (d. 820) and Mālik ibn Anas (d. 796).

The Autobiography of Yūsuf al-Baḥrānī

(1696–1772)

Introduction

Given his background and scholarly education, Yūsuf ibn Aḥmad al-Baḥrānī might well have lived a quiet, uneventful life; he came from a wealthy merchant family, and his grandfather engaged in Bahrain's most important area of commerce, the pearl trade. Instead, he was destined to live in turbulent times in a region and era often ignored by western scholarship on Middle Eastern history. As his name indicates, he was born on the island of Bahrain in the Persian Gulf, in a Shiʿite community at the very edges of the waning Persian Safavid dynasty's effective political control. When he was five, the region was shaken by tribal wars. Soon afterward, Bahrain was besieged three times by the Omani Yaʿriba dynasty. At the conclusion of the final siege, Bahrain fell and came under Omani control. A counterattack by the Safavids failed, but eventually they regained Bahrain through negotiations and the payment of a large sum to the Omanis. Next the Huwala Arab tribes again attacked from the west and captured Bahrain. The region was thrown into further disorder by the fall of the Safavid dynasty that had ruled from 1501 to 1722. Fleeing these troubles, al-Baḥrānī traveled to Qaṭīf in what is now eastern Saudi Arabia, then across the Arabian peninsula to Mecca. He returned for a time to Qaṭīf and Bahrain but finally fled to southern Iran. There, however, his luck was no better: in Shiraz he got caught up in a local rebellion and left for Fasā, only to have that region be struck by an unspecified disaster. Finally, in his old age he sought refuge in Karbalāʾ in southern Iraq, the site of the martyrdom of the Imam Ḥusayn, grandson of the Prophet Muhammad, one of the defining moments of history for Shiʿite Islam. Here the turmoil that had followed al-Baḥrānī his whole life suddenly ceased. His financial situation improved, and he became respected as both a scholar and a teacher. Composing this account of his life in 1768 at the age of seventy-two, he wrote from the perspective of a secure and peaceful dotage.

The author's autobiography constitutes the final section of his biographical dictionary of Shiʿite scholars titled *The Pearl of Bahrain* (Lu'lu'at al-Baḥrayn). He wrote the work as a scholarly legacy to his two nephews and framed the entire opus as an *ijāza,* or certificate of study, for them in which he detailed his links with earlier generations of Shiʿite scholars. The *ijāza* was a document that transferred the authority to teach a given work or a given body of knowledge, similar to the role of the university degree in modern times. The extension of the *ijāza* from a simple signed statement into a larger document at times involved, as here, the recording of the transmission of that authority back through the teacher to his own teachers, their teachers, and so forth. *The Pearl of Bahrain* is thus a scholarly biographical compendium, on the one hand, and a family-oriented document, on the other, for in it al-Baḥrānī presents the Shiʿite tradition of the study of law and *ḥadīth,* establishes his own place within that tradition, justifies his own authority, and formally passes on the tradition to his two nephews, the recipients of this *ijāza.*

One striking feature of this short autobiographical section is al-Baḥrānī's repeated mentions of his financial state, debts, losses, and taxes and the abundant use of metaphors of commerce and acquisition such as in this verse of poetry quoted by the author:

> Your nearness is my wealth, despite a lack of riches,
> and your distance my poverty, despite abundant wealth.

If we understand the autobiographical act as an attempt to evaluate one's life by searching for its central or enduring meaning, we may read al-Baḥrānī's text as a literal stock-taking. The central metaphor for his life is accumulation, and through this metaphor he describes his life as a double quest: on the one hand, to acquire material and worldly property, including money, land, date palms, wives, and dependents, and, on the other, to accumulate religious knowledge as embodied in certificates of study, books, and treatises.

Bibliography

al-Baḥrānī, Yūsuf ibn Aḥmad. *Lu'lu'at al-Baḥrayn.* Ed. Muḥammad Ṣādiq Baḥr al-ʿUlūm. Najaf: Maṭbaʿat al-Nuʿmān, 1966. 442–49.

Stewart, Devin J. "Capital, Accumulation, and the Islamic Academic Biography." *Edebiyât: Special Issue—Arabic Autobiography,* N.S. 7, no. 2 (1997): 345–62.

An Account of the Life of the Author and the Events That Have Befallen Him
[*Lu'lu'at al-Baḥrayn,* pp. 442–49]

Let us now fulfill the promise we made above that we would relate the conditions of this miserable wretch, who is guilty of many sins and shortcomings, the author of this *ijāza*. So I say:

I was born in the year 1107 [1695–96 C.E.].[1] My brother, Shaykh Muḥammad—may God prolong his presence [in this world]—was born in 1112 [1700–1] in the village of Māḥūz, for our father was residing there in order to attend the lessons of his teacher Shaykh Sulaymān, who has been mentioned above. I was about five years old then and in that year the battle between the Huwala and ʿUtūb tribes took place.[2] The ʿUtūb had been causing great havoc in Bahrain and the [Safavid] ruler [Shah Sulṭān Ḥusayn] could do nothing to stop them. So the Shaykh al-Islām, Shaykh Muḥammad ibn ʿAbd Allāh ibn Mājid, wrote to the Huwala entreating them to oppose the ʿUtūb. A large force from the Huwala tribe came and there was a great battle. The land was ravaged right up to the fortress, affecting everyone, notables and commoners, until God finally caused the ʿUtūb to be defeated. My father—may God have mercy on him—wrote some verses describing and dating this battle, but I only remember the last line, which includes the date and reads as follows:

> The year of the battle of the tormented tribe
> is "they scattered it" [*shattatūhā*], so reckon the sum.[3]

I was raised in the lap of my grandfather, the late Shaykh Ibrāhīm—may God bless his soul. He was involved in pearling and the pearl trade. He was noble, pious, generous, and merciful, and would spend all of his income on his guests, relatives, and petitioners. He neither hoarded nor jealously guarded anything from others. Since my father had not had any sons before me, my grandfather took me in and raised me. He had a teacher come to the house to teach me the Qur'ān, and he himself taught me how to write. His script and that of my father were extremely fine and beautiful. After this, I attended the lessons of my father—may God bless his soul—but at the time I had no great desire to study for I was still overcome by the ignorance of youth.

Under my father's supervision I read *Drops of Dew* [a work on basic Arabic syntax],[4] most of *The Son of the Versifier* [an intermediate commentary on Arabic syntax],[5] most of al-Niẓām on morphology,[6] and the beginning of al-Quṭbī [on logic][7] until the Khārijites [the Omani Yaʿriba dynasty] came to seize the land of Bahrain.[8] The earth shook and everything came to a standstill while preparations were made to do battle with these vile men.

The first year they came to seize it they returned disappointed, for they were unable to do so. Nor were they able to succeed the second time a year later, despite the help they received from all of the Bedouin and outlaws. The third time, however, they were able to surround Bahrain by controlling the sea, for Bahrain is an island. In this way they eventually weakened its inhabitants and then took it by force. It was a horrific battle and a terrible catastrophe, for all the killing, plunder, pillage, and bloodshed that took place.

After the Khārijites had conquered it and granted the inhabitants safe passage, the people—especially the notables—fled to al-Qaṭīf and other regions. Among them was my father—God have mercy upon him—accompanied by his dependents [i.e., wives] and children, who traveled with them to al-Qaṭīf. But he left me in Bahrain in the house we owned in al-Shākhūra because some chests filled with bundles of our possessions, including books, gold coins, and clothes, were hidden there. He had taken a large portion of our possessions up to the fortress in which everyone had planned to [take refuge] when we were besieged, but he had left some behind in the house, stored in hiding places. Everything in the fortress was lost after the Khārijites took it by force, and we all left the fortress with nothing but the clothes on our backs. So when my father left for al-Qaṭīf, I remained in Bahrain; he had ordered me to gather whatever books remained in the fortress and save them from the hands of the Khārijites. I did manage to save a number of books that I found there along with some that were left in the house, which I sent to him a few at a time. These years passed in an utter lack of prosperity.

I then traveled to al-Qaṭīf to visit my father and stayed there two or three months, but my father grew fed up with sitting in al-Qaṭīf because of the large number of dependents he had with him, the miserable conditions, and his lack of money, so he grew determined to return to Bahrain even though it was in the hands of the Khārijites. Fate, however, intervened between him and his plans, for the Persian army, along with a large number of Bedouins, arrived at that time to liberate Bahrain from the hands of the Khārijites. We followed the events closely and waited to see the outcome of these disasters; eventually the wheel of fortune turned against the Persians, they were all killed, and Bahrain was burned. Our house in the village [of al-Shākhūra] was among those burned. My father's anguish—may God have mercy on him—increased further with this. He had spent a considerable sum to have it built and its loss was the death of him. He fell ill and the illness lasted for two months. He died on the date mentioned above [January 14, 1719, at the age of forty-seven]. When death approached, he summoned me and said, "I will never forgive you if you should ever sit down to eat even once without your brothers and sisters around you." This was because my siblings were from other mothers and most of them were small children whose mothers had died and who had no one else to turn to. I had no choice but to allow myself to be saddled with dependents and the burden of all these siblings, both the smaller ones and the older ones.[9]

I stayed thus in al-Qaṭīf for about two years after the death of my father—may God have mercy on him—studying with Shaykh Ḥusayn al-Māḥūzī, mentioned above. Under him I read some of al-Quṭbī and a great deal from the beginning of the Old Commentary on *al-Tajrīd*.[10] During this time, I was traveling back and forth to Bahrain in order to take care of the date palms we owned there and gather the harvest, then returning to al-Qaṭīf to study. [This continued] until Bahrain was taken from the hands of the Khārijites by treaty, after a great sum had been paid to their commander, because of the Persian king's weakness and impotence, and his empire's decline through bad administration. I returned to Bahrain and stayed there five or six years engaged in my studies both in group lessons and individually with our peerless, most accomplished professor Shaykh Aḥmad ibn ʿAbd Allāh al-Bilādī, who is mentioned above, and then, after his death, with Shaykh ʿAbd Allāh ibn ʿAlī.

During that period I traveled to perform the pilgrimage to God's Sacred House, and I gained the honor of visiting the Prophet Muhammad and his noble descendants—may the blessings of God the Omniscient Ruler be upon them. I then traveled to al-Qaṭīf again to study the traditions of the Imams in detail with our professor, Shaykh Ḥusayn mentioned above, since he had remained in al-Qaṭīf and had not returned to Bahrain with the others. I studied with him, reading some of the *Tahdhīb* [Revision; of Muḥammad ibn al-Ḥasan al-Ṭūsī, d. 1067] and checking for errors with the texts of other students. Then I returned to Bahrain and matters grew very difficult for me as a result of the many debts I incurred which burdened and worried me because of my numerous dependents and my general lack of funds.

It then happened that Bahrain was ruined by the Huwala Bedouin who conquered it and became its rulers—for reasons it would take too long to explain—after the Afghanis had conquered the kingdom of the [Safavid] Shah Sulṭān Ḥusayn [r. 1694–1722] and killed him. I fled to Iran and stayed for a while in Kirmān. I then came back as far as Shiraz, and God—glory be to Him—granted us success and blessings, and caused the heart of its governor at that time, Mīrzā Muḥammad Taqiyy, who subsequently rose in rank until he became Taqiyy Khān, to have sympathy for us. He was most noble and generous toward us—may God reward him generously. I stayed for a while in the protection of his rule, teaching in his college of law and serving as the Friday prayer leader for the town. During that time I wrote a number of treatises and many responsa to legal questions. I was free to study until the storms of time, which allow neither rest nor rest themselves, swept through the region, shattered its society, scattered its inhabitants, plundered its wealth, and dishonored its women.[11] Time wreaked havoc with its conditions, and I left that region to go to a village, settling in the township of Fasā, after I had sent my dependents back to Bahrain. I then acquired new dependents [i.e., got married] in that village and stayed there engaged in study. I wrote the book *al-Ḥadā'iq al-nāḍira* [The Priceless Gardens] up to the chapter on ablutions there, while at the same time engaging in farming to earn a living and to avoid becoming indebted to others. The administrator in charge of the region, Mīrzā Muḥammad ʿAlī—may God have mercy on him—was extremely friendly toward me, very attentive and generous. He did not impose any land tax on me during my stay.

[This continued] until the town was struck by fateful events which scattered its inhabitants to other regions and killed its administrator, Mīrzā Muḥammad ʿAlī. The book I just mentioned [i.e., *al-Ḥadā'iq al-nāḍira*] remained untouched and the spiders of forgetfulness spun their webs over it. The disasters that befell me because of this destruction caused most of my books and a great deal of my property to be lost. I fled to al-Iṣṭihbānāt and remained there, striving to recover from bitter times and awaiting the opportunity to travel to the High Threshholds [the Shiʿite shrines of Iraq] and to settle in the vicinity of the Imams descended from the Prophet, until God—glory be to Him—granted me success in drinking the nectar from this cup. I went to Iraq and stayed in Karbalā' the Blessed—may God the Exalted bless him who is buried there, his forebears and his descendants—intending to stay until my death, without regret for what I had lost after having gained the honor of arriving there and patiently to endure the easy and difficult times brought on by fate, as has been said:

> Your nearness is my wealth, despite a lack of riches,
> and your distance my poverty, despite abundant wealth.

God—glory be to Him—granted, through His extreme generosity and all-encompassing bounty, and His continual gifts to His sinning, wrong-doing servant, the opening of the doors of providence toward every horizon, and—praise be to God—I became well-to-do and without worries.

I engaged in research, teaching, and writing, and began to finish my book *al-Ḥadā'iq al-nāḍira* mentioned above. The volumes which I have already completed are the section on ritual purity, in two volumes, the section on prayer, in two volumes, the section on alms and the section on fasting, in one volume, and the section on pilgrimage, in one volume. Praise and glory be to God! No book like this has ever been written among the Twelver Shiʿites, nor has anyone written anything of its kind, for it contains all the scriptural texts related to each legal question, all the opinions of earlier scholars, and all of the subsidiary issues relating to each question except those I may have overlooked inadvertently. This method is followed in the parts I wrote in Karbalā', but the first part, which I wrote in Iran, though it presents the legal questions fully and provides the necessary evidence, does not include all of the *ḥadīth,* though it mentions them collectively, and the same may be said for the opinions of earlier scholars. On the whole, our aim is that the reader not need to consult any other traditions or works of legal derivation [*kutub istidlāl*]. Therefore, it has become a large work, as extensive as a sea filled with elegant pearls. While writing it, I also wrote a number of treatises in answer to questions, which will all be mentioned below, in addition to[12] the work, *Salāsil al-ḥadīd fī taqyīd Ibn Abī Ḥadīd* [Iron Chains to Fetter Ibn Abī Ḥadīd].[13]

I shall conclude by mentioning the works I have completed from long ago and recently.

[Al-Baḥrānī here lists thirty additional works.]

Notes

1. In the village of al-Shākhūra.

2. The Huwala were a prominent group of Arabian tribes noted as excellent seafarers who were, in general, allied with the Safavid regime of Persia against other tribal groups in the region.

3. The date is found by adding together the numerical values of the letters in the word *shattatūhā:* sh (300) + t (400) + t (400) + w (6) + h (5) + a (1) = A.H. 1112 (= 1700–1 C.E.).

4. *Qaṭr al-nadā* (Drops of Dew), by Hishām al-Anṣārī (d. 1360).

5. *Ibn al-nāẓim,* a commentary on *Alfiyyat Ibn Mālik* by his son Badr al-Dīn (d. 1287).

6. Al-Niẓām al-Nīsābūrī (d. ca. 1310).

7. Quṭb al-Dīn al-Rāzī (d. 1365).

8. The invaders, known in contemporary European sources as the "Muscat Arabs," were the Yaʿriba dynasty (1624–1749) who ruled from their capital at Rustāq in Oman. They were Khārijites, belonging to a sect that first arose during the first great civil war of the nascent Islamic Empire (656–61). The birth of the movement is dated to the Battle of Siffin in 657, when some of the supporters of ʿAlī, the cousin and son-in-law of the Prophet, deserted him after he had engaged in unsuccessful negotiations with the forces of his enemy, Muʿāwiya. They became known as the Khārijites, or "Deserters." Adherents of the sect subsequently settled in eastern Arabia and have dominated the region of Oman until the present day. The Yaʿriba contingent recognized their leader as Imām, both political and spiritual leader. See S. B. Miles, *The Countries and Tribes of the Persian Gulf* (London: Frank Cass, 1966), 201–64.

9. The author would have been about twenty-four years old at this time.

10. *Tajrīd al-ʿaqā'id,* the famous work on dogma by Naṣīr al-Dīn al-Tūsī (d. 1274); the "Old Commentary" is the *Tashyīd* by Maḥmūd ibn ʿAbd al-Raḥmān al-Iṣfahānī

(d. 1348); see Carl Brockelmann, *Geschichte der arabischen Litteratur* (Leiden: E. J. Brill, 1943–49), Supp. Vol. I:925–26.

11. Probably the unsuccessful rebellion of 1744 led by Taqiyy Khān against Nādir Shāh; al-Baḥrānī reports that he was Friday prayer leader in Shiraz when Nādir Shāh, whom he describes as an oppressive tyrant, took the throne in 1735.

12. Reading *wa-* for *fī* in the text.

13. A rebuttal to Ibn Abī Ḥadīd's famous commentary on the *Nahj al-balāgha,* the popular collection of ʿAlī's speeches and sayings.

The Autobiography of ʿAlī Mubārak

(1824–1893)

Introduction

ʿAlī Mubārak was born in a small village in northern Egypt in 1824. In the opening passages of his autobiography, he recounts a childhood so filled with misadventures that he might well be termed an Egyptian Tom Sawyer. He leaves his teachers when they beat him, frustrates all of his father's efforts to educate him at home, works at five different occupations, runs away from home and from various employers, is brought home against his will several times, lies to his parents and employers alike, lands in prison once, is placed under "house arrest" by his parents, and, finally, against the will of his entire family, enrolls in a government elementary school and is selected to become a student at one of the new European-style secondary schools in Cairo—all by the age of twelve![1]

Eventually he was sent to France as part of an educational delegation that included two sons of the Egyptian ruler Muḥammad ʿAlī and studied there for five years (1844–50), first in Paris and then in Metz. On his return to Egypt he embarked on a tempestuous political career during which he fell in and out of favor with members of the royal family and, over several decades, held the posts of minister of public works, minister of education, and minister of charitable foundations for various periods. He was an ardent reformer and modernizer who personally helped to redesign Egypt's central irrigation system, railway system, and institutions of higher education. His two best-known literary works are his encyclopedic historical and geographic description of Egypt in twenty volumes, *al-Khiṭaṭ al-Tawfīqiyya,* and his four-volume didactic novel, *ʿAlam al-Dīn,* neither of which is available in translation.

Mubārak's autobiography appears in his *Khiṭaṭ*—a genre of geographic description that originated in the Middle Ages in which the author describes cities and villages, arranged alphabetically, and cites their major monuments and characteristics, important historical events that occurred there, and the biographies of famous persons who were born, resided, or died there. The whole is thus a combination of geographic, historical, and biographical knowledge and is one of several genres that reflect the universalist encyclopedic impulse typical of medieval Islamic scholarship.

Mubārak includes his own life story precisely where it should be found: under the entry for his natal village, al-Birinbāl al-Jadīda (New Birinbāl). He opens his account quite modestly by stating that since he has listed all other persons of note under their appropriate headings, he shall therefore proceed to include his own life story under that of his birthplace. The account is rather lengthy and is recounted in the first person. Mubārak's writing is rather modern in taste regarding which aspects of his childhood he chooses to recount to his readers and at the same rather traditional in literary style. It is almost ironic that this distinctly modern autobiography, which presages much of what was to happen in that genre of Arabic literature over the next century, came into being within the framework of one of the last examples of the *khiṭaṭ* genre. The only subsequent example of the *khiṭaṭ* genre of real significance has been *Khiṭaṭ al-Shām* (The Description of Syria), by Muḥammad Kurd ʿAlī (1876–1953). Following the example of Mubārak, he included a short autobiography in his *Khiṭaṭ,* published in 1928, but later produced a greatly expanded, more modern version titled *Mudhakkirāt* (Memoirs) in four volumes published between 1948 and 1951. Selections of this later work have appeared in an English translation by Khalil Totah.

In his autobiography, ʿAlī Mubārak never allows the latter part of his life to be foreshadowed in the chronological unfolding of his narrative. The reader is always left in suspense about how various trials and tribulations will be resolved. Mubārak is also liberal in his portrayal of feelings. At one point when he is lying sick in the hospital and thinks that he might die, he portrays his father's leave-taking as follows: "He looked at me and I looked at him, he kissed me and I kissed him, he wept and I wept, and finally he said farewell and went on his way, him sighing and me crying. Our state was like that described in the verse:

> Could perhaps the sorrows which now beset me
> Conceal behind them approaching release?"

Each hardship he endures, however, leads him (at least in his autobiography) to derive some positive lesson from what he has undergone and to face the future even more resolutely.

ʿAlī Mubārak's autobiography provides a fascinating account not only of the internal politics of Egypt during a dramatically eventful period but also of an exuberant personality whose early poverty and simple origins fostered a deep desire to provide basic education and modern technological advances to the masses.

Bibliography

Fliedner, Stephan. *ʿAlī Mubārak und seine Ḫiṭaṭ: Kommentierte Übersetzung der Autobiographie und Werkbesprechung.* Berlin: Klaus Schwarz, 1990.

Kurd ʿAlī, Muḥammad. *Khiṭaṭ al-Shām* (Description of Syria). 6 vols. Damascus: Maṭbaʿat al-Mufīd, 1925–28. [The autobiography appears in vol. 6, pp. 411–42.]

———. *Memoirs, a Selection.* Trans. Khalil Totah. Washington, D.C.: American Council of Learned Societies, 1954.

———. *Mudhakkirāt* (Memoirs). 4 vols. Damascus: Maṭbaʿat al-Turkī, 1948–51.

Mubārak, ʿAlī. *ʿAlam al-Dīn.* 4 vols. Alexandria: Maṭbaʿat Jarīdat al-Maḥrūsa, 1882.

———. *al-Khiṭaṭ al-tawfīqiyya al-jadīda li-Miṣr al-Qāhira wa-muduniha wa-bilādihā al-qadīma wa-l-mashhūra* (The New Description in Honor of Tawfīq of Cairo, Egypt, and Her Old and Famous Cities and Towns). Būlāq: al-Maṭbaʿa al-Kubrā al-Amīriyya, 1888–89. 9:37–61.

Reynolds, Dwight F. "Childhood in One Thousand Years of Arabic Autobiography." *Edebiyât: Special Issue—Arabic Autobiography,* N.S. 7, no. 2 (1997): 379–92.

The Childhood of ʿAlī Mubārak
[*al-Khiṭaṭ,* vol. 9, pp. 37–42]

In describing each village we have taken it upon ourself to mention, to the best of our ability, those who were born or raised there and those who died or are buried there from among the famous or those renowned for some important matter (good or otherwise). We have also mentioned those who have obtained high rank or an honored position from His Highness the khedive as well as others from the family and forebears of Muḥammad [ʿAlī]. It is therefore appropriate that we should make mention here of our own biography and the stages of our life that they may become known—and perhaps they shall not be without some value:

New Birinbāl [Birinbāl al-Jadīda, located in the Nile Delta] was my birthplace and where I grew up. I was born in the year 1239 [1824] according to what I have been told by my father and my late elder brother, al-Ḥājj Muḥammad, who died in the month of Ramadan 1293 [1876]. My father's name was Mubārak ibn Mubārak ibn Sulaymān ibn Ibrāhīm al-Rūjī. My brother told me that our distant forefather was from the area of al-Kūm wa-l- Khalīj, a village on the "sea" of Ṭanāḥ, and that because of an economic crisis which occurred there, our family scattered to different villages. The Baḥālṣa [branch of the] family went to live in the region of Damūh and some of the others went to the region of al-Mawāmana. There are none left in the original village except the descendants of Ghayṭās.

My great-great-grandfather, Ibrāhīm al-Rūjī, went to live in the region of New Birinbāl where he was respected and venerated. He was the prayer leader of the village, its preacher, and its judge. After his death, his son Sulaymān succeeded him in that position, and after Sulaymān, his son Mubārak. When my grandfather Mubārak was blessed with the birth of my father, he named him after himself, and bequeathed to him the position of his forefathers. So it was with most members of the family. The family is known in that village even now as the family of the shaykhs [religious leaders]. The family had so many branches that the village had an entire neighborhood of them containing nearly two hundred souls. They were judges, preachers, prayer leaders, officiators at marriages, and the weighers and measurers of the village harvests. They had income but no landholdings, so they did not suffer any of the fiscal obligations levied upon the peasants, nor did they have any affiliation with the local authorities.

They remained thus until the villagers could no longer farm the land. Then the tax system was reorganized and the authorities forced upon our family liability for some farmlands and then demanded the taxes which [they claimed] were due.[2] The authorities fined them and threatened them with imprisonment and beatings just like the peasants. They spent what money they had and sold their livestock and household furnishings. Overwhelmed by the situation, and unaccustomed to such abuse, they saw no alternative but to flee. So they left the village and dispersed to various other villages. My father settled in the village of Ḥammādiyyīn in Sharqiyya province.

I was at that time about six years old. Before our departure I had begun to learn to read and write from a blind man in Birinbāl whose name was Abū ʿAsr, but he then passed away. Due to the lack of hospitality in the region of Ḥammādiyyīn our stay there was not pleasant and we did not remain long. We then traveled to the Samāʿna Arabs, also in Sharqiyya province. They were tent-dwelling Bedouin with no men learned in religion among them, so they received my father with generosity and hospitality. They benefited from him and he in turn benefited from them a great deal. They began to consult him in all religious matters, for he was a righteous man, pious, well schooled in religious law, and well mannered. Their affection for him increased tremendously, so much so that they built a mosque and appointed him prayer leader.

When he was thus comforted and relieved of his troubles, he turned his attention to my education and at first taught me himself. He then turned me over to a teacher by the name of Shaykh Aḥmad Abū Khaḍir who was originally from the area of Kurdī, a village near Birinbāl. At that time he was living in a small village near the camps of these Arabs and my father sent me an allowance for my upkeep at the shaykh's home. I returned home only on Fridays and out of fear of the shaykh I never returned [to him] empty-handed. I stayed on with him for about two years, and to begin with I completed my memorization of the Qur'ān. Then, because of the many beatings he gave me, I left and refused to go back to him. So I began to study again with my father, but due to the large amount of work he had, and all the various distractions which diverted his attention from me, I took to playing and neglecting my studies and forgot what I had memorized. My father feared what might come of all this and was about to force me to return to that teacher, but I refused and resolved to run away from home if he did not relent.

I had seven sisters, but my mother had no male children other than myself, though I did have half brothers through women other than my mother. When my parents understood that I indeed intended to run away, they grew concerned and more sympathetic toward me, and asked me what I wished to do regarding my education. It would not do for someone from a learned family to remain without an education. I chose at that time not to become a religious scholar but rather to become a civil servant, for I had noticed the fine appearance of the civil servants, their status, and their close relations with the authorities. My father had a friend who was a civil servant, so he entrusted me to him. He was a district secretary and lived in the region of Akhaywa. I found him to be a man of fine appearance, well dressed, and who wrote in a beautiful hand, so I stayed with him for a while. I had an allowance from my father that sufficed for my upkeep, so I lived with him in his home and settled in among his children. It turned out, however, that although he appeared quite well-off, he was in fact in dire domestic straits. He had three wives, and more children than food, which meant that I went to sleep starving with hunger most of my days there. Most of his instruction, what little there was of it, took place in the house in front of the women. He rarely went out to work, and when he did go out he would take me along as company, from which I did not benefit at all but rather was of service to him. On top of all that, he used to torment me constantly, until one day when we were in the village of Manājāt, he asked me in front of the school principal and others what one times one is. When I answered two he struck me with a coffee-roasting pan and split my head open. Those present rebuked him. I went to my father to complain, but I obtained nothing from him but further pain.

That day was the festival of Our Master Aḥmad al-Badawī [a Sufi saint], so I ran away with all the people heading toward Maṭariyya near Manzila intending to catch up with an aunt of mine there, but on the way, I took ill with cholera in the village of Ṣān al-Ḥajar. One of the inhabitants of the village whom I did not know took me in and I lay ill in his home for forty days. They asked about my family, but I told them I was an orphan, completely alone in the world. During this time, my father and one of my brothers had been searching for me throughout the villages. My brother was eventually guided to where I was in Ṣān, but I caught sight of him from a distance and ran away. I stayed in Minyat Ṭarīf where a Bedouin man took me in, but I only stayed with him a short while. I left and happened to come across a brother of mine in our home village of Birinbāl to which he had returned. A few days later, the brother who had been searching for me found us; he tricked me and took me back to my father.

My situation was becoming a real problem for them. They had done everything they could as far as providing an education was concerned, and they began to suggest Qur'ānic reciters and Qur'ān school, but I wouldn't agree to this. I told them that I had received nothing from teachers except beatings. The civil servant had been of no use to me except as wasted time and torment; indeed, he had been the one who benefited from using me as a servant. Then it was suggested to my father that he send me to a friend of his who was a surveyor and this idea pleased me.

When I got to know him I grew to like him, and by accompanying him I earned some of the money which he took in payment from people. I stayed with him three months, but because of my youth and lack of knowledge about what is good for one and what is harmful, I revealed his secrets and divulged what he took in payment from people on the side. For this, he threw me out and I ended up living at home again, studying with my father.

My father used to take me along with him when collecting the government levies imposed upon the Bedouin and with which he was entrusted. I also used to handle the writing of the accounts and some of the calculations.

Then, after about a year, he made me an assistant to a civil servant in the district office of [the town of] Abū Kabīr at a salary of fifty piasters. I would write out fair copies of the notebooks for him. I stayed with this civil servant about three months. All my clothes were worn out and I was soon in very dire straits indeed, for I had not yet received any of my salary except for the food I ate in his house. Then one day he entrusted me to collect the revenues of Abū Kabīr. I collected them, took out the amount due me as my salary, and wrote him a note as a receipt and placed it in the money sack. When he found it he grew angry with me, but kept it to himself. The commissioner in Abū Kabīr at that time was ʿAbd al-ʿĀl Abū Sālim from Minyat al-Namrūṭ, and he informed the commissioner of this incident.

It happened that the commissioner's office was required to send a person to the armed forces, so they tricked me into it. They agreed to send me to the military service to meet this requirement. They called for me when I was completely unsuspecting and the commissioner ordered me to go to the prison to write up the names of the prisoners. He sent a man from the commissioner's guards to accompany me. When I entered the prison, they brought an iron fetter and placed it on my neck and I was left a prisoner there. I was overcome with the greatest fear. For twenty days or so I was kept in the filth and refuse of the prisoners. I began to weep and wail so much that the guard took pity on me due to my young age and moved me closer to the door. I gave him a small amount of the money which had been the reason for my imprisonment and through him sent news to my father.

My father went to His Highness the khedive who was in the area of Minyat al-Qamḥ where he presented my story in detail in a formal written petition. The khedive then ordered my release. My father had the order in his hand, but before he reached me, a friend of the guard's from the service of the commissioner of cotton production in the area of Abū Kabīr came to him and informed him that the commissioner needed a salaried secretary to work for him. The guard, taking pity on me, pointed me out to him, described my outstanding qualities and fine penmanship, and told him of my miserable situation. The servant approached me and asked me to write something on a piece of paper so that the commissioner could see my handwriting. I wrote a petition and took great care in doing it, and handed it to the servant with a gold piece worth twenty piasters and promised him more than that as well if he would but open a path for me to his master.

He took it and after a short while came back with an order for my release and took me to the commissioner, a man by the name of ʿAnbar Effendi. I looked at him: he was black, an Abyssinian—like a slave! But he was magnanimous, noble, and dignified. I saw the shaykhs and the governors of towns standing before him as he addressed his instructions to them, so I waited until they withdrew, then entered and kissed his hand. He spoke to me in fine, eloquent Arabic, saying, "Do you wish to be a secretary in my service? You will receive your daily food and a monthly salary of seventy-five piasters." I said yes, then withdrew from his presence and sat with the servants.

Because of the shaykhs who presented themselves to him, I came to know a number of the most famous men of that area, men possessed of riches, servants, entourages, and slaves. I was greatly surprised to see them standing before him and obeying his orders. I had never seen such a thing before, nor had I heard of its like. I had thought rather that the authorities were chosen exclusively from the Turks, as was the practice in those days, and I was both amazed and confused about the reason which would cause eminent men to remain standing in front of a slave and to kiss his hand. I grew intent on discovering the reason for this; it was one of my main motives for remaining with him.

The next day my father arrived with the order from His Highness the khedive and I greeted him and ushered him into the presence of the commissioner and introduced him. ʿAnbar Effendi smiled cheerfully at my father, asked him to be seated, and made him feel welcome. My father was handsome, fair-complexioned, eloquent, gracious, with all the signs of righteousness and piety. My father asked about me and the commissioner answered, "I have chosen him to be with me and have granted him a salary. If you are in agreement, then it will be so." My father thanked him and agreed that I should remain with him. He told the commissioner about our origins and our current conditions, then left the audience with the commissioner quite content.

When I sat with my father that night I turned the conversation to the subject of the commissioner and said, "The commissioner cannot be a Turk for he is black." He answered me that it was possible he was an emancipated slave. "Could a slave then become a governor when even the most powerful men of this region are not governors, let alone the slaves?" I asked. His answers did not convince me. He said that perhaps the reason for this was the commissioner's fine manners and education. "But," I said, "what knowledge does he have?" "Perhaps he lived at the al-Azhar university and studied there," he answered. "And does learning in al-Azhar lead to a governorship? Who leaves al-Azhar a governor?" I asked. "We are all slaves of God," my father replied, "and God, may He be glorified, raises up whomsoever He desires." "Agreed," I said, "but there must be reasons for all of this." Then he began to preach to me and tell me stories and recite poems which did not convince me at all, and finally he advised me to stay in the commissioner's service and to obey his orders.

Two days later my father departed and left me there. Then another idea occurred to me. Writing accounts and drawing a salary were the reason for my imprisonment and being forced to wear neck-irons, I said to myself, and the commissioner had indeed delivered me from that; but what if the commissioner in turn dealt with me as the secretary had? Who would deliver me then? These ideas remained in my mind and my concern was to be done with all of this and everything like it. I wanted a position which did not mean suffering indignities and which would not bring with it constant fear of ruin.

In the meantime, I grew friendly with a servant of the commissioner's and began to gather information about his master and the reason for his high rank. I gleaned enough information from him that I could piece it all together.

The servant told me that his master, the commissioner, had been bought by a generous woman of noble rank and that his mistress had enrolled him in the Qaṣr al-ʿAynī school when the khedive Muḥammad ʿAlī had opened the schools and had had boys enrolled. He told me that they studied calligraphy, mathematics, Turkish, and other things there, and that the government authorities were selected from these schools. At that moment I resolved to enter such a school. I asked him whether any peasants ever made it into these schools, and he told me that only those who have "connections" enter them. This made me think even more about the idea. After that my interest never abated. I asked about Qaṣr al-ʿAynī, the way there, and what life there was like. He told me about all of this. He spoke highly of the fine living conditions, the food, the uniforms, and the hospitality. My desire to go increased. I wrote down everything he told me about the way to the school, the distance, and the names of the towns along the way.

The idea eventually occurred to me simply to escape and make my own way to the school, so I asked for permission to visit my family and was given fifteen days' leave.

I traveled until, on Saturday, I arrived at Banī ʿIyād, a village on my route. There I came upon a group of children led by a tailor, each of whom had an inkstand and pens. I sat with them beneath a tree and we talked. It turned out that they were pupils from the elementary school at Minyat al-ʿAzz. This seemed to me a good sign. When they saw my penmanship, they found it to be finer than their own, and some of them said to the others, "If he were to join the elementary school, he would be a *chāwīsh.*" "That would be easy for him," the tailor said. "Even the penmanship of our *bashchāwīsh* does not equal his."

So I asked them what a *chāwīsh* and a *bashchāwīsh* were.[3] They explained to me that they were the best pupils in the elementary school. I began to ask for information about the elementary school and what it was like, and the tailor began to describe it in glowing terms, enticing me to join it. He explained to me that the outstanding students from the elementary schools continued on to the secondary schools even if they did not have "connections." This was my most ardent hope, so I wasted no time in going with them and entering the elementary school.

As it turned out, the principal was an acquaintance of my father's and wished to prevent me from becoming one of the pupils. He went to great lengths to dissuade me in order to please my father, but I would not listen to him and stayed on at the elementary school for fifteen days. The principal sent for my father. When he arrived, the principal explained the situation to him and showed him that I was very determined, having even said to the principal that if he did not enroll me I would file a complaint against him. But he and my father devised a trick to seize me when the other pupils and I would be caught unawares. My father waited till I went out for a walk at lunchtime; then he abducted me, took me back to our village, and there imprisoned me in the house for about ten days. All the while my mother cried—for me and because of me—and implored me to refrain from anything which would cause me to leave them again. She asked me to swear that I would not attempt to leave again, so I promised her that I would refrain from this for her sake and they then released me.

We had some sheep and I was charged with taking them out to graze. My parents thus thought to keep me far from a writing career which might mean me leaving them again. I remained thus for some time until their concerns were calmed and they came to believe that I had given up my plan, despite the fact that it never left me. I was only concealing it until I could take advantage of an opportunity to escape. One night I waited till they were all asleep and, taking my inkstand and other things, I left, fearful of being caught. I headed toward Minyat al-ʿAzz. That was the last time I lived with my parents.

It was a moonlit night so I walked till it grew light and entered Minyat al-ʿAzz around midmorning. The principal did not see me until I was in the midst of all the children in the Qurʾān school. I was forced to avoid leaving by day or night for fear of being abducted again. Later my father came and used every possible means of persuading me, he and the principal both, but to no avail. Eventually he went home without achieving his goal, but he continued to visit frequently hoping to take me from the Qurʾān school until ʿIṣmat Effendi, the principal of the *maktab al-khānqāh,* came to select the best students for the Qaṣr al-ʿAynī school: I was among those chosen. My father went and complained to ʿIṣmat Effendi, but he said to him, "Here is your son before you; it is his choice." They gave me the choice and I chose the school. At this my father wept greatly and a group of teachers and others implored me to change my mind, but I did not listen to them. It was decreed by God, and there is no escape from what He has decreed.

I entered the Qaṣr al-ʿAynī school in the year 1251 [1835–36] and at that time I was just entering adolescence.[4] I was placed in the class of Burʿī Effendi, but I found the school to be not at all what I had imagined. In fact, because of its recent establishment, the areas of responsibility were unclear, and teaching and education were of little concern. Instead, the major concern was with teaching military marching drills, which were held in the dormitories every morning and noon and after meals. All those who supervised the students tormented them with beatings, different types of abuse, and countless insults. There was no end to the favoritism and they neglected their duties in matters such as providing food and other essentials. The furnishings of the barracks consisted only of grass floormats and blankets of heavy wool made in Bulaq. I hated the food given us so much that I ate only cheese and olives. Burʿī Effendi looked after me more than he did the others, so the small amount of money I had, I placed in his care.

When I saw what conditions were like, I was unable to bear it and felt that I had done myself wrong by entering schools which were in this state. Then, due to the change in climate from that to which I was accustomed, and the great number of thoughts and misgivings which beset me, I fell ill with mange rashes all over my body. I was therefore placed in the infirmary where I came down with even more illnesses. They began to despair for my life, but God preserved me.

At this point my father came and asked to see me, but they would not allow him in. So he offered one of the attendants fifty gold pieces if he would secretly bring me out of the infirmary and save me from the condition I was in. I knew nothing of this until one of the attendants broke the iron window in the room I was in and informed me of my father's wishes and that he was waiting for me outside the school grounds. The attendant wanted to lower me down to him from the window so he could get his reward. At first I was inclined to comply, to go with my father and leave the school. I had seen such great hardship there and almost no teaching, and I had experienced such hunger in the infirmary that I had even sucked the bones others had finished with. But then I thought of the punishment for running away, and the fact that they used to chase down the students who ran away and arrest their families and lock them up and abuse them, so I restrained myself from going with him.

He tried several ploys to make the matter easier for me, but I refused. "Let me be patient with God's decree," I said, "for I am the one who has wronged myself." To the attendant I said, "Give my father my greetings and ask him to pray for me and to give my mother greetings from me." But then my father bribed his way into where I was. He looked at me and I looked at him, he kissed me and I kissed him, he wept and I wept, and finally he said farewell and went on his way, him sighing and me crying. Our state was like that described in the verse:

Could perhaps the sorrows which now beset me
Conceal behind them approaching release?

Later I recovered, returned to the school, and worked hard at my studies. I never fell ill again.

Toward the end of the year 1252 [1837] they transferred me to the school of Abū Zaʿbal and they turned Qaṣr al-ʿAynī into a private medical school which it still is today. The school administration at Abū Zaʿbal was the same as that at Qasr al-ʿAynī except that they did have some small concern for teaching because the directorship had been given to the late Ibrāhīm Bey Raʾfat.

The heaviest and most difficult subjects for me were geometry, arithmetic, and grammar. I regarded these subjects as talismanic charms and everything the teachers said about them as incomprehensible as magical spells. I remained thus for some time until the late Ibrāhīm Bey Raʾfat gathered together the slow students at the end of the third year after our transfer and made them into a separate class. I was one of them, in fact, the last of them. He appointed himself teacher for this class and in the very first lesson he gave us he explained the aims of geometry with complete clarity and concision. He explained the importance of boundaries and the designations placed at the beginnings of the diagrams, and explained that the letters were used like names for the shapes and their parts just as we use names for people; and how just as a person may choose for his son any name he wishes, whoever analyzes the diagrams may choose whichever letters he wishes.

The excellence of his explanations unlocked my mind and I understood everything he said. His method of teaching was what opened the door for me. I did not leave that first lesson without having learned something, and this was true of all of his lessons—quite the contrary from the other teachers, for they did not possess his methods. Their persistence in their approach was the obstacle which had prevented me from understanding all along!

Within the first year I had completed all of geometry and arithmetic and had become the best in my class. In grammar I became an outstanding student because I did not have to change teachers and was not subjected to the bad teaching methods of the others. Ra'fat Bey began to cite me as an example and to use my success at his hands as an indication of the poor teaching of the other teachers, showing that poor teaching was indeed the cause of the lack of progress among the students.

In that year, 1255 [1839–40], they selected from among us those students who would go on to the School of Engineering in Būlāq, and I was among the ones they chose. I stayed there five years and took all of the courses offered. I was always first and at the head of my class.

There I studied elementary algebra with the late Ṭā'il Effendi, as well as mechanics, dynamics, and mechanical design. I studied advanced algebra with him and with the late Muḥammad Abū Sinn; differential calculus and astronomy with the late Maḥmūd Pasha al-Falakī; hydraulics with the late Daqla Effendi; topography and hydrography with the late Ibrāhīm Effendi Ramaḍān; chemistry, physics, mineralogy, geology, and mechanical engineering with the late Aḥmad Bey Fā'id; descriptive geometry, sectioning, and sampling technologies for wood and stone, and surveying[5] in part with Ibrāhīm Effendi Ramaḍān, and in part with the late Salāma Pasha, as well as the essentials of cosmography.

Due to the lack of printed books on these and other subjects at that time, the students used to copy their lessons from the teachers in notebooks, each one according to his ability to take down what the teachers said. At that time the teachers put forth their greatest efforts in teaching, but it was rare for any one student to have taken down everything that had been presented in his notebook, especially all the figures and diagrams. For that reason, after some time had passed or when the students left the school, it was difficult for them to recall what they had studied, and they lost much of what they learned.

Toward the end of my period at the School of Engineering they began publishing some books in lithographs, and the students made use of them and benefited from them. Later, little by little, books grew more plentiful, so that now all of the proofs are printed with their figures and diagrams and it has become easy to deal with them and to recall what is in them.

Then in the year '60 [1844], His Highness the khedive decided to send his noble sons to the kingdom of France to study. An order was issued to select a group from among the best of the advanced students in the schools to accompany them. The late Sulaymān Pasha [= Joseph Sève] the Frenchman came to the School of Engineering to select a group of its students, and I was among them. The headmaster at that time was Lambert Bey. He wished to keep me at the School of Engineering to become a teacher there. But I explained to Sulaymān Pasha that I wished to travel with the others. The headmaster tried to persuade me and turned me over to the teachers to keep me from leaving. "If you remain here," they said, "you will receive a salary immediately and be given an allowance, but if you travel you will still be a student and you will miss this opportunity." My opinion, however, was that traveling with the sons of Muḥammad ʿAlī would bring me honor, status, and knowledge. So I insisted on traveling, despite the fact that I knew that my family was poor, and that they would have benefited from my teacher's salary, and were even counting on this. But I felt that "An abundance delayed is worth more than a pittance today." It all happened just as I wished, praise be to God, and we did indeed travel to that country.

My monthly salary was, like my companions, two hundred fifty piasters, and I set aside half of it for my family to be paid to them in Egypt each month. This had been my habit with them ever since I entered school.

We lived in Paris for two years in a single house reserved for us. The teachers for all of our lessons, as well as the prefect and overseer, were sent from the French War Ministry because our mission was of a military nature. We studied military science every day.

A point worth mentioning here is that the background knowledge of each of the members of our mission was quite different: some of us had knowledge only of military matters, such as those who had been taken from the artillery, cavalry, or infantry; and some had knowledge of mathematics but did not know French, such as those who had been taken from the Polytechnical School like myself; and others knew French—some of these were even teachers of French in the schools of Egypt. The overseer chose to lump together in one group those who were advanced in mathematics and those advanced in French, a group in which I was included. He ordered the teachers to give everyone lessons in French without differentiating between those who understood that language and those who did not. They did this and turned over those who did not understand to those who did, so that they could learn from them after the presentation of the lessons. But the ones who knew French were sparing about giving us lessons so that they might be the only ones to make progress. For a while we simply did not understand the lessons, until we began to fear that we would fall far behind, at which point we began to complain and ask that the system be changed and that we be taught in a language we could understand. The overseer, however, would not listen to our complaints, so we stopped attending class for several days.

As a result, they locked us up and wrote a report about us to His Highness, Muḥammad ʿAlī, who then issued an order that we be told to obey and that whoever did not obey would be sent back in irons to Egypt. We feared the outcome of all of this, so I directed my efforts and focused my thoughts in a way which brought me quite good results as well as knowledge of the French language: I asked about books for children and they told me of one so I purchased it and strove to memorize it. I got to work memorizing and studying, staying awake at night, scarcely lying down to rest, and sleeping but a short while. This has remained a habit of mine until now. I learned the book by heart along with its meaning, and then I memorized a large portion of a history book with its meaning as well. I also memorized the names of the geometric shapes along with the terminology, all of this in the first three months.

It was customary that the examination be at the beginning of each three-month period. I now turned to the lessons which were given by the teachers. My memorization produced great results for me. I became the best student in the entire delegation, switching places on and off with Ḥammād Bey and ʿAlī Pasha Ibrāhīm. When the late Ibrāhīm Pasha, the general of all of Egypt, came to Paris, he and the French general attended our examinations, along with the son of their king, and the nobles of France, as well as a group of the wives of the most important men. They praised us all lavishly and then distributed prizes amongst us three. The late Ibrāhīm Pasha handed me my prize himself, it was the second prize, a book of geography by the Frenchman Malte-Brun along with the accompanying atlas as a gift from him. We were invited to eat with our general, Ibrāhīm Pasha, and when he returned to Egypt he praised us to His Highness [Muḥammad ʿAlī] and to others.

After exactly two years, the top three from our delegation, that is myself, Ḥammād Bey, and ʿAlī Pasha Ibrāhīm, were appointed to the school of artillery and military engineering which was located near Metz also in the kingdom of France. In addition, we were awarded the rank of second lieutenant. We stayed in that city for two years. There we studied light and heavy fortifications, civil and military marine and terrestial construction, explosives, military strategy, and all that goes along with that, including a review of all that we had previously learned, summarized concisely by our new teachers. Our examinations there took place after two years and I placed fifteenth among approximately seventy-five students.

We were then assigned to different regiments. I was in the Third Regiment of Military Engineers but stayed there less than a year. The late Ibrāhīm Pasha wished us to remain in the military until we had exhausted its benefits and then travel throughout the European countries so that we might see what we could discover, by thus applying both knowledge and practice, about the actual conditions, situations, and customs of these nations. This was the intended plan, but God desired other than what the Pasha desired, for he then passed into the mercy of Almighty God. In the year '66 [1849–50], the late ʿAbbās Pasha was appointed to head the government of Egypt and the three of us were asked to return to Egypt.[6]

[This section of ʿAlī Mubārak's autobiography covering his birth to his return to Egypt at the age of twenty-six constitutes approximately one-fifth of the text. In the remainder of the text, he describes the vicissitudes of his political career and his role as reformer in Egyptian public life. He fared well during the reign of ʿAbbās I, holding a number of key government posts in education and public works, but was removed from his various positions during the reign of Saʿīd through the intervention of jealous rivals whose actions he sums up in a quoted verse of poetry: "Like the second wives of a beautiful first wife, they say of her face / Out of envy and spite, that it is unlovely." He provides a dramatic description of his forced departure from the school where he had served as rector: students and colleagues line the riverbank as he boards the ferryboat "weeping and mourning as if they were sons mourning the death of their father, so much so that I too began to cry!" Yet as he surveys the ranks of students, he is proud of the work he has done.

During this period, Mubārak was sent abroad for two years in government service—in virtual exile—to the Crimea, Constantinople, and finally Anatolia. He sums up the experience with typical aplomb by noting, after a vivid description of the hardships he endured, that he had at least learned Turkish, seen new places, and met new people. With the establishment of a new administration under the khedive Ismāʿīl he rose to the pinnacle of his political career, at one point being in charge of Egypt's railroads, government schools, public works, and charitable foundations, in addition to being chief engineer in charge of the Nile Barrages. He then lost all but one of these posts in a clash with his rival, the finance minister Ismāʿīl Ṣiddīq. He later managed to regain some of his political status when the khedive Ismāʿīl was ousted and replaced by Tawfīq I and even, though to a lesser degree, remained a key political figure during and after the ʿUrābī rebellion.

Mubārak describes himself most enthusiastically as a reformer and a civil engineer. Long passages are devoted to his plans, some successful and some not, for reforming the school system, improving Egypt's waterways and irrigation system, creating new boulevards and neighborhoods in Cairo complete with gas streetlights and modern sewers, and implementing new textbooks he wrote for teaching mathematics and engineering more effectively, as well as for effecting the financial reform of his ministries, establishing new printing presses, creating a national library, building slaughterhouses and bridges, revitalizing agriculture in the Fayyoum oasis, and other undertakings.

In between these projects, which he describes in loving detail, we catch glimpses of his private life. He marries the orphaned and impoverished daughter of a former teacher out of regard for the education he had received from her father. He tells of his first visit back to his home village after his return from France; in the middle of the night he reaches his family home and has a tearful reunion with his mother, whom he has not seen for fourteen years. At the death of his first wife, he marries another woman, also an orphan, whose rightful inheritance had been seized by her stepmother, and describes in great detail the legal proceedings and the political maneuvering in the highest social circles that occurred subsequent to his attempt to reclaim her inheritance—an affair that reached almost scandalous proportions for that period. At times he grows so frustrated with government service that he vows to return to his village and farm for the rest of his life, but each time some new opportunity arises. He falls deeply in debt several times and tries out a number of private business ventures.

Toward the end of his narrative, the momentous historical events in Egypt during the period from the 1860s to the 1880s begin to dominate his story. He helps to survey the land to be leased to the new Suez Canal Company and at the inauguration of the Suez Canal was placed in charge of the transportation and well-being of the foreign guests, for which he received medals from the governments of Egypt, France, Prussia, and Austria. Thereupon quickly follow the extended financial crises of Ismāʿīl's later reign, various desperate attempts to reorganize the ministries on more financially sound principles, the increasing political and military presence of foreign powers, and finally the ʿUrābī rebellion, the arrival of British and French warships in Alexandria, and the disastrous military defeat of the Egyptian forces. Mubārak's autobiography ends in 1888, with the author once again serving in the Ministry of Education in the newly formed government of Muṣṭafā Riyāḍ, and Egypt fully under England's colonial control.]

Notes

1. Although Mubārak's account is notable for the number of misadventures he underwent at such an early age, the idea of recounting such childhood escapades has a long history in Arabic autobiographical writing. See Dwight F. Reynolds, "Childhood in One Thousand Years of Arabic Autobiography," *Edebiyât: Special Issue—Arabic Autobiography,* N.S. 7, no. 2 (1997): 379–92.

2. This passage is problematic. It appears that a general agricultural failure occurred, perhaps due to the increasing infertility of the soil. Apparently, in a reorganization of the tax system, the author's family was saddled with fiscal liability for lands that were no longer producing enough to pay the taxes due on them. The family thus found their resources impounded toward the unpaid taxes. This interpretation follows Stephan Fliedner's translation of *inkasarat ʿalayhā amwāl al-dīwān* as "the tax regime was re-ordered" (Stephan Fliedner, *ʿAlī Mubārak und seine Hiṭaṭ* [Berlin: Klaus Schwarz, 1990], 11) and takes the term *ṭīn /aṭyān* to refer to plots of agricultural land.

3. Turkish terms denoting rank.

4. The author was eleven years old at this point.

5. Literally "shadow and sighting"; my thanks to Joseph Lowry for this suggested reading.

6. Although Mubārak writes that ʿAbbās I ascended to the throne in A.H. 1266 (1849–50), ʿAbbās in fact became ruler of Egypt in 1264 (1848).

Conclusion

This survey of roughly one hundred forty texts has revealed certain dimensions of the Arabic autobiographical tradition, but only at the cost of obscuring others. These texts came into being in different historical periods and diverse societies. By seeking a sense of the whole, the present study has perforce focused primarily on shared elements and historical connections and has not attempted to situate each text deeply within the specific context of the individual life and literary production of each author. Such detailed analysis would, in any case, go far beyond the scope of a single study. The larger view presented here, however, provides critical insights that will allow for more accurate assessments of individual texts when analyzed principally in their specific historical milieus.

There are clearly far more premodern Arabic autobiographies in existence than have previously been assumed; however, the works included in this study represent only a portion of the tradition as a whole. What portion they represent cannot be known with any certainty at this time. Judging from this partial view, the evidence seems to indicate that the production of Arabic autobiographies continued at a steady pace over the millennium extending from the ninth to the nineteenth centuries and over a broad geographic expanse. Arabic autobiographers were well aware, certainly no later than the twelfth to fourteenth century, of the "autobiographical act" and of certain precedent-setting texts. At certain points, historical clusters of autobiographies were produced by circles of authors who either knew each other personally or read each other's texts; in some cases, an autobiography by a particularly influential or respected figure motivated the writing of an entire sequence of autobiographical texts. In at least one period, the fifteenth and sixteenth centuries, a sense of "autobiographical anxiety" emerged that motivated authors to pen elaborate defenses of autobiographical writing. The larger sociopolitical reasons for this anxiety have yet to be fully explored.

The body of texts examined here exhibits a range of form and content difficult to refer to as a single "genre" or as a formal category. Curiously, even in cases in which direct personal links between authors and earlier autobiographical texts can be demonstrated, no fixed form for autobiographical representation emerges. Texts produced within the historical clusters are as formally diverse as the tradition taken as a whole. In contrast, biography, a far more common literary genre, developed within forms that maintained a stronger sense of constraint than their autobiographical counterparts. It seems clear that biographers within a single lineage (e.g., scholars of the Ḥanbalī school of law, Sufi mystics, etc.) established conventions for later generations; for autobiographers, in contrast, each generation found earlier precedents but not binding formal models. This may be a consequence of the relative infrequency of autobiographies and the resulting ad hoc nature of each example. Although these texts do not display a limited set of shared formal characteristics, they were consistently grouped together as a category by medieval and early modern Arabic writers. The best approximation of that category seems to be understanding these texts as resulting from the same literary act: the act of "interpreting," "representing," or "portraying" oneself in written form.

Despite a general awareness of autobiography as a distinct category of writing, it never became an "organized science" to the degree that biography and prosopography did. In part this may be a direct result of the differing natures of the two endeavors: biography and prosopography in the Arabo-Islamic tradition were both essentially cumulative and ever expanding. Compilers and redactors freehandedly amended, expanded, and rewrote biographical accounts to suit different contexts and even different political purposes. Autobiographies could not be rewritten with nearly the same freedom without fundamentally altering their status as texts. As we have noted above, however, in regard to such texts as those by Ibn Sīnā, ʿAbd al-Laṭīf al-Baghdādī, and Ibn al-ʿAdīm, anthologizers did rework certain autobiographies in a number of creative ways by appending additional material, inserting passages and commentary, or quoting only extracts of the original. In essence, autobiographical texts were sometimes manipulated to fit the practices of biography and prosopography.

Personality and Self

Autobiographers in the Arabic tradition appear to have made independent choices concerning how much of what we would term their "private" lives to include in their works. Literary convention seems neither to have encouraged nor to have hindered such expression; but the elements that we as twenty-first-century individuals most associate with the realm of "private" life were never the central focus of premodern Arabic autobiographical texts. This study has attempted to approach these texts from a perspective relatively uncolored by modern preconceptions, analyzing instead four sets of recurring features that may help in uncovering the modes of self-representation these authors used to construct their individual identities: portrayals of childhood failures, portrayals of emotion through the description of action, dream narratives as reflections of moments of authorial anxiety, and poetry as a discourse of emotion. These represent but a handful of many possible approaches to this highly diverse body of texts.[1]

While these texts at first glance look less "personal" than modern autobiographies (Arabic or western), they are not therefore less "individuating." They are, in fact, each replete precisely with the specific details of an individual life. In many cases, they clearly communicate a strong sense of the author's personality. There may be many ways in which the medieval and premodern texts in this corpus differ from modern examples, but to attribute this difference to a less developed sense of "individual identity" would certainly be neither accurate nor intellectually useful.

Cultures in different historical periods foreground different characteristics and behaviors as being more closely tied to the innermost identity of their members: piety, poetry, sexuality, handwriting, class, ethnicity, emotions, citizenship, and other concepts have all had their day at one time or another, in one culture or another, as reflections or constituents of the "self." Any study that purports to examine the concept of "personhood" in a particular period of any society would have to be based on a broader foundation than a corpus consisting only of autobiographical texts. Autobiographical writings may offer a particularly rich source, but they provide only a portion of the data needed to address larger questions: Which elements of human behavior are seen as significant to individual identity? Is the human personality seen as essentially unchanging or fluid? Is the human "self" seen as an organic whole such that an individual's characteristic manner of being (*bios*) is commensurate with the individual? Or does the "self" exist in a bifurcated state (inner/outer, private/public)? And if so, what is the perceived relationship between these elements? Direct reflections? Mirror images? Are they elements that coexist in relative harmony, or are they by definition in conflict?

Only a partial answer to these questions can be offered based on the surveyed texts. These authors portray themselves both as distinct individuals and as participants in various significant relationships. The relationships most clearly foregrounded in these texts are "vertical" or "genealogical" connections. In the context of the family these reach back in time to parents, grandparents, and more distant ancestors, on the one hand, and forward in time through children and grandchildren, on the other; this is paralleled in the sphere of education by the meticulously noted relationships with teachers and the mention of students. In contrast, there are strikingly few portrayals of "lateral" relationships with siblings, fellow students, friends, and colleagues. The only clear exceptions to this principle are autobiographers who wrote their texts based on their relationship with famous figures of their time, such as ʿImād al-Dīn's relationship with his patron, Saladin.

It was the purpose of many of these authors to demonstrate their part in the passage of history—and a major element in the concept of history was the transmission of authority, legitimacy, and descent. This can be seen in realms as diverse as genealogy, religious authority, political legitimacy, scholarly knowledge, and mystical enlightenment; by contrast, artistic genius in poetry and music was far less likely to be understood in this paradigm. Thus a great deal of the material in these autobiographical texts serves to locate the authors in their appropriate channels of transmission. Yet, to be part of this larger flow of transmission did not hinder the understanding of oneself as an individual. One rather common motif in medieval Arabic scholarly literature, for example, is the author's claim to have provided in a given work ideas and insights that are unique and unprecedented in his field. Equally common is the writer who complains that he cannot find other minds of his caliber or other figures at his moral or spiritual level.

Did this paradigm of "genealogical" transmission also apply to the concept of character? If character were understood primarily as an enduring, inherited template, then the careful documentation of earlier generations of one's family and, to a lesser extent, the documentation of one's offspring would be of more significance than the documentation of friendships or relationships with siblings. This perhaps explains why far more attention is paid in these texts to describing the personalities of the author's parents, grandparents, and even uncles than to describing those of siblings or friends.[2] Yet these same autobiographers often mention ways in which they, as adults, differ from their childhood selves; the author's own character undergoes clear transformation in many of these texts.

The image derived from these autobiographies of the personality as part inherited and yet also changing is echoed in medieval Arabo-Islamic theoretical writings on the question of human character. The scholar Abū Ḥayyān al-Tawḥīdī (d. 1023) in his "Treatise on Life" (*Risālat al-ḥayāt*) treats the various elements of a person's character as being divided into two categories: "Some of these dispositions can be caused to disappear through conscious effort [*riyāḍa*] or can at least be somewhat attenuated, while the other portion constitute the very form of the soul and one therefore cannot hope to rid oneself of them or to purify them."[3] A variety of terms are used in this discussion: *ṭabʿ* (innate nature), *akhlāq* (character/personality), *ʿayn* (essence), *ṣifāt* (characteristics), *fiṭra* (temperament/nature) and *sajīya* (disposition). Although coming to a complete understanding of the individual terms is a complicated undertaking, Abū Ḥayyān and a number of his contemporaries are in agreement as to this dual aspect of human personality—some aspects of a person's personality undergo growth and transformation, while others remain fixed and unchanging.[4]

Western societies of the late twentieth and early twenty-first century are also characterized by a dichotomy in the conceptualization of the self, but the division cuts along the axis of public and private. This distinction appears to have become more and more clearly drawn in recent centuries. Ironically, as Habermas and others have pointed out, the modern western "private" self emerges historically with the very literary genres that make the "private" public—diaries, journals, memoirs, autobiographies—and in tandem with fictionalized "private" lives in the form of the novel.[5] The emergence of the modern western sense of "private" takes place most decidedly in public.

It does not seem that premodern Arabic autobiographies existed in the same tension-filled space between the public and private, or that this bifurcation of the self is a formulation that would have made any sense to these authors. It is not at all clear that premodern Arabic autobiographers would have interpreted western-style confessions and detailed accounts of love and sex as being any more indicative of an "inner" self than the driest of Arabic autobiographical writings. Accounts of sexual encounters, desires, practices, and techniques would not have been unfamiliar to them, but they would have found these discussions strangely misplaced and more fitting to books of erotica such as *The Delights of Hearts* or *The Perfumed Garden,* or to books on the theory of love, such as *The Ring of the Dove.*[6] They would certainly have had difficulty accepting a psychology that placed sexual behavior at the very center of the formation of personality and selfhood. For a sense of the "inner" self, they would have searched for evidence of intellectual, spiritual, or mystical experience and the cultivated expression of emotion in poetry.

Literary Conventions

Arabic autobiography emerged from the context of historical and biographical literature. Although it never slavishly adopted the forms of history and biography, it maintained some of the basic techniques of those intellectual fields. Arabic autobiographies demonstrate a concern with historical fact and truth that immediately involves methods of establishing the authority for certain statements. The historical conventions for asserting authoritative accounts of events in Arabic literature, however, bear little resemblance to modern western "realist" conventions found in western historical writings, including biographies and autobiographies.[7]

Perhaps the single most significant discrepancy between the two practices is the role of narrative as a means of apprehending and presenting a life: the life as *story*. Out of the kaleidoscopic mix of experience and memory, the western autobiographer has traditionally opted to couch the entire span of life in a single, rather cohesive tale, imposing the structure of the metanarrative on the whole. The surge in popularity in the writing of autobiographies and the concomitant rise of the novel in European literatures reveals the two genres to be very close siblings, with the structure of the *Bildungsroman* so closely resembling that of many autobiographies that only the (hotly disputed) issue of truth versus fiction at times separates them. Some scholars see this interaction between autobiography and novel flowing more strongly in one direction, and some the other. It would appear that Rousseau's groundbreaking achievement may only have been possible in the wake of the publication of a half century of fictional lives. Arguing for the flow of influence in the other direction, Roy Pascal, for example, finds that "the nineteenth-century novels that delve deep into childhood, from Dickens and the Brontës onwards, are unimaginable without the great autobiographies [of Rousseau, Goethe, Franklin, Gibbon, and Wordsworth]."[8] The modern hybridization and convergence of the autobiographical novel and the fictionalized autobiography may be the true culmination of the western autobiography/novel tradition. In contrast, this subjection of the facts and shorter anecdotal episodes to a larger narrative structure is found in only a handful of premodern Arabic autobiographies.

A second point of comparison between Arabic and western practices is closely connected to the western notion of life as narrative: chronological order. Although some of the narratives given canonical status in western culture are not revealed in simple, chronological order (e.g., Homer), western autobiographies, from the Middle Ages onward, display a distinct propensity toward linear narration. Chronological structure even figures in many modern western definitions of autobiography. Yet there is nothing inherently natural about linear chronologism: human memory is not linear and indeed is far more susceptible to associative linkages. The act of reconstructing the past from the author's present is not a chronological or linear process, and even primary experience is not decoded linearly but rather with many mental leaps forward and backward in time. Chronological linearity as an instrument of coherence and authority is fundamentally tied to massive cultural shifts in the European Renaissance and Enlightenment.

Arabic autobiographers, in contrast, had at their disposal a rich palette of literary conventions for asserting the veracity of an account, such as providing outside authoritative testimony for points that readers might doubt if recounted only on the authority of the author, as well as alternative conventions for portraying emotions and inner motivations, such as poetry, visions, and dreams. For many Arab autobiographers, the intellectual techniques of categorization and enumeration served as the primary format for communicating information about a human life. The common western convention of dividing the autobiographical narrative into chapters derives historically from fictional discourse (such as that of episodic romances) or the practice of theater (scenes and acts) rather than from the structures of real-life experience or historical writing. When Arabic autobiographers included divisions in their texts, they most often did so according to rational criteria, such as dividing the time line into periods such as years (similar to a chronicle) or according to thematic organization, devoting separate chapters to teachers, publications, family history, and so forth.

The Status of Arabic Autobiographies as Texts

The authors of premodern Arabic autobiographies assumed that their autobiographical texts would be read in conjunction not only with selections of their poetry but also with their other intellectual or artistic productions. The autobiography did not represent a unique moment for self-representation but rather a frame or summation for revealing a certain portrait of the whole, a context within which one's work would then be placed and evaluated. In this framework it was most important to portray one's place within the larger transmission of knowledge from respected sources of the past, through the present, into the future. It was important to establish one's family background as this would not ordinarily be expressed in one's other works. It was equally significant to delineate one's acquired authority by carefully listing one's teachers and the works one had studied. It was also of consequence to establish the degree to which one had contributed to this body of knowledge by presenting the quantity and quality of one's intellectual or artistic production; this occasionally extended to presenting or reporting the testimony of one's peers as to one's status and worth. If one had been accused of wrongdoing, misinterpreted, or slandered, here was a framework within which one could launch a defense by guiding the reader to a proper understanding of one's actions or words, or to a proper interpretation of one's published work.

Amid all these concerns there existed also the urge to present a personal self as the source of these works or deeds; but it was not necessary to do this entirely in this one text, for one's poetry, personal correspondence, formal epistles, sermons, dream accounts, entertaining anecdotes, travel journals, and so forth, all also served in part to express oneself to the larger world and to future generations. Often these other types of text were transmitted alongside the autobiography itself.

Some Arabic autobiographers penned rather dry autobiographies while at the same time making remarkable disclosures about themselves in their other writings, as did Ibn Ḥajar al-ʿAsqalānī and Abū Shāma. In some autobiographical works this urge toward the personal is distinctly foregrounded, and in others it plays a very marginal role. Some Arabic autobiographies therefore pose a serious challenge to any methodology that might attempt to read them as closed texts, as complete statements on their own. At one level they are indeed complete representations and to some degree they circulated as such; at another level, however, many of them were never conceived of as wholly isolated representations.

Some medieval and early modern Arabic autobiographies do not possess the "boundedness" or "insularity" of more recent examples but rather emerge from a literary context in which various types of borrowing, imitation, reworking, unattributed quotation, and allusion—virtually every possible form of intertextuality—were commonplace. Even the physical object of the "book" did not possess the definition it later came to possess, with multiple works by the same author or a random selection of smaller works often being bound into a single volume. However carefully these authors may have constructed their autobiographical works, and however lengthy these may be, only a few of the autobiographers represented here would ever have conceived of a reader who would select this, and only this, work from among their writings for study or analysis. Although compilations of biographical and prosopographical materials were extremely common, no such collection of autobiographies was ever attempted. One can certainly read and analyze texts from the genre of "writing a *tarjama* of oneself" in isolation and even find them fascinating, instructive, and at times emotionally moving. It is, however, the other level, the level at which these texts act as lenses through which to view the author's assembled literary corpus, that probably far more closely resembles the understanding shared by premodern Arab autobiographers and their readers, an understanding akin to a premodern "autobiographical pact."[9]

The spectacular explosion in popularity of the autobiography in Europe from the late eighteenth century onward is presumably linked to social forces that eventually affected—through the political and cultural contacts of the colonial era—the similar burst of popularity the autobiography experienced in twentieth-century Arabic literature. Modern Arabic autobiography is in fact often relegated to the status of a genre that has simply been "borrowed" from the West; however, this should not be assumed a priori without careful documentation and analysis. Ṭāhā Ḥusayn's influential childhood memoirs published in 1926–27 have at times been explained as a result of his studies in Europe; he was also, however, the single most influential Arab literary historian of his day and possessed a vast and intimate knowledge of pre-Islamic, classical, and medieval Arabic literature. His detailed and personal account of his childhood may at first glance seem to be a borrowing from modern European tradition, though this view becomes more difficult to maintain when it is asked which European texts might have influenced him. When viewed as part of the Arabic autobiographical tradition, however, his autobiography seems to be the culmination of a centuries-long chain of texts that included more and more intimate anecdotal material about the periods of the author's childhood and youth. Indeed, when viewed in this manner, the strangely "classical" characteristics of the third-person voice, the highly stylized language, and the pedagogical tone all seem familiar rather than foreign elements.

Long before the genre had taken hold in European literatures in its modern, most recent form, the idea of writing an account or an interpretation of one's life was an accepted intellectual and literary endeavor in Arabo-Islamic culture. Autobiographers writing in Arabic left behind representations of their lives specifically crafted as texts for subsequent generations.

Into the Twentieth Century

In 1898, when Egypt's poet laureate, Aḥmad Shawqī, published the first volume of his four-volume anthology, *al-Shawqiyyāt,* he included a brief autobiography that not only traced his personal life but also included a discussion of those classical Arab poets who most strongly influenced him. In addition, he identified some of the European literature he had read. This autobiography sparked a heated debate in the press concerning the role of traditional grammatical and linguistic correctness versus innovation and western influence in the Arabic poetic tradition. The series of articles criticizing Shawqī's work, together with published responses to them, developed into a public forum for discussing the many social and cultural changes now recognized as the Arab *nahḍa,* or "Renaissance," of the second half of the nineteenth century. Shawqī's most vociferous and most famous critic was Muḥammad al-Muwayliḥī, himself a famous writer, and best known as the author of *Ḥadīth ʿĪsā ibn Hishām,* a collection of piquant social criticisms couched in the medieval genre of the picaresque *maqāmāt.*[10]

The element that is usually remembered from this debate is the linguistic conservatism of Shawqī's critics and their fundamental argument that the Arabic poetic tradition did not need, indeed should not be subjected to, innovation of any kind. Similar criticisms were leveled against al-Yāzijī, Jubrān Khalīl Jubrān (Kahlil Gibran), and others. A forgotten element of the debate is that al-Muwayliḥī wrote two articles specifically criticizing Shawqī's autobiography, taking him to task first for even having written an autobiography and second, given that he did write one, for having included personal information in that text.

Briefly, al-Muwayliḥī charged that (1) Shawqī had, by writing an autobiography, praised himself rather than leave it to others to praise him; (2) Shawqī had written this account of himself in prose, whereas, as a poet, he should let his poetry stand as his sole public voice; (3) he had done what no other Arab poet had done by including an autobiography in his poetic anthology;[11] and (4) Shawqī had found new and innovative ideas while pursuing his education in Europe and such foreign influence was repugnant, particularly in the realm of poetry in which the Arabs excelled and far surpassed westerners:

> The Gracious Poet has, in his introduction, treated himself in a way that earlier poets did not do in their collected works; indeed, they left it to others to speak of them. The most we have observed among Arab authors is that if they wished to speak of themselves, they spoke only of their literary origins and not of their personal [genealogical] origins. They might, for example, mention from whom they had learned, whom they had met, and what they had studied and memorized. As for our Gracious Poet, well, he lists four personal origins for himself, and does not list a single literary origin, when he says:
>
> > "I am thus Arab, Turkish, Greek and Circassian by my grandmother on my father's side. . . . Four origins gathered into a single branch: *It is not impossible for God/to gather the whole world into one.*"[12]

Finally, al-Muwayliḥī criticized Shawqī for writing of his memories of childhood encounters with the khedive (the ruler of Egypt) and other notables, for these memories, he claimed, reveal the poet's arrogance and vanity.

Thus Muḥammad al-Muwayliḥī in 1898–99 cast at Aḥmad Shawqī many of the charges against which al-Suyūṭī, Ibn Ṭulūn, al-Shaʿrānī, and others had sought to defend themselves in the introductions to their autobiographies four centuries earlier. Al-Muwayliḥī's articles were angrily refuted by the Lebanese literary critic and pan-Arabist thinker Amīr Shakīb Arslān. Though Shawqī and Arslān eventually won the day, no Arabic autobiographies were published for an entire generation until the appearance of Ṭāhā Ḥusayn's *al-Ayyām* in 1926–27. After that, the floodgates opened.

Strangely enough, although *al-Shawqiyyāt* has gone through more than a dozen new editions and reprints, Shawqī's autobiography has never been reprinted as part of the collection. Where Aḥmad Shawqī's autobiography once stood, an introduction by Muḥammad Ḥusayn Haykal has been substituted in every subsequent printing. Al-Muwayliḥī's articles, however, anthologized in al-Manfalūṭī's *Mukhtārāt* (Literary Selections), became obligatory reading in many public schools of the Arab world for decades.

Arslān, perhaps to prove his point, went on to write his own autobiography in 1931, but by that time the point was moot and autobiographies were being written and published at an ever-increasing rate.[13]

The present study ends here in the first decades of the twentieth century. Although political and cultural engagement with the West led to rapid and complex transformations in the genre of Arabic autobiography, echoes of the literary conventions of the premodern tradition are still found in many texts even from recent decades. Literary figures such as Bint al-Shāṭi' and Muḥammad Qarah ʿAlī insert samples of their own poetry into their autobiographies much as premodern Arabic autobiographers did.[14] The literary critic Amīr Shakīb Arslān includes in the preface to his autobiography a list of predecessors that includes al-Suyūṭī, Ibn Sīnā, Ibn Khaldūn, and Lisān al-Dīn Ibn al-Khaṭīb as several of those authors themselves did.[15] Anīs Frayḥa addresses his autobiography to his son Riḍā much as ʿAbd al-Laṭīf al-Baghdādī, Ibn al-Jawzī, Abū Ḥayyān al-Andalusī, al-Baḥranī, Princess Salmé, and Ṭāhā Ḥusayn addressed their works to family members of the next generation.[16] Some twentieth-century Arabic autobiographers, beginning with Ṭāhā Ḥusayn himself, continue to write in the third person. Muslim religious scholars such as Shaykhs ʿAbd al-Ḥamīd Maḥmūd, Muḥammad Mitwallī Shaʿrāwī, and ʿAbd al-Ḥalīm Kishk have produced autobiographies that are so close to the conventions of classical Arabic autobiography that one recent writer has termed them "*tarjama*-reflexes."[17] Modern Arab scholars and writers have even written self-authored biographical notices for inclusion in biographical dictionaries as Ibn al-ʿAdīm and others did for Yāqūt in the thirteenth century.[18] And at least one Arabic autobiographer has produced texts in both the traditional and the modern mode: the Syrian scholar Muḥammad Kurd ʿAlī (1876–1953) first produced a short, traditional version of his life story in the mid-1920s that was included as the final section of his *Khiṭaṭ al-Shām* (Description of Syria) in open imitation of ʿAlī Mubārak who had published his *Khiṭaṭ* of Egypt three decades earlier and included his autobiography. Kurd ʿAlī then expanded his text into a four-volume work twenty years later and rewrote it in a manner marked by a much greater use of linear narrative and a far more modern literary style.[19] In short, although twentieth-century Arabic autobiographies display many formal characteristics not found in premodern Arabic texts, a degree of continuity can yet be discerned, testifying to the strength and impact of earlier literary practices of "interpreting the self."

Notes

1. A demonstration of a wide variety of approaches to individual texts from this tradition can be found in the ten articles included in *Edebiyât: Special Issue—Arabic Autobiography,* ed. Dwight F. Reynolds, N.S. 7, no. 2 (1997).

2. See, for example, the works of ʿUmāra al-Yamanī and Usāma Ibn Munqidh for detailed descriptions of uncles coupled with a nearly complete absence of any mention of siblings.

3. Claude France Audebert, "La Risālat al-Ḥayāt d'Abū Ḥayyān al-Tawḥīdī," *Bulletin d'Études Orientales* 18 (1964): 155; cf. M. I. Kīlānī, *Trois epîtres d'Abū Ḥayyān al-Tawḥīdī* (Damascus: Institut Français de Damas, 1951). Quoted passage translated by Dwight F. Reynolds.

4. Audebert, "La Risālat," 155 n. 2.

5. Jürgen Habermas, *The Structural Transformation of the Public Sphere: An Inquiry into a Category of Bourgeois Society,* trans. Thomas Berger and Frederick Lawrence (Cambridge, Mass.: MIT Press, 1989), 49; Dipesh Chakrabarty, "Postcoloniality and the Artifice of History: Who Speaks for 'Indian' Pasts?" *Representations* 37 (1992): 1–26.

6. Aḥmad al-Tifāshī, *Les délices des coeurs,* trans. René Khawam (Paris: Editions Phébus, 1981); ʿUmar al-Nafzāwī, *The Perfumed Garden,* trans. Richard Burton (London: Neville Spearman, 1975); Ibn Ḥazm, *The Ring of the Dove: A Treatise on the Art and Practice of Arab Love,* trans. A. J. Arberry (London: Luzac, 1953).

7. Debate over the role of these same realist narrative conventions in shaping western conceptualizations of history has come to the fore in recent works such as Hayden White, *The Content of the Form: Narrative Discourse and Historical Representation* (Baltimore: Johns Hopkins University Press, 1987).

8. Roy Pascal, *Design and Truth in Autobiography* (Cambridge, Mass.: Harvard University Press, 1960), 52.

9. Philippe Lejeune, "The Autobiographical Pact," trans. Katherine Leary, in *On Autobiography* (Minneapolis: University of Minnesota Press, 1989), 3–30. "In effect, the autobiographical pact is a form of contract between author and reader in which the autobiographer explicitly commits him or herself not to some impossible historical exactitude but rather to the sincere effort to come to terms with and to understand his or her own life," Paul John Eakin, foreword to *On Autobiography,* ix.

10. The *maqāma* genre originated with the writings of Badīʿ al-Zamān al-Hamadhānī (d. 1008) and consists of short tales recounted in rhymed prose with intermittent passages of verse. Although the genre went through many transformations over the centuries, the typical *maqāma* plot revolved around two central characters: the honest but somewhat plodding narrator and the rascally but silver-tongued hero, a sort of medieval con artist, who outwits the narrator and those around him time and again.

11. The charge is essentially correct: out of all of the autobiographers surveyed here, other than Shawqī, only ʿUmāra al-Yamanī (d. 1175) is remembered primarily as a poet.

12. Muṣṭafā Luṭfī al-Manfalūṭī, *Mukhtārāt al-Manfalūṭī* (Cairo: n.p., 1912), 149.

13. Amīr Arslān, *al-Sīra al-dhātiyya* (Beirut: Dār al-Ṭalīʿa, 1969).

14. Muḥammad Qarah ʿAlī, *Suṭūr min ḥayātī* (Beirut: Mu'assasat Nawfal, 1988); Bint al-Shāṭi' [= ʿĀ'isha ʿAbd al-Raḥmān], *ʿAlā jisr bayna al-ḥayāh wa-l-mawt* (Cairo: al-Hay'a al-ʿAmma al-Miṣriyya li-l-Kitāb, 1967).

15. Arslān, *Sīra dhātiyya,* 17.

16. Anīs Frayḥa, *Isma' yā Riḍā* (Listen to me, Riḍā) (Beirut: Dār al-Maṭbū'āt al-Muṣawwara, [1956] 1981).

17. Tetz Rooke, *"In My Childhood": A Study of Arabic Autobiography* (Stockholm: Stockholm University, 1997), 92–97. See, for example, 'Abd al-Ḥamīd Kishk, *Qiṣṣat ayyāmī: mudhakkirāt al-Shaykh Kishk* (Cairo: al-Mukhtār al-Islāmī, n.d.); Muḥammad Mitwallī al-Sha'rāwī, *Ḥayātī: min Daqādūs ilā al-wizāra* (Alexandria: Qāyitbay, 1992); 'Abd al-Ḥalīm Maḥmūd, *al-Ḥamdu li-llāh hādhihi ḥayātī* (Cairo: Dār al-Ma'ārif, [1976] 1985).

18. See Shafīq Jabrī, Nawāl al-Sa'dāwī, and Samīḥ Qāsim in R. B. Campbell [Kāmbil], *A'lām al-adab al-'arabī al-mu'āṣir, siyar wa-siyar dhātiyya* (Beirut: Orient-Institut der Deutschen Morgenländishen Gesellschaft, 1996), 421–23, 726–27, 1077–78. [Cited in Rooke, *"In My Childhood,"* 119]

19. Muḥammad Kurd 'Alī, *Mudhakkirāt,* 4 vols. (Damascus: Maṭba'at al-Turkī, 1948–51).

AN ANNOTATED GUIDE TO ARABIC AUTOBIOGRAPHICAL WRITINGS (NINTH TO NINETEENTH CENTURIES C.E.)

This annotated guide is ordered chronologically by the autobiographer's death date. Each entry includes the author's name, with the most commonly used element(s) in boldface, birth and death dates, and a brief characterization of the author and the autobiography (except those translated in this volume), followed by bibliographic information about the Arabic text, translation(s) if available, and occasional secondary sources that deal directly with the autobiographical text. In cases of autobiographies that were once widely known and cited but appear now to have been lost, references are given that may help in locating the missing texts. Bracketed entries for "autobiographies" cited by other scholars that do not in fact exist, or do not appear to be autobiographical, are also included. Translations are generally provided for the titles of autobiographical texts but not for other sources.

Toward the end of our project, an enigmatic ennumeration of Arabic autobiographers published in a work titled *Itḥāf al-nubalā'* by Rāshid al-Zahrānī was brought to our attention. This list is transmitted from an apparently unpublished study by the contemporary Saudi scholar Bakr ibn ʿAbd Allāh Abū Zayd titled *Kitāb al-Naẓā'ir*. It gives the names and death dates of 126 Arabic autobiographers (40 of whom are twentieth-century authors who do not fall within the time frame of this study) but includes no citations to the works themselves. It offers particularly thorough coverage for the Arabian peninsula, a region not well represented in other sources, from the seventeenth century to the present. Where this listing supplemented our own research, those names have been added with page references to *Itḥāf al-nubalā'* (hereafter *IN*).

It is our hope that this necessarily preliminary list will be of use to scholars of autobiography and, indeed, that it will be supplemented and augmented by further research in this new and fertile area of scholarship.

Abbreviations

EI^1/*EI*^{2}	*Encyclopaedia of Islam.* Leiden: E. J. Brill. 1st ed., 1913–16, 2d ed., 1960–.
GAL	Carl Brockelmann, *Geschichte der arabischen Litteratur* (Leiden: E. J. Brill, 1898–1902; *Supplementband* 1937–42; rev. ed. 1943–49).
GAS	*Geschichte des arabischen Schrifttums.* Ed. Fuat Sezgin. Leiden: E. J. Brill, 1967–98.
Ibn Ṭūlūn	*Al-Fulk al-mashḥūn fī aḥwāl Muḥammad Ibn Ṭūlūn.* Damascus: Maṭbaʿat al-Taraqqī, 1929.
IN	Rāshid ibn Shaʿbān ibn Aḥmad al-Zahrānī, *Itḥāf al-nubalāʾ bi-siyar al-ʿulamāʾ.* Riyadh: Dār al-Ṣumayʿī li-l-Nashr wa-l-Tawzīʿ, 1996.
Maqqarī	*Nafḥ al-ṭīb min ghuṣn al-Andalus al-raṭīb.* Ed. Iḥsān ʿAbbās. Beirut: Dār Ṣādir, 1968.
Qifṭī	Ibn al-Qifṭī, *Taʾrīkh al-ḥukamāʾ.* Ed. J. Lippert. Leipzig: Dieterich, 1903.
Sakhāwī	*Al-Jawāhir wa-l-durar fī tarjamat Shaykh al-Islām Ibn Ḥajar.* Cairo: Wizārat al-Awqāf, al-Majlis al-Aʿlā li-l-Shuʾūn al-Islamiyya, wa-Lajnat Iḥyāʾ al-Turāth al-Islāmī, 1986.
Shaʿrānī	*Laṭāʾif al-minan wa-l-akhlāq fī wujūb al-taḥadduth bi-niʿmat Allāh ʿalā al-iṭlāq.* Cairo: ʿĀlam al-Fikr, 1938–39.
Suyūṭī	*Jalāl al-Dīn al-Suyūṭī.* Ed. Elizabeth M. Sartain. Cambridge: Cambridge University Press, 1975.
ʿUyūn	Ibn Abī Uṣaybiʿa, *ʿUyūn al-anbāʾ fī ṭabaqāt al-aṭibbāʿ.* Ed. Nizār Riḍā. Beirut: Dār Maktabat al-Ḥayāt, 1965.
Yāqūt^1	*Irshād al-arīb ilā maʿrifat al-adīb,* also known as *Muʿjam al-udabāʾ.* Ed. D. S. Margoliouth. Leiden: E. J. Brill, 1907–32.
Yāqūt^2	*Muʿjam al-udabāʾ: irshād al-arīb ilā maʿrifat al-adīb.* Ed. Iḥsān ʿAbbās. Beirut: Dār al-Gharb al-Islāmī, 1993.

Authors (by date of death)

Ninth Century

[Muḥammad ibn ʿUmar **al-Wāqidī** (b. 130/747, d. 207/823)

Although Tarif Khalidi mentions an autobiography by the historian al-Wāqidī, no such text appears to exist; the reference is, rather, to isolated *khabar*-anecdotes in the first person attributed to an unlikely chain of transmitters. Tarif Khalidi, *Arabic Historical Thought in the Classical Period* (Cambridge: Cambridge University Press, 1994): 44 n. 46.]

Abū ʿAbd Allāh Ḥārith ibn Asad al-ʿAnazī **al-Muḥāsibī** (b. ca. 165/781, d. ca. 243/857)

Early ascetic and mystic whose brief account of conversion to the mystical path is prefaced to his *Kitāb al-Naṣāʾiḥ* (The Book of Advice), also known as *al-Waṣāyā* (The Bequests). The text, which provides no dates or specific references to events in his life, is available in multiple Arabic editions. Translated passages appear in Louis Massignon, *Essai sur les origines du lexique technique de la mystique musulmane* (Paris: P. Guethner, 1922); and Margaret Smith, *An Early Mystic of Baghdad: A Study of the Life and Teaching of Ḥārith b. Asad al-Muḥāsibī* (London: Sheldon Press, 1935 [rpt. 1977]).

Abū Zayd **Ḥunayn ibn Isḥāq** al-ʿIbādī (b. 194/809, d. 260/873 or 264/877)

Christian Arab physician and translator of Greek works. His autobiography is quoted, apparently in full, in *ʿUyūn*, 257–74. It is translated in this volume. See also Michael Cooperson, "The Purported Autobiography of Ḥunayn ibn Isḥāq." *Edebiyât: Special Issue—Arabic Autobiography* N.S. 7, no. 2 (1997): 235–49.

Abū ʿAbd Allāh Muḥammad ibn ʿAlī **al-Ḥakīm al-Tirmidhī** (b. before 215/830, d. between 292 and 297/905 and 910)

Controversial religious figure influential on later philosophers and mystics. His autobiography is published in *Khatm al-awliyāʾ*, ed. ʿUthmān Yaḥyā (Beirut: Buḥūth wa-dirāsāt bi-idārat maʿhad al-ādāb al-sharqiyya, al-Maṭbaʿa al-Kāthūlīkiyya, 19, 1965 = Recherches publiées sous la direction de l'Institut des lettres orientales de Beyrouth, vol. 19, Imprimérie Catholique, 1965:14–32). It is translated in this volume. Another English translation appears in Bernd Radtke and John O'Kane, *The Concept of Sainthood in Early Islamic Mysticism: Two Works by al-Ḥakīm al-Tirmidhī* (Richmond, Surrey: Curzon Press, 1996), 15–36.

[Aḥmad ibn Ismāʿīl ibn Ibrāhīm **Ibn al-Khaṣīb** (d. 290/903)

Secretary/administrator (*kātib*) and poet. He is cited in *IN*, 23, as an autobiographer (out of chronological order and with no death date). The reference may be to an anthology of his prodigious correspondence mentioned by Yāqūt: "For the most part, he wrote about himself to his friends; he and Ibn al-Muʿtazz wrote wonderous letters and epistles to each other." Yāqūt adds, however, quoting Ibn al-Nadīm, that Ibn al-Khaṣīb also wrote "a *Kitāb Ṣifat al-nafs* (Book on the Description of the Soul/Self)"(*Yāqūt*[1] 1: 377–78; *Yāqūt*[2] 1:199–201). This possibly autobiographical work does not survive.]

Tenth Century

Abū l-Qāsim al-Ḥasan ibn Faraj, known as **Ibn Ḥawshab** (d. 302/914)

A convert from Imāmī Shiʿism to Ismāʿīlī Shiʿism and a missionary/agent provocateur (*dāʿī*) in Yemen. The original text is lost, but an extract preserved in al-Qāḍī al-Nuʿmān, *Risālat iftitāḥ al-daʿwa*, ed. Wadad al-Qāḍī (Beirut: Dār al-Thaqāfa, 1970), 32–62, describes his conversion and early missionary work. See "Ibn Ḥawshab," Wilferd Madelung, *EI*[2] 6:438–39.

Abū Bakr Muḥammad ibn Zakariyyā' **al-Rāzī** (b. 250/854, d. 313/925 or 323/935)

Famous physician and philosopher (Latin *Rhazes*). His autobiography appears in *Rasā'il falsafiyya li-Abī Bakr Muḥammad ibn Zakariyā al-Rāzī = Abi Bakr Mohammedi filii Zachariae Raghensis [Razis] opera philosophica* (Cairo: al-Maktaba al-Murtaḍiyya, 1939), 98–111. A French translation by Paul Kraus has been published as "Raziana I: La Conduite du philosophe," *Orientalia*, N.S. 4 (1935): 300–34. In it he describes his life, beliefs, and learning as a response to critics who claim that he does not live the life of a philosopher as exemplified by Socrates.

Abū Jaʿfar Aḥmad ibn Yaʿqūb Yūsuf, known as **Ibn al-Dāya** al-Baghdādī (b. ca. 245/859, d. 330 or 40/941 or 51)

Scholar of astronomy, philosophy, and history and author of a biography of Aḥmad ibn Ṭūlūn, ruler of Egypt (r. 868–84). His *Kitāb al-Mukāfa'a* (The Book of Compensation), ed. Aḥmad Amīn and ʿAlī Jarīm (Cairo: al-Maṭbaʿa al-Amīriyya, 1941), which deals with the comic and tragic vicissitudes of life, includes anecdotes from his own life and that of his father (who served the famous musician Ibrāhīm al-Mahdī until the latter's death).

Abū al-Faḍl **Jaʿfar** ibn ʿAlī **al-Ḥājib** (b. ca. 260/873, d. ca. 342/954)

Devoted servant, then chamberlain, to the first Fāṭimid caliph, al-Mahdī. His autobiography, compiled by one Muḥammad ibn Muḥammad al-Yamanī, is in the third person when the compiler is narrating and in the first person when Jaʿfar himself speaks. It is a lively account, covering the flight of al-Mahdī from Syria to North Africa in the years 902–5. The Arabic text was edited by Wladimir Ivanow et al., *Bulletin of the Faculty of Arts, Egyptian University* 4, no. 2 (1936): 107–33, and translated into English by Wladimir Ivanow in *Ismaili Tradition Concerning the Rise of the Fatimids* (London: Oxford University Press, 1942), 184–223. Marius Canard's French translation, "L'autobiographie d'un chambellan du Mahdī ʿObeidallāh le

Fāṭimide," *Hespèris* 39 (1952): 279–329, is reprinted in *Marius Canard: Miscellanea Orientalis* (London: Variorum, 1973).

Abū Bakr Muḥammad ibn al-Ḥasan ibn Yaʿqūb al-ʿAṭṭār **Ibn Miqsam** (d. 354/965)

Grammarian and Qur'ān reciter, cited in *IN*, 22, as an autobiographer. The text in question may be his lost *Kitāb Akhbār nafsih* (The Book of Information about Himself), which appears under the amended title, *Kitāb (al-)ikhtiyār nafsihi*, in *GAS* 9:149–50. See also *EI*² Supplement, 393.

Abū ʿAlī Ismāʿīl ibn al-Qāsim **al-Qālī** (b. 288/901, d. 356/967).

Renowned grammarian and lexicographer. Brief autobiographical remarks, primarily concerning his teachers and studies, occasioned by the questions of his student and biographer al-Zubaydī (d. 378–79/989), are recorded by the latter in his biographical compendium of grammarians, the *Ṭabaqāt al-naḥwiyyīn wa-l-lughawiyyīn*, ed. Muḥammad Abū al-Faḍl Ibrāhīm (Cairo: Muḥammad Sāmī Amīn al-Khānjī al-Kutubī, 1954).

Eleventh Century

ʿAlī ibn Muḥammad ibn al-ʿAbbās **Abū Ḥayyān al-Tawḥīdī** (b. ca. 215/927, d. after 400/1009)

Major prose writer and littérateur, cited as an autobiographer in *IN*, 22. The text remains unidentified.

Abū al-Ḥasan ibn ʿAbd Allāh **Ibn Sīnā** (b. 370/980, d. 428/1036)

Famous physician and philosopher (Latin *Avicenna*). His well-known autobiography describes his youth and adolescence and ends when he reaches adulthood. The Arabic text has been preserved in *ʿUyūn*, 437–59 and *Qifṭī*, 413–17. English translations have been published by A. J. Arberry, *Avicenna on Theology* (London, 1951): 9–24; William Gohlman, *The Life of Ibn Sina: A Critical Edition and Annotated Translation* (Albany: SUNY Press, 1974); and Dimitri Gutas, *Avicenna and the Aristotelian Tradition: Introduction to Reading Avicenna's Philosophical Works* (Leiden: E. J. Brill, 1988), 22–30.

Abū ʿAlī Muḥammad al-Ḥasan b. al-Ḥasan **Ibn al-Haytham** (b. ca. 354/965, d. ca. 430/1039)

Famous scholar of medicine, mathematics, and physics (Latin *Alhazen*). Written in 417/1026 when he was sixty, his autobiography describes his spiritual-philosophical quest for Truth and his scholarly life. Skeptical of religious beliefs, he follows a path based on Aristotelian philosophy and rational deduction and science. The Arabic text is preserved in *ʿUyūn*, 550–60.

[Abū al-Rayḥān Muḥammad ibn Aḥmad **al-Bīrūnī** (b. 362/973, d. after 442/1050)

Famous mathematician, astronomer, geographer, historian, and translator. Despite references to an autobiography by al-Bīrūnī, only the following are extant: (1) 17 lines of verse giving a chronological list of his patrons, preserved in Yāqūt and cited by A. S. Khan, *A Bibliography of the Works of al-Bīrūnī* (New Delhi: Indian National Science Academy, 1982), 53, as part of a lost work, *Majmūʿ min al-ashʿār* (Collection of Verses); and (2) an autobibliography of 138 works in *Risāla fī fihrist kutub Muḥammad ibn Zakarīyā al-Rāzī*, ed. Paul Kraus (Paris: Imprimerie Orientaliste au Calame, 1936).]

ʿUthmān b. Saʿīd **al-Dānī** (b. 371/982, d. 444/1053)

Malikite jurist whose terse account of his birth, travels, and studies appears in Yāqūt, in the first person, as copied and transmitted by his student, Sulaymān ibn Najjāḥ al-Muʾayyadī. See *Yāqūt*[1] 5:35–37; *Yāqūt*[2] 4:1603–4.

Abū al-Ḥasan ʿAlī **Ibn Riḍwān** (b. 388/998, d. 453/1061)

Physician and medical scholar. His autobiography is unusual for the inclusion of prosaic details of the author's life: his lowly origins, early struggles, and unhappy domestic life; the death of all of his children; and being robbed by an orphan he attempted to adopt. It also includes an account of a typical day in his life. The Arabic text is preserved in *Qifṭī*, 294, 298–300, 443–45; and *ʿUyūn* 2:99–105. Excerpts are translated in Michael W. Dols, *Medieval Islamic Medicine: Ibn Riḍwān's Treatise "On the Prevention of Bodily Ills in Egypt"* (Berkeley: University of California Press, 1984), 54–66.

[ʿAlī ibn Aḥmad **Ibn Ḥazm** (b. 384/994, d. 456/1064)

Religious scholar and belletrist of Islamic Spain. His treatise on love, *Ṭawq al-ḥamāma fī al-ulfa wa-l-ullāf* (The Ring of the Dove on Lovers and Love), which includes a handful of autobiographical anecdotes, is regarded as an autobiography in Iḥsān ʿAbbās, *Fann al-sīra* (Beirut: Dār al-Thaqāfa, 1956); and Yaḥyā I. ʿAbd al-Dāyim, *al-Tarjama al-dhātiyya fī al-adab al-ʿarabī al-ḥadīth* (Beirut: Dār Iḥyāʾ al-Turāth al-ʿArabī, 1956).]

Al-Muʾayyad fī al-Dīn Hibat Allāh **al-Shīrāzī** (b. 330s/990s, d. 470/1077)

Missionary/agent provocateur (*dāʿī*) for the Shiʿite Fatimid dynasty of Egypt. This book-length autobiography is a lively account of the adventures of the author from 1038 to 1060 in southern Iran, in Cairo, and battling the Turks in Iraq. Its three sections appear to have been composed at different times. Excerpts from the *Sīrat al-Muʾayyad fī al-dīn dāʿī al-duʿāt*, ed. M. K. Ḥusayn (Cairo: Dār al-Kutub, 1949), are translateed in Jawad Muscati and Khan Bahadur Moulvi, *Life and Lectures of the Grand Missionary Al-Muayyad-Fid-Din al-Shirazi* (Karachi: Ismailia Assocation of West Pakistan, 1950), and in this volume.

Abū ʿAlī al-Ḥasan ibn Aḥmad **Ibn al-Bannāʾ** (b. 396/1005, d. 471/1079)

Baghdadi scholar of little renown, a fragment of whose personal diary survives. The extant text, which runs from August 3, 1068, to September 4, 1069, consists of first-person, laconic, unpolished, personal jottings, clearly not intended for publication in this form. It describes political and social events and includes conversations with travelers and merchants and discussions of unusual occurrences. It has been edited and translated by George Makdisi, "Autograph Diary of an Eleventh-Century Historian of Baghdad," *BSOAS* 18 (1956): 9–31, 239–60; 19 (1957): 13–48, 281–303, 426–443.

ʿAbd Allāh **Ibn Buluggīn** (b. 447/1056, d. after 487/1094)

The last Zirid Berber prince of Granada, who ruled 465/1073–483/1090. His autobiography is divided into twelve chapters: the first four chapters deal with the history of his family, and the remaining eight deal with his own life. The final chapter is an intimate and moving summation of his life written from exile in Morocco. *Mudhakkirāt al-amīr ʿAbd Allāh ākhir mulūk banī zīri bi-Gharnāṭa al-musammā bi-kitāb al-tibyān*, ed. E. Lévi-Provençal (Cairo: Dār al-Maʿārif, 1955), has been translated into English by Amin T. Tibi as *The Tibyān: Memoirs of ʿAbd Allāh b. Buluggīn, Last Zīrid Amīr of Granada* (Leiden: E. J. Brill, 1986).

Abū al-Aṣbagh ʿĪsā ibn Sahl **al-Asadī** al-Tustarī (d. 486/1093)

Jurist identified as an autobiographer in *IN*, 23. The text remains unidentified. See *GAL* 1, 383, and *GAL* Suppl. 1, 661.

Twelfth Century

Abū Ḥāmid Muḥammad **al-Ghazālī** (b. 450/1058, d. 505/1111)

Famous religious thinker whose autobiography describes his lifelong pursuit of truth and the dramatic spiritual crisis that leads him to explore and reject several schools of thought before finally choosing the mystical path. *Al-Munqidh min al-ḍalāl* (Cairo: al-Maktab al-Fannī, 1961) has been translated as "Deliverance from Error" by W. Montgomery Watt in *The Faith and Practice of Al-Ghazālī* (London: Allen and Unwin, 1953).

Abū al-Qāsim ʿAlī ibn Jaʿfar al-Baghdādī al-Siqillī **Ibn al-Qaṭṭāʿ** (b. 433/1041, d. 514/1121)

An anthologist, historian, and grammarian whose autobiography, according to Ibn Khallikān (d. 681/1282), was appended to the end of his anthology of Arabo-Sicilian poetry, *al-Durra al-khaṭīra fī shuʿarāʾ al-jazīra.* This work survives only in abridged redactions, none of which contain the autobiography. The various redactions have been collated and edited by

Béchir Baccouche as *al-Durra al-khaṭīra fī shuʿarāʾ al-jazīra: Anthologie des poètes arabo-siciliens* (Beirut: Dār al-Gharb al-Islāmī, 1995). See also Ibn Saʿīd (d. 1286) below.

ʿ**Abd al-Ghāfir** ibn Ismāʿīl **al-Fārisī** (b. 451/1059, d. 529/1135)
Religious scholar and historian whose autobiography is appended to his unpublished work, *al-Siyāq li-taʾrīkh Nīsābūr* (see *GAL* Suppl. 1:623). A published abridgment by Ibrāhīm ibn Muḥammad al-Azhar al-Sarifīnī (d. 1243), *al-Muntakhab min al-siyāq li-taʾrīkh Nīsābūr*, ed. Muḥammad Kāẓim al-Maḥmūdī (Qom: Jamāʿat al-Mudarrisīn, 1983), includes a two-page abridged version of the autobiography (pp. 754–56).

[Abū al-Fatḥ Muḥammad ibn ʿAbd al-Karīm ibn Aḥmad Tāj al-Dīn **al-Shahrastānī** (b. 479/1086, d. 548/1153).
Historian and philosopher of religion. Guy Monnot (*EI*² 9:215) has characterized the preface to al-Shahrastānī's *Mafātīḥ al-asrār wa-maṣābīḥ al-abrār*, ed. Muḥammad ʿAlī Adharshab (Teheran: Iḥyā-i Kitāb, 1997): 103–7, as autobiographical, but the passages in question provide only sparse personal information that pertains to the writing of the larger work and little else.]

ʿAbd Allāh ibn Ibrāhīm **al-Ḥijārī** (d. 549/1155)
Historian whose autobiography was included in his work *Kitāb al-Mushib fī gharīb al-maghrib* according to Ibn Saʿīd (d. 685/1286) below.

Ibn al-Imām (d. 550/1155)
Author whose autobiography was included in his work *Simṭ al-jumān* according to Ibn Saʿīd (d. 685/1286) below.

Abū Bakr ibn ʿAlī **al-Baydhaq** al-Ṣinhājī (d. after 559/1164)
Berber companion and chronicler of Ibn Tūmart (founder of the Almohad dynasty). Strictly speaking, this is a memoir of the career of Ibn Tūmart as told by his close companion, although the author appears as a character throughout. In the extant fragments, he provides no information about his life beyond his experiences with Ibn Tūmart. A French translation was published by E. Lévi-Provençal as *Documents inédits d'histoire almohade* (Paris: P. Geuthner, 1928), 75–224; an Arabic edition, *Kitāb Akhbār al-mahdī ibn Tūmart* (Algiers: al-Muʾassasa al-Waṭaniyya li-l-Kitāb, 1982), has appeared more recently.

Ẓāhir al-Dīn Abū al-Ḥasan ʿAlī ibn Zayd **al-Bayhaqī** (b. 493/1100, d. 565/1169)
Historian and religious scholar. The complete autobiography is not ex-

tant, but excerpts are preserved in Yāqūt, who quotes al-Bayhaqī in the first person from a text he copied. Quoted passages cover al-Bayhaqī's birthdate, education, travels, career, and publications. Briefly mentioned are a visit to his mother, who had memorized the Qur'ān and mastered its exegesis, and her subsequent death. *Yāqūt*[1] 5:208–13; *Yāqūt*[2] 4:1759–68.

Samaw'al ibn Yaḥyā **al-Maghribī** (b. 520/1126, d. 569/1174)

Jewish scholar who converted to Islam and became an anti-Jewish polemicist. The autobiography is appended to his treatise against Judaism. It gives an account of his parents, his childhood and education, his growing doubts about the claims of Judaism, and finally a series of visions of the Prophets Samuel and Muhammad that ultimately lead to his conversion. The Arabic text and English translation are found in *Samau'al al-Maghribī: Ifḥām al-Yahūd "Silencing the Jews,"* ed. and trans. Moshe Perlmann (New York: American Academy for Jewish Research, 1964).

ʿUmāra ibn Abī l-Ḥasan **al-Ḥakamī al-Yamanī** (b. 515/1121, d. 569/1175)

Poet, historian, and politician. His book-length autobiography recounts anecdotes, in roughly chronological order, about his childhood and extended family, his travels from Yemen to Egypt, his political and poetic career in Egypt under the Fatimids, various viziers of Egypt, and finally his unsuccessful attempts to gain the favor of Saladin, who had him crucified on charges of heresy and treason. Passages from *Kitāb fīhi nukat al-ʿaṣriyya fī akhbār al-wuzarāʾ al-miṣriyya* (Contemporary Anecdotes on News of the Ministers of Egypt), ed. Hartwig Derenbourg (rpt. Cairo: Maktabat Matbūlī, [1897] 1991), are summarized or translated in *ʿOumāra du Yémen: sa vie et son oeuvre,* ed. Hartwig Derenbourg (Paris: E. Leroux, 1897–1904).

Usāma ibn Munqidh (b. 488/1095, d. 573/1188)

Syrian nobleman, poet, and warrior during the Crusades. This is one of the best-known medieval Arabic autobiographies in the West. It was written when Usāma was ninety years old and contains anecdotes from his adventures in the Crusades arranged thematically and associatively, rather than chronologically. One section describes the strange social, medical, legal, and sexual customs of the Europeans he encountered in the Crusader cities. *Kitāb al-Iʿtibār,* ed. Philip K. Hitti (Princeton: Princeton University Press, 1930), is published in an English translation by Philip K. Hitti as *An Arab-Syrian Gentleman and Warrior in the Period of the Crusades: Memoirs of Usāmah Ibn-Munqidh* (New York: Columbia University Press, 1929; rpt. Princeton: Princeton University Press, 1987).

Aḥmad ibn ʿAlī **Ibn Ma'mūn** (b. 509/1115, d. 586/1191)

Judge, grammarian, and lexicographer. The full text is lost, but excerpts are preserved by Yāqūt, who copied from Ibn Ma'mūn's original. These recount his education and early years, including an account of a childhood friend and his older brother. Ibn Ma'mūn was appointed to a judgeship in his mid twenties, became a powerful political figure, but was then imprisoned for eleven years. The text closes by relating this reversal of his fortunes. *Yāqūt*[1] 2:51–57; *Yāqūt*[2] 1:448–53.

Thirteenth Century

Abū al-Faraj ʿAbd al-Raḥmān **Ibn al-Jawzī** (b. 511/1116, d. 597/1201)

Jurist, historian, and preacher. This text consists of advice from the author to his son, but the third section recounts the author's own childhood and young adulthood in exemplary terms. *Laftat al-kabad ilā naṣīḥat al-walad* (The Turning of the Heart toward Advising One's Son), ed. ʿAbd al-Ghaffār Sulaymān al-Bindarī (Beirut: Dār al-Kutub al-ʿIlmiyya, 1987).

ʿImād al-Dīn al-Kātib al-Iṣfahānī (b. 519/1125, d. 597/1201)

Personal secretary/chancellor to Saladin and historian. His *al-Barq al-shāmī* (The Syrian Thunderbolt), a professional diary of sorts, is written as a historical account of Saladin's reign and includes not only narrative accounts of Saladin's actions but also official letters, poems, and memorandums, all told with a distinctly autobiographical voice emphasizing al-Iṣfahānī's role in the events. Al-Suyūṭī (d. 909/1505) and al-Shaʿrānī (d. 973/1565), see below, both refer to it as al-Iṣfahānī's *tarjama* of himself. *Al-Barq al-shāmī*, vol. 3, ed. Muṣṭafā al-Hayarī, and vol. 5, ed. Fāliḥ Ḥusayn (ʿAmmān: ʿA. H. Shuman, 1986–87). Only two of the seven volumes of *al-Barq* have survived, but a condensed version, the *Sanā* by al-Bundarī, gives a summary of the whole: al-Fatḥ ibn ʿAlī al-Bundarī, *Sanā al-barq al-shāmī*, ed. Ramazan Şeşen (Beirut: Dār al-Kitāb al-Jadīd, 1971).

Abū Muḥammad **Rūzbihan** ibn Abī Naṣr al-Fasā'ī **al-Baqlī** al-Shirāzī (b. 522/1128, d. 606/1209)

Sufi mystic and Qur'ān commentator. His spiritual autobiography was written in 557/1181–82 when he was fifty-five. It is in the first person and recounts his visionary encounters with God, angels, prophets, and Sufi figures. In the first fifth of the text, which is the autobiographical memoir proper, Rūzbihan describes how he was overwhelmed by a vision at the age of fifteen and thereafter abandoned his vegetable shop for a year of wandering in the desert. Abridged versions of the Arabic text are available in *Ruzbihan al-Bakli ve kitab Kaşf al-asrar'i ile Farsca bazi Şiirleir*, ed. Nazif Hoca (Istanbul: Edebiyat Fakultesi Matbaası, 1971), and in "Kashf al-asrār," ed.

Paul Nwyia, in *al-Machriq* 64 (1970): 385–406. The text exists, however, in two complete manuscripts and is being edited for publication by Javad Nurbakhsh. For a recent English translation based on these manuscripts, see Rūzbihan Baqlī, *The Unveiling of Secrets: Diary of a Sufi Master*, trans. Carl Ernst (Chapel Hill, N.C.: Parvardigar Press, 1997), 9–26.

[**Al-Malik** Muḥammad ibn ʿUmar **al-Manṣūr** (b. 567/1171–2, d. 617/1220)
Ruler of Ḥamāh and historian. There are numerous autobiographical remarks in his chronicle glorifying Saladin. Regrettably, only a final section survives in *Miḍmār al-ḥaqā'iq wa-sirr al-khalā'iq*, ed. Ḥasan Ḥabashī (Cairo: Ālam al-Kutub, 1968), passim. See Angelika Hartmann, *EI*[2] 6:429–30.]

Yāqūt al-Ḥamawī (b. 575/1179, d. 622/1229)
Prominent biographer and encyclopedist. He appended his autobiography to the end of his monumental biographical compendium, *Irshād al-arīb.* It is mentioned by al-Suyūṭī (d. 909/1505), Ibn Ṭūlūn al-Dimashqī (d. 953/1546), and al-Shaʿrānī (d. 973/1565), see below, but has since been lost.

Muwaffaq al-Dīn Abū Muḥammad **ʿAbd al-Laṭīf** ibn Yūsuf **al-Baghdādī** (b. 557/1162, d. 629/1231)
Grammarian, lexicographer, philosopher, and physician. The autobiography appears to have been part of a larger work titled *Ta'rīkh* (History, or Diary), composed for his son, Sharaf al-Dīn Yūsuf. The complete work has not survived, but excerpts are preserved in *ʿUyūn*, 683–96. Selections are translated in this volume, and an extensive English paraphrase appears in George Makdisi, *The Rise of Colleges: Institutions of Learning in Islam and the West* (Edinburgh: Edinburgh University Press, 1981), 84–88. See also Shawkat Toorawa, "Language and Male Homosocial Desire in the Autobiography of ʿAbd al-Laṭīf al-Baghdādī," *Edebiyât: Special Issue—Arabic Autobiography*, N.S. 7, no. 2 (1997): 251–65.

Muḥyī al-Dīn **Ibn al-ʿArabī** (b. 560/1165, d. 638/1240)
One of the most important figures in postclassical Sufism. He is often cited for the strongly autobiographical nature of his writings, but no single text presents itself as an autobiography per se. See *Rūḥ al-quds fī munāṣaḥat al-nafs* (Damascus: Maṭbaʿat al-ʿIlm, 1964); *al-Durra al-fākhira fī dhikr man intafa'tu bihi fī ṭarīq al-ākhira* (see Austin below); and *al-Futūḥāt al-makkiyya*, 12 vols. (Cairo: al-Hay'ah al-Miṣriyya li-l-Kitāb, 1972–91). English translations of the first two appear in R. W. J. Austin, *Sufis of Andalusia: The Rūḥ al-Quds and al-Durrah al-fākhirah of Ibn ʿArabī* (Berkeley: University of California Press, 1972 [London: Allen and Unwin, 1971]).

Kamāl al-Dīn ʿUmar ibn Hibat Allāh **Ibn al-ʿAdīm** (b. 588/1192, d. 660/1262)

Aleppan scholar and historian. The complete autobiography that Ibn al-ʿAdīm wrote at the behest of his friend and biographer Yāqūt has not survived, but passages are cited in *Yāqūt*[1] 6:18–46 and *Yāqūt*[2] 5:2068–91 and are translated in this volume. See also Nuha N. N. Khoury, "The Autobiography of Ibn al-ʿAdīm as Told to Yāqūt al-Rūmī," *Edebiyât: Special Issue—Arabic Autobiography*, N.S. 7, no. 2 (1997): 289–311.

ʿAbd al-Raḥmān ibn Ismāʿīl al-Maqdisī **Abū Shāma** (b. 599/1202, d. 665/1268)

Damascene jurist and historian. His complete autobiography is translated in this volume: *Al-Dhayl ʿalā al-rawḍatayn*, ed. Muḥammad Kawtharī as *Tarājim rijāl al-qarnayn al-sādis wa-l-sābiʿ* (Cairo: Dār al-Kutub al-Malikiyya, 1947), 37–39; see also an edition from a different manuscript, *Tarjamat Abī Shāma manqūla min Dhayl kitāb al-rawḍatayn*, ed. and trans. Barbier de Meynard, in *Recueil des Historiens des Croisades*, 5:207–16 (Paris: Imprimerie Nationale, 1872–1906). See also Joseph Lowry, "Time, Form, and Self: The Autobiography of Abū Shāma." *Edebiyât: Special Edition—Arabic Autobiography*, N.S. 7, no. 2 (1997): 313–25.

Manṣūr ibn Salīm **al-Hamadānī** al-Iskandarānī Wajīh al-Dīn Abū al-Muẓaffar **Ibn al-ʿImādiyya** (b. 607/1210, d. 673/1275)

Muḥtasib (inspector of the markets) of Alexandria who is identified as an autobiographer in *IN*, 25. The text remains unidentified.

Saʿd al-Dīn ibn Ḥamawiyya **al-Juwaynī** (b. 592/1196, d. 674/1276)

Damascene military commander and historian. The original text does not survive but appears to have been a historical chronicle with a highly autobiographical tone. Claude Cahen has pieced together the fragments preserved in later sources that include first-person passages relating to the birth of the author's father, the author's political exploits, opinions of various personalities, and his eventual retirement from his military career to become a Sufi. Claude Cahen, "Une source pour l'histoire ayyubide: Les mémoires de Saʿd al-dīn ibn Ḥamawiya al-Juwaynī," *Bulletin de la Faculté des Lettres de Strasbourg*, 7 (1950): 320–37; rpt. in *Les peuples musulmans dans l'histoire médievale* (Damascus: Institut Français de Damas, 1977), 457–82.

Ṣafī al-Dīn ibn Abī al-Manṣūr **Ibn Ẓāfir** (b. 595/1198, d. 682/1283)

Sufi mystic identified by al-Shaʿrānī (d. 973/1565—see below) as an autobiographer. The author figures in many of the entries in a collection of biographies of saintly men he encountered, purportedly penned for his son, Ibrāhīm, but the focus remains biographical. It is not clear, however, that this is the text intended by al-Shaʿrānī. See *La Risāla de Ṣafī al-Dīn ibn Abī Manṣūr ibn Ẓāfir: Biographies des maîtres spirituels connus par un cheikh égyptien du VIIe/XIIe siècle,* ed. and trans. Denis Gril (Cairo: Institut Français d'Archéologie Orientale du Caire, 1986).

Abū al-Ḥasan ʿAlī ibn Mūsā **Ibn Saʿīd al-Maghribī** (b. 610/1208, d. 685/1286)

Andalusian man of letters and biographer. Al-Maqqarī (2:262) reports that in his autobiography, included in *al-Mughrib fī ḥulā al-Maghrib,* Ibn Saʿīd cites three previous autobiographers and their works as predecessors: Ibn al-Imām (d. 550/1155), *Simṭ al-jumān;* al-Ḥijārī (d. 549/1155), *al-Mushib;* and Ibn al-Qaṭṭāʿ (d. 433/1041) *al-Durra* (see above). Extant editions of the *Mughrib,* however, do not contain Ibn Saʿīd's autobiography.

Abū al-Rabīʿ **al-Mālaqī**. Identified as an autobiographer by al-Shaʿrānī (d. 973/1565—see below), perhaps Abū al-Ḥasan ʿUbaydallah ibn Aḥmad ibn Abī al-Rabīʿ (b. 599/1202, d. 648/1289), the author of an unpublished *al-Barnāmaj* (see *GAS* Suppl. 1:547).

Fourteenth Century

[Al-Ḥasan ibn Yūsuf **Ibn al-Muṭahhar al-Ḥillī** (b. 648/1250, d. 726/1325)

Religious scholar identified as an autobiographer in *IN,* 25. The reference may be to his entry on himself in *Khulāṣat al-aqwāl fī maʿrifat al-rijāl,* but this consists only of an autobibliography, with no further information.]

ʿAbd Allāh ibn Muḥammad **Ibn Farḥūn** (d. 729/1327)

Identified as an autobiographer in *IN,* 25. The text has not been identified.

Abū al-Fidāʾ al-Ayyūbī: Ismāʿīl ibn ʿAlī ibn Muḥammad ibn Muḥammad ibn ʿUmar Ayyūb al-Malik al-Muʾayyad (b. 672/1273, d. 732/1331)

Ruler of the city-state of Ḥamāh who wrote a political and military chronicle of his reign. The text, however, contains little in the way of personal information. An English translation is offered in P. M. Holt, *The Memoirs of a Syrian Prince: Abū al-Fidāʾ Sultan of Ḥamāh (672–732/1273–1331)* (Wiesbaden: Franz Steiner, 1983).

Abū l-Makārim Rukn al-Dawla Aḥmad ibn Muḥammad ibn Aḥmad ʿAlāʾ al-Dīn al-Biyābānakī **al-Simnānī** (b. 659/1261, d. 736/1336)

Major Sufi religious figure. The text is translated in this volume. *Al-ʿUrwa li-ahl al-khalwa wa-l-jalwa,* ed. Najīb Māyil-i Hirawī (Teheran: Mawla, 1983), 396–400. See also Jamal J. Elias, *The Throne Carrier of God: The Life and Thought of ʿAlāʾ al-Dawla al-Simnānī* (Albany: SUNY Press, 1995).

Jamāl al-Dīn Abū al-Ḥajjāj Yūsuf ibn ʿAbd al-Raḥmān al-Quḍāʿī **al-Mizzī** al-Kalbī al-Dimashqī (b. 654/1256, d. 742/1341)

Damascene religious scholar identified as an autobiographer in *IN*, 26. The text has not been identified.

Athīr al-Dīn Muḥammad **Abū Ḥayyān al-Gharnāṭī** al-Jayyānī al-Nafzī al-Andalusī (b. 654/1256, d. 745/1344)

Grammarian and religious scholar. Later authors such as Ibn Ḥajar (d. 852/1449) and al-Suyūṭī (d. 909/1505) write that his autobiography was quite lengthy and was written as an act of mourning after the untimely death of his daughter Nuḍār, considered by contemporaries a scholar in her own right. The text of his *al-Nuḍār fī al-maslāt ʿan Nuḍār* (Book of Purest Gold on Consolation for Nuḍār) is no longer extant.

Abū ʿAbd Allāh Muḥammad ibn Aḥmad ibn ʿUthmān **al-Dhahabī** (b. 672–3/1274, d. 748/1348)

Famous biographer and historian identified as an autobiographer in *IN*, 26. The text has not been identified.

Al-Ṣalāḥ Abū al-Ṣafī Khalīl **Ibn Aybak al-Ṣafadī** (b. 696–97/1297, d. 764/1363)

Renowned biographer, cited as an autobiographer by al-Sakhāwī (d. 902/1497—see below). The text has not been identified.

ʿAbd al-Raḥīm ibn al-Ḥasan **al-Isnawī** al-Shāfiʿī (b. 704–5/1305, d. 772/1370)

Biographer whose autobiography, according to *IN*, 26, is found in his *Ṭabaqāt al-Shāfiʿiyya*, which has been published in facsimile, *Ṭabaqāt al-Shāfiʿiyya* (Baghdad: Riʾāsat Dīwān al-Awqāf, 1970–71), and in a version edited by ʿAbd Allāh al-Jabbūrī (Riyadh: Dār al-ʿUlūm li-l-Ṭibāʿa wa-l-Nashr, 1981).

Muḥammad ibn ʿAbd Allāh ibn Saʿīd ibn ʿAlī ibn Aḥmad al-Salmānī [= **Lisān al-Dīn ibn al-Khaṭīb**] (b. 713/1313, d. 775/1374)

Scholar and political figure. Written in 1369, his autobiography includes a brief history of his family, an account of his life and career, lists of his teachers and writings, and many samples of his poetry and correspondence. The text appears in his *al-Iḥāṭa fī akhbār Gharnāṭa* (The Complete Source on the History of Granada), ed. Muḥammad ʿAbd Allāh ʿInān (Cairo: Maktabat al-Khānjī, 1978), 4:438–640.

Ibrāhīm ibn ʿAbd al-Raḥīm **Ibn Jamāʿa** (b. 725/1325, d. 790/1388)

Religious scholar who served as Shāfiʿite grand *qāḍī* (judge) of Cairo and later Damascus. He studied with al-Mizzī (d. 742/1341) and al-Dhahabī (d. 772/1370); see above. His autobiography is mentioned by al-Sakhāwī (d. 902/1427—see below), but the text remains unidentified.

Fifteenth Century

Abū Zayd ʿAbd al-Raḥmān ibn Muḥammad **Ibn Khaldūn** (b. 732/1332, d. 808/1406)

Famous political figure, historian, and social theorist. He originally included his autobiography as an appendix to his historical work, *al-ʿIbar*, and later expanded and published it as an independent book. It includes an account of his family and education, as well as detailed memoirs of his political career, including his encounter with Tamerlane. *Al-Taʿrīf bi-Ibn Khaldūn wa-riḥlatih gharban wa-sharqan* (An Account of Ibn Khaldūn and His Travels West and East) (Cairo: Lajnat al-Taʾlīf wa-l-Tarjama wa-l-Nashr, 1951). A partial English translation by Walter Fischel appears in *Ibn Khaldūn and Tamerlane* (Berkeley: University of California Press, 1952).

Ṣārim al-Dīn Ibrāhīm ibn Muḥammad ibn Aydamir **Ibn Duqmāq** al-Qāhirī (d. 809/1407)

Historian cited in *Sakhāwī* as an autobiographer. The text remains unidentified.

Muḥammad ibn Abī Bakr ibn ʿAbd al-ʿAzīz ibn Muḥammad **al-ʿIzz Ibn Jamāʿa** (d. 819/1416)

Member of the prominent Ibn Jamāʿa family of jurists. Al-Sakhāwī writes that "he wrote a fascicle [*juz*ʾ] which he called *Ḍawʾ al-shams fī aḥwāl al-nafs* [The Light of the Sun, Concerning the States of the Self] in which he included an account of himself [*dhakara fīhā tarjamat nafsih*]," but the text remains unidentified.

Abū al-Ṭayyib **Taqī al-Dīn** Muḥammad ibn Aḥmad ibn ʿAlī **al-Fāsī** (b. 775/1373, d. 832/1429

Religious scholar and historian of Mecca. Al-Suyūṭī (d. 909/1505), Ibn Ṭūlūn (d. 953/1546), and al-Shaʿrānī (d. 973/1565), see below, all refer to his autobiography, which includes a detailed account of his education, teachers, publications, and quotations from others regarding his publications. *Al-ʿIqd al-thamīn fī taʾrīkh al-balad al-amīn* (Cairo: Maṭbaʿat al-Sunna al-Muḥammadiyya, 1958–1969), 1:331–63. There is also a shorter autobiography, written in the third person, in al-Fāsī's supplement to a work by Ibn Nuqṭa (d. 628/1231), *Dhayl al-Taqyīd fī ruwāt al-sunan wa-l-masānīd*, ed. Kamāl Yūsuf al-Ḥūt (Beirut: Dār al-Kutub al-ʿIlmiyya, 1990), 1: 60–69.

Muḥammad ibn Muḥammad ibn Muḥammad ibn ʿAlī ibn Yūsuf **Ibn al-Jazarī** (b. 751/1350, d. 833/1429)

Religious and legal scholar. A brief account of his birth, studies, travels, teachers, students, and books appears in his *Ghāyat al-nihāya fī ṭabaqāt al-qurrāʾ*, ed. Gotthelf Bergsträsser (Cairo: Maktabat al-Khānjī, 1933), 2:247–51.

ʿAbd Allāh al-Turjumān al-Andalusī [**Fray Anselmo Turmeda**] (b. 753/1352, d. 835–6/1432?)

Mallorcan convert to Islam. The autobiography is translated in this volume. *Tuḥfat al-adīb fī al-radd ʿalā ahl al-ṣalīb*, ed. Maḥmūd ʿAlī Ḥamāya (Cairo: Dār al-Thaqāfa li-l-Ṭibāʿa wa-l-Nashr, 1983). A more reliable Arabic text with Spanish translation appears in Mikel de Epalza, *Fray Anselm Turmeda (ʿAbdallah al-Taryuman) y su polemica islamo-cristiana: Edición, traducción y estudio de la Tuhfa*, 2d ed. (Madrid: Hiperion, 1994).

Sirāj al-Dīn Ismāʿīl ibn Abī Bakr **Ibn al-Muqrī al-Yamanī** (b. 765/1363, d. 837/1433).

Scholar and poet identified as an autobiographer by al-ʿAydarūs (d. 1037/1628—see below). The text remains unidentified.

Aḥmad ibn ʿAlī ibn Muḥammad [= **Ibn Ḥajar**] **al-ʿAsqalānī** (b. 773/1372, d. 852/1449)

Major religious scholar, particularly in *ḥadīth* studies. One autobiography appears in *Rafʿ al-iṣr fī quḍāt Miṣr* (History of the Judges of Egypt) (Cairo: al-Maṭbaʿa al-Amīriyya, 1957), 85–88, and is translated in this volume. See also the autobiographical notices and passages in his *al-Durar al-kāmina, Inbāʾ al-ghamr, al-Muʿjam al-mufahras*, and *al-Muʿjam al-muʾassas* (*IN*, 27–28).

Ibrāhīm ibn Aḥmad ibn Nāṣir Abū Isḥāq ibn Shihāb Abī al-ʿAbbās al-Muqaddasī al-Nāṣirī **al-Bāʿūnī** al-Dimashqī al-Ṣāliḥī al-Shāfiʿī (b. 777/1376, d. 870/1465)

Prominent scholar, *khaṭīb* (official preacher) first at the Umayyad mosque in Damascus and later at the al-Aqṣā in Jerusalem, identified as an autobiographer in *Sakhāwī*. The text remains unidentified.

Abū ʿAbd Allāh al-Qurashī—cited in *Shaʿrānī* as an autobiographer and tentatively identified as the religious scholar Abū ʿAbd Allāh Muḥammad **Abū al-ʿAbbās** ibn ʿĪsā al-ʿUbbādī **al-Tilimsānī** (d. 871/1467). The text remains unidentified.

Abū Zayd ʿAbd al-Raḥmān ibn Makhlūf al-Thaʿālabī **al-Jazāʾirī** (b. 785/1383, d. 875/1470–71)

Identified as an autobiographer in *IN*, 28. The text remains unidentified.

Burhān al-Dīn Ibrāhīm ibn ʿUmar **al-Biqāʿī** (d. 885/1480)

Scholar and commentator who adapted the *Isagoge* of Porphyry; cited in *IN*, 28. The text is unidentified but may be one of the works mentioned by the editor or al-Biqāʿī's *al-Qawl al-mufīd fī uṣūl al-tajwīd*, ed. Khayr Allāh al-Sharīf (Beirut: Dār al-Bashāʾir al-Islāmiyya, 1995), 7–14.

Al-Shams Muḥammad ibn Muḥammad ibn al-Khiḍr **al-ʿAyzarī** al-Dimashqī

Cited in *Sakhāwī* as an autobiographer and tentatively identified as Muḥammad ibn Muḥammad ʿAbd Allāh ibn Khayḍar Sulaymān ibn Dāwūd ibn Ḍumayda, known as al-Khayḍari (b. 821/1418, d. 894/1489), who was a student of Ibn Ḥajar (d. 852/1449—see below) and a personal acquaintance of al-Sakhāwī (d. 902/1497—see below). Al-Sakhāwī's lengthy but extremely negative biographical entry on al-Khayḍarī in his *al-Ḍawʾ al-lāmiʿ* contains passages that suggest that he had seen an autobiography in the author's own hand. *Al-Ḍawʾ al-lāmiʿ* (Cairo: Maktabat al-Qudsī, 1934–36), 9:117–124.

Shihāb al-Dīn Abū al-ʿAbbās Aḥmad al-Barnusī [= **Zarrūq**] (b. 846/1442, d. 899/1493)

Moroccan Sufi around whose teachings the Zarrūqiyya Sufi order emerged. Entertaining anecdotes of his childhood, travels, and education appear in an untitled *fahrasa* and *al-Kunnāsh fī ʿilm ʾāsh*, both still in manuscript. Selected passages appear in translation in *Zarrūq the Sufi: A Guide in the Way and a Leader to the Truth*, by Ali Fahmi Khushaim (Tripoli, Libya: General Company for Publication, 1976).

Muḥammad ibn ʿAbd al-Raḥmān ibn Muḥammad ibn Abī Bakr al-Shāfiʿī [= **al-Sakhāwī**] (b. 830/1427, d. 902/1497)

Scholar of *ḥadīth* and the compiler of a major biographical dictionary. A detailed account of his education, teachers—particularly Ibn Ḥajar (d. 852/1449—see above)—publications, and citations of praise from contemporaries appears in his biographical compendium, *al-Ḍawʾ al-lāmiʿ li-ahl al-qarn al-tāsiʿ* (Cairo: Maktabat al-Quds, 1934–36), 8:2–32.

Sixteenth Century

Abū al-Fatḥ **Shams al-Dīn** Muḥammad ibn Muḥammad ibn ʿAlī ibn ʿAṭiyya al-ʿAwfī **al-Mizzī** al-Shāfiʿī (d. 906/1500)

Scholar identified as an autobiographer in *Ibn Ṭūlūn* (d. 953/1546—see below). The text remains unidentified. See *GAL*, Suppl. 2:908.

Jamāl al-Dīn Yūsuf **Ibn ʿAbd al-Hādī** al-Ḥanbalī (b. 840/1436, d. 909/1503)

Prominent Damascene scholar who, according to Ibn Ṭūlūn (d. 953/1546—see below), wrote at length of himself "in his compendium of Ḥanbalī scholars in his book on the praiseworthy qualities [*manāqib*] of the Imām Aḥmad ibn Ḥanbal." This text remains unidentified.

ʿAbd al-Raḥmān ibn Abī Bakr ibn Muḥammad al-Khuḍayrī [= **Jalāl al-dīn al-Suyūṭī**] (b. 849/1445, d. 909/1505)

Judge, legal scholar, and prolific author. His lengthy autobiography is divided into more than twenty sections covering his birth, family, father, town of origin, studies, teachers, books, clashes with contemporaries, and other topics. One extract is translated in this volume. The Arabic text is published in Elizabeth Sartain, *Jalāl al-Dīn al-Suyūṭī*, 2 vols. (Cambridge: Cambridge University Press, 1975). See also Kristen Brustad, "Imposing Order: Reading the Conventions of Representation in al-Suyūṭī's Autobiography," *Edebiyât: Special Issue—Arabic Autobiography*, N.S. 7, no. 2 (1997): 327–44.

ʿĀʾisha bint Yūsuf **al-Bāʿūniyya** (d. 922/1516)

Scholar, Sufi mystic, and author. First-person passages by her quoted in later biographical sources suggest a lost autobiographical text. See Muḥammad al-Ghazzī, *al-Kawākib al-sāʾira bi-aʿyān al-miʾa al-ʿāshira* (Beirut: al-Maṭbaʿa al-Amīrikāniyya, 1945–59), 1:287–92; see also ʿAbd al-Ḥayy Ibn al-ʿImād, *Shadharāt al-dhahab fī akhbār man dhahab* (Cairo: Maktabat al-Qudsī, 1931–33), 8:111–13; and passages cited in ʿUmar Mūsā Bāshā, *Taʾrīkh al-adab al-ʿarabī: al-ʿaṣr al-mamlūkī* (Beirut: Dār al-Fikr al-Muʿāṣir, 1989), 437–42.

ʿAbd al-Raḥmān ibn ʿAlī al-Zabīdī [= **Ibn al-Daybaʿ**] (b. 866/1462, d. 944/1537)

Religious scholar and historian. His short autobiography covers his childhood, education, teachers, and three pilgrimages to Mecca. The Arabic text and a German summary appear in Rudolf Sellheim, "Die Autobiographie des Ibn ad-Daybaʿ," *Folia Rara: Wolfgang Voight LXV Diem Natalem Celebranti* [= Verzeichnis der Orientalischen Handschriften in Deutschland, Supplementband 19] (Wiesbaden: Franz Steiner, 1976): 111–19.

Muḥammad ibn ʿAlī ibn Aḥmad [= **Ibn Ṭūlūn al-Dimashqī**] (b. 880/1473, d. 953/1546)

Scholar of law and government official. This fifty-page autobiography includes descriptions of the author's birth, education, scholarly works, and posts held, as well as a collection of marriage sermons, letters, and selected poetry. *Al-Fulk al-mashḥūn fī aḥwāl Muḥammad Ibn Ṭūlūn* (The Loaded Pontoon on the Life of Muḥammad Ibn Ṭūlūn) (Damascus: Maṭbaʿat al-Taraqqī, 1929).

Zayn al-Dīn al-ʿĀmilī [= **al-Shahīd al-thānī**] (b. ca. 911/1506, d. 965/1558)

Twelver Shiʿite jurist of southern Lebanon. Fragments of the autobiography (no longer extant), covering his birth, education, teachers, and travels, were preserved in a biography by his student: ʿAlī ibn Muḥammad al-ʿĀmilī, *Bughyat al-murīd fī kashf ʿan aḥwāl al-Shaykh Zayn al-Dīn al-Shahīd,* which survives in truncated form as part of *al-Durr al-manthūr* (Qom: Maktabat al-Marʿashī al-Najafī, 1978), 2:157–82.

Aḥmad ibn Muṣṭafā ibn Khalīl al-Dīn **Ṭaşköprüzādeh** (b. 901/1495, d. 968/1561)

Ottoman scholar, professor, and judge. His brief autobiography covers his father's dream of his birth, his education, teaching, books, and remarks on going blind. It is included as the last of the 522 collected biographies in his *al-Shaqāʾiq al-nuʿmāniyya fī ʿulamāʾ al-dawla al-ʿuthmāniyya* (Beirut: Dār al-Kitāb al-ʿArabī, 1975), 325–31.

ʿAbd al-Wahhāb ibn Aḥmad **al-Shaʿrānī** (b. 897/1492, d. 973/1565)

Sufi shaykh. This massive autobiography lists each of his blessings from God individually, covering family, childhood, education, spiritual journey, career, personal traits, wives, children, professional rivalries, and much more. The *Laṭāʾif al-minan wa-l-akhlāq fī wujūb al-taḥadduth bi-niʿmat Allāh ʿalā al-iṭlāq* (The Book of Gracious Merits and Virtues Bestowed on Me by God and the Absolute Obligation of Recounting His Blessings) (Cairo: ʿĀlam al-Fikr, 1938–39) has been translated into Italian as *Il Libro dei Doni,* ed. and trans. Virginia Vacca (Naples: Istituto Orientale, 1972), Serie Orientalistica, Testi vol. 13. See also Dwight F. Reynolds, "Shaykh ʿAbd al-Wahhāb al-Shaʿrānī's Sixteenth-century Defense of Autobiography," *Harvard Middle Eastern and Islamic Review* 4, no. 1–2 (1997–98): 122–37.

Aḥmad ibn Muḥammad **Ibn Ḥajar al-Haytamī** (b. 909/1504, d. 974/1567)

Prominent jurist and prolific author, particularly of works against popular religious practices, festivals, music, joking, and frivolity. Extant fragments of his autobiography, in ornate rhymed prose, covering his teachers, education, and professional posts are preserved in ʿAbd al-Qādir al-ʿAydarūs, *al-Nūr al-sāfir ʿan akhbār al-qarn al-ʿāshir,* ed. Muḥammad Rashīd Afandī al-Ṣaffār (Baghdad: al-Maktaba al-ʿArabiyya, 1934), 289–91.

Seventeenth Century

ʿ**Abd al-Qādir** ibn Muḥammad ibn Yaḥyā **al-Ṭabarī** al-Makkī (d. 1033/1623–24)

Schoolteacher and close friend of the governor of Mecca, identified as an autobiographer in *IN*, 29. The text remains unidentified.

Abū Bakr ibn Abī al-Qāsim ibn Aḥmad ibn Muḥammad al-Ḥusaynī, commonly known as **Ibn al-Ahdal** al-Yamanī (b. 984/1576, d. 1035/1626)

Sufi and scholar from a prominent southwestern Arabian family, identified as an autobiographer in *IN*, 30. The autobiography may be in his unpublished *Nafḥat al-mandal fī tarājim sādāt al-ahdal.*

Abū al-ʿAbbās Aḥmad ibn Aḥmad ibn Aḥmad ibn ʿUmar **al-Tanambaktī** al-Sūdānī al-Takrūrī, commonly known as **Bābā al-Tanambaktī** or **Aḥmad Bābā** (b. 936/1556, d. 1032/1627)

Prominent West African religious scholar. His autobiography is in the unpublished *Kifāyat al-muḥtāj li-maʿrifat man laysa fī al-Dībāj*, which is, according to John Hunwick, very similar to the biography in al-Bartallī's *Fatḥ al-shakūr* (pers. com., December 28 1999). Muḥammad ibn Abī Bakr al-Ṣiddīq al-Bartallī, *Fatḥ al-shakūr fī maʿrifat aʿyān ʿulamāʾ al-takrūr*, ed. Muḥammad al-Kattānī (Beirut: Dār al-Gharb al-Islāmī, 1981).

ʿAbd al-Qādir ibn ʿAbd Allāh **al-ʿAydarūs** (b. 978/1570, d. 1037/1628)

Sufi scholar of Arabian origin, born and lived in India. His autobiography is included under the year of his birth in his biographical dictionary, *al-Nūr al-sāfir ʿan akhbār al-qarn al-ʿāshir*, ed. Muḥammad Rashīd Afandī al-Ṣaffār (Baghdad: al-Maktaba al-ʿArabiyya, 1934), 334–343, and is translated in this volume.

[**Aḥmad** ibn Abī al-Fatḥ Shihāb al-Dīn al-Ḥakamī **al-Maqqarī** (b. ca. 986/1577, d. 1041/1632)

Noted historian of Islamic Spain. Although autobiographical passages in *Rawḍat al-ās al-ʿāṭirat al-anfās fī dhikr man laqītuhu min aʿlām al-ḥaḍratayn Marrākush wa-Fās* (Rabat: al-Maṭbaʿa al-Malakiyya, 1964) include a great deal of information about the author's life and education, the focus is on other scholars' lives. He is identified as an autobiographer in *IN*, 30.]

[Abū Zayd al-Sayyid ʿAbd al-Raḥmān ibn Muḥammad al-Jazūlī **al-Tamanārtī** (d. 1060/1650)

Berber religious scholar. His *Fawāʾid al-jamma bi-isnād ʿulūm al-umma* (French translation Col. Justinard, *Fawaid Al Jamma Bi ʿOuloumi Al Oumma* [Chartres: Durand, 1953] is a list of teachers (*mashyakha*) but filled with personal observations. The French translation covers approximately one-third of the Arabic text.]

Muḥammad ibn Muḥammad Badr al-Dīn al-ʿĀmirī **Najm al-Dīn al-Ghazzī** al-Shāfiʿī (b. 977/1570, d. 1061/1651)

Scholar and biographer. His autobiography, which originally appeared in his biography of his father, the *Bulghat al-wājid fī tarjamat shaykh al-islām al-wālid,* is no longer extant, but extracts are preserved in the notice devoted to him in al-Muḥibbī (d. 1111/1700—see below), *Khulāṣat al-athar fī aʿyān al-qarn al-ḥādī ʿashar* (Beirut: Maktabat Khayyāṭ, 1966), 189–200. It appears to have been a traditional *tarjama* but is notable for its use of *ḥadith* and passages about the author's mother. See also the autobiographical passages in al-Ghazzī's *al-Kawākib al-sāʾira bi-aʿyān al-miʾa al-ʿāshira,* ed. Jibrāʾīl Sulaymān Jabbūr, 3 vols. (Beirut: al-Maṭbaʿa al-Amrīkāniyya, 1945–59).

Ḥajjī Khalīfa, Muṣṭafā ibn ʿAbd Allāh, **Kātib Çelebī** b. 1017/1609, d. 1067/1657)

Ottoman Turkish historian and bibliographer. He is identified as an Arabic autobiographer in *IN,* 30, but the only extant autobiography is in Ottoman Turkish. See *Mīzān al-ḥaqq fī ikhtiyār al-aḥaqq,* ed. Moriz Wickerhauser, in *Wegweiser zum Verständnis der türkischen Sprache: Eine deutsch-türkische Chrestomathie* (Vienna: Kaiserlich-Königlichen Hof- und Staatsdruckerei, 1853), 159–67, and translated into English as *The Balance of Truth,* by G. L. Lewis (London: Allen and Unwin, 1957). An autobiographical note that appears at the end of part 1 of *Sullam al-wuṣūl ilā ṭabaqāt al-fuḥūl* may originally have been composed in Arabic. See *GAL* Suppl. 2:636–37.

Shihāb al-Dīn Aḥmad ibn Muḥammad ibn ʿUmar **al-Khafājī** (b. 979/1571, d. 1069/1659)

Cairene religious scholar and man of letters. His autobiography includes an enumeration of teachers and contemporaries, as well as details about his birth, education, and family history, all in rhymed prose. *Rayḥānat al-alibbāʾ wa-zahrat al-ḥayāt al-dunyā,* ed. ʿAbd al-Fattāḥ Muḥammad al-Ḥilw (Cairo: ʿĪsā al-Bābī al-Ḥalabī, 1967), 2:281–411.

Aḥmad ibn ʿAlī al-Dimashqī **al-Khalwatī**, commonly known as **Ibn Sālim al-ʿUmarī al-Ḥanbalī** (d. 1086/1657–6)

Identified as an autobiographer in *IN,* 30. The text remains unidentified.

Abū ʿAbd Allāh Mahammad [*sic*] ibn Aḥmad **Mayyāra** (b. 997/1591, d. 1071/1662).

Muslim religious scholar and author of Jewish descent. Autobiographical details are mentioned in his *fahrasa,* included as part of his unpublished

Naẓm al-durar wa-l-la'ālī (mss. Rabat 855 and 3702 Z). See Charles Pellat, *EI*[2] 6:932–33.

Muḥsin Fayd **al-Kāshānī** (b. 1007/1598, d. 1091/1680)

Prolific Shiʿite mystic, philosopher, and *ḥadīth* scholar. His biographer mentions that al-Kāshānī wrote an independent autobiography titled *Sharḥ al-ṣadr* (Opening Up the Heart) in 1685 and cites al-Kashānī's own description of it: "a summary of my conditions and the disasters that have befallen me during my life, during my travels and sojourns, my studies and teaching, my pleasures and pains, my obscurity and fame, my loneliness and companionship." See Yūsuf ibn Aḥmad al-Baḥranī, *Lu'lu'at al-Baḥrayn* (Najaf: Maṭbaʿat al-Nuʿmān, 1966), 130. The text apparently has not have survived.

Muḥammad Jamāl al-Dīn ibn Abī Bakr ibn Aḥmad **al-Shillī** al-Ḥaḍramī (b. 1030/1621, d. 1093/1682)

Biographer, historian, and astronomer. His autobiography is a traditional self-*tarjama* that cites examples of earlier autobiographers and "speaking of God's Bounty" as motivations for writing an autobiography. In his biographical compendium, *al-Mashraʿ al-rāwī fī manāqib al-sādat al-kirām āl Abī ʿAlawī*, ed. Muḥammad al-Shāṭirī (Beirut: n.p., 1982), 38–41, the autobiography is located at the end of the section devoted to Muḥammads, rather than alphabetically.

Muḥammad b. al-Ḥasan al-Ḥurr **al-ʿĀmilī** (b. 1033/1624, d. 1099/1688)

Prominent Shiʿite jurist and *ḥadīth* scholar. A terse account of his life, travels, studies, and books, ending with selections of his poetry, appears in his biographical dictionary, *Amal al-ʿāmil fī tarājim ʿulamā' jabal ʿĀmil* ed. Aḥmad al-Ḥusaynī (Baghdad: Maktabat al-Andalus, 1965–66), 1:141–54.

Abū ʿAlī al-Ḥasan **al-Yūsī** (b. 1040/1631, d. 1102/1691)

Innovative and influential Moroccan Sufi thinker. One of his works, *al-Fahrasa*, is a lengthy autobiography; however, only the introduction and first section have survived and these are unpublished. Selections are cited in Jacques Berque, *Al-Yousi: Problèmes de la culture marocaine au XVIIème siècle* (Paris: Mouton, 1958), and in ʿAbd al-Kabīr al-ʿAlawī al-Mudghirī, *Al-Faqīh Abū ʿAlī al-Yūsī: namūdhaj min al-fikr al-maghribī fī fajr al-dawla al-ʿalawiyya* (Muḥammadiyya, Morocco: Maṭbaʿat Faḍāla, 1989). See *al-Fahrasa*, mss. in al-Khizāna al-Ḥasaniyya nos. 1183, 5470, and 5995; and ms. in al-Khizāna al-ʿAmma, no. 1234 K. A second and more famous text, *al-Muḥāḍarāt* (Rabat: Maṭbūʿāt Dār al-Maghrib li-l-Ta'līf wa-l-Tarjama wa-l-Nashr, 1976), contains many autobiographical passages. Both are remarkable for the author's frank discussions of childhood misdeeds, the pleasures of his conjugal sex life, and other intimate details of his personal life.

ʿAlī ibn Muḥammad **al-ʿĀmilī** (d. 1103/1692)

Shiʿite scholar and biographical compiler. His autobiography includes traditional information on his family and education but also describes strange occurrences and adventures during his travels, his efforts to preserve his books, and a poignant lament at the death of his son. *Al-Durr al-manthūr,* ed. Aḥmad al-Ḥusaynī (Qom: Maktabat al-Marʿashī al-Najafī, 1978), 2:238–59.

Eighteenth Century

Muḥammad Amīn ibn Faḍl Allāh **al-Muḥibbī** (b. 1061/1651, d. 1111/1700)

Historian identified as an autobiographer in *IN,* 31. The reference may be to the selections of al-Muḥibbī's prose and poetry appended, without an autobiographical narrative of any sort, to the end of his *Nafḥat al-rayḥāna,* ed. Muḥammad al-Ḥilw (Cairo: Dār Iḥyāʾ al-Kutub al-ʿArabiyya, 1967–69), 5:49–79.

Niʿmat Allāh **al-Jazāʾirī** (b. 1050/1640, d. 1112/1701)

Shiʿite author and jurist. His autobiography is included as the epilogue to his *al-Anwār al-nuʿmāniyya* (Tabriz: Sharikat-i Chāp, 1958–62), 4:302–26, a collection of treatises on ethics, dogma, education, love theory, and other topics and covers his studies and accomplishments, but also highlights his sufferings in a humorous style. An English translation by Devin J. Stewart is published in "The Humor of the Scholars: The Autobiography of Niʿmat Allāh al-Jazāʾirī (d. 1112/1701)," *Iranian Studies* 22 (1989): 47–50.

Al-Ḥasan ibn ʿAlī ibn Yaḥyā al-**ʿUjaymī** (b. 1049/1639–40, d. 1113/1701–2)

Meccan religious scholar and historian identified as an autobiographer in *IN,* 31. The text remains unidentified.

Aḥmad ibn Muḥammad **al-Manqūr** al-Tamīmī al-Najdī (b. 1067/1656–57, d. 1125/1701–2)

Najdī scholar of religion and science identified as an autobiographer in *IN,* 31. The text remains unidentified.

Mulla Aḥmad ibn Abī Saʿīd al-Ḥanafī al-Ṣāliḥī al-Amīṭhawī **Jīwan** (b. 1047/1637, d. 1130/1717)

Religious scholar and tutor to the Mughal emperor Awrangzīb (Aurangzeb). There is, according to A. S. Bazmee Ansari in *EI*² 2:558, a detailed autobiographical note in his unpublished *Manāqib al-awliyāʾ.* A short extract is quoted in ʿAbd al-Ḥayy al-Laknawī (d. 1304/1886—see below), *Nuzhat* *al-khawāṭir wa-bahjat al-masāmī wa-l-nawāẓir* (Beirut: Dār Ibn Ḥazm, 1999), 691–92.

Aḥmad ibn Qāsim **al-Būnī** (d. 1139/1726–27)
Identified as an autobiographer in *IN*, 31. The text remains unidentified.

Al-Qāsim ibn al-Ḥusayn ibn Muṭahhir **al-Jurmūzī** al-Ṣanʿānī (b. 1100/1688, d. 1146/1733–4)
Identified as an autobiographer in *IN*, 31. The text remains unidentified.

Aḥmad ibn ʿAlī **al-Manīnī** (b. 1100/1688, d. 1172/1759)
Identified as an autobiographer in *IN*, 31. The text remains unidentified.

Abū Saʿīd Muḥammad ibn Muṣṭafā ibn ʿUthmān **al-Khādimī** (b. 1113/1701, d. 1186/1772)
Sufi author identified as an autobiographer in *IN*, 31. The text remains unidentified. See *GAL* Suppl. 2:663–64.

Yūsuf ibn Aḥmad **al-Baḥrānī** (b. 1107/1696, d. 1186/1772)
Prominent Shiʿite jurist and *ḥadīth* scholar. His autobiography is found in his biographical compendium, *Luʾluʾat al-Baḥrayn*, ed. Muḥammad Ṣādiq Baḥr al-ʿUlūm (Najaf: Maṭbaʿat al-Nuʿmān, 1966), 442–49, and is translated in this volume.

Muḥammad ibn al-Ṭayyib **al-Qādirī** (b. 1124/1712, d. 1187/1773)
Moroccan scholar. His extensive autobiography, principally an autobibliography with some references to himself and family, is in *Iltiqāṭ al-durar (wa-mustafād al-mawāʾiẓ wa-al-ʿibar min akhbār wa-aʿyān al-miʾa al-ḥādiya wa-al-thāniya ʿashar)*, ed. Hāshim al-ʿAlawī al-Qāsimī (Beirut: Manshūrāt Dār al-Āfāq al-Jadīda, 1983), 449–92. He also wrote a *fihrist*, which is unpublished.

ʿAbd al-Raḥmān ibn ʿAbd al-Karīm **al-Anṣārī** (b. 1124/1712, d. 1197/1781)
Historian and man of letters. His brief third-person autobiographical notice is notable for its listing of the dates of his wedding and his children's births, weddings, and so forth; his daughters are given separate entries in the larger work. *Tuhfat al-muḥibbīn wa-al-aṣḥāb fī maʿrifat mā li-al-madīniyyīn min al-ansāb*, ed. Muḥammad al-ʿArūsī al-Miṭwī (Tunis: al-Maktaba al-ʿAtīqa, 1970), 27–29.

Mīr Ghulām ʿAlī ibn Nūḥ al-Ḥusaynī al-Wāsiṭī **Āzād Bilgrāmī** (b. 1116/1704, d. 1200/1786).
Religious scholar, accomplished poet, and historian. Āzād Bilgrāmī's autobiography forms part of his *Tasliyat al-fuʾād*, itself incorporated into a

larger biographical work on Indian religious scholars. In it he describes his education, travels, and works. His account is notable for its poetic turn of phrase, especially in the description of his journey to Mecca and Medina and his experiences there, which take up a large part of the autobiography. See Āzād Bilgrāmī, *Ṣubḥat al-marjān fī āthār Hindustān*, ed. Amīn ibn Ḥasan al-Ḥalwānī (lithograph, Bombay, 1886), 118–23. For references to his other works, including autobiographies in Persian, see A. S. Bazmee Ansari, *EI*² 1:808.

Muḥammad Khalīl ibn ʿAlī ibn Muḥammad ibn Muḥammad **al-Murādī** al-Dimashqī (b. 1173/1759, d. 1206/1791)
Damascene historian and biographer. An account written in ornate rhymed prose, including references to his father, family, education, and many poems, but few personal details, is appended to *ʿArf al-bashām fī man waliya fatwā Dimashq al-Shām*, ed. Muḥammad Muṭīʿ al-Ḥāfiẓ and Riyāḍ ʿAbd al-Ḥalīm Murād (Damascus: Maṭbaʿat Majmuʿat al-Lugha al-ʿArabiyya, 1979), 144–214. He states, however, that he has written at length about his own life in another work with details of his travels, studies, writings, trials and tribulations, and so forth (p. 151). The latter text is unidentified.

Nineteenth Century

Aḥmad **Ibn ʿAjība** (b. 1160/1747 or 1161/1748, d. 1224/1809)
Ḥadīth scholar and Sufi shaykh. His autobiography covers his childhood, education, teachers, wives, children, dramatic conversion to Sufism at the age of 46, period of imprisonment, and religious beliefs. The Arabic text is unpublished but has been translated into French by J.-L. Michon, *L'autobiographie (fahrasa) du soufi marocain Ahmad ibn ʿAgiba (1747–1809)* (Leiden: E. J. Brill, 1969); rpt. of *Arabica* 15–16, 1968–69. Michon cites three extant mss.: D 1845 in the Bibliothèque générale de Rabat and two in private hands (pp. 22–24).

Abū al-Qāsim **al-Zayyānī** (b. 1147/1734, d. 1249/1809)
Historian and civil servant who wrote a lengthy, panoramic account of his life and the events he witnessed, including much nonautobiographical historical and geographical information. *Al-Tarjumāna al-kubrā fī akhbār al-maʿmūr barran wa-baḥran*, ed. ʿAbd al-Karīm al-Filālī (Rabat [?]: Wizārat al-Anbāʾ, 1967).

Abū al-Rabīʿ Sulaymān ibn ʿAbd Allāh **al-Ḥawwāt** (b. 1160/1747, d. 1232/1816)
Historian, biographer, and poet. This book-length, first-person account covers the author's life and family, including his father, his father's four

wives, his mother, his education, and a variety of events in his adult career. *Thamarat unsī fī al-taʿrīf bi-nafsī* (The Fruit of My Familiarity in Knowing Myself) (Shafshawan: Wizārat al-Thaqāfa, Markaz al-Dirāsāt wa-l-Buḥūth al-Andalusiyya, 1996). He also penned an unpublished *kunnāsha*, a type of literary daybook (*Thamarat*, 16).

Muḥammad ibn Aḥmad **al-Muʿaskarī** al-Jalīlī, known as **Abū Raʿs** (b. 1150/1737, d. 1239/1823)

Religious scholar. This book-length autobiography includes details of his family history, teachers, travels, conversations with scholars, and discussions of theological issues and an autobibliography. *Fatḥ al-ilāh wa-minnatih fī al-taḥadduth bi-faḍl rabbī wa-niʿmatih: ḥayāt Abī Raʾs al-dhātiyya wa-al-ʿilmiyya* (Algiers: al-Muʾassasa al-Waṭaniyya li-l-Kitāb, 1990).

[**Aḥmad** ibn Zayn al-Dīn **al-Aḥsāʾī al-Baḥrānī** (b. 1166/1753, d. 1240/1826)

Identified as an Arabic autobiographer in *IN*, 32. The only published text located, however, was composed in Persian.]

ʿAbd al-Raḥmān [Abdul Rahaman] (b. ca. 1176/1762, d. 1245/1829)

West African captured at twenty-one and sold into slavery in the United States. Freed at sixty-six, he attempted to return with his family to West Africa but died after arriving in Liberia. He wrote a short autobiography in Arabic that was translated and published in American newspapers in 1828. See Allan Austin, *African Muslims in Antebellum America: A Sourcebook* (New York: Garland, 1984), 121–55.

Muḥammad ibn ʿAlī **al-Shawkānī** (b. 1173/1860, d. 1250/1834)

Historian and jurist. Numerous autobiographical passages are to be found throughout his works, the most important in *al-Badr al-ṭāliʿ bi-maḥāsin man baʿd al-qarn al-sābiʿ*, 2 vols. (Cairo: Maṭabaʿat al-Saʿāda, 1929). His *Dhikrayāt* (Beirut: Dār al-ʿAwda, 1983) focuses on others rather than himself.

Maḥmūd ibn ʿAbd Allāh **Shihāb al-Dīn al-Ālūsī** (b. 1217/1803, d. 1270/1850)

Literary scholar. His autobiography incorporates biographies of his principal teachers, examples of their poetry, and enumerations of his own qualities and motivations, all in rhymed prose (*sajʿ*). It is located in the opening section of his literary compendium, *Kitāb gharāʾib al-ightirāb wa-nuzhat al-albāb* (Baghdad: Maṭbaʿat Shāhbandar, 1909), 2–26.

Abū Bakr al-Ṣiddīq [Edward Donellan] (b. 1208–9/1794. d. 1850)

Originally from Timbuktu, orphaned at four, captured and sold into slavery at fourteen, he lived the rest of his life in the West Indies, where he kept plantation accounts in Arabic. He wrote two short accounts of his life in Arabic in 1834 and 1835, including a vivid description of his childhood, education, travels, capture, and enslavement. See Ivor Wilks, "Abū Bakr al-Ṣiddīq of Timbuktu," in *Africa Remembered: Narratives by West Africans from the Era of the Slave Trade*, ed. Philip Curtin (Madison: University of Wisconsin Press, 1968), 152–69; and Allan Austin, *African Muslims in Antebellum America: A Sourcebook* (New York: Garland, 1984), 553–57.

Muḥammad ʿAyyād **al-Ṭanṭāwī** (b. 1215/1801, d. 1278/1861)

According to Yaḥyā Ibrāhīm ʿAbd al-Dāyim, *al-Tarjama al-dhātiyya fī al-adab al-ʿarabī al-ḥadīth* (Beirut: Dār Iḥyāʾ al-Turāth al-ʿArabī, 1975), 45–52, al-Ṭanṭāwī wrote an autobiography at the request of a Russian friend during his sojourn in Saint Petersburg where he taught Arabic at the university beginning in 1840. The text remains unidentified.

ʿUmar ibn Saʿīd (b. ca. 1184/1770, d. 1281/1864)

West African originally from Futa Toro, captured and sold into slavery in North America, arriving in South Carolina in 1807. He composed an autobiography in Arabic in 1831 of which two differing translations were published in American newspapers (1848 and 1864). A later, final autobiography referred to in 1869 has never been found. The earlier autobiography, covering his childhood, education, capture, and life as a slave, is published in facsimile and in English translation in Marc Shell and Werner Sollers, eds., *The Multilingual Anthology of American Literature* (New York: New York University Press, 2000), 58–93.

[Rifāʿa Rāfiʿ ibn Badawī ibn ʿAlī **al-Ṭahṭawī** (b. 1215/1801, d. 1290/1873)

Religious scholar and reformist. His travel account of the five years he spent in France is classified by some Arab scholars as the beginning of the modern Arabic autobiographical tradition. *Takhliṣ al-ibrīz ilā talkhiṣ Bārīz* (The Purification of Gold in the Description of Paris Told) (Cairo: Dār al-Ṭibāʿa al-Khidaywiyya, 1835) has been translated into French by Anouar Louca as *L'Or de Paris* (Paris: Sindbad, 1988).]

Aḥmad Fāris **al-Shidyāq** (b. 1219/1804, d. 1305/1887)

Author, poet, and linguist. *Al-Sāq ʿalā al-sāq fī mā huwa l-Fariyāq* (Thigh over Thigh on the Question of Who Am I), 2 vols. (Paris: Benjamin Duprat, 1855). His fascinatingly idiosyncratic, satirical autobiography is framed as a comic discussion of the war between the sexes but generally follows the author's life story in a wild, Rabelaisian amalgam of styles. See also Paul Starkey, "Fact and Fiction in *al-Sāq ʿalā al-Sāq*," in *Writing the Self: Autobiographical Writing in Modern Arabic Literature*, ed. Robin Ostle, Ed de Moor, and Stefan Wild (London: Saqi Books, 1998), 30–38.

Abū al-Ḥasanāt **Muḥammad ibn ʿAbd al-Ḥayy al-Laknawī** al-Hindī (b. 1264/1848, d. 1304/1886).

Scholar and author. Autobiographical passages appear in many of his works. In the introduction to his *al-Siʿāya fī kashf mā fī sharḥ al-wiqāya*, 2 vols. in 1 (Lahore: Suhail Academy 1976), 41–42, al-Laknāwī writes: "I have mentioned a part of my autobiography [*tarjamat nafsī*] in *al-Nāfiʿ al-kabīr li-man yuṭāliʿ al-jāmiʿ al-ṣaghīr*, in *al-Taʿlīqāt al-sinniyya ʿalā al-fawāʾid al-bahiyya*, and in the introduction to *al-Taʿlīq al-mumajjad ʿalā muwaṭṭā al-imām muḥammad*. Now I wish to mention [another] necessary part."

Mikhāyil **Mishāqa** (b. 1214–15/1800, d. 1284–85/1888)

Historian and scholar. His text, written in 1873, includes elements of his family and personal history but treats primarily the chaotic political events of his time. Portions were published as *Muntakhabāt min al-jawāb ʿalā iqtirāḥ al-aḥbāb* (Selections from a Response to a Suggestion by Loved Ones) (Beirut: Mudīriyyat al-Āthār, 1955) and translated into English by W. M. Thackston, Jr., as *Murder, Mayhem, Pillage and Plunder: The History of Lebanon in the 18th and 19th Centuries by Mikhāyil Mishāqa* (Albany: SUNY Press, 1988).

ʿAlī ibn Sulaymān al-Dimnatī **al-Būjumʿawī** ʿAlī (b. 1234/1819, d. 1306/1889)

Identified as an autobiographer in *IN*, 33. The text remains unidentifed.

Al-Nawāb Muḥammad **Ṣadīq** ibn **Ḥasan Khān** al-Qannūjī al-Būfālī (b. 1248/1832, d. 1306/1889)

Well-known Arabian religious scholar identified as an autobiographer in *IN*, 33. The text remains unidentified.

ʿAlī Mubārak (b. 1239/1824, d. 1312/1893)

Statesman, reformer, and engineer. His memoirs, written in 1889, are a remarkable account of his childhood misadventures, education, travel in France, and political career. The text was originally published in *al-Khiṭaṭ al-tawfīqiyya al-jadīda li-miṣr al-qāhira wa-mudunihā wa-bilādihā al-qadīma wa-l-mashhūra* (The New Description in Honor of Tawfīq of Cairo, Egypt, and Her Old and Famous Cities and Towns) (Bulaq, Egypt: al-Maṭbaʿa al-Kubrā al-Amīriyya, 1888–89), 9:37–61, then separately a year after his death as *Taʾrīkh ḥayāt al-maghfūr lahu ʿAlī Mubārak Bāshā* (History of the Life of the Late ʿAlī Mubārak Pasha), ed. Muḥammad Bāshā al-Ḥakīm (Cairo: Muḥammad Bey Durrī, 1894). An extract is translated in this volume.

Muḥammad ibn ʿUthmān ibn Yūsuf al-Ḥusaynī Jalāl = **Muḥammad Bey ʿUthmān Jalāl** (b. ca. 1242/1826, d. 1315–16/1898).

Government official, civil servant, accomplished translator and author. Muḥammad ʿUthmān Jalāl's autobiography was written at the request of

ʿAlī Mubārak (d. 1312/1893—see above) for inclusion in his *Khiṭaṭ*. It is a chronological account of his studies, government appointments, and descriptions of the translations he undertook, interspersed with personal observations about the people he encountered and the problems he faced. It includes many lines of verse occasioned by situations in his daily life. The text is in ʿAlī Mubārak, *al-Khiṭaṭ al-tawfīqiyya al-jadīda li-miṣr al-qāhira wa-muduniha wa-bilādihā al-qadīma wa-l-mashhūra* (Bulaq, Egypt: al-Maṭbaʿa al-Kubrā al-Amīriyya, 1888–1889), 17:62–65.

Nubar Nubarian Pasha (b. 1240/1825, d. 1318/1899)

Ethnically Armenian Ottoman statesman, born in Turkey, educated in France, who served in Egyptian government. His memoirs, written between 1890 and 1894 in French and covering the period 1842–79 from his arrival in Egypt to the deposing of the khedive Ismāʿīl are primarily a political memoir rather than a personal autobiography. *Mémoires de Nubar Pacha,* introd. and notes Mirrit Butros Ghali (Beirut: Librairie du Liban, 1983).

Twentieth Century [texts cover late nineteenth century]

ʿĀʾisha ʿIṣmat **al-Taymūriyya** (b. 1255–56/1840, d. 1319–20/1902)

Female author and poet. An autobiographical introduction is prefaced to her allegorical narrative, *Natāʾij al-aḥwāl fī al-aqwāl wa-l-afʿāl* (The Results of a Life in Words and Deeds) (Cairo: Maṭbaʿat Muḥammad Afandī Muṣṭafā, 1888). It describes her childhood aversion to the domestic education offered by her mother and her love of the world of books and learning opened up to her by her father. This section has been translated by Marilyn Booth as "The Results of Circumstances in Words and Deeds," in *Opening the Gates: A Century of Arab Feminist Writing,* ed. Margot Badran and Miriam Cooke (London: Virago, 1990): 126–28.

Ibrāhīm Fawzī Pasha (b. 1265/1849, d. after 1321/1902)

Egyptian military officer. His memoirs, which begin in 1874 with his recruitment by General Gordon to serve in Sudan, are a lively account covering his service with Gordon, his imprisonment for slave trading, his participation in the ʿUrābī rebellion against British rule in Egypt, and the Mahdists' siege of Khartoum, which he survived. *Kitāb al-Sūdān bayn ayday Gordon wa-Kitchener* (The Sudan under Gordon and Kitchener), 2 vols. (Cairo: al-Muʾayyad, 1902). See also Eve M. Troutt Powell, "Waving His Own Flag: Ibrāhīm Fawzī Pasha's Narrative of the Sudan," *Edebiyât: Special Issue—Arabic Autobiography,* N.S. 7, no. 2 (1997): 363–78.

Muḥammad ʿAbduh (b. 1265–66/1849, d. 1323/1905)

Islamic reformer and author. His autobiography was written sometime after 1892 at the urging of a western friend. Only the introduction and the first chapter were completed, and then, much later, a second chapter. There are multiple Arabic editions; see, for example, *al-Aʿmāl al-kāmila li-l-Imām Muḥammad ʿAbduh* (The Complete Works), ed. Muḥammad ʿAmāra (Beirut: al-Muʾassasa al-ʿArabiyya li-l-Dirāsa wa-l-Nashr, 1972), 2:315–37.

Aḥmad ʿUrābī (b. 1257/1840–41, d. 1329/1911)

Military officer. His firsthand account of leading the Egyptian rebellion against the British in 1882 also includes a brief account of birth and childhood. There are multiple Arabic editions; see, for example, *Mudhakkirāt al-Zaʿīm Aḥmad ʿUrābī* (Cairo: Dār al-Maʿārif, 1983).

Yaʿqūb Ṣanūʿ (b. 1255/1839, d. 1330/1912)

Jewish dramatist, considered the father of modern Egyptian theater. His autobiography covers his career in Egyptian theater and his political difficulties and subsequent exile to France. The original text remains unpublished, but see the references in Irene L. Gendzier, *The Practical Visions of Yaʿqūb Ṣanūʿ* (Cambridge: Cambridge University Press, 1966), 15, 154 (nn. 34, 35); and Rosella Dorigo Ceccato, "Autobiographical Features in the Works of Yaʿqūb Ṣanūʿ," in *Writing the Self: Autobiographical Writing in Modern Arabic Literature,* ed. Robin Ostle, Ed de Moor, and Stefan Wolf (London: Saqi Books, 1998), 51–60. There is a French translation titled *Ma vie en vers et mon théâtre en prose* (Paris: Montgeron, 1912).

Al-Zubayr Raḥma(t) Manṣūr **Pāshā** (b. 1246/1831, d. 1331/1913)

Trader and political figure. His autobiography, taken down in 1900, covers the second half of the nineteenth century and is a lively account of his experiences as de facto ruler of Baḥr al-Ghazāl (the upper White Nile) in the Sudan. See Naʿūm Shuqayr, *Taʾrīkh al-Sūdān,* ed. Muḥammad Ibrāhīm Abū Salīm (Beirut: Dār al-Jīl, 1981), 258–89. A German translation of the text by Martin Thilo is titled *Ez-Ziber Rahmet Paschas Autobiographie. Ein Beitrag zur Geschichte des Sudan* (Bonn and Leipzig: K. Schroeder, 1921).

Jurji Zaydān (b. 1278/1861, d. 1332/1914)

Historian, novelist, and publisher. His memoirs are a frank personal account of his childhood, education, and family and include nostalgic portrayals of Beirut during a period of increasing western cultural presence. Though written in 1908, they cover only the years up to 1883 and were not published until 1966. *Mudhakkirāt Jurjī Zaydān,* ed. Ṣalāḥ al-Dīn Munajjid (Beirut: 1966); pt. 2, *al-Madrasa al-kulliyya,* ed. Nabīh Amīn Fāris, *al-Abḥāth* 20 (1967): 323–55. There is an English translation by Thomas Philipp, *The Autobiography of Jurji Zaidan* (Washington, D.C.: Three Continents Press, 1990).

Muḥammad Farīd (b. 1285/1868, d. 1338/1919)
Political figure. His daily diary covering political and personal events was first published posthumously in the Egyptian journal *Kull shay' wa-l-dunyā*, January 16–March 20, 1935. The full text covers the period 1891–1919: *Awrāq Muḥammad Farīd* (Cairo: al-Hay'a al-ʿĀmma li-l-Kitāb, 1978–86). It was translated into English by Arthur Goldschmidt, Jr., as *The Memoirs and Diaries of Muḥammad Farīd, an Egyptian Nationalist Leader (1868–1919)* (San Francisco: Mellen University Research Press, 1992). See also ʿAbd al-ʿAẓīm Muḥammad Ramaḍān, *Mudhakkarāt al-siyāsiyyīn wa-l-zuʿamāʾ fī Miṣr 1891–1981* (Beirut: al-Waṭan al-ʿArabī; Cairo: Maktabat Matbūlī, 1984), 35–50.

ʿAlī ibn Ḥasan al-Bilādī **al-Baḥrānī** (b. 1275/1858, d. 1340/1922)
Shiʿite religious scholar. This text is a short academic portrayal covering his studies, writings, and a rather detailed account of his main teacher, his father-in-law. It appears in his biographical compendium, *Anwār al-badrayn fī tarājim ʿulamāʾ al-Qaṭīf wa-l-Ahsāʾ wa-l-Baḥrayn* (Najaf: Maṭbaʿat al-Nuʿmān, 1957), 270–74.

Emily [Emilie] Ruete, née **Princess Salmé** (b. 1260/1844, d. 1342/1924)
Omani princess. Her memoirs are an intimate portrayal of life in the sultan's palace of Zanzibar and the author's meeting and elopement with a German official. They were written in German sometime after 1875 and first published in 1886: *Memoiren ein arabischen Prinzessin* (Berlin: H. Rosenberg, 1886). Recent English translations include *An Arabian Princess between Two Worlds*, ed. E. van Donzel (Leiden: E. J. Brill, 1993), and *Memoirs of an Arabian Princess from Zanzibar* (New York: Markus Weiner, 1989).

ʿAbd al-Qādir ibn Aḥmad ibn Badrān (d. 1336/1927)
Religious scholar identified as an autobiographer in *IN*, 34. The text remains unidentified.

Muḥammad ibn al-ʿArabī **Ibn Abī Shanab** (= **Ben-Shneb**) (b. 1286/1869, d. 1347/1929)
Accomplished teacher and scholar of Arabic and Islam. The very brief third-person autobiography he submitted to a journal for publication was published porthumously. See *Majallat al-Maʿhad al-ʿIlmī al-ʿIrāqī* (= *Revue de l'Academie Arabe de Damas*) 10, nos. 3–4 (March–April 1930): 238–39.

Aḥmad Shawqī (b. 1285/1868, d. 1351/1932)
Neoclassical poet. His brief memoirs cover his childhood among the Turco-Circassian nobility of Cairo, his explorations in western literature, and the primary influences on his artistic life. They were published as the

preface to the first edition of his collection of poetry, *al-Shawqiyyāt* (Cairo: Maṭbaʿat al-Adab, 1898). Later deemed arrogant and elitist, the text was dropped from all subsequent editions.

Abū al-ʿAbbās Aḥmad ibn Muṣṭafā al-ʿAlawī **Ibn ʿAlīwa** (b. 1289/1869, d. 1352–53/1934).

Important Sufi shaykh and poet. After Ibn ʿAlīwa's death, the spiritual autobiography that he had dictated to one of his disciples sometime after 1923 was discovered among his papers. It recounts his rise from a modest life as a cobbler to his devoted membership of the Darqāwī-Shādhilī order and includes many intimate details, such as his mother's great love for him, periods of intense loneliness, his difficulties with his wives, and his inner struggles. The autobiography ends in 1910. He would later become the shaykh of an order that came to be known as the ʿAlawī Darqāwī-Shādhilī. The Arabic text is in ʿAddah Bin-Tunis (= ibn Tunis), *al-Rawḍa al-saniyya* (Mostaganem, 1936), 9–27. It is translated in full, "except for abridgements here and there to avoid repetitions," and supplemented with "other quotations which help to complete it," in the study by Martin Lings, *A Sufi Saint of the Twentieth Century, Shaikh Ahmad al-ʿAlawi: His spiritual Heritage and Legacy*, rev. ed. (Berkeley: University of California Press, 1971), 48–78 (properly, pp. 48–56, 58–59, 60–63, 66–70, 74–78).

Rashīd Riḍā (b. 1282/1865, d. 1343/1935)

Islamic reformer and author. Although a traditionally subdivided text treating family, origins, education, professional opinions and disputes, and defense of his ideas, his autobiography also includes a section analyzing his personality and a detailed discussion of his religious views. The text covers his life to about 1900 and was published as an appendix to part 1 of *Kitāb al-manār wa-l-Azhar* (The Book of *al-Manār* and *al-Azhar*) (Cairo: Maṭbaʿat al-Manār, 1934), *al-Manār* being the influential religious journal Riḍā edited and al-Azhar the famed Islamic university.

Hudā Shaʿrāwī (b. 1296/1879, d. 1367/1947)

Feminist activist and political leader. Her autobiography is a compelling account of her childhood and youth, her education in Arabic, Turkish, and French, her early marriage against her will, and her struggle for women's rights. Written in the 1940s, the text covers the years 1879 to 1924: *Mudhakkirāt Hudā Shaʿrāwī* (Cairo: Dār al-Hilāl, 1981). In her English translation, *Harem Years: The Memoirs of an Egyptian Feminist* (London: Virago Press, 1986), Margot Badran has "reordered" the text to preserve the "natural flow" of the narrative.

Muḥammad Kurd ʿAlī (b. 1293/1876, d. 1372/1953)
Historian, journalist, and intellectual. His fifteen-page, traditional autobiography covers his childhood and education and the vicissitudes of his career as a journalist and writer under the Ottoman regime. It was appended to volume 6 of *Khiṭaṭ al-Shām* (Description of Syria) (Damascus: Maṭbaʿat al-Mufīd, 1925–28), 411–25. Kurd ʿAlī later published a greatly expanded version titled *Mudhakkirāt* (Memoirs) in 4 volumes (Damascus: Maṭbaʿat al-Turkī, 1948–51), selections from which are translated by Khalil Totah in *Memoirs, a Selection* (Washington, D.C.: American Council of Learned Societies, 1954).

Bābakr Badrī (b. 1278/1861, d. 1374/1954)
Sudanese nationalist. The first half of his autobiography covers his childhood, the Mahdist rebellion, and his career as teacher and champion of women's education. The complete text was published posthumously in 2 volumes, 1959 and 1961; part 1 covers the years to shortly after 1900; part 2 begins after World War I: *Taʾrīkh ḥayātī* (Sudan: Maṭbaʿat Miṣr, 1959–61). An English translation is titled *The Memoirs of Babikr Bedri*, vol. 1, trans. Yousef Bedri and George Scott (London: Ithaca Press, 1969); vol. 2, trans. Yusuf Bedri and Peter Hogg (New York: Oxford University Press, 1980).

Sharaf al-Dīn ʿAbd al-Ḥayy al-Ḥusayn ibn al-Sayyid Yūsuf al-Musāwī **al-ʿĀmilī** (b. 1290/1873, d. 1377/1957).
Influential Shiʿite religious scholar and author. Sharaf al-Dīn's extensive autobiography—some two hundred published pages—is an engaging account of his education, travels, and accomplishments, supplemented by many passages of verse by admirers and observations about the political scene in the Middle East from the late nineteenth to the early twentieth century. The autobiography appears in his posthumously published *Bughyat al-rāghibīn fī silsilat āl Sharaf al-Dīn*, ed. Sayyid ʿAbd Allāh Sharaf al-Dīn (Beirut: al-Dār al-Islāmiyya, 1991), 2:63–254.

ʿAbd al-Raḥmān Shukrī (1886–1958)
Poet and intellectual. Although framed as the thoughts and reflections of a young man who is *not* the author, it has been deemed autobiographical by later literary historians. *Kitāb al-Iʿtirāfāt, wa-huwa qiṣṣat nafsī* (The Book of Confessions, Which Is the Story of Myself) (Alexandria: Maṭbaʿat Jurjī Gharzūzī, 1916).

Ṭāhā Ḥusayn (b. 1304/1889, d. 1378/1973)
Author, scholar, and government minister. This moving account of the blind author's childhood in a southern Egyptian village up to his move to

Cairo to study at the al-Azhar university is available in multiple Arabic editions as volume 1 of *al-Ayyām* (The Days). Volume 1, originally published in 1926–27, covers to 1903; the other volumes cover later periods in his life. The full text is available in English translation as *The Days—Taha Hussein: His Autobiography in Three Parts* (Cairo: American University Press, 1997); and volume 1 as *An Egyptian Childhood,* trans. E. H. Paxton (London: Routledge, 1932).

GLOSSARY

ʿAbbāsids — Dynasty that ruled 750 to 1258 C.E.; their claim to the caliphate was challenged by a number of other regimes such as the Spanish Umayyads in the ninth century and the North African Fatimids in the tenth.

aḥwāl (sing. *ḥāl*) — Lit. "states" or "conditions"; used along with *aṭwār* (stages) to refer to the stages in a person's life history.

akhbār (see *khabar*) — Lit. "reports" or "news"; an account of an event often accompanied by an *isnād* (sequence of transmitters) and sometimes by a poem composed about the event.

akhbārī — Adj., refers to the narration of history through a series of individual reports of events (*akhbār*) rather than the assimilation of these accounts into a single synthesized narrative created by the historian; as a noun it can refer to any of a number of early historians who compiled verses, genealogies, and historical reports.

al-Azhar — Mosque and later university established by the Shiʿite Fatimid dynasty in Cairo in 972; after the fall of the Fatimids and reinstatement of Sunnī Islam in Egypt with the ascension of Saladin, it came to be recognized as the preeminent academic institution of Sunnī Islam.

aṭwār (sing *ṭawr*) — Lit. "stages"; used along with *aḥwāl* (states) to refer to a person's life history.

barnāmaj (pl. *barāmij*)	Originally Persian; in Islamic Spain and North Africa the term in Arabic indicated among other meanings a biography or an autobiography, particularly among religious scholars and Sufi mystics.
bey	Turkish title of nobility also used in Arab countries during the Ottoman and modern periods.
Būyids	Persian dynasty of the tenth and early eleventh century that seized political power from the ʿAbbāsids while retaining nominal allegiance to the authority of the caliph.
caliph	Lit. "successor"; the head of the Islamic community following the death of the Prophet Muhammad in 632 C.E.; in the early centuries the caliph was both the political and the spiritual head of the community, but each of these two functions became diluted with the passage of time, and in some periods the caliph was nothing more than a figurehead, while other social groups and figures wielded temporal and/or religious power.
dāʿī (pl. *duʿāt*)	Missionary of Ismāʿīlī Shiʿism during the Middle Ages.
dīwān	Among other meanings, the collected poetry of an author published as a single anthology.
fahrasa/fihrist (pl. *fahāris*)	Originally Persian, used to mean an index, a bibliography, and, in Islamic Spain and North Africa, a biography or an autobiography, particularly of a religious scholar or Sufi figure.
Fatimids	Ismāʿīlī Shiʿite dynasty that ruled parts of North Africa and later Egypt from the late ninth century to 1171 C.E.
ḥadīth	Account of a statement or action of the Prophet Muhammad passed down with an *isnād* (sequence of transmitters).
ḥāl	See *aḥwāl*
ijāza	Certificate of authorization passing on to a second party the right to teach, lecture on, or claim mastery of a specific work or body of work.

ikhwāniyyāt	Lit. "fraternal correspondence"; writings among members of a Sufi brotherhood, for example; within a *tarjama* or *sīra,* a section of the text including sample letters written by the subject of the biography or autobiography.
Īlkhānids	Mongol dynasty that ruled in Persia from the thirteenth through the fifteenth century C.E.
Imāmīs (also known as "Twelvers")	Main branch of Shiʿite Islam that recognizes the spiritual authority of a chain of twelve Imāms (leaders) from among the descendants of the Prophet Muhammad through ʿAlī, his cousin and son-in-law. ʿAlī is recognized as the fourth caliph by Sunnī Muslims, but Shiʿites recognize him as the immediate spiritual successor to Muhammad himself and the first of the Imāms.
Ismāʿīlīs (also known as "Seveners")	Branch of Shiʿite Islam that, with the Imāmīs, recognizes a series of Imāms beginning with ʿAlī but, unlike the Imāmīs, recognizes only seven such figures, rather than twelve. The split occurred over whether the sixth Imām's elder son, Ismāʿīl, or younger son, Mūsā, would become the seventh Imām; the Imāmīs recognized the latter and the Ismāʿīlīs the former, hence their name.
isnād	Sequence of transmitters for a *khabar* or a *ḥadīth* (e.g., "I heard this from so-and-so who heard it from so-and-so who heard it from his father who was with the Prophet—Upon him be Peace and God's Blessings—when he said the following . . .").
karamāt (sing. *karāma*)	Miracles or wonders performed by God in response to the prayers of a particularly pious believer.
khabar (pl. *akhbār*)	Account or report; see *akhbār.*
khaṭīb	Person appointed by mosque or state authorities to deliver the official Friday oration ("sermon") during congregational prayer services.
khedive	Title used for the ruler of Egypt in the nineteenth century.

maghāzī Lit. "raids"; originally, the historical accounts of the campaigns of the early Islamic community during the lifetime of the Prophet Muhammad; later, often used as a synonym for the *sīra,* or biography, of the Prophet.

manāmāt Lit. "dreams"; in a biography or an autobiography, a discrete section recounting the dreams of the subject of the text and dreams that others had relating to him or her; interchangeable with *manāẓir.*

manāqib Term of unclear origin that came to mean "virtues"; often used in the title of biographies of spiritual figures.

manāẓir Lit. "visions"; in a biography or an autobiography, a discrete section recounting the visions of the subject of the text and visions that others had relating to him or her; interchangeable with *manāmāt.*

mashyakha List of teachers; sometimes an independent work, otherwise the section listing the subject's teachers and what he or she studied with them in a biography or an autobiography (see also *muʿjam* and *thabat*).

muʿjam Lit. "collection"; in the context of a biography or autobiography, a list of teachers (see *mashyakha*).

mujtahid Jurist with the authority to make broad rulings on difficult questions in religious law.

Muʿtazilite N.; any of a number of theologians who advocated free will, divine justice, and allegorical interpretations of the Qur'ān; most prominent during the eighth through twelfth centuries.

pasha Turkish title of nobility used in some Arab countries in Ottoman and modern times.

qudwa Example for emulation; righteous figure after whose words and actions one should pattern one's own life; most commonly used in reference to the Prophet Muhammad.

Qur'ān Divine scripture of Islam, believed by Muslims to have been revealed in inimitable Arabic to the Prophet Muhammad between

	610 and 632 C.E. and regarded as God's final revelation to humankind.
rasā'il (sing. *risāla*)	Letters or correspondence; in a biography or an autobiography, a discrete section containing samples of the subject's correspondence.
riḥla	Lit. "travel" or "journey"; a popular literary genre of first-person travel accounts; in a biography or an autobiography, a discrete section detailing the subject's travels.
Safavids	Shiʿite dynasty that extended its control overall of Persia during the reign of its founder, Ismāʿīl (d. 1524), and ruled there until 1737.
Shiʿite	Member of one of two main branches of Islam [cf. Sunnī] that recognize the spiritual authority of a chain of Imāms from among the descendants of the Prophet Muhammad through his daughter, Fāṭima, and ʿAlī, his cousin and son-in-law; ʿAlī is recognized as the fourth caliph by Sunnī Muslims, but Shiʿites recognize him as the immediate spiritual successor to Muhammad himself and the first of the Imāms; the term comes from the phrase *shīʿat ʿAlī*, the "party of ʿAlī" or "supporters of ʿAlī."
sīra (pl. *siyar*)	From the Arabic verb *sāra*, "to go," meaning, inter alia, (1) behavior or conduct; (2) path or travel; (3) an independent work consisting of a biography or an autobiography; (4) a polemical or ideological stance; and (5) a legal work addressing the conduct of war and international relations.
sīra dhātiyya	Lit. "self-*sīra*"; twentieth-century neologism used to translate the western concept "autobiography" in modern Arabic literary writings (see also *tarjama shakhṣiyya*).
Sufism	Mystical tradition of Islamic piety and thought that gave rise in the Middle Ages to organized orders emphasizing varying degrees of asceticism, group ritual, ecstatic experience, and esoteric teachings.
Sunnī	Member of one of the two main branches of Islam (cf. Shiʿite) that recognizes the au-

	thority of the historical caliphs, including the Umayyads and ʿAbbāsids, as heads of the Islamic community, in contrast to Shiʿite recognition of a line of spiritual leaders known as Imāms; the term comes from the idea of the *sunna* (words and deeds) of the Prophet Muhammad that is accorded a spiritual authority second only to that of the Qurʾān.
ṭabaqāt	Lit. "classes" or "generations" (sing. *ṭabaqa*); a work providing biographical information organized into "notices" or "entries" (*tarājim,* sing. *tarjama*) about a specific social group.
tafsīr	Exegetical commentary on the Qurʾān.
tarjama (pl. *tarājim*)	Originally Aramaic with multiple meanings in Arabic: (1) to translate from one language to another; (2) to give a text a title; (3) to subdivide a text into sections with subheadings; (4) to interpret or analyze a text; and (5) a biographical or an autobiographical notice included in a larger work.
tarjama shakhṣiyya	Lit. "personal biographical notice"; a twentieth-century neologism used to translate the western concept "autobiography" in modern Arabic literary writings (see also *sīra dhātiyya).*
thabat	List of teachers (see *mashyakha* and *muʿjam*) and later, in some regions, a biographical entry similar to a *tarjama,* definition 5.
ṭawr	See *aṭwār.*
Umayyads	Arab dynasty of caliphs that ruled in the eastern Mediterranean from 661 to 750 C.E.; an extension of this family who later ruled in Spain from 756 to 1031.
Yaʿruba (also Yaʿriba)	Seventeenth- and eighteenth-century dynasty of Oman.

REFERENCES

ʿAbbās, Iḥsān. *Fann al-sīra*. Beirut: Dār al-Thaqāfa, 1956.

———, ed. *Muʿjam al-udabāʾ*. Beirut: Dār al-Gharb al-Islāmī, 1993.

ʿAbd Allāh al-Turjumān. *Tuḥfat al-adīb fī al-radd ʿalā ahl al-ṣalīb*. Ed. Maḥmūd ʿAlī Ḥamāya. Cairo: Dār al-Thaqāfa li-l-Ṭibāʿa wa-l-Nashr, 1983.

ʿAbd al-Dāyim, Yaḥyā Ibrāhīm. *al-Tarjama al-dhātiyya fī al-adab al-ʿarabī al-ḥadīth*. Beirut: Dār Iḥyāʾ al-Turāth al-ʿArabī, 1975.

ʿAbd al-Sattār, Muʾayyad. *al-Sīra al-dhātiyya: dirāsa naqdiyya*. Uddevalla, Sweden: Dār al-Manfā, 1996.

ʿAbd al-Wāḥid, ʿAlī, ed. *Muqaddimat Ibn Khaldūn*. 2d ed. Cairo: Lajnat al-Bayān al-ʿArabī, 1965.

Abiad, Malik. "Origine et développement des dictionnaires biographiques arabes." *Bulletin d'Études Orientales* 31 (1979): 7–15.

Abū Fidāʾ al-Ayyūbī. *The Memoirs of a Syrian Prince: Abū Fidāʾ Sultan of Ḥamāh (672–732/1273–1331)*. Trans. P. M. Holt. Wiesbaden: Franz Steiner, 1983.

Abu-Lughod, Lila. *Veiled Sentiments: Honor and Poetry in a Bedouin Society*. Berkeley: University of California Press, 1986.

Abū Saʿd, Aḥmad. *Adab al-raḥalāt* . Cairo: n.p., 1961.

al-Ahwānī, ʿAbd al-ʿAzīz. "Kutub barāmij al-ʿulamāʾ fī al-Andalus." *Majallat maʿhad al-makhṭūṭāt al-ʿarabiyya* 1 (May 1955): 91–120.

Akroyd, Joyce, trans. *Told Round a Brushwood Fire: The Autobiography of Arai Hakuseki*. Princeton: Princeton University Press, 1979.

ʿAlī, ʿAbdullah Yūsuf. *The Meaning of the Holy Qurʿan*. Brentwood, MD: Amana Corp., 1991.

ʿAlī, Muḥammad Qarah. *Suṭūr min ḥayātī*. Beirut: Muʾassasat Nawfal, 1988.

Allen, Roger. "The Beginnings of the Arabic Novel." In *Cambridge History of Arabic Literature: Modern Arabic Literature*, ed. M. M. Badawi, 180–92. Cambridge: Cambridge University Press, 1992.

ʿAlwash, Jawad Ahmad. *Umara al-Yamani the Poet*. Baghdad: al-Maʿārif Press, 1971.

al-ʿĀmilī, ʿAlī. *al-Durr al-manthūr*. 2 vols. Ed. Aḥmad al-Ḥusaynī. Qom: Maktabat al-Marʿashī al-Najafī, 1978.

Ansari, A. S. Bazmee. "Āzād Bilgrāmī." EI[2] 1:808.

Arberry, A. J. *Avicenna on Theology.* London: Murray, 1951.

———. *The Ring of the Dove.* London: Luzac, 1953.

Armistead, Samuel. "An Anecdote of King Jaume I and Its Arabic Cogener." In *Cultures in Contact in Medieval Spain: Historical and Literary Essays Presented to L. P. Harvey,* ed. David Hook and Barry Taylor, 1–8. London: King's College, 1990.

Arslān, Amīr. *al-Sīra al-dhātiyya.* Beirut: Dār al-Ṭalīʿa, 1987.

Auchterlonie, Paul. *Arabic Biographical Dictionaries: A Summary Guide and Bibliography.* Durham: Middle East Libraries Committee, 1987.

Audebert, Claude France. "La Risālat al-Ḥayāt d'Abū Ḥayyān al-Tawḥīdī." *Bulletin d'Études Orientales* 18 (1964): 147–95.

Austin, Allan. *African Muslims in Antebellum America: A Sourcebook.* New York: Garland, 1984.

Austin, R. W. J. *Sufis of Andalusia: The Rūḥ al-Quds and al-Durrah al-fākhirah of Ibn ʿArabī.* Berkeley: University of California Press, 1972. [London: Allen and Unwin, 1971].

Baccouche, Béchir. *al-Durra al-khaṭīra fī shuʿarā al-jazīra: Anthologie des poètes arabo-siciliens.* Beirut: Dār al-Gharb al-Islāmī, 1995.

Badawi, M. M. *Short History of Modern Arabic Literature.* Oxford: Clarendon, 1993.

Badran, Margot. "Expressing Feminism and Nationalism in Autobiography: The Memoirs of an Egyptian Educator." In *De/Colonizing the Subject: The Politics of Gender in Women's Autobiography,* ed. Sidonie Smith and Julia Watson, 270–93. Minneapolis: University of Minnesota Press, 1992.

———. *Feminists, Islam and Nation: Gender and the Making of Modern Egypt.* Princeton: Princeton University Press, 1995.

———. Introduction to *Harem Years: The Memoirs of an Egyptian Feminist (1879–1924),* trans. and ed. Margot Badran, 7–22. London: Virago Press, 1986.

Badran, Margot, and Miriam Cooke, eds. *Opening the Gates: A Century of Arab Feminist Writing.* London: Virago Press, 1990.

al-Baḥrānī, Yūsuf. *Lu'lu'at al-Baḥrayn.* Najaf: Maṭbaʿat al-Nuʿmān, 1966.

Barbier de Meynard, C. *Recueil des historiens des Croisades, historiens orientaux.* Paris: Imprimerie National, 1872–1906.

Bartallī, Muḥammad ibn Abī Bakr al-Ṣiddīq. *Fatḥ al-shakūr fī maʿrifat aʿyān ʿulamāʾ al-Takrūr.* Ed. Muḥammad al-Kattānī. Beirut: Dār al-Gharb al-Islāmī, 1981.

al-Baydhaq, Abū Bakr. *Documents inédits d'histoire almohade.* Trans. E. Lévi-Provençal. Paris: P. Geuthner, 1928.

Berkey, Jonathan. *The Transmission of Knowledge in Medieval Cairo: A Social History of Islamic Education.* Princeton: Princeton University Press, 1992.

Berque, Jacques. *Al-Yousi: Problèmes de la culture marocaine au XVIIème siècle.* Paris: Mouton, 1958.

Bint al-Shāṭi' [ʿĀ'isha ʿAbd al-Raḥmān]. *ʿAlā jisr bayna al-ḥayāh wa-l-mawt.* Cairo: al-Hay'a al-ʿĀmma al-Miṣriyya li-l-Kitāb, 1967.

Blois, François de. *Burzōy's Voyage to India and the Origin of the Book of Kalīlah wa Dimnah.* London: Royal Asiatic Society, 1990.

Bowring, Richard, trans. *Murasaki Shikibu: Her Diary and Poetic Memoirs.* Princeton: Princeton University Press, 1982.

Bravmann, M. M. *The Spiritual Background of Early Islam: Studies on Ancient Arab Concepts.* Leiden: E. J. Brill, 1972.

Brock, Arthur J. *Greek Medecine, being extracts illlustrative of medical writers from Hippocrates to Galen.* London: Dent and Sons, 1929.

Brockelmann, Carl. *Geschichte der arabischen Litteratur.* Vols. 1–2, Supplement vols. 1–3. Leiden: E. J. Brill, 1943–49.

Brustad, Kristen. "Imposing Order: Reading the Conventions of Representation in al-Suyūṭī's Autobiography." *Edebiyât: Special Issue—Arabic Autobiography,* N.S. 7, no. 2 (1997): 327–44.

al-Bundarī al-Fatḥ. *Sanā al-barq al-shāmī.* Ed. Ramazan Şeşen. Beirut: Dār al-Kitāb al-Jadīd, 1971.

al-Budayrī, Aḥmad al-Ḥallāq. *Ḥawādith Dimashq al-yawmiyya,* A.H. *1154–1175.* Ed. Aḥmad ʿIzzat ʿAbd al-Karīm. Cairo: Maṭbaʿat Lajnat al-Bayān al-ʿArabī, 1959.

Burckhardt, Jacob. *The Civilization of the Renaissance in Italy.* Trans. S. G. C. Middlemore. London: Harrap, 1929.

Burckhardt, Titus. "Le Sheikh al-ʿArabī Ad-Darqāwī: Extraits de ses lettres." *Études Traditionnelles* 394 (March–April 1966): 60–80.

———. "Le Sheikh Ad-Darqāwī: Nouveaux extraits des ses lettres." *Études Traditionnelles* 402–3 (July–October 1967): 192–210.

———. "Extracts from the Letters of Shaikh Al-ʿArabī Ad-Darqāwī." *Studies in Comparative Religion.* London: Winter, 1967.

Burns, Robert I. "The King's Autobiography: the Islamic Connection." In *Muslims, Christians, and Jews in the Crusader Kingdom of Valencia,* 285–88. Cambridge: Cambridge University Press, 1984.

Bushnell, Charles. Introduction to *University Library of Autobiography,* 15 vols.; vol. 2: *The Middle Ages and Their Autobiographers.* New York: F. Tyler Daniels, 1918; rpt. National Alumni, 1927.

Cachia, Pierre. *An Overview of Modern Arabic Literature.* Edinburgh: Edinburgh University Press, 1990.

Cahen, Claude. "ʿAbdallaṭīf al-Baghdādī, portraitiste et historien de son temps: Extraits inédits de ses Mémoires." *Bulletin d'Études Orientales* 23 (1970): 101–28.

———. "Une source pour l'histoire ayyubide: Les mémoires de Saʿd al-dīn ibn Ḥamawiya al-Juwaynī." *Bulletin de la Faculté des Lettres de Strasbourg* 7 (1950): 320–37; rpt. in *Les peuples musulmans dans l'histoire médievale,* 457–82. Damascus: Institut Français, 1977.

Calvet, Agustín. *Fray Anselmo Turmeda: Heterodoxo español (1352–1423–32?).* Barcelona: Casa Editorial Estudio, 1914.

Campbell [Kāmbil], R. B. *Aʿlām al-adab al-ʿarabī al-muʿāṣir, siyar wa-siyar dhātiyya.* Beirut: Orient-Institut der Deutschen Morgenländischen Gesellschaft, 1996.

Canard, Marius. *Marius Canard: Miscellanea Orientalis.* London: Variorum, 1973.

Cardano, Girolamo. *The Book of My Life.* Trans. J. Stoner. New York: Dutton, 1930.

Carlock, Mary Sue. "Humpty Dumpty and Autobiography." *Genre* 3 (1970): 345–46.

Caskel, Werner. *Ǧamharat an-nasab: Das genealogische Werk des Hišam ibn Muḥammad al-Kalbī.* Leiden: E. J. Brill, 1966.

Ceccato, Rosella Dorigo. "Autobiographical Features in the Works of Yaʿqūb Ṣanūʿ." In *Writing the Self: Autobiographical Writing in Modern Arabic Literature,* ed. Robin Ostle, Ed de Moor, and Stefan Wild, 51–60. London: Saqi Books, 1998.

Chakrabarty, Dipesh. "Postcoloniality and the Artifice of History: Who Speaks for 'Indian' Pasts?" *Representations* 37 (1992): 1–26.

Chamberlain, Michael. *Knowledge and Social Practice in Medieval Damascus, 1190–1350*. Cambridge: Cambridge University Press, 1994.

Coe, Richard N. *When the Grass Was Taller: Autobiography and the Experience of Childhood.* New Haven, Conn.: Yale University Press, 1984.

Cooperson, Michael. *The Heirs of the Prophet in the Age of al-Ma'mūn.* Cambridge: Cambridge University Press, 2000.

———. "Ibn Ḥanbal and Bishr al-Ḥāfī: A Case Study in Biographical Traditions." *Studia Islamica* 86, no. 2 (1997): 71–101.

———. "The Purported Autobiography of Ḥunayn ibn Isḥāq." *Edebiyât: Special Issue—Arabic Autobiography,* N.S. 7, no. 2 (1997): 235–49.

Cranston, Edwin A., trans. *The Izumi Shikibu Diary: A Romance of the Heian Court.* Cambridge, Mass.: Harvard University Press, 1969.

Crone, Patricia, and Friedrich W. Zimmermann, *The Epistle of Sālim B. Dhakwān.* Oxford: Oxford University Press, 1999.

Daftary, Farhad. *The Ismailis: Their History and Doctrines.* Cambridge: Cambridge University Press, 1990.

al-Damurdashī, Aḥmad. *al-Damurdashī's Chronicle of Egypt, 1688–1755.* Trans. and annot. Daniel Crecelius and ʿAbd al-Wahhāb Bakr. Leiden: E. J. Brill, 1991.

Dankoff, Robert. *Seyahatname: The Intimate Life of an Ottoman Statesman Melek Ahmad Pasha (1588–1662) as Portrayed in Evliya Celebi's "Book of Travels."* Albany: SUNY Press, 1991.

Ḍayf, Shawqī. *al-Raḥalāt* [= *Funūn al-adab al-ʿarabī: al-fann al-qaṣaṣī IV*]. Cairo: Dār al-Maʿārif, 1969.

———. *al-Tarjama al-shakhṣiyya.* Cairo: Dār al-Maʿārif, 1956.

Derenbourg, Hartwig. *ʿOumâra du Yémen, sa vie et son oeuvre.* 2 vols. Paris: Leroux, 1897.

Dilthey, Wilhelm. *Der Aufbau der geschichtlichen Welt in den Geisteswissenschaften.* Frankfurt: Suhrkamp, 1970.

Dols, Michael W. *Medieval Islamic Medicine: Ibn Riḍwān's Treatise "On the Prevention of Bodily Ills in Egypt."* Berkeley: University of California Press, 1984.

Eakin, Paul John. Foreword to Philippe Lejeune, *On Autobiography,* vii–xxviii. Trans. Katherine Leary. Minneapolis: University of Minnesota Press, 1989.

Elias, Jamal J. 1997. "The *Ḥadīth* Traditions of ʿĀ'isha as Prototypes of Self-Narrative." *Edebiyât: Special Issue—Arabic Autobiography,* N.S. 7, no. 2 (1997): 215–33.

———. *The Throne Carrier of God: The Life and Thought of ʿAlā' al-Dawla al-Simnānī.* Albany: SUNY Press, 1995.

Elisséeff, Nikita. *Nūr al-Dīn: Un grand prince musulman de Syrie au temps des croisades.* Damascus: Institut Français de Damas, 1967.

Ende, Werner. "Neue arabische Memoirenliteratur zur Geschichte des modernen Iraq." *Der Islam* 49 (1972): 100–9.

de Epalza, Miguel (Mikel). *Fray Anselm Turmeda (ʿAbdallah al-Taryuman) y su polemica islamo-cristiana: Edición, traducción y estudio de la Tuhfa.* 2d ed. Madrid: Hiperion, 1994.

———."Nuevas aportaciones a la biografía de Fray Anselmo Turmeda (Abdallah al-

Tarchumān)." *Analecta Sacra Tarraconensia: Revista de Ciencias Histórico-Eclesiásticas* 38 (1965): 87–158.

Fahd, Toufic. "Inventaire de la littérature onirocritique arabe." In *La divination arabe,* 330–63. Leiden: E. J. Brill, 1966; rpt. Paris: Sindbad, 1987.

———. *La divination arabe.* Leiden: E. J. Brill, 1966; rpt. Paris: Sindbad, 1987.

Farīd, Muḥammad. *The Memoirs and Diaries of Muḥammad Farīd, an Egyptian Nationalist Leader (1868–1919).* Trans. Arthur Goldschmidt, Jr. San Francisco: Mellen University Research Press, 1992.

al-Fāsī, ʿAbd al-Ghāfir. *al-Muntakhab min al-siyāq li-ta'rīkh Nīsābūr.* Ed. Muḥammad Kāẓim al-Maḥmūdī. Qom: Jamāʿat al-Mudarrisīn, 1983.

Fischel, Walter J. *Ibn Khaldūn and Tamerlane.* Berkeley: University of California Press, 1952.

Fleischer, Cornell H. *Bureaucrat and Intellectual in the Ottoman Empire: The Historian Muṣṭafā ʿAlī (1541–1600).* Princeton: Princeton University Press, 1986.

Fliedner, Stephan. *ʿAli Mubārak und seine Ḫiṭaṭ: Kommentierte Übersetzung der Autobiographie und Werkbesprechung.* Berlin: Klaus Schwarz, 1990.

Fragner, Bert G. *Persische Memoirliteratur als Quelle zur neueren Geschichte Irans.* Wiesbaden: Franz Steiner, 1979.

Frayḥa, Anīs. *Ismaʿ yā Riḍā.* Beirut: Dār al-Maṭbūʿāt al-Muṣawwara, [1956] 1981.

Gabrieli, F. *Arab Historians of the Crusades.* Trans. E. J. Costello. Berkeley: University of California Press, 1969.

Georgescu, Constantin. "A Forgotten Pioneer of the Lebanese 'Nahḍah': Salīm al-Bustānī." Ph.D. diss., New York University, 1978.

Gendzier, Irene L. *The Practical Visions of Yaʿqūb Ṣanūʿ.* Cambridge: Cambridge University Press, 1966.

al-Ghamdi, Saleh. "Autobiography in Classical Arabic Literature: An Ignored Genre." Ph.D. diss., Indiana University, 1989.

al-Ghazālī, Abū Ḥāmid Muḥammad. *al-Munqidh min al-ḍalāl.* Cairo: al-Maktab al-Fannī, 1961.

al-Ghazzī, Muḥammad. *al-Kawākib al-sā'ira bi-aʿyān al-mi'a al-ʿāshira.* 3 vols. Beirut: al-Maṭbaʿa al-Amrīkāniyya, 1945–59.

Gibb, H. A. R. "Al-Barq al-Shāmī: The History of Saladin by the Kātib ʿImād ad-Dīn al-Iṣfahānī." *Wiener Zeitschrift zur Kunde des Morgenlandes* 52 (1953): 93–115.

———. "The Arabic Sources for the Life of Saladin." *Speculum* 25 (1950): 58–72.

———. "Islamic Biographical Literature." In *Historians of the Middle East,* ed. Bernard Lewis and P. M. Holt, 54–58. London: Oxford University Press, 1962.

Gohlman, William E. *The Life of Ibn Sina: A Critical Edition and Annotated Translation.* Albany: SUNY Press, 1974.

Goitein, S. D. "Individualism and Conformity in Classical Islam." In *Individualism and Conformity in Classical Islam,* ed. Amin Banani and Spyros Vryonis, 3–17. Wiesbaden: Otto Harrassowitz, 1977.

Goldziher, Ignaz. "The Appearance of the Prophet in Dreams." *Journal of the Royal Asiatic Society* (1912): 503–6.

———. *Muslim Studies.* Trans. C. R. Barber and S. M. Stern. 2 vols. London: George Allen and Unwin, 1967.

Gouda, Yehia, trans. *Dreams and Their Meanings in the Old Arab Tradition.* New York: Vantage Press, 1991.

von Grunebaum, Gustave. "Die Wirklichkeitsweite der früharabischen Dichtung. Eine literaturwissenschaftliche Untersuchung." *Wiener Zeitschrift für die Kunde des Morgenlandes,* Beiheft 3 (1937).

———. *Medieval Islam: A Study in Cultural Orientation.* Chicago: University of Chicago Press, 1946.

———. "Self-Expression: Literature and History." In *Medieval Islam: A Study in Cultural Orientation,* 258–93. Chicago: University of Chicago Press, 1956.

von Grunebaum, Gustave, and R. Callois, eds. *The Dream and Human Societies.* Berkeley: University of California Press, 1966.

Gusdorf, Georges. "Conditions and Limits of Autobiography." Trans. James Olney [orig. pub. 1956]. In *Autobiography: Essays Theoretical and Critical,* ed. James Olney, 28–48. Princeton: Princeton University Press, 1980.

Gutas, Dimitri. *Avicenna and the Aristotelian Tradition: Introduction to Reading Avicenna's Philosophical Works.* Leiden: E. J. Brill, 1988.

———. *Greek Thought and Arabic Culture: The Graeco-Arabic Translation Movement in Baghdad and Early ʿAbbāsid Society (2nd–4th/8th–10th Centuries).* London: Routledge, 1998.

Habermas, Jürgen. *The Structural Transformation of the Public Sphere: An Inquiry into a Category of Bourgeois Society.* Trans. Thomas Berger and Frederick Lawrence. Cambridge, Mass.: MIT Press, 1989.

Hafsi, Ibrāhīm. "Recherches sur le genre Ṭabaqāt dans la littérature arabe." *Arabica* 23 (1976):227–65; 24 (1977):1–41, 150–86.

Hartmann, Angelika. "al-Malik al-Manṣūr." *EI²* 6:429–30.

Häusler, Martina. *Fiktive ägyptische Autobiographien der zwanziger und dreissiger Jahre.* Frankfurt: Peter Lang, 1990.

Haywood, John. *Modern Arabic Literature 1800–1970.* New York: St. Martin's Press, 1971.

Heath, Peter. *The Thirsty Sword: Sīrat ʿAntar and the Arabic Popular Epic.* Salt Lake City: University of Utah Press, 1996.

Heinrichs, Wolfhart. "Prosimetrical Genres in Classical Arabic Literature." In *Prosimetrum: Cross-Cultural Perspectives on Narrative in Prose and Verse,* ed. Joseph Harris and Karl Reichl, 249–75. Suffolk: Boydell and Brewer, 1998.

Hinds, Martin. *Studies in Early Islamic History.* Ed. Jere Bacharach, Lawrence I. Conrad, and Patricia Crone. Studies in Late Antiquity and Early Islam, 4. Princeton: Darwin Press, 1996.

Hitti, Philip. Introduction to Usāma ibn Munqidh, *Kitāb al-Iʿtibār.* Baghdad: Maktabat al-Muthannā, 1964. 1–43.

Hodgson, M. G. S. *The Venture of Islam.* 3 vols. Chicago: University of Chicago Press, [1974] 1984.

Hopkins, J. F. P. "Geographical and Navigational Literature." In *The Cambridge History of Arabic Literature: Religion, Learning, and Science in the ʿAbbasid Period,* ed. M. J. L. Young, J. D. Latham, and R. B. Serjeant, 301–27. Cambridge: Cambridge University Press, 1990.

Horn, Paul. *Die Denkwurdigkeiten schah Tahmasp's des Ersten von Persien.* Strassburg: K. J. Trubner, 1891.

Hourani, Albert. *Arabic Thought in the Liberal Age: 1798–1939.* Oxford: Oxford University Press, 1962. [2d ed. Cambridge: Cambridge University Press, 1983]

Humphreys, R. Stephen. *Islamic History: A Framework for Inquiry*. Rev. ed. Princeton: Princeton University Press, 1991.

Hussein, Taha [= Ṭāhā Ḥusayn]. *An Egyptian Childhood, the Autobiography of Taha Hussein*. Trans. E. H. Paxton. London: Routledge, 1932.

———. *ʿIlm al-ijtimāʿ*. Vol. 8 of *al-Majmūʿa al-kāmila li-muʾallafāt Ṭāhā Ḥusayn*. Beirut: Dār al-Kitāb al-Lubnānī, 1973.

Ibn Abī Dunyā. *Morality in the Guise of Dreams: Ibn Abī al-Dunya, a Critical Edition of Kitāb al-manām*. Ed. Leah Kinberg. Leiden: E. J. Brill, 1994.

Ibn Abī Uṣaybiʿa. *ʿUyūn al-anbāʾ fī ṭabaqāt al-aṭibbāʾ*. Ed. Nizār Riḍā. Beirut: Dār Maktabat al-Ḥayāh, 1965.

———. *ʿUyūn al-anbāʾ fī ṭabaqāt al-aṭibbāʾ*. Ed. Bāsil ʿUyūn al-Sūd. Beirut: Dār al-Kutub al-ʿIlmiyya, 1998.

Ibn ʿAjība, Aḥmad. *L'autobiographie (Fahrasa) du Soufi Marocain Ahmad ibn ʿAgîba (1747–1809)*. Trans. J.-L. Michon. Leiden: E. J. Brill, 1969. [Rpt. from *Arabica* 15–16: 1968–69].

Ibn Buluggīn. *Mudhakkirāt al-amīr ʿAbd Allāh ākhir mulūk Banī Zīrī bi-Gharnāṭa al-musammāt bi-Kitāb al-Tibyān*. Ed. E. Lévi-Provençal. Cairo: Dār al-Maʿārif, 1995.

———. *The Tibyān: Memoirs of ʿAbd Allāh b. Buluggīn, last Zirid amīr of Granada*. Trans. Amin Tibi. Leiden: E. J. Brill, 1986.

Ibn Ḥajar al-ʿAsqalānī. *Uns al-hujar fī abyāt Ibn Ḥajar*. Beirut: Dār al-Rayyān li-l-Turāth, 1988.

Ibn Ḥazm. *The Ring of the Dove: A Treatise on the Art and Practice of Arab Love*. Trans. A. J. Arberry. London: Luzac, 1953.

Ibn Hishām. *The Life of Muhammad: A Translation of Isḥāq's Sīrat Rasūl Allāh*. Trans. Alfred Guillaume. London: Oxford University Press, 1955.

Ibn al-ʿImād, ʿAbd al-Ḥayy. *Shadharāt al-dhahab fī akhbār man dhahab*. 8 vols. Cairo: Maktabat al-Qudsī, 1931–33.

Ibn al-Jawzī, ʿAbd al-Raḥmān. *Mashyakhat Ibn al-Jawzī*. Ed. M. Maḥfūẓ. Beirut: Dār al-Gharb al-Islāmī, 1980.

———. *Ṣayd al-khāṭir*. Amman: Maktabat Dār al-Fikr, 1987.

Ibn Kathīr, Ismāʿīl ibn ʿUmar. *al-Bidāya wa-l-nihāya*. 14 vols. Cairo: al-Maṭbaʿa al-Salafiyya, 1932.

Ibn Khaldūn. *The Muqaddimah*. 3 vols. Trans. F. Rosenthal. New York: Pantheon, 1958.

Ibn Munqidh, Usāma. *An Arab-Syrian Gentleman and Warrior in the Period of the Crusades: Memoirs of Usāmah Ibn-Munqidh*. Trans. Philip K. Hitti. Princeton: Princeton University Press, 1987.

Ibn al-Qaṭṭāʿ, ʿAlī. *al-Durra al-khaṭīra fī shuʿarāʾ al-jazīra*. Ed. Bashīr al-Bakkūsh. Beirut: Dār al-Gharb al-Islāmī, 1995.

al-Iṣfahānī, ʿImād al-Dīn al-Kātib. *al-Barq al-shāmī*. Amman: Muʾassasat ʿAbd al-Ḥamīd Shūmān, 1987.

———. *Kharīdat al-qaṣr*. Damascus: al-Maṭbaʿa al-Hishāmiyya, 1964.

Ismāʿīl, ʿIzz al-Dīn. *al-Adab wa-funūnuh*. 3d ed. Cairo: Dār al-Fikr al-ʿArabī, 1965.

ʿIyāḍ, al-Qāḍī. *Madhāhib al-ḥukkām fī nawāzil al-aḥkām*. Ed. Muḥammad ibn Sharīfa. Beirut: Dār al-Gharb al-Islāmī, 1990.

Jaʿfar al-Ḥājib. "L'autobiographie d'un chambellan du Mahdī ʿObeidallāh le Fātimide." Trans. Marius Canard. *Hespéris* 39 (1952): 279–329.

al-Jundī, Anwar. *al-Aʿlām al-alf*. Cairo: Maṭbaʿat al-Risāla, 1957.

Juynboll, J. H. A. "Ibn Miḳsam." *EI*² Supp.: 393.

Kafadar, Cemal. "Self and Others: The Diary of a Dervish in Seventeenth-Century Istanbul and First-Person Narratives in Ottoman Literature." *Studia Islamica* (1989): 121–50.

al-Kattānī, ʿAbd al-Ḥayy. *Fihris al-fahāris wa-muʿjam al-maʿājim wa-al-mashyakhāt wa-al-musalsalāt.* 2d ed. Beirut: Dār al-Gharb al-Islāmī, 1982–86.

Katz, Jonathan G. *Dreams, Sufism, and Sainthood: The Visionary Career of Muhammad al-Zawāwī.* Leiden: E. J. Brill, 1996.

———. "Visionary Experience, Autobiography, and Sainthood in North African Islam." *Princeton Papers in Near Eastern Studies* 1 (December 1992): 85–118.

Kawash, Sabri K. "Ibn Ḥajar al-Asqalānī (A.D. 1372–1449): A Study of the Background, Education, and Career of an ʿĀlim in Egypt." Ph.D. diss., Princeton University, 1969.

Kay, Henry Cassels. *Yaman: Its Early Medieval History.* London: E. Arnold, 1892.

Kedouri, Elie. *Arabic Political Memoirs and Other Studies.* London: Cass, 1974.

Kīlānī, M. I. *Trois epîtres d'Abū Ḥayyān al-Tawḥīdī.* Damascus: Institut Français de Damas, 1951.

al-Khafājī, Shihāb al-Dīn. *Rayḥānat al-alibbāʾ wa-zahrat al-ḥayāt al-dunyā.* Ed. ʿAbd al-Fattāḥ Muḥammad al-Ḥilw. Cairo: ʿĪsā al-Bābī al-Ḥalabī, 1967.

Khalidi, Tarif. *Arabic Historical Thought in the Classical Period.* Cambridge: Cambridge University Press, 1994.

Khan, M. A. M. "A Unique Treatise on the Interpretation of Dreams by Ibn Sina." In *Avicenna Commemoration Volume,* 255–307. Calcutta: Iran Society, 1956.

Khoury, Nuha N. N. "The Autobiography of Ibn al-ʿAdīm as Told to Yāqūt al-Rūmī." *Edebiyât: Special Issue—Arabic Autobiography,* N.S. 7, no. 2 (1997): 289–311.

Kilpatrick, Hilary. "Autobiography and Classical Arabic Literature." *Journal of Arabic Literature* 22 (1991): 1–20.

———. "The Egyptian Novel from Zaynab to 1980." *Cambridge History of Arabic Literature: Modern Arabic Literature,* ed. M. M. Badawi, 223–69. Cambridge: Cambridge University Press, 1992.

Kinberg, Leah. "The Legitimization of *Madhāhib* through Dreams." *Arabica* 32 (1985): 47–79.

———. "Literal Dreams and Prophetic *Ḥadīth* in Classical Islam—A Comparison of Two Ways of Legitimization." *Der Islam* 70 (1993): 279–300.

———. "The Standardization of Qur'ān Readings: The Testimonial Value of Dreams." *The Arabist: Budapest Studies in Arabic* 3–4 (1991): 223–38.

Kishk, ʿAbd al-Ḥamīd. *Qiṣṣat ayyāmī: mudhakkirāt al-shaykh Kishk.* Cairo: al-Mukhtār al-Islāmī, 1986.

Klemm, Verena. *Die Mission des fāṭimidischen Agenten al-Muʾayyad fī d-dīn in Šīraz.* Frankfurt: Peter Lang, 1989.

Kramer, Martin, ed. *Middle Eastern Lives: The Practice of Biography and Self-Narrative.* Syracuse: Syracuse University Press, 1991.

Kurd ʿAlī, Muḥammad. *Khiṭaṭ al-Shām.* 6 vols. Damascus: Maṭbaʿat al-Mufīd, 1925–28.

———. *Memoirs, a Selection.* Trans. Khalil Totah. Washington, D.C.: American Council of Learned Societies, 1954.

———. *Mudhakkirāt.* 4 vols. Damascus: Maṭbaʿat al-Turkī, 1948–51.
Lamoreaux, John C. "Dream Interpretation in the Early Medieval Near East." Ph.D. diss., Duke University, 1999.
Latour, Bruno. *We Have Never Been Modern.* Cambridge, Mass.: Harvard University Press, 1993.
Leder, Stefan. *Das Korpus al-Haiṯam b. ʿAdī (st. 207/822). Herkunft, Überlieferung, Gestalt früher Texte der ahbār Literatur.* Frankfurt: Vittorio Klostermann, 1991.
Lejeune, Philippe. "The Autobiographical Pact." Trans. Katherine Leary. In *On Autobiography,* 3–30. Minneapolis: University of Minnesota Press, 1989.
Lewis, Bernard. "First-Person Narrative in the Middle East." In *Middle Eastern Lives,* ed. Martin Kramer, 20–34. Syracuse: Syracuse University Press, 1991.
———. "Ibn al-ʿAdīm." *EI*² 3:695–96.
Lewis, G. L., trans. *The Balance of Truth.* London: Allen and Unwin, 1957.
Lings, Martin. *A Sufi Saint of the Twentieth Century, Shaikh Ahmad al-ʿAlawi: His Spiritual Heritage and Legacy.* Rev. ed. Berkeley: University of California Press, 1971.
Löfgren, Oscar. "ʿAydarūs." *EI*² 1:780–82.
Loth, Otto. "Ursprung und Bedeutung der Ṭabaqāt." *Zeitschrift der Deutschen Morgenländischen Gesellschaft* 23 (1869): 593–614.
Lowry, Joseph E. "Time, Form, and Self: The Autobiography of Abū Shāma." *Edebiyât: Special Issue—Arabic Autobiography,* N.S. 7, no. 2 (1997): 313–25.
Madelung, Wilfred. "Manṣūr al-Yamanī." *EI*² 6:438–39.
Maḥmūd, ʿAbd al-Ḥalīm. *al-Ḥamdu li-llāh hādhihi ḥayātī.* Cairo: Dār al-Maʿārif, [1976] 1985.
Maimonides. *A Guide for the Perplexed.* Trans. E. F. Schumacher. New York: Harper and Row, 1977.
Makdisi, George. "Autograph Diary of an Eleventh-Century Historian of Baghdad." *Bulletin of the School of Oriental and African Studies* 18 (1956): 9–31, 239–60; 19 (1957): 13–48, 281–303, 426–43.
———. "The Diary in Islamic Historiography." In *Islamic and Middle Eastern Societies,* ed. Robert Olson, 3–28. Brattleboro, Vt.: Amana Books, 1987.
———. *The Rise of Colleges: Institutions of Learning in Islam and the West.* Edinburgh: Edinburgh University Press, 1981.
Malti-Douglas, Fedwa. *Blindness and Autobiography: al-Ayyām of Ṭāhā Ḥusayn.* Princeton: Princeton University Press, 1988.
al-Manfalūṭī, Muṣṭafā Luṭfī. *Mukhtārāt al-Manfalūṭī.* Cairo: n.p., 1912.
Mano, Eiji. *Bābur-nāma (Vaqāyiʿ).* 2 vols. Kyoto: Syokado, 1995, 1996.
al-Maqdisī, Anīs. *Taṭawwur al-asālīb al-nathriyya fī al-adab al-ʿarabī.* Beirut: Sarkis Press, 1935.
al-Maqqarī, Aḥmad. *Nafḥ al-ṭīb min ghuṣn al-Andalus al-raṭīb.* Ed. Iḥsān ʿAbbās. Beirut: Dār Ṣādir, 1968.
al-Maqrīzī, Aḥmad. *al-Khiṭaṭ.* Cairo: Maṭbaʿat al-Nīl, 1906–8.
Maraldo, John C. "Rousseau, Hakuseki, and Hakuin: Paradigms of Self in Three Autobiographers." In *Self as Person in Asian Theory and Practice,* ed. Roger T. Ames, 57–86. New York: SUNY Press, 1994.
Marmura, Michael E. "Plotting the Course of Avicenna's Thought." *Journal of the American Oriental Society* 111, no. 2 (1991): 333–42.
Massé, Henri. "ʿImād al-Dīn." *EI*² 4:1157–58.

Massignon, Louis. *Essai sur les origines du lexique technique de la mystique musulmane.* Paris: P. Geuthner, 1922.
Masud, Muhammad Khalid. "Al-Ḥakīm al-Tirmidhī's *Buduww Sha'n.*" *Islamic Studies* (Islamic Research Institute, Islamabad, Pakistan) 4 (1965): 315–43.
May, Georges. *L'autobiographie.* Paris: Presses Universitaires de France, 1979.
Meyerhof, Max. "Autobiographische Bruchstücke Galens auz arabischen Quellen." *Sudhoffs Archiv für Geschichte der Medizin* 22 (1929): 72–86.
Miles, S. B. *The Countries and Tribes of the Persian Gulf.* London: Frank Cass, 1966.
Miller, Marilyn J. *The Poetics of Nikki Bungaku: A Comparison of the Traditions, Conventions, and Structure of Heian Japan's Literary Diaries with Western Autobiographical Writings.* New York: Garland, 1985.
Misch, Georg. *Geschichte der Autobiographie.* 4 vols. Bern and Frankfurt: A. Francke and Gerhard Schultke-Bulmke, 1949–69.
Monés, Hussain. "Ibn al-Imām." *EI*[2] 3:807.
Moraux, Paul. *Galien de Pergame: Souvenirs d'un médecin.* Paris: Belles Lettres, 1985.
Morray, David. *An Ayyubid Notable and His World: Ibn al-ʿAdīm and Aleppo as Portrayed in His Biographical Dictionary of People Associated with the City.* Leiden: E. J. Brill, 1994.
Mottahedeh, Roy. *Loyalty and Leadership in an Early Islamic Society.* Princeton: Princeton University Press, 1980.
al-Mu'ayyad al-Shīrāzī. *Sīrat al-Mu'ayyad fī al-Dīn dāʿī al-duʿāt.* Ed. M. K. Husayn. Cairo: Dār al-Kutub, 1949.
Mubārak, ʿAlī. *ʿAlam al-Dīn.* 4 vols. Alexandria: Maṭbaʿat Jarīdat al-Maḥrūsa, 1882.
———. *al-Khiṭaṭ al-tawfīqiyya al-jadīda li-Miṣr al-Qāhira wa-muduniha wa-bilādihā al-qadīma wa-l-mashhūra.* Būlāq: al-Maṭbaʿa al-Kubrā al-Amīriyya, 1888–89.
Mubārak, Zākī. *al-Nathr al-ʿarabī fī al-qarn al-rābiʿ.* Cairo: Dār al-Maʿārif, 1966.
———. *La prose arabe au IVe siècle de l'Hégire (Xe siècle).* Paris: Maisonneuve, 1931.
al-Mudghirī, ʿAbd al-Kabīr al-ʿAlawī. *Al-Faqīh Abū ʿAlī al-Yūsī: namūdhaj min al-fikr al-maghribī fī fajr al-dawla al-ʿalawiyya.* Muḥammadiyya, Morocco: Maṭbaʿat Faḍāla, 1989.
al-Muḥibbī, Muḥammad. *Khulāṣat al-athar fī aʿyān al-qarn al-ḥādī ʿashar.* 4 vols. Beirut: Maktabat Khayyāṭ, 1966.
Mūsā, ʿUmar Bāshā. *Tārīkh al-adab al-ʿarabī: al-ʿaṣr al-mamlūkī.* Beirut: Dār al-Fikr al-Muʿāṣir, 1989.
Muscati, J., and K. Moulvi. *The Life and Lectures of the Grand Missionary Al-Mu'ayyad-fid-din Al-Shirazi.* Karachi: Ismailia Association of West Pakistan, 1950.
al-Nafzāwī, ʿUmar. *The Perfumed Garden.* Trans. Richard Burton. London: Neville Spearman, 1975.
Naim, C. M., trans. *Zikr-i Mir: The Autobiography of the Eighteenth-Century Mughal Poet, Mir Muhammad Taqi "Mir" (1723–1810).* New Delhi: Oxford University Press, 1999.
Nubarian Pasha, Nubar. *Mémoires de Nubar Pacha.* Introd. and notes, Mirrit Butros Ghali. Beirut: Librairie du Liban, 1983.
Oberhelman, Steven M. *The Oneirocriticon of Achmet: A Medieval Greek and Arabic Treatise on the Interpretation of Dreams.* Lubbock: Texas Tech University Press, 1991.

Olney, James, ed. *Autobiography: Essays Theoretical and Critical.* Princeton: Princeton University Press, 1980.

Omori, Annie Shepley, trans. *Diaries of Court Ladies of Old Japan.* Tokyo: Kenkyusha, [1935] 1961.

Ostle, Robin, Ed de Moor, and Stefan Wild, eds. *Writing the Self: Autobiographical Writing in Modern Arabic Literature.* London: Saqi Books, 1998.

Pascal, Roy. *Design and Truth in Autobiography.* Cambridge, Mass.: Harvard University Press, 1960.

Pedersen, J. *The Arabic Book.* Princeton: Princeton University Press, 1984.

Pellat, Charles. "Fahrasa." *EI*² 2:743–44.

———. "Manāḳib." *EI*² 6:349–57.

Philipp, Thomas. "The Autobiography in Modern Arab Literature and Culture." *Poetics Today* 14, no. 3 (Fall 1993): 573–604.

———. *The Autobiography of Jurji Zaydan.* Washington, D.C.: Three Continents Press, 1990.

Poonawalla, Ismail. "Al-Mu'ayyad fī 'l-Dīn." *EI*² 5:270.

Porter, Roy, ed. *Rewriting the Self: Histories from the Renaissance to the Present.* New York: Routledge, 1997.

Pouzet, Louis. "Maẓāhir al-sīra al-dhātiyya fī kitāb tarājim al-qarnayn al-sādis wa-l-sābiʿ li-Shihāb al-Dīn Abī Shāma al-Maqdisī al-Dimashqī." *Annales du Départment des Lettres Arabes, Institut de Lettres Orientales, Université Saint-Joseph* 1 (1981): 25–35.

al-Qāḍī, Wadād. "Biographical Dictionaries: Inner Structures and Cultural Significance." In *The Book in the Islamic World: The Written Word and Communication in the Middle East,* ed. George N. Atiyeh, 93–122. Albany: SUNY Press, 1995.

al-Qāḍī al-Nuʿmān. *Risālat iftitāḥ al-daʿwa.* Ed. Wadād al-Qāḍī. Beirut: Dār al-Thaqāfa, 1970.

Rabbat, Nasser. "My Life with Ṣalāḥ al-Dīn: The Memoirs of ʿImād al-Dīn al-Kātib al-Iṣfahānī." *Edebiyât: Special Issue—Arabic Autobiography,* N.S. 7, no. 2 (1997): 267–87.

Radtke, Bernd, and John O'Kane. *The Concept of Sainthood in Early Islamic Mysticism: Two Works by al-Ḥakīm al-Tirmidhī.* Richmond, Surrey: Curzon Press, 1996.

Ramaḍān, ʿAbd al-ʿAẓīm Muḥammad. *Mudhakkirāt al-siyāsiyyīn wa-l-zuʿamāʾ fī Miṣr 1891–1981.* Beirut: al-Waṭan al-ʿArabī; Cairo: Maktabat Matbūlī, 1984.

al-Rāzī, Muḥammad. "Raziana I: La conduite du philosophe." Trans. Paul Kraus. *Orientalia* N.S. 4 (1935): 300–334.

———. *Risāla fī fihrist kutub Muḥammad ibn Zakariyyāʾ al-Rāzī.* Ed. Paul Kraus. Paris: Imprimerie Orientaliste au Calame, 1936.

Reinhart, Kevin. *Before Revelation: The Boundaries of Muslim Moral Thought.* Albany: SUNY Press, 1995.

Reynolds, Dwight F. "Childhood in One Thousand Years of Arabic Autobiography," *Edebiyât: Special Issue—Arabic Autobiography,* N.S. 7, no. 2 (1997): 379–92.

———. *Heroic Poets, Poetic Heroes: The Ethnography of Performance in an Arabic Oral Epic Tradition.* Ithaca: Cornell University Press, 1995.

———. "Introduction." *Edebiyât: Special Issue—Arabic Autobiography,* N.S. 7, no. 2 (1997): 207–14.

———. "Prosimetrum in 19th- and 20th-Century Arabic Literature." In *Prosimetrum: Cross-Cultural Perspectives on Narrative in Prose and Verse,* ed. Joseph Harris and Karl Reichl, 277–94. Suffolk: Boydell and Brewer, 1998.

———. "Shaykh ʿAbd al-Wahhāb al-Shaʿrānī's Sixteenth-Century Defense of Autobiography." *Harvard Middle Eastern and Islamic Review* 4, nos. 1–2 (1997–98): 122–37.

Richter-Bernburg, Lutz. "Observations on ʿImād al-Dīn's al-Fatḥ al-qussī fī-al-fatḥ al-qudsī." In *Studia Arabica et Islamica: Festschrift for Iḥsān ʿAbbās on His Sixtieth Birthday.* ed. Wadad al-Qadi, 373–79. Beirut: American University of Beirut, 1981.

Roded, Ruth. *Women in the Islamic Biographical Dictionaries: From Ibn Saʿd to Who's Who.* Boulder: Lynne Rienner, 1994.

Rooke, Tetz. *"In My Childhood": A Study of Arabic Autobiography.* Stockholm: Stockholm University, 1997.

Rosenthal, Franz. "Die arabische Autobiographie." *Studia Arabica* 1 (1937): 1–40.

———. *A History of Muslim Historiography.* 2d rev. ed. Leiden: E. J. Brill, 1968.

———. "Ibn Ḥadjar al-ʿAsḳalānī." *EI*² 3:776–78.

al-Ṣadr, Ḥasan. *Taʾsīs al-shīʿa li-ʿulūm al-islām.* Baghdad: Sharikat al-Nashr wa-l-Ṭibāʿa al-ʿIrāqiyya, 1951.

Said, Edward. *Beginnings.* Baltimore: Johns Hopkins University Press, 1987.

al-Sakhāwī, Shams al-Dīn Muḥammad. *Iʿlān bi-l-tawbīkh li-man dhamma al-taʾrīkh.* Damascus: al-Qudsī, 1930.

Salama-Carr, Myriam. *La traduction à l'époque abbaside : l'école de Hunayn ibn Ishaq et son importance pour la traduction.* Paris: Didier, 1990.

Salmé [Emily Ruete]. *An Arabian Princess between Two Worlds: Memoirs, Letters Home, Sequels to My Memoirs, Syrian Customs and Usages.* Ed. E. van Donzel. Leiden: E. J. Brill, 1992.

———. *Raised in a Harem: Memoirs of an Arabian Princess from Zanzibar, Emily Ruete, Born Salmé, Princess of Zanzibar and Oman.* New York: Marcus Weiner, 1989.

Samawʾal al-Maghribī. *Ifḥām al-yahūd, Silencing the Jews.* Ed. and trans. Moshe Perlmann. New York: American Academy for Jewish Research, 1964.

Samsó, Julio. "Turmediana: I. Trasfondo cultural islámico en la obra catalana de Anselmo Turmeda; II. En torno a la "Tuḥfa" y al "Libre de bons amonestaments." *Boletín de la Real Academia de Buenos Letras de Barcelona* 34 (1971–72): 51–85.

Sartain, E. M. *Jalāl al-Dīn al-Suyūṭī.* 2 vols. Cambridge: Cambridge University Press, 1975.

Scaglione, Aldo. "The Mediterranean's Three Spiritual Shores: Images of Self between Christianity and Islam in the Later Middle Ages." In *The Craft of Fiction: Essays in Medieval Poetics,* ed. Leigh A. Arrathoon, 453–73. Rochester, Mich.: Solaris Press, 1984.

Sellheim, Rudolf. "Die Autobiographie des Ibn ad-Daybaʿ." *Folia Rara: Wolfgang Voight LXV Diem Natalem Celebranti* [= Verzeichness der orientalischen Handschriften in Deutschland, Supplementband 19]. Wiesbaden: Franz Steiner, 1976. 111–19.

al-Shahrastānī, Muḥammad. *Mafātīḥ al-asrār wa-maṣābīḥ al-abrār.* Ed. Muḥammad ʿAlī Adharshab. Teheran: Iḥyā-i Kitāb, 1997.

al-Shaʿrānī, ʿAbd al-Wahhāb. *Il Libro dei Doni.* Ed. and trans. Virginia Vacca. Serie Orientalistica, Testi Vol. 13. Naples: Istituto Orientale, 1972.

———. *Laṭā'if al-minan wa-l-akhlāq.* Cairo: ʿĀlam al-Fikr, 1976.

Shaʿrāwī, Hudā. *Harem Years: The Memoirs of an Egyptian Feminist (1879–1924).* Trans., ed., and introd. Margot Badran. London: Virago Press, 1986.

al-Shaʿrāwī, Muḥammad Mitwallī. *Ḥayātī: min Daqādūs ilā al-wizāra.* Alexandria: Qāy-itbay, 1992.

Shell, Marc, and Werner Sollors, eds. *The Multilingual Anthology of American Literature.* New York: New York University Press, 2000.

al-Shidyāq, Aḥmad Fāris. *al-Sāq ʿalā al-sāq fī mā huwa al-Faryāq.* 2 vols. Paris: Benjamin Duprat, 1855.

Shryock, Andrew. "History and Historiography among the Belqa Tribes of Jordan." Ph.D. diss., University of Michigan, 1993.

———. *Nationalism and the Genealogical Imagination: Oral History and Textual Authority in Tribal Jordan.* Berkeley: University of California Press, 1997.

al-Simnānī, ʿAlā' al-Dawla. *Al-ʿUrwa li-ahl al-khalwa wa-l-jalwa.* Ed. Najīb Māyil-i Hirāwī. Teheran: Mawla, 1983.

Smith, Margaret. *An Early Mystic of Baghdad: A Study of the Life and Teaching of Ḥārith b. Asad al-Muḥāsibī,* A.D. *781*–A.D. *857.* London: Sheldon Press, 1935 [rpt. 1977].

Starkey, Paul. "Fact and Fiction in *al-Sāq ʿalā al-Sāq.*" In *Writing the Self: Autobiographical Writing in Modern Arabic Literature,* ed. Robin Ostle, Ed de Moor, and Stefan Wild, 30–38. London: Saqi Books, 1998.

Stewart, Devin J. "Capital, Accumulation, and the Islamic Academic Biography." *Edebiyât: Special Issue—Arabic Autobiography,* N.S. 7, no. 2 (1997): 345–62.

———. "The Humor of the Scholars: The Autobiography of Niʿmat Allāh al-Jazā'irī (d. 1112/1701)." *Iranian Studies* 22 (1989): 47–50.

Strohmaier, Gotthard. "Ḥunayn ibn Isḥāq und die Bilder." *Klio* 43–45 (1965): 525–33.

Tabbaa, Yasser. "The Transformation of Arabic Writing: Part I, Qur'ānic Calligraphy." *Ars Orientalis* 21 (1991): 119–48.

Ṭahmās Khān. *Tahmas Nama: The Autobiography of a Slave.* Abr. and trans. P. Setu Madhana Rao. Bombay: Popular Prakashan, 1967.

———. *Ṭahmāsnāmah.* Ed. Muhammad Aslam. Lahore: Panjab University, 1986.

Ṭahmāsp, Shāh. *Tazkīra-i Shāh Ṭahmāsp.* Teheran: Intishārāt-i Sharq, 1984.

al-Tamanārtī, ʿAbd al-Raḥmān. *Fawaid Al Jamma Bi ʿOuloumi Al Oumma.* Trans. Léopold V. Justinard. Chartres: Durand, 1953.

Tamari, Stephen. "Teaching and Learning in Eighteenth-Century Damascus: Localism and Ottomanism in an Early Modern Arab Society." Ph.D. diss., Georgetown University, 1998.

Thackston, Wheeler M., trans. *Murder, Mayhem, Pillage and Plunder: The History of Lebanon in the 18th and 19th Centuries by Mikhāyil Mishāqa.* Albany: SUNY Press, 1988.

Thackston, Wheeler M., trans. *The Bāburnāma.* Oxford: Oxford University Press, 1996.

Tietze, Andreas. "Muṣṭafā ʿAlī's Counsel for Sultans of 1581." *Österreichische Akademie der Wissenschaften, Philosophisch-Historische Klasse Denkschriften.* Bd. 137, Bd. 158. Vienna, 1979, 1982.

al-Tifāshī, Aḥmad. *Les délices des coeurs.* Trans. René Khawam. Paris: Editions Phébus, 1981.

al-Tirmidhī, Abū ʿAbd Allāh Muḥammad. "Buduww sha'n Abī ʿAbd allāh." In *Khatm al-awliyā'*, ed. ʿUthmān Yaḥyā, 14–32. Buḥūth wa-dirāsāt bi-idārat maʿhad al-ādāb al-sharqiyya fī Bayrūt, 19. Beirut: al-Maṭbaʿa al-Kāthūlīkiyya, 1965.

Todorov, Tzvetan. *Genres in Discourse*. Trans. Catherine Porter. Cambridge: Cambridge University Press, 1990.

Toorawa, Shawkat M. "The Educational Background of ʿAbd al-Laṭīf al-Baghdādī." *Muslim Education Quarterly* 13, no. 3 (1996): 35–53.

———. "Language and Male Homosocial Desire in the Autobiography of ʿAbd al-Laṭīf al-Baghdādī." *Edebiyât: Special Issue—Arabic Autobiography*, N.S. 7, no. 2 (1997): 251–65.

Troutt Powell, Eve M. "Waving His Own Flag: Ibrāhīm Fawzī Pasha's Narrative of the Sudan." *Edebiyât: Special Issue—Arabic Autobiography*, N.S. 7, no. 2 (1997): 363–78.

Usāma ibn Munqidh. *An Arab-Syrian Gentleman and Warrior in the Period of the Crusades*. Trans. Philip K. Hitti. New York: Columbia University Press, 1929; rpt. Princeton: Princeton University Press, 1987.

Vajda, Georges. "De la transmission orale du savoir dans l'Islam traditionnel." In *La transmission du savoir en Islam, VIIe–XVIIIe siècles*, ed. Nicole Cottart, 1–9. London: Variorum Reprints, 1993.

Vernet, Juan. *La cultura hispanoárabe en Oriente y Occidente*. Barcelona: Ariel, 1978.

Waddell, Norman, trans. "Wild Ivy: The Spiritual Autobiography of Hakuin Ekaku." *Eastern Buddhist* 15, no. 2 (1982): 71–109; 16, no. 1 (1983): 107–39.

Watt, W. Montgomery. *The Faith and Practice of Al-Ghazālī*. London: Allen and Unwin, 1953.

White, Hayden. *The Content of the Form: Narrative Discourse and Historical Representation*. Baltimore: Johns Hopkins University Press, 1987.

Wickerhauser, Moriz. *Wegweiser zum Verständnis der türkischen Sprache. Eine deutsch-türkische Chrestomathie*. Vienna: Kaiserlich-Königlichen Hof- und Staatsdruckerei, 1853.

Wu, Pei-Yi. *The Confucian's Progress: Autobiographical Writings in Traditional China*. Princeton: Princeton University Press, 1990.

Yāqūt al-Rūmī. *Irshād al-arīb ilā maʿrifat al-adīb (Muʿjam al-udabā')*. 7 vols. Ed. D. S. Margoliouth. Cairo: Hindiyya Press, 1907–26.

———. *Muʿjam al-udabā': irshād al-arīb ilā maʿrifat al-adīb*. Ed. Iḥsān ʿAbbās. Beirut: Dār al-Gharb al-Islāmī, 1993.

Young, M. J. L. "Arabic Biographical Literature." In *Cambridge History of Arabic Literature: Religion, Learning, and Science in the ʿAbbasid Period*, ed. M. J. L. Young, J. D. Latham, and R. B. Serjeant, 311–12. Cambridge: Cambridge University Press, 1990.

———."Medieval Arabic Autobiography." In *Cambridge History of Arabic Literature: Religion, Learning, and Science in the ʿAbbasid Period*, ed. M. J. L. Young, J. D. Latham, and R. B. Serjeant, 183–87. Cambridge: Cambridge University Press, 1990.

al-Yūsī al-Ḥasan. *al-Muḥāḍarāt*. Rabat: Maṭbūʿāt Dār al-Maghrib li-l-Ta'līf wa-l-Tarjama wa-l-Nashr, 1976.

Zonis, Marvin. "Autobiography and Biography in the Middle East: A Plea for Psychopolitical Studies." In *Middle Eastern Lives: The Practice of Biography and*

Self-Narrative, ed. Martin Kramer, 60–88. Syracuse: Syracuse University Press, 1991.

al-Zubaydī, Muḥammad. *Ṭabaqāt al-naḥwiyyīn wa-l-lughawiyyīn.* Ed. Muḥammad Abū al-Faḍl Ibrāhīm. Cairo: Dār al-Maʿārif, 1973.

al-Zubayr Raḥma(t). *Ez-Ziber Rahmet Paschas Autobiographie; ein Beitrag zur Geschichte des Sudan.* Bonn and Leipzig: K. Schroeder, 1921.

CONTRIBUTORS

Kristen E. Brustad is associate professor of Arabic language, literature, and culture in the Department of Middle Eastern Studies at Emory University.

Michael Cooperson is assistant professor of Arabic language and literature in the Department of Near Eastern Languages and Civilizations at the University of California, Los Angeles.

Jamal J. Elias is associate professor of Islamic Studies in the Department of Religion at Amherst College.

Nuha N. N. Khoury is associate professor of Islamic Art in the History of Art and Architecture Department at the University of California, Santa Barbara.

Joseph E. Lowry is visiting professor of Middle East Studies in the Department of Middle East Studies at New York University.

Nasser Rabbat is the Aga Khan professor of Islamic Architecture at the Massachusetts Institute of Technology.

Dwight F. Reynolds is associate professor of Arabic language and literature in the Department of Religious Studies at the University of California, Santa Barbara.

Devin Stewart is associate professor of Arabic and Islamic Studies in the Department of Middle Eastern Studies at Emory University.

Shawkat M. Toorawa is assistant professor of Arabic literature and Islamic Studies at Cornell University.

INDEX

ʿAbbās, Iḥsān, 68n2; *Fann al-sīra,* 2, 27, 260
ʿAbbās II, 7, 27
ʿAbbās Pasha (ʿAbbās I), 238, 240n6
ʿAbbāsids: caliphs as patrons for Ḥunayn ibn Isḥāq and his rivals, 107–8, 111–17, 118n3; defined, 289; Ibn al-ʿ Adīm as emissary to court of, 166
ʿAbd Allāh (al-ʿAydarūs's brother), 214
ʿAbd Allāh ibn ʿAlī, 220
ʿAbd Allāh Ibn Nāʾilī, 160
ʿAbd Allāh ibn Salām, 200, 201n1
ʿAbd Allāh al-Minūfī, 205
ʿAbd Allāh al-Turjumān (Fray Anselmo Turmeda), 194–95, 270; conversion autobiography, 47, 65, 194–95; —, translated text, 196–200
ʿAbd al-ʿAzīz ibn ʿAbd al-Salām, 183, 187n12
ʿAbd al-Dāyim, Yaḥyā Ibrāhīm, 14n28, 25–26, 49n16, 260, 281
ʿAbd al-Ghāfir, 67
ʿAbd al-Jabbār, al-Qāḍī, 63
ʿAbd al-Laṭīf al-Baghdādī, 156–57, 265; autobiography, 54, 84, 97, 156–57, 242, 265; —, translated text, 158–64
ʿAbd al-Malik al-Yamanī, 213–14
ʿAbd al-Raḥmān (Abū Shāma's grandfather's uncle), 182, 187n7
ʿAbd al-Raḥmān ("Prince"), 280; slave memoir, 56, 57, 280
ʿAbd al-Raḥmān al-Anbārī, 158
ʿAbduh, Muḥammad, 27, 283–84
ʿAbd al-Wāḥid, ʿAlī, 72
Abū al-ʿAbbās al-Tilimsānī (Abū ʿAbd Allāh al-Qurashī), 270
Abū al-ʿAbbās Aḥmad (sultan of Tunis), 199
Abū ʿAbd Allāh al-Qurashī (Abī al-ʿAbbās al-Tilimsānī), 65
Abū Bakr al-Ṣiddīq (Edward Donellan), 281; slave memoir, 56–57, 280–81
"Abū Bakr al-Ṣiddīq of Timbuktu" (Wilks), 281
Abū Dawūd, the tailor, 127
Abū al-Faḍl Hibat Allāh, 169
Abū al-Fidāʾ al-Ayyūbī, 267
Abū Ghānim Muḥammad, Jamāl al-Dīn, 169–70
Abū Ḥayyān al-Gharnāṭī (Abū Ḥayyān al-Andalusī), 268; autobiography, 2, 55, 65, 77, 268
Abū Kālījār, 132–33, 137–39, 140, 144n7
Abū Khaḍir, 227–28
Abu-Lughod, Lila, 102n45
Abū al-Najīb, 158, 160
Abū al-Qāsim, *History of Damascus,* 182
Abū Sālim, ʿAbd al-ʿĀl, 229
Abū Shāma, 179–81, 248, 266; autobiography, 11n2, 24, 33n29, 54, 179–81, 266; —, additional text added by another hand, 181, 187n15; —, age as motivation for writing, 78; —, citation of Qurʾān 93:11, 62; —, cited in preface to al-Suyūṭī's autobiography, 2, 11n1, 65; —, dream narrative, 90, 92–93; —, translated text, 182–86; *Book of the Two Gardens,* 54, 179; *Sequel to the Book*

Egypt: ʿAbd al-Laṭīf's time in, 161–62, 164; autobiographical writings from, discussed by Misch, 21; Ibn al-ʿAdīm as emissary to Mamluk court in Cairo, 166; ʿImād al-Dīn in Cairo, 150–51; modern politically-oriented autobiographies, 26–27, 34n41, 285 (*see also individual political figures*); Mubārak's childhood and political career in, 224, 225–26; novel's place in literature of, 102n43; women scholars from, biographical compendiums of, 40

Egyptian Childhood, An, the Autobiography of Taha Hussein (Paxton, trans.), 14n24, 288

Ekaku, Hakuin, 32

Elisséeff, Nikita, 72

emotions, portrayal of in autobiography, 74, 243, 247; by al-ʿAydarūs, 209, 213; devices used by al-Suyūṭī, 87–88; grief over family deaths, 77–78 (*see also* grief); in the historical text of Abū Shāma's *Sequel,* 180; by Ibn al-ʿAdīm, 167, 175–77; by Ibn Buluggīn, 74, 76–77; by ʿImād al-Dīn, 152; by Mu'ayyad, 133, 143; by Mubārak, 225, 234; use of poetry to express, 94–99, 167, 209, 213, 245, 247

Ende, Werner, 34n41

endowments, charitable (*awqāf*), 189, 191–92; conferred by al-Simnānī, 191–92

envy, role of in Ḥunayn ibn Isḥāq's tribulations, 109–11

epistles, formal, as a constituent part of a *tarjama,* 43

espionage, al-Mu'ayyad autobiography as story of, 132

Essai sur les origines du lexique techniques de la mystique musulmane (Massignon), 257

execution(s): of "enemies of God," ʿImād al-Dīn's refusal to perform, 152–53; of Ḥunayn ibn Isḥā, miraculous intervention into, 108; of al-Simnānī's uncle, 188; of ʿUmāra al-Ḥakamī al-Yamanī, 65, 95–96, 263

exemplary life: connotation of in the term *sīra,* 39, 40 (see also *sirā*); as al-Suyūṭī's motivation for writing an autobiography, 3

explanation, text(s) of, 25; *tarjama* as a, 42

Ez-Ziber Rahmet Paschas Autobiographie (Thilo, trans.), 284

"Fact and Fiction in *al-Sāq ʿalā al-Sāq*" (Starkey), 281

faḍā'il, as term associated with biographies of religious figures, 38

Fahrasa, al- (al-Yūsī), 276–77

fahrasa (fihrist) (pl. *fahāris),* 38, 42, 48n8; defined, 290

Fā'id, Aḥmad Bey, 235

Faith and Practice of Al-Ghazālī, The (al-Ghazālī; Watt, trans.), 261

al-Falakī, Maḥmūd Pasha, 235

family history (genealogy): account of as a constituent part of a *tarjama,* 42; accounts of in autobiographies, 8, 243–44, 247; —, of Abū Shāma, 182–83; —, of Ibn Buluggīn, 53, 261; —, of Mubārak, 226–27; —, of al-Suyūṭī, 4; collections of compiled from oral to written form, 36–37; of Ibn al-ʿAdīm, in Yāqūt's compilation, 165–68, 169–70, 172, 173

family relationships, 8, 78–79, 88, 243–44, 252n2; of al-ʿAydarūs with his father, 208, 209, 210; of al-ʿAydarūs with his mother, 210; of al-Baḥrānī with his father and grandfather, 218, 219–20; of al-Baḥrānī with his siblings, 219–20; dreams of family members: effect on autobiographers, 92–93; —, as prophecies about the autobiographer, 93, 102n42; grief over deaths (*see* grief); of Ibn al-ʿAdīm with his father, 167; of Mubārak with his father, 225, 227, 229, 230–31, 232–33, 234; of al-Tirmidhī with his father, 121

Fann al-sīra (ʿAbbās), 25, 27, 260

Faqīh Abū ʿAlī al-Yūsī, Al- (al-Mudghirī), 276

al-Fārābi, Abū Naṣr, 84, 162

Farīd, Muḥammad, 27, 285

al-Fārisī, ʿAbd al-Ghāfir, 1, 53, 65, 262

al-Fāsī, Taqī al-Dīn, 2, 67, 269

Faṣīḥ (Thaʿlab), 158

fast, Ramadan, breaking of, 134–35, 143n2

Fatḥ al-ilāh wa-minnatih fī al-taḥadduth bi-faḍl rabbī wa-niʿmatih (al-Muʿaskarī), 280

Fatḥ al-shakūr (al-Bartallī), 274

Fatimids, 95–96, 132; defined, 290

Fawā'id al-jamma bi-isnād ʿulūm al-umma (al-Tamanārtī), 274–75

fidelity, discussion of in Ibn Ḥazm's autobiography, Qur'ān 93:11 quoted in context of, 61–62

fihrist. See *fahrasa* (*fihrist*)

103n55, 251; —, by Usāma ibn Munqidh, 78; —, used to express emotions, 94–99, 167, 209, 213, 245, 247; selections of as a constituent part of a *tarjama*, 43, 50n24; written by ʿUmāra, ʿImād al-Dīn's knowledge of, 54
political activists, white, 19th-century slave memoirs written at instigation of, 7–8, 56
political autobiographies, 58, 65–66; modern Egyptian, 26–27, 34n41, 285 (*see also individual political figures*)
political family history, Ibn Buluggīn's autobiography as a, 53
political figures, *manāqib* works written about, 38
politics, Mubārak's career in Egypt, 224, 225–26, 238–39
Polo, Marco, 195
pool from which the faithful will drink on the Day of Resurrection, 186, 187n14
portents of the future, dreams acting as, 90, 93
Porter, Roy, 33n6
power, as a concern of the young al-Simnānī: effect of conversion on, 189, 190; as subject of Satan's temptation, 192–93
Practical Visions of Yaʿqūb Ṣanūʿ (Gendzier), 284
pride: modesty combined with in al-ʿAydarūs's autobiography, 208–9, 211–12; not a motive for autobiography for al-Shaʿrānī, 68; not a motive for autobiography for al-Suyūṭī, 3; when speaking of one's self, use of Qur'ān 93:11 as a disclaimer of, 61–62
prison: Ḥunayn ibn Isḥāq in, 109; Mubārak's time in as a youth, 229–30
private life/personal life, 74–79 (*see also* emotions; family relationships; self, portrayal in Arabic autobiography); of Abū Shāma, revelation of in historical text of the *Sequel*, 180; of the adult Mubārak, glimpses of in autobiography, 239; not focused on in premodern Arabic autobiography, 30, 242–43; symbolic dreams as not pertaining to, 90
prophecies, in dreams, 89, 91, 93, 102n42
prose: ʿImād al-Dīn's introduction of new style of, 149; relationship to poetry, 36, 94, 99
prosopography, Arabic, as an "organized science," 242
"Purported Autobiography of Ḥunayn ibn Isḥāq" (Cooperson), 257

al-Qāḍī al-Fāḍil, 161, 162
al-Qāḍī ʿIyāḍ, 42
al-Qādirī, Muḥammad, 278
al-Qālī, 259
Qāmūs fī al-lugha, Al- (al-Shīrāzī), 81
Qānṣūh al-Sharafī, role in "house of ill repute" incident, 204, 206
Qarawiyyīn Mosque, in Fez Morocco, manuscript discovered in library of, 62
qarīb (relative), letters in used in poem by Ibn al-ʿAdīm, 176, 178n9
qaṣīda (formal ode), 94; composed by ʿUmāra al-Yamanī, 95–96
Qaṣr al-ʿAynī school, Mubārak at, 231–32, 233–34
al-Qaṭṭān al-Miṣrī, 81
Qawl al-mufīd fī uṣūl al-tajwīd, Al- (al-Biqāʿī), 271
al-Qifṭī, biographical compendium of scientists and physicians, Ibn Sīnā's text in, 60, 61
al-Qudūrī, *al-Mukhtaṣar*, 172, 178n8
qudwa, defined, 292
Qur'ān: ʿAbd al-Laṭīf questioned about by al-Qāḍī al-Fāḍil, 161; allegorical interpretation of advocated by the Muʿtazilites, 63; commentaries drawn on by al-Suyūṭī, 1; defined, 292; first known cursive-script manuscript, 178n7; material for development of Arabo-Islamic beliefs and practices about dreams and their interpretation, 88–89; quotations from used in al-Shaʿrānī's defense of autobiography, 67; reciters, biographical compendiums of, 40; seen as untranslatable, 42, 49n18
Qur'ān, memorization of, 80, 100n14; by Abd al-Laṭīf, 158; by Abū Shāma, 183; by every male in Ibn al-ʿAdīm's family, 165–66; by Ibn al-ʿAdīm, 171; by Mubārak, 228; by al-Simnānī, 191; by al-Tirmidhī, 121
Qur'ān, verses quoted: 3:138, 206; 7:43, 162; 9:41, 144n5; 13:31, 161; 27:62, 193; 27:64, 193; 39:71, 161; 40:60, 193; 41:44, 143n3; 61:13, 210; 84:15, 144n4; 93:11: connected with act of autobiogra-

Salāsil al-ḥadīd fī taqyīd Abī Ḥadīd (al-Baḥrānī), 222, 223n13
Salmé, Princess (Emily Ruete), 285; autobiography, 77, 79, 285; —, written in German, 7, 8, 13n15
salvation: seen by al-ʿAydarūs as reward for pious efforts, 208; sought in Islam by ʿAbd Allāh al-Turjumān, 198–99
Samau'al al-Maghribī: Ifḥām al-Yahūd "Silencing the Jews" (Perlmann, ed. and trans.), 263
Samawʿal al-Maghribī, 64, 91–92, 263; autobiography, 24, 45, 47, 53, 65, 263
Sanā al-barq al-shāmī (al-Bundarī), 146–55, 263
Ṣanūʿ, Yaʿaqūb, 284
Sāq ʿalā al-sāq, Al- (al-Shidyāq), 10, 14n26, 58, 281–82
Sarakhsī, *Mabsūṭ*, 178n8
Sarashina, Heian literary diary, 32
sar-guzasht, as Persian term for autobiographical text, 60
al-Sarifīnī, Ibrāhīm ibn Muḥammad al-Azhar, 262
Sartain, Elizabeth, 202
Satan (the Devil): al-Simnānī's confrontation with, 189, 192–93; as a source of dreams, 89
Sayf al-muhannad fī sīrat al-malik al-Mu'ayyad, Al- (al-ʿAynī), 39
Scaglione, Aldo, 29
School of Engineering, in Būlāq, Mubārak at, 235–36
scriptural language, Arabic as a, 6
self, portrayal in Arabic autobiography, 3–6, 30, 47, 77–78, 242–45; additional portrayal in other writings, 247–48; essentialization of in Ibn Buluggīn's autobiography, 74–77, 78–79; historicization of, 79–87; —, in Ibn Ḥajar's autobiography, 80–83, 86–87; Rosenthal's critique of, 24
self, portrayal in autobiography: attempts to define "true" autobiography in terms of, 73–74; Misch's and Rosenthal's approach to and critique of, 20, 24; western expectations of, 19, 29, 72–73
self, public *versus* private, modern and premodern conceptualizations of, 29, 79–80, 245
self-denial, advocated and practiced by al-Tirmidhī, 119, 121–23
self-effacement, found in descriptions of childhood in Arabic autobiographies, 80–88
Sequel to the Book of the Two Gardens (*Dhayl kitāb al-rawḍatayn*) (Abū Shāma), 2, 11n1, 179, 180–81 (*see also* Abū Shāma, autobiography)
"Seveners." *See* Ismāʿīlīs
sex/sexual relations, 79–80; discussion of in Arabic books, 75, 78, 245; discussion of in western literature, 245; in dreams, interpretation of, 90
Shadharāt al-dhahab fī akhbār man dhahab (Ibn al-ʿIād), 272
Shādhbakht academy, Ibn al-ʿAdīm as professor at, 173–74
al-Shāfiʿī, 215n3; legal tradition, 40, 49n11, 215n3; use of name as pun in poem by al-ʿAydarūs, 212–13
shāfiʿī: meaning, 215n3; used as pun in poem by al-ʿAydarūs, 212–13
al-Shahīd al-thānī (Zayn al-Dīn ibn ʿAlī al-ʿĀilī) (d. 1558), 56, 273
al-Shahrastānī, 262
al-Shahrazūrī, Ḍiyā' al-Dīn, 151
shakwā (ode of complaint), composed by ʿUmāra al-Yamanī, 95
Shams al-Dīn Muḥammad b. ʿUmar al-Sallāwī al-Dimashqī, 80–81, 83
Shaqā'iq al-nuʿmāniyya fī ʿulamā' al-dawla al-ʿuthmāniyya (Taşköprüzādeh), 273
Sharaf al-Dīn, 180
al-Sharaf ibn Ra'īs, 186
al-Sharaf al-Ṣarkhadī, 186
al-Shaʿrānī, ʿAbd al-Wahhāb, 273; autobiography, 4, 26, 56, 66, 87, 273; —, introduction used to defend writing an autobiography, 250; —, as a spiritual autobiography, 47, 65; —, use and expansion of al-Suyūṭī's list, 65–66; discussions of autobiography, 39, 55, 67–68; —, on ʿImād al-Dīn, 55, 145, 264
Shaʿrāwī, Hudā, 8, 27, 286
Sharḥ al-ṣadr (al-Kāshānī), 276
al-Sharīf ʿUmar ibn Ḥamza, 159
al-Shārʿī, Qāsim al-, ʿAbd al-Laṭīf al-Baghdādī's association with, 97, 161, 162, 163
shattatūhā, reckoning a date by, 218, 222n3
al-Shawkānī, 280
Shawqī, Aḥmad, 285–86; anthology of poetry, autobiography prefaced to, 58,

Text:	10/12 Baskerville
Display:	Baskerville
Composition:	Binghamton Valley Composition
Printing and binding:	Edwards Brothers

Interpreting the ...
autobiography in the Arabic liter
tradition /
31516000716801

SAUK VALLEY COMMUNITY COLLEGE
LIBRARY
DIXON, IL 61021